D1590701

THE I TATTI
RENAISSANCE LIBRARY

James Hankins, General Editor

# PONTANO

# THE VIRTUES AND
# VICES OF SPEECH

ITRL 87

GIOVANNI GIOVIANO
PONTANO
◆ ◆ ◆
THE VIRTUES AND
VICES OF SPEECH

EDITED AND TRANSLATED BY

G. W. PIGMAN III

THE I TATTI RENAISSANCE LIBRARY
HARVARD UNIVERSITY PRESS
CAMBRIDGE, MASSACHUSETTS
LONDON, ENGLAND
2019

Series design by Dean Bornstein

First printing

*Library of Congress Cataloging-in-Publication Data*

Names: Pontano, Giovanni Gioviano, 1429–1503, author. | Pigman, G. W.,
editor, translator. | Container of (expression): Pontano, Giovanni Gioviano,
1429–1503. De sermone. | Container of (expression): Pontano, Giovanni
Gioviano, 1429–1503. De sermone. English (Pigman)
Title: The virtues and vices of speech / Giovanni Gioviano Pontano ; edited and
translated by G. W. Pigman III.
Other titles: I Tatti Renaissance library ; 87.
Description: Cambridge, Massachusetts : Harvard University Press, 2019. |
Series: The I Tatti Renaissance library ; 87 | Text in Latin with English
translation on facing pages ; introduction and notes in English. | Includes
bibliographical references and index.
Identifiers: LCCN 2018017735 | ISBN 9780674987500 (alk. paper)
Subjects: LCSH: Rhetoric, Medieval—Early works to 1800. | Virtue—Early
works to 1800. | Aristotle—Influence—Early works to 1800.
Classification: LCC PA8570.P5 A2 2019 | DDC 808—dc23 LC record available at
https://lccn.loc.gov/2018017735

# Contents

꽃꽃꽃

# Introduction

꿹꿹꿹

## *Pontano's Life*

Giovanni Pontano (Ioannes Iovianus Pontanus) was born in Cerreto di Spoleto on May 7, 1429, and spent his first years in this Umbrian village.[1] After his father was killed in civil strife, his mother, Cristiana, and her mother, Leonarda — both strong-minded women to judge from the stories Pontano tells of them in *De sermone* (5.4.2–3, 6.4.14) — took him and his sister, Aurienta, to Perugia, where his uncle Tommaso (5.2.41) was chancellor of the university and where he studied with Guido Vannucci (5.2.40).[2] Civil strife drove Pontano from Perugia in 1447, but he remained attached to his *patria*. After spending most of his life in Naples, he still refers to Plautus as "our Umbrian comic poet" (2.5.2; cf. 4.4.2).

In 1448 Pontano entered Naples in the entourage of Alfonso V of Aragon, who had conquered the kingdom of Naples in 1442.[3] Except for diplomatic and military missions, he spent the rest of his life there. When seventy, he still recalled with pride that in Naples at twenty-four he had been judged to excel at literary studies, even among men who had grown old in them.[4] He studied Greek with Gregorio Tifernate (5.2.30) and attended lectures by George of Trebizond but, more important, enjoyed the protection and friendship of Antonio Beccadelli (il Panormita, 1.18.4), the founder of the humanist academy, which, after the latter's death, became the Accademia Pontaniana.[5]

Under Alfonso, Naples became a center for humanism, and in *De sermone* Pontano recalls his cordial relations with one of Alfonso's most illustrious clients, Lorenzo Valla (1.18.6). Several of Pontano's friends and associates in the Accademia Pontaniana fig-

ure in *De sermone*: Marino Brancaccio (4.3.14), Tristano Caracciolo (4.10.4), Girolamo Carbone (4.10.2), Angelo Colocci (6.2.43), Antonio De Ferrariis (il Galateo, 1.30.2), Pietro Golino (Petrus Compater, 4.3.36), Peto Fundano (6.2.9), Benet Gareth (il Cariteo, 4.3.30), Francesco Elio Marchese (6.2.1), Giovanni Pardo (1.30.3), Francesco Pucci (4.3.38), Enrico Puderico (4.3.12), Jacopo Sannazaro (Actius Sincerus, 6.2.7–8), Suardino Suardo (6.2.12), Pietro Summonte (4.3.36), and Marino Tomacelli (2.13.6). *De sermone* ends at the deathbed of Compater, one of Pontano's closest friends, who acknowledges the pleasantness of conversation among friends and acquaintances — the main subject of the treatise.

For almost fifty years Pontano served the Aragonese kings of Naples in many capacities. His first diplomatic job was in 1450, when he accompanied Panormita on a mission to establish a league against Milan. After lecturing on Latin poets and historians, Pontano was appointed by Alfonso around 1456 to tutor his nephew, Juan, the illegitimate son of Juan II of Aragon. Around 1463 Pontano became tutor to Alfonso, duke of Calabria, son and heir of Ferdinando I of Naples. As a soldier and diplomat, he served the Aragonese in the first conspiracy of the barons (1458–65) and wrote the history of the war, *De bello Neapolitano*. He accompanied the duke of Calabria in a war in Romagna (1467–68), and in *De sermone* he recalls a tribute paid to him as Alfonso's tutor by Federico, then count of Urbino and captain general of the league (5.2.65). Appointed Alfonso's principal secretary in 1482, Pontano also accompanied him in the war of Ferrara (1482–84) and played an important role in negotiating the peace treaty.[6] In 1486 in Rome, he negotiated the peace treaty that ended the second conspiracy of the barons, and in *De sermone* he recalls with pride that Pope Innocent VIII praised him for his truth and trustworthiness (2.2.24).[7] In 1486 Pontano became Ferdinando's prime minister, a post that he retained under Alfonso II and Ferdinando II. After Charles VIII of France entered Naples (February 22,

1495), Pontano, with the consent of Ferdinando II, who had fled, handed over the keys of the city to the French king. Francesco Guicciardini notoriously and unjustly accused him of vituperating the Aragonese kings in a speech at the investiture of Charles as king of Naples.[8] During the last eight years of his life, Pontano lived in retirement, although not completely withdrawn from public affairs. Four months before his death on September 17, 1503, he wrote a letter on behalf of the people of Naples to Louis XII justifying their surrender to the Spanish after being abandoned by the French.[9]

The last years of Pontano's life were saddened not only by the catastrophic end of the kingdom of Naples but also by the deaths of friends and family. His wife, Adriana Sassone, fifteen years his junior and only forty-nine, died on March 1, 1490, after twenty-nine years of marriage. *De sermone* 5.2.46 is a touching tribute to his affection for her. His son Lucio, for whom he had written the lovely lullabies in *De amore coniugali* 2.8–19, died in 1498 at the age of twenty-nine, accidentally poisoned. His infant son by the girlfriend whom he calls Stella died before 1496, and Stella herself died after that year. Two of Pontano's daughters, Aurelia (5.2.46) and Eugenia (5.2.45), did survive him, but Lucia Marzia had died years earlier at fourteen. At the end of 1501, the death of Compater "inflicted a huge wound on my old age" (6.4.20).

Although his retirement from politics was an extraordinary period of literary productivity despite his personal and public griefs, Pontano had been composing works in verse and prose since his youth. His poetry comprises many genres and meters: erotic poems influenced by Panormita's *Hermaphroditus* and Latin love elegy (*Parthenopeus*); Vergilian eclogues; didactic poems on citrus trees (*De hortis Hesperidum*), weather (*Meteorum liber*), and astrology (*Urania*); religious hymns for his pupil, Juan of Aragon, who had been destined for the church (*De laudibus divinis*); Horatian lyric (*Lyra*); epitaphs for friends and relatives (*De tumulis*); Catullan

hendecasyllables (*Baiae*); and two collections of elegiacs, one concerning his wife and children (*De amore coniugali*), the other, Stella (*Eridanus*).[10] Pontano's reputation as an extraordinary poet began during his own lifetime—in 1486 Innocent VIII crowned him a poet laureate—and continues to this day.

Pontano's prose is also varied and distinguished. It includes two astrological works (*Commentationes super centum sententiis Ptolemaei* and *De rebus coelestibus*); a treatise on the use of the letter *h* and other orthographical matters (*De aspiratione*); dialogues ranging from Lucianic satire to theology (*Charon, Antonius, Actius, Asinus, Aegidius*); a treatise of political philosophy for his pupil, Alfonso duke of Calabria (*De principe*); a history of the first conspiracy of the barons (*De bello Neapolitano*); and several treatises of moral philosophy (*De obedientia, De liberalitate, De beneficentia, De magnificentia, De splendore, De conviventia, De immanitate, De prudentia, De fortuna,* and *De magnanimitate*).[11] Pontano did not live to finish revising these last three works or *De sermone*.

## De sermone[12]

Although Pontano did not polish *De sermone* completely or provide Books 2 to 6 with prefaces, as Summonte indicates in his own preface ("Appendix One"), he had substantially completed it about a year before his death.[13] Since he does not include it among his works in progress in a letter of June 1, 1499, to Battista Spagnoli,[14] he probably began composition after that date.[15] He completed it in 1502, the date that he wrote at the very end of the work in his manuscript, probably early in the year, since the last paragraph refers to the death of Compater (November 17, 1501) as recent, and surely before May 7, 1502, his seventy-third birthday, since he says in the preface to the first book that he was seventy-two at the time of writing (1.pr.1); for he most likely wrote this preface after he had completed the work as a whole. In his manuscript, now Vi-

enna, Österreichische Nationalbibliothek, Cod. 3413, between the end of *De bello Neapolitano* and *De sermone* 1.1, Pontano left folia 146 to 151 and 153 blank.[16] The preface to the first book occupies 152r except for the last four words, which appear at the top of 152v, the rest of which is blank. The preface immediately looks different from the rest of the manuscript: it is written in a slightly larger hand, and the lines are longer. Furthermore, the manuscript gives hardly any indication of the plan stated in the preface to dedicate each book to a different person. Pontano left space for a preface or addition only before the third book, and he left a row of dots for a dedicatee only on the last page of the manuscript, a page that looks as if it was written later than what preceded it, since it is in a slightly larger hand with shorter lines, follows a page left half blank, and is a conclusion to the entire work. Finally, it is worth recalling that Pontano did not write the dedication of *De fortuna* to Gonzalo de Córdoba until the last four months of his life, although he had completed the treatise in 1501.[17]

The preface refers to the partition of the kingdom of Naples between the French and the Spanish, which began in the summer of 1501 and introduced a conflict between the two resolved only with the abandonment of Naples by Louis XII of France in 1503, by which time Pontano had completed *De sermone*. A passage canceled from 3.17.16 refers to the expulsion of Federico I of Naples from the kingdom (September 6, 1501) as not many months earlier. In 4.3.36 and 4.10.5 Pontano refers to Compater as if still alive but mentions his death in the last book (6.4.20 and 6.4.37). I find nothing before 3.17.16 that dates the first part of the work, so I take the letter to Spagnoli (June 1, 1499) as the *terminus post quem* and Pontano's seventy-third birthday (May 7, 1502) as the *terminus ante quem* for his composition of *De sermone*.

The only indication that Pontano might not have completed the rest of the work when he wrote the preface to the first book is the reference to "several" books (1.pr.3), since one might have ex-

pected him to say six if he knew that was the number he had decided upon. For Pontano did not decide that *De sermone* was to
consist of six books until late in its composition. But it was in fact
Pontano, not Summonte, who divided the work into six books and
indicated the points at which those books were to begin; these
beginnings are correctly indicated in the first edition. Since there
has been considerable confusion and misunderstanding on this
subject, it is necessary to clarify the division into books that Pontano indicated in the manuscript.[18]

The manuscript does reveal Pontano's hesitations over the
number of books and their beginnings and endings. At the end of
the second book, halfway down 184r, he wrote, "FINIS."; the
second half of the page and all of 184v–85r are blank. At the top of
186r he wrote, "Liber ~~secundus: Quartus~~ Tertius."[19] Apparently
Pontano originally intended the first two books to be one, since —
in addition to canceling "secundus" — he canceled the end of what
became the first book, replacing it with "de qua insequenti libro
disseremus," when he added "lib'. 2." in the margin.[20] Moreover, at
some point he apparently intended the third book to be the fourth,
since — in addition to canceling "Quartus" — he canceled "Lib III.,"
which he had written in the margin before 2.3.[21] At this stage he
intended the fifth book to begin with 3.15, since in the margin he
wrote and canceled "lib .V." At another stage he appears to have
intended the fifth — or even a seventh — book to begin with 4.11,
since in the margin he wrote and canceled "lib. vii." and apparently
canceled the "ii" of "vii" before canceling the two words. He may
have thought of beginning the sixth book at 5.4, since four lines
before in the margin he wrote and canceled "VI" (without "liber"
or an abbreviation for it). Finally, when he wrote "Nam de ironicis
insequenti libro disputabitur" (2.17.8), he did not know that that
section would appear in the sixth book.[22]

But there should be no doubt that by the time Pontano finished
his work on *De sermone* he intended it to contain six books, begin-

ning and ending as they do in the *editio princeps*. He clearly stated (1.pr.3–4) that the preface to Book 1 is the dedication only to Book 1 and not to the work as a whole, so the first book begins with 1.pr and not 1.1. As we have just seen, he explicitly indicated the beginnings of Books 2 and 3, as well as the ending of 2. And he explicitly indicated the beginnings of Books 4, 5, and 6, as well as the ending of 6. Pontano added all three beginnings in the margins. The first two occur before what were already new paragraphs, but the last requires signs for a new paragraph: "L. IIII." (184v), ".V. liber." (218v), and ".VI. liber." (229v).[23] It took Pontano time to determine on six books, but this division represents his plan, not Summonte's.

Of all of these divisions into books, the beginning of what is now the third book is probably the most significant. It is apparently the only division that Pontano made while he was composing, as opposed to while he was revising—since, as discussed above, he wrote "FINIS" in the middle of the last page of the preceding book, left pages blank, and wrote "Liber secundus" in the center at the top of a page. (He indicated the beginnings of Books 2, 4, 5, and 6 in the margins.) Originally, then, Pontano intended Books 1 and 2 to be the first book, and Book 3 the second.

As we shall see shortly, such a division simultaneously points to the Aristotelian structure of *De sermone* and highlights the subject that Pontano considered central to his treatise, the formation of the *vir facetus*. For although most appreciated as a collection of witticisms, *De sermone* is first and foremost a treatise of Aristotelian moral philosophy about the virtues and vices of speech. In 1.4.3 Pontano presents the treatise as a continuation of his other studies of the moral virtues and insists on the concept that guides him, the Aristotelian doctrine that every moral virtue is a mean between two extremes, an excess and a deficiency, both of which are vices.[24] *De sermone* provides an inventory of the kinds of speech in

- INTRODUCTION -

social situations, and Aristotle, "who has discussed the moral virtues most skillfully" (6.3.1), is Pontano's guide throughout. At one point he explains his method as exploring at greater length and a bit more searchingly subjects treated by Aristotle (2.7.5). Chapter 2.6 ("What Aristotle thinks about this subject") and sections 2.7.1–4 are a detailed summary of Aristotle's discussion of the mean of veracity and its extremes of ostentation and self-deprecation (1127a14–b22). Although Pontano does not say so, chapter 1.26 borrows heavily from Aristotle's discussion of the unnamed mean most resembling friendship and its extremes of contentiousness and obsequiousness (1126b11–27a6).

A review of Aristotle's classification of the three virtues of sociability will clarify the structure of De sermone and Pontano's innovations with respect to Aristotelian theory.[25] Aristotle is not simply describing types of behavior and character. When he discusses the virtues of sociability, he is explicitly arguing for his general theory that every virtue is a mean between two extremes (1127a15–17). He is more systematic about classification than Pontano, who takes Aristotle's theory as a given and is more concerned with describing types of social behavior than with arranging them into triads of mean, excess, and deficiency.

Aristotle divides the three similar means that concern "intercourse in words and actions of some kinds" (1128b5–6) in two: one mean concerns truth, and the other two, pleasantness. Pleasantness concerns either amusements or the other social activities. Aristotle excludes truthfulness about agreements or about things pertaining to justice and injustice from this discussion of truth, since they belong to a different virtue, namely justice itself (1127a33–b3). He is not talking about keeping promises or lying about what other people have done but rather about how people represent themselves. Consequently, in this section of the Nicomachean Ethics, "candor" or "sincerity" is sometimes a more appropriate translation for ἀλήθεια than "truth." The ἀληθευτικὸς—the

xiv

truthful, candid, or sincere person — calls things by their own names and neither augments nor diminishes himself, whereas the boaster (ἀλαζών), either for gain or with no end in view, pretends to more than he has, and the self-deprecator (εἴρων) pretends to less.

Aristotle's other two means concern pleasantness (τὸ ἡδύ). The second mean, which is concerned with aspects of social life other than amusements, has no name but most resembles friendship — friendship without passion or affection (1126b19–25). This virtue becomes clearer when opposed to its extremes. The obsequious (ἄρεσκοι), to give pleasure, praise everything and oppose nothing, while the grumpy and contentious (δύσκολοι καί δυσέριδες) do not care about giving pain and oppose everything. So the person between the obsequious and the grumpy will be appropriately tolerant or vexed by others and prefer to give pleasure and avoid giving pain but will be guided by nobler considerations if necessary. The mean that concerns amusements (παιδιά) is wittiness (εὐτραπελία). Witty people joke in a tasteful, tactful way, avoiding the excesses of the buffoon (βωμολόχος), who will say anything to raise a laugh, indifferent to giving pain. The witty or tactful say and listen to things appropriate to upright, freeborn people. The boors and austere people (ἄγροικοι καὶ σκληροί) are deficient in a sense of humor; they say nothing funny and are vexed by those who do (1127b33–28b4).

Pontano's final division of De sermone into books follows, to a certain extent, Aristotle's arrangement of the virtues and vices of sociability into three triads. After some introductory topics, the first book contains an overview of them, just as Aristotle gives an overview in Book 2 before the detailed discussion in Book 4. The end of Pontano's first book is a closer examination of the first triad discussed by Aristotle, the unnamed mean that is closest to friendship with its extremes of obsequiousness and contentiousness. The second book is devoted to Aristotle's second triad, the mean

of veracity and its extremes of ostentation and dissimulation/self-deprecation. The third book takes up Aristotle's third and final triad, the mean of wittiness and its extremes of buffoonery and agresticity.[26] Books 4, 5, and 6, taking Cicero's and Quintilian's discussions of joking as points of departure, then discuss various topics involving wittiness.

In one crucial way, however, Pontano's original division of the Aristotelian part of *De sermone* more accurately reflects his conception of the virtues and vices of speech than his final division. For Pontano does not accept Aristotle's subdivision of the virtues of sociability. Instead of placing the means like friendship and wittiness together as means concerning pleasantness, as Aristotle does, Pontano groups the mean like friendship with veracity as means concerning truth and opposes them to wittiness, the mean concerning pleasantness. Consequently, Pontano's original division into a first book devoted to veracity and the mean like friendship and a second book devoted to wittiness made his reorganization of the means structurally apparent. By placing almost everything involving the virtues and vices of speech except for wittiness in one, long introductory book, the original division also emphasized Pontano's primary concern in *De sermone*. *Facetudo* and the formation of the *vir facetus* were the subject of all the books except for the first.

Although Pontano explicitly argues against (3.19–20) Cicero's view that there is no art of witticism and openly disagrees with (5.2.1–7) the definition of *urbanity* given by Domitius Marsus and accepted and enlarged by Quintilian, he does not indicate that he is disagreeing with Aristotle's subdivision of the virtues of sociability. A few pages into *De sermone* Pontano argues, in good Aristotelian fashion, that the mean governs all human activity, including speech (1.5), and turns Aristotle's almost casual remark that life includes rest (1127b33) into a desire for repose and restoration given to man by nature (1.6). The next section, "Urbanity and

truth are deservedly praised," lays the foundation for the virtues of sociability.

> Therefore urbanity is deservedly praised, and many seek intercourse and intimacy with urbane and witty men. And because right reason presides over the handling and administering of affairs and is the special friend of truth, so those who cultivate truth are commended by all and held most valuable. When moderation and what is called the mean are added to this pursuit of the true and the pleasant and to the motions and affections of the mind toward these things, there will directly emerge things worthy of good men and freeborn citizens. (1.7.1–2)

This section suggests that Pontano is proposing two means of sociability—truth and urbanity—in place of Aristotle's three means, one of truth and two of pleasantness. Since *urbanitas* and *urbanus* are words chosen by Giovanni Argiropulo, Leonardo Bruni, and Giannozzo Manetti, the three fifteenth-century translators of the *Nicomachean Ethics*, to refer to Aristotle's mean of wittiness, Pontano is initially dividing social intercourse into truthfulness and wittiness, the former associated with the serious business of life and the latter with relaxation.[27] In fact, in this passage Pontano seems to identify urbanity with the pleasant.

By classifying wittiness and the unnamed virtue similar to friendship under the pleasant and opposing these two means to truthfulness, Aristotle is emphasizing the distinction between how one represents oneself to others and how one otherwise interacts with them. Pontano draws the line differently—between truthful self-representation and truthful interaction with others, on the one hand, and witty, pleasant conversation on the other. When he turns to truth and truthfulness, he indicates that he is not talking about philosophical or mathematical truth (1.13.2). He does not indicate, however, that he is not restricting himself to Aristotle's

truth, the mean between self-deprecation and boasting, since he includes not only boasting but also adulation, the excess to the unnamed virtue that resembles friendship, in the behavior avoided by the truthful man. In fact, adulation is the first vice opposed to truth that Pontano proceeds to consider (1.14). Initially, Pontano intended to discuss only wittiness and truth and not to say anything about the third virtue (1.13.3), but at 1.22.3–4 he returns to the unnamed virtue resembling friendship with an apology for investigating it.

Like Aristotle, Pontano places this virtue between contentiousness and obsequiousness, but unlike Aristotle, he shifts the emphasis to gratifying and advising (1.25). The person who acts in accord with the mean between them is more concerned with approving the good behavior of others and admonishing their bad behavior than with being pleasant or unpleasant. Pontano specifies the nobler considerations that Aristotle vaguely refers to — praising and encouraging morality and blaming and discouraging immorality. Consequently, Pontano classifies this unnamed virtue under truthfulness instead of pleasantness. His truth "is particularly involved in speech and conversation and both in praising and commending oneself and others and in blaming and censuring the base" (2.2.11). Pontano's reclassification around sincere praise and blame — both of self and others — replaces Aristotle's distinction between self-representation and interaction with others. It also gives a more prominent place to wittiness among the virtues of sociability.

Pontano was a lover of words, and he coined one for wittiness: *facetudo*.[28] The coinage underlines the importance of the concept in his discussion of speech, for he retains the terms used by the fifteenth-century translators of the *Nicomachean Ethics* for the people who embody the extremes of wittiness, the *scurra* (buffoon) and the *rusticus/agrestis* (rustic/agrestic).[29] But Argiropulo, Bruni, and Manetti do not use *facetus* to refer to the witty man ($\epsilon \dot{v} \tau \rho \acute{a} \pi \epsilon \lambda o s$).[30]

In fact, Pontano takes pains to distinguish the *facetus* from the *urbanus* (urbane) and the *comes* (affable), the words that the translators use for Aristotle's witty man. For Pontano, *urbanitas* involves more than pleasant, witty speech; it encompasses the well-bred manners of the freeborn man, such things as rising for an elder or escorting a magistrate home from court (1.12.1–2). In a lengthy section (1.28), he prefers affability (*comitas*) for the unnamed virtue that most resembles friendship, not for wittiness.

What, then, constitutes wittiness? At the beginning of the final book Pontano sums up his ideal of the witty man:

> Thus the witty man I am now training will be pleasant and cheerful when telling jokes, and will have a calm face composed to refresh, pleasing and elegant, when responding, with a voice neither languid nor coarse but virile and glad, urbane in motion as one who shows neither any sign of the country nor the overrefinement of the city. He will shrink from buffoonishness as if from a cliff and relegate obscenity to parasites and mimes. He will use caustic and mordant sayings in such a way that, unless provoked and irritated, he does not bite or taunt back, yet never moves away from the honorable and that composure of mind characteristic of a freeborn man. (6.1.1)

This ideal is very Aristotelian (*Nicomachean Ethics* 1127b33–28b4). Wit serves to restore men from the fatigues of labor. The witty man avoids the excesses of the buffoon and the deficiencies of the agrestic. His mockery is appropriate to a freeborn man (ἐλευθέριος; Pontano's *ingenuus*). Aristotle's other central component of wittiness—tact (ἐπιδεξιότης)—appears a bit later in the chapter, when Pontano mentions that the witty man uses discrimination (6.1.4). An earlier chapter on *delectus* (3.6) shows how similar it is to decorum: the witty man is guided by right reason and jokes in a way appropriate to the speaker, the audience, and

the occasion. The witty man, to use an old-fashioned word, speaks and acts in ways appropriate to a gentleman.

In this chapter, "What kind of man the witty man ought to be" (6.1), Pontano adds some particulars to his Aristotelian ideal from the second most important source for *De sermone*, Cicero's *De oratore*.[31] The witty man will tell fables and pleasant stories (*De sermone* 5.4 2; *De oratore* 2.264) and make use of *sententiae* (4.3.38–39; 2.248), verses (4.3.36; 2.257), and proverbs (4.3.34; 2.258). This chapter is typical of Pontano's procedure throughout the treatise. Aristotle provides the conceptual framework; Cicero provides particulars about different kinds of witticisms. Pontano's sense of decorum leads him to reject parts of Cicero's account of wit, since they are "more appropriate to an orator trying to win a lawsuit than to the kind of decent and dignified mental relaxation we seek" (3.18.11).

On only one occasion does Pontano set out Cicero's view in detail — before proceeding to disagree with it (3.19). Julius Caesar Strabo, the main speaker on wit in *De oratore*, begins his discussion by distinguishing two kinds of witticism, one spread over the entire speech, the other sharp and brief (2.218). His principal reason for making the distinction, however, is to deny art any role in wit: nature makes men witty narrators and imitators, and repartee occurs almost faster than thought (2.219). Quintilian, whose discussion of wit in *Institutio oratoria* 6.3 closely follows *De oratore*, would not dare to say that it completely lacks art, since it does observe some rules, but declares that it mainly depends on nature and the moment (6.3.11). Pontano goes much further in "Art is highly effective for inventing witticisms and funny stories" (3.20), arguing that there is just as much an art of wittiness as one of speaking (rhetoric) or of reasoning (logic). The difference between Pontano and Cicero is not as great as the one between Pontano and Caesar, for Pontano (unlike Quintilian) does not allude to Crassus' objection to Caesar: there is no real art of discourse but one does ob-

serve things that are effective in speaking (*De oratore* 2.232). Caesar yields and delivers a well-ordered speech on witticisms.

Unlike Caesar, Pontano gives no structural importance to the two kinds of witticisms, although the second half of *De sermone*, beginning with 3.17, frequently turns to *De oratore* for ideas and phrases. Pontano expands Cicero's brief statement that "the place and region, as it were, of the laughable . . . are restricted to a sort of baseness or deformity" (2.236) by enumerating several kinds of baseness and deformity (4.1.2). He devotes a chapter (4.4) to Cicero's remark that one must not mock especially wicked, miserable, or powerful men (2.237). In the next (4.5) he takes bits from *De oratore* 2.240–41 to reiterate his point that the witty man must practice moderation. He develops a passing observation, about suiting facial expressions to the kind of joke (2.289), into a chapter about the appropriateness of face, gesture, and voice (4.8). But Pontano is perhaps most indebted to Cicero when he provides places from which witticisms are to be drawn (3.17 and 4.3), although he indicates that he must seek the places for witticisms differently from Cicero, since he is not trying to win over judges but "to relax the mind urbanely and mirthfully" (3.21.1).[32]

One can more clearly see the almost haphazard use that Pontano makes of *De oratore* by contrasting his practice with Castiglione's. For although Bernardo Bibbiena, the principal speaker on witticisms in *Il Cortegiano*, does begin his discourse with Pontano's insistent theme that men naturally seek repose and recreation, Castiglione owes much more to Cicero than to Pontano.[33] After this initial chapter, Bibbiena discusses deformity as the source of the laughable and warns against making fun of the miserable, wicked, or powerful (2.46). (Pontano, by contrast, discusses these two topics from *De oratore* 2.236–37 in different places [4.1.2 and 4.4].) The rest of Bibbiena's discourse follows Cicero's division into two kinds of witticisms—those spread throughout a speech and brief, sharp remarks (*De oratore* 2.218). And Bibbiena follows

more than this principal division; he also, for the most part, considers the material within "urbane and pleasant continuous narration" (2.48–56) and short, sharp sayings (2.57–83) in the same order in which it appears in *De oratore*. It is not until Castliglione reaches practical jokes (*burle*, 2.84), his addition to Cicero's two types of witticism, that he breaks with the order of *De oratore*.

Castiglione makes no mention of the Aristotelian virtues and means of sociability, although like Aristotle, Cicero, and Pontano, he is very concerned with decorum (e.g., 2.50, 67). What Castiglione shares in particular with Pontano (and not with Cicero) is a focus on gentility. Castiglione, after all, is writing about "the form of courtiership most appropriate to a gentleman living in the court of princes" (1.1), and in the discussion of *facezie* he insists that the courtier must always preserve "the dignity of the gentleman" (2.50). Aristotle's tactful, witty man will say things appropriate to a freeborn man (*Nicomachean Ethics* 1128a18–32), but Pontano emphasizes this point much more insistently. For example, as we have seen, when Pontano initially sets forth his distinction between truth and urbanity, he says that when the mean is joined to their pursuit, "there will directly emerge things worthy of good men and freeborn [*ingenuis*] citizens" (1.7.1). In fact, *ingenuus* and *ingenuitas* appear thirty-nine times in *De sermone* (and not once in the excursus on wit in *De oratore*). Although Pontano speaks disparagingly of the flattery (1.14.1) and mendacity (2.14.5) of courtiers, his freeborn witty man is an ancestor of Castiglione's gentleman-courtier.

But Pontano is not trying to fashion an ideal courtier or commemorate the court of the Duchess of Urbino. He tells us that he has dedicated each book of *De sermone* to a different person, as if he were having a discussion with the men of letters in Italy, so that there would be more consolers for the losses and sorrows attendant upon the French and Spanish invasions of the peninsula (1.pr.3). And loss and sorrow do hang over the work, as Pontano did not live to dedicate Books 2 to 6 to anyone and concluded the

work with the deathbed of one of his closest friends, Petrus Compater. In his dying exhortation, Compater insists that conversations about God are the most pleasant of all but that "all conversations among acquaintances and friends" are very pleasant (6.4.37). The emphasis is just as much upon the pleasures of sociability as the consolations of religion. In fact, *De sermone*, a treatise on the Aristotelian virtues of sociability, is also an extended tribute to friendship and conversation in the Accademia Pontaniana.

I appreciate the support given to me by the Division of the Humanities and Social Sciences at Caltech to obtain a scan of Pontano's autograph manuscript and to examine it in Vienna. I am immensely indebted to Julia Haig Gaisser and James Hankins, who have improved every page of the translation and made many other helpful suggestions. They are not responsible, of course, for my errors or occasional obstinacy in refusing their advice.

## NOTES

1. For accounts of Pontano's life see Monti Sabia 1998, 7–27, and Kidwell 1991. The year of Pontano's birth, long thought to be 1426, was established by Monti 1962–63 and confirmed by a letter discovered by Monti Sabia 1986. The origin of "Iovianus," the name that Pontano assumed in the academy that was to become the Accademia Pontaniana, is obscure.

2. More information about people mentioned in this introduction may be found in the notes to the section of *De sermone* indicated in the text.

3. For Pontano's recollections of Alfonso, see Monti Sabia, D'Alessandro, and Iacono 1998 (17–19, on *De sermone*).

4. *De prudentia* (Pontano 1508, B8v). The autobiographical sketch in this work is most easily accessible in Monti Sabia 1998, 74–75 (Italian translation, 84–85).

5. See Furstenberg-Levi 2016 for the "Antonian Portico," as Pontano calls it (6.4.22).

6. See Pontano 2012a for the letters that he wrote first as secretary to Alfonso's wife, Ippolita Maria Sforza (1475–82), and then as secretary to Alfonso (1482–95).

7. In the passage of *De prudentia* cited earlier, Pontano indicates that twice (in 1486 and 1492) he made peace between Ferdinando and the pope. For an account of Pontano's diplomatic activities after the peace of 1486, see Bentley 1987, 176–94.

8. For rebuttals of Guicciardini (*Storia d'Italia* 2.3), see Kidwell 1991, 1–14, and Monti Sabia 1998, 22–23.

9. Monti Sabia 1980, 312–14.

10. *Baiae* (Pontano 2006) and *De amore coniugali* and *Eridanus* (Pontano 2014) are available in the I Tatti Renaissance Library, as is Panormita's *Hermaphroditus* (Beccadelli 2010).

11. The first two dialogues are available in the I Tatti Renaissance Library (Pontano 2012b), and the other three are in press.

12. *De sermone* has traditionally been translated as "On Conversation," but "On Speech" gives a better idea of the breadth of Pontano's concerns. The title used for this volume, *The Virtues and Vices of Speech*, alludes to Pontano's general statement, "I have turned to writing about those things, whether virtues or vices, that occur in discourse" (1.pr.2), and to his project of analyzing speech from the perspective of the Aristotelian mean.

13. Studies of *De sermone* include Walser 1908; Luck 1958; Lupi 1955; Tateo 1972, 94–109; Tateo 1975; Tateo 2006; Ferroni 1980; Alfano 2000; Bistagne 2000; and Quondam 2007, 35–131.

14. Percopo 1907, 59.

15. Monti 1962–63, 235–44.

16. For the few words that he added later to the bottom of the page, see the textual note to 1.pr.4.

17. Tateo in Pontano 2012c, 62.

18. The problems begin with Lupi and Risicato's apparatus criticus (Pontano 1954) and spread to Pighi 1954, 485; Lupi 1955, 386–87; and Bistagne (Pontano 2008, 67).

19. For more details see the textual note at the end of Book 2. For what follows see the textual notes at the beginning and end of Book 1 and the beginning of Books 4, 5, and 6, as well as the ones to the titles of 2.3 and 3.15.

20. In the manuscript, 2.1 begins a new paragraph but not a new page. The only book that does begin on a new page is the third. Also, in the first sentence of the third book Pontano changed "superiore libro" to "primo libro," and the new cross-reference is correct; see note to 3.1.1. Finally, Summonte also took a stab at dividing the first book at 1.26, which does not begin a new paragraph: he wrote "LIB. II." and partially erased it.

21. Once again, 2.3 begins a new paragraph in the manuscript, as does 3.15.

22. Later he changed "insequenti libro" to "alibi expressius," but neither he nor Summonte caught "ut superiore libro ostendimus" (5.2.1), which refers to 3.8.1. I have fudged this slip by translating "as I showed in a previous book," although Pontano probably meant "the previous book." The only other "superiore libro" (4.11.16) refers to the previous book (3.22.4).

23. Although Lupi and Risicato state that these three marginal additions are in Summonte's hand, they are not. It is easiest to see at the beginning of Book 4, where Summonte wrote "LIB. IIII." below Pontano's "L. IIII." The hands are clearly different, and Summonte always — on the slips inserted into the manuscript before the beginnings of books, as well as in the text itself, and in the same hand — writes "LIB." roman numeral in capitals, whereas Pontano is inconsistent: "lib'. 2.," "Liber Tertius," "L. IIII." ".V. liber.," and ".VI. liber."

24. *Nicomachean Ethics* 1106b8–7a8. Courage, for example, is the mean between the excess of rashness and the deficiency of cowardice (1107a33–b1).

25. *Nicomachean Ethics* 1108a19–30 offers an outline; the fuller discussion occurs at 1126b11–28b9. The most important difference between the two passages is that initially one of the virtues is called friendship (1108a28)

but later, Aristotle says, it has been assigned no name but most resembles friendship (1126b19–20).

26. See the note to 3.8 for *agresticity*.

27. Argiropulo's and Bruni's translations both appear in Aristotle 1505; see F7r and 3B6v for *urbanitas*. Manetti's translation has never been printed, and it is not clear how well-known it was. Since Manetti made it in Naples, sometime between 1455 and 1458, at the bidding of Alfonso I (Botley 2004, 69–70, 78–79), Pontano may have known about it. See Aristotle 1455–59, ca. 1473, 169v for *urbanitas*.

28. Actually he coined three, although he does not make much use of *facetitas* or *faceties*, which is attested earlier (see note to 1.12.9). On language as a major theme in Pontano's *Dialogues*, see Gaisser (Pontano 2012b, xxi–xxiv).

29. Pontano does, however, devote a section to distinguishing *agrestitas* (his coinage) from *rusticitas* (3.8). Argiropulo uses *rusticus* (Aristotle 1505, F6v–7r), Bruni, *agrestis* and *rusticus* (Aristotle 1505, 3B6v), and Manetti, *agrestis* (Aristotle 1455–59, ca. 1473, 169v–70r). For the buffoon all three use only *scurra*.

30. Manetti does use *faceti* to translate Aristotle's χαρίεντες (*Nicomachean Ethics* 1128a15; Aristotle 1455–59, ca. 1473, 170r), and Donato Acciaiuoli uses *facetum* when commenting on Aristotle's "man who mocks well" (τὸν εὖ σκώπτοντα: 1128a25; Aristotle 1560, 75v).

31. For an excellent analysis of Cicero's account of wit (*De oratore* 2.219–90), see Leeman, Pinkster, and Nelson 1981–89, 3:172–212. Pontano also made use of Cicero's discussion of joking and conversation in *De officiis* 1.103–5, 132–37, and related several of Cicero's jokes told by Macrobius (*Saturnalia* 2.3).

32. For the rhetorical meaning of *locus* and *place*, see note to 3.17.

33. In fact, it appears to me that Pontano's influence on Castiglione is often exaggerated, although it is clear initially. Bibbiena begins by declaring that man "da natura è tirato al piacere, ed appetisce il riposo e 'l recrearsi" (2.45), which appears to adapt Pontano's "Natura enim duce ad requietem trahimur ac voluptatem" (1.6.1), especially since Bibbiena, like

Pontano, proceeds to the games and festivals instituted by ancient kings, the Romans, and other peoples, and to the recreations of laborers. Furthermore, versions of four jokes appear in both works (see notes to 4.3.9, 4.3.11, 4.11.24, and 5.2.44). In Castiglione (2.82) Alfonso V of Aragon's remark about not putting faith in dreams is introduced with information not in Pontano (5.2.44). The other jokes appear in Poggio, Poliziano, or Machiavelli, and one should not forget that jokes are often handed down by word of mouth. The retort that Castiglione is most likely to have borrowed from Pontano occurs at *De sermone* 4.11.25, since the other sources refer to Rinaldo degli Albizi, not Palla Strozzi. Finally, in the printed edition of *Il Cortegiano*, Castiglione does not refer to Pontano, although manuscript versions do twice, but neither refers to *De sermone*. At 2.35 Sannazaro's verses were originally Pontano's, and, oddly, Cato's joke from Cicero (*De oratore* 2.279) was originally attributed to Pontano before being restored to Cato in the printed edition (*Il Cortegiano* 2.77). Transcriptions of five early manuscripts of *Il Cortegiano* are available on the web (Pugliese et al.). Vian's notes to *Il Cortegiano* 2.42–96 (Castiglione 1894, 176–252) provide many useful parallels between Castiglione and Pontano and thoroughly document Castiglione's dependence on *De oratore*. See also Floriani 1976, 136–42, Ferroni 1980, and Bistagne (Pontano 2008, 57–63).

*Chapter Headings*

## Book One

## Liber Secundus

## Book Two

## Book Three

## Book Four

IOANNIS IOVIANI PONTANI
AD M. ANTONIUM SABELLICUM
DE SERMONE LIBRI SEX


SIX BOOKS ON SPEECH
BY GIOVANNI GIOVIANO PONTANO
DEDICATED TO
MARCANTONIO SABELLICO

# LIBER PRIMUS[1]

## [Praefatio]

1 Annum agimus, M. Antoni Sabellice,[2] tertium ac septuagesimum et eum quidem nequaquam ociosum aut desidem, quando ocio illo frui, quod suapte natura concessum est senectuti, per Italiae turbationes non licet, discursante per Aemiliam, Hetruriam, Latium, Campaniam, Apuliam ac Brutiam Gallorum exercitu, meque ipso de rebus non modo familiaribus verum de vita ipsa solicito. Nam ut desidem agamus vitam ante acta aetas docere satis potuit in tot tantisque occupationibus, docet etiam praesens; quae ne per ignaviam transeat volumina a me scripta diversis etiam de rebus ac disciplinis ostendunt.

2 Itaque vagantibus per Italiam Gallicis, ne dicam eam vastantibus, copiis regnumque Neapolitanum hinc Gallis ipsis, illinc Hispanis occupantibus, a maximis doloribus nos merito labefacientibus animum ac mentem nostram omnino avertimus, quodque mirum fortasse videri possit, convertimus ad scribendas eas sive virtutes sive vitia quae in sermone versantur — non autem aut oratorio aut poetico sed qui ad relaxationem animorum pertinet — atque ad eas quae facetiae dicuntur — id est ad civilem quandam urbanamque consuetudinem domesticosque conventus hominum inter ipsos, non utilitatis tantum gratia convenientium sed iucun-
3 ditatis refocillationisque a labore ac molestiis. Divisimus autem pervestigationem eam in plures libros; quodque solari literarum studiosum hominem ipsorum esset literatorum proprium, quasi dissertatio haec inter literatos qui in Italia florent haberetur, libros ipsos non uni inscripsimus sed compluribus, quo plures habeamus iacturae nostrae nostrorumque dolorum consolatores.

# BOOK ONE

## [Preface]

I am in my seventy-third year, Marcantonio Sabellico, and it is not 1
at all a leisurely or indolent one, since the disturbances in Italy do
not allow me to enjoy that leisure naturally granted to old age, seeing that the French army is running over Emilia, Etruria, Latium,
Campania, Apulia, and Bruttium and that I am anxious not only
for my property but also for my life.[1] For my past life, spent in so
many great occupations, was able to show well enough just how
indolent is the manner of life I lead, as does my present life; the
volumes I have written, which even now concern diverse matters
and disciplines, show whether it is passing away in idleness.[2]

And so, while the French troops are roaming through, not to 2
say devastating, Italy, and the French themselves occupy one part
of the kingdom of Naples and the Spanish another, I have turned
my intellect and mind entirely from the very great sorrows that
naturally are shaking me. Although it may perhaps appear strange,
I have turned to writing about those things, whether virtues or
vices, that occur in discourse — not however in oratorical or poeti-
cal discourse but in the kind that tends to relax our minds — and
to those things called jokes. Such jokes occur in civil and urbane
intercourse and in private meetings of men among themselves, and
are not only useful but also pleasant, and provide refreshment
from work and annoyance. Furthermore, I have divided this inves- 3
tigation into several books. Since consoling the student of letters is
the concern of men of letters, as if this discussion were being held
among the eminent men of letters in Italy, I have inscribed these
books not to one man but to many, so that we may have more
consolers of our loss and sorrows.[3]

4    Tu librum hunc accipe et ad iucunda tantum animum cogitatio-
nesque tuas verte; neque enim te ad complorationem invitamus
sed ad risum atque festivitatem, neque nos ipsos a dolore avertimus, quo te ipsum reliquosque invitemus ad lacrimas, sed ut sciatis nos neque consolatione etiam in summis erumnis indigere et ut
vos ipsos intelligatis Italicis a vastionibus contemplandis a me
averti. Tu vero, M. Antoni,[3] quod tuum est quodque literatorum
omnium proprium, id et contemplare et age, ut arbitrere, cogites,
scias non pauca hominum consiliis atque actionibus geri posse,[4]
rerum tamen omnium summam ad deum optimum maximum referendam esse; qui vero secus arbitrentur vanos eos esse homines
ac maxime futiles.[5]

: I :

*Rationem atque orationem esse homini a natura tributam.*

1 Et rationem homini natura dedit, quo animal ipsum perficeret, et
orationem; atque altera, mente quidem duce, coelitibus maxime
eum esse similem voluit; utraque vero coeteris praestare animali-
2 bus summa etiam cum excellentia et dignitate. Itaque ratione quidem ipsa homines seque suaque et metiuntur et componut omnia,
oratione autem et conciliationem a natura insitam conservant
tuenturque et, quae ratio ipsa dictat, ea explicant atque eloquun-
tur, sive ad usum spectent atque ad seria sive ad iocum ac voluptatem, quando absque illa ratio manca quaedam res esset maximeque imbecilla, cum hominis praesertim vita in actionibus versetur
civilique in congregatione et coetu, cuius oratio ipsa totiusque humanae societatis vinculum sit praecipuum ac sine ea ad summi
boni adeptionem perveniri nullo modo queat.

4

Accept this book and turn your mind and thoughts only to  4
pleasant things. For I am not urging you to lamentation but to
laughter and mirth. Nor do I turn away from sorrow to urge you
and others to tears, but so that you might know that I do not need
consolation even amid the utmost distress, and so that you might
understand that I am turning you away from contemplating the
devastations of Italy. But you, Marcantonio, consider and do what
is appropriate for you and all men of letters: observe, ponder, and
know that not a few things can be done by men's deliberations
and actions, and yet the perfection of all things must be ascribed
to God, the best and greatest. Without doubt, those who think
otherwise are vain and worthless men.

: I :

*Reason and speech were given to man by nature.*

Nature gave man, in order to perfect this animal, both reason and  1
speech. She wanted him, by means of the former, with the mind
as guide, to be as similar as possible to the celestial beings and, by
means of both, to surpass the other animals with the greatest excellence and dignity.[4] And so, with reason men measure and order  2
themselves and all their affairs, but with speech they preserve and
protect the bond of union that has been engrafted by nature, and
they explain and declare what reason itself dictates, whether relating to the useful and serious or to jest and pleasure. Without
speech reason is a maimed and completely weak thing, since man's
life is particularly occupied with actions and with civil assemblies
and meetings, of which speech itself is the foremost bond, as it is
of all human society, and without which it is by no means possible
to attain the highest good.

3   Ut autem ratio ipsa dux est ac magistra ad actiones quasque
dirigendas, sic oratio illorum ministra est omnium quae mente
concepta rationcinandoque agitata depromuntur in medium, cum
sociabiles, ut dictum est, nati simus sitque vivendum in multitudine; quae quo maior est ac frequentior, eo in illa huberior est
copia eorum omnium quibus vita indigeat, quando nascentibus
hominibus inopia data est comes; qua e re vita ipsa longe aptior
redditur atque habilior tum ad assequendas virtutes tum ad felici-
tatem comparandam.

4   Igitur ut ratio dux est ac magistra dirigendis actionibus virtuti-
busque comparandis, oratio vero mentis est interpres rationisque
ipsius instrumentum quasi quoddam (siquidem consultationes,
consilia, ratiocinationes ipsae denique dissertionibus constant, dis-
sertiones vero verbis), sic eadem ipsa oratio instrumentum quoque
rationi et quasi materiam sumministrat in qua versetur. Nam si
laudantur recte qui loquuntur dicuntque apposite quod sentiunt,
improbentur necesse est qui male atque incomposite.


:   2   :

*Virtutem et vitium versari etiam circa orationem.*


1   Quod si ubicunque laudi locus suus est ac vituperationi, illic et
virtuti et vitio, nimirum et in oratione virtus ac vitium sedem sibi
constituent aliquam ut, quemadmodum in agendis rebus, sic in
explicandis quae animo menteque concepta sunt, sententiis item
dicendis atque in habenda oratione sive ad multos sive apud paucos, modus mensuraque servanda sit ac mediocritas illa quae
virtutes constituit estque in omni vitae genere merito laudanda.

2   Etenim graviter alii quae sentiunt explicant ac composite, inepte

Moreover, as reason itself is the leader and guide for the direc- 3
tion of every action, so speech is the minister of all those things
that are conceived by the mind, considered by meditating, and
made public, since we are born sociable, as they say, and must live
among the multitude.[5] The greater and larger this is, the more
abundant the supply of all those things that life requires, since
want is given as a companion to men at birth. As a result, life itself
is rendered much more convenient and more able both to acquire
virtues and to obtain happiness.

Therefore, as reason is the leader and guide for directing actions 4
and obtaining virtues, and speech is the interpreter of the mind
and the instrument, as it were, of reason itself (since consultations, deliberations, and, finally, reasonings themselves consist of
discourses and discourses in turn consist of words), so likewise
speech itself provides to reason the instrument and also, so to
speak, the material on which to act. For if those who aptly say and
speak what they feel are rightly praised, those who do so poorly
and awkwardly must be censured.

: 2 :

*Virtue and vice also apply to speech.*

Now if every topic provides a place for praise and blame, and in 1
that place also one for virtue and vice, no doubt in speech too virtue and vice will make a place for themselves, so that, just as in the
conduct of affairs, so in explaining those things conceived by intellect and mind, and likewise in stating opinions and in making a
speech before many or few people, a limit and measure must be
observed, as well as the mean that determines the virtues and must
deservedly be praised in every kind of life. For some explain what 2

alii ac ieiune: hique ut inepti levesque improbantur, illi contra
commendantur ut graves atque compositi. Ergo et in oratione
quoque virtus sibi locum comparavit illumque ipsum cum dignitate et laude.

∶ 3 ∶

*Maximam esse vim atque auctoritatem orationis.*

1  Nec vero populosissimis in civitatibus amplissimisque in administrationibus non maximum sibi peperisse locum summamque auctoritatem eos constat qui inter coeteros essent elocutione praeci-
2  pue clari; inde ea qui pollerent oratores dicti. Sed nos hac in parte
de ea quae oratoria sive vis facultasque sive ars dicitur nihil omnino loquimur, verum de oratione tantum ipsa communi quaque
homines adeundis amicis communicandis negociis in quotidianis
praecipue utuntur sermonibus, in conventibus, consessionibus,
congressionibus familiaribusque ac civilibus consuetudinibus. Qua
e re alia quadam hi ratione commendantur quam qui oratores dicuntur atque eloquentes.

∶ 4 ∶

*Maximam esse in hominibus orationis varietatem*
*ac diversitatem.*

1  Nec vero natura in hoc quoque a se ipsa discessit aut ab ea, quae
sua ipsius propria est, varietate ac dissimilitudine. Cum aliorum
sermones severi sint ac subtristes, aliorum iucundi et lepidi, huius

8

they think gravely and in an orderly manner, others ineptly and meagerly; the latter are censured as inept and slight, but the former are commended as grave and orderly. And so in speech too virtue has obtained a place for itself and done so with dignity and praise.

## : 3 :

### *The power and authority of speech are very great.*

And indeed it is known that in the most populous states and the largest administrations the people who acquired the greatest position and highest authority for themselves were especially celebrated among all others for expressing themselves. Therefore those who excelled at it were called orators. But in this part I am not talking at all about what is called the power, skill, or art of oratory but only about common speech and the one that men use when addressing friends and imparting affairs, especially in daily discourse, in meetings, gatherings, encounters, familiar and civil intercourse. And so these men are commended in a different way than those who are called orators and eloquent.

## : 4 :

### *The variety and diversity of speech in men are very great.*

But in this area also nature has not departed from itself or from that variety and difference that are characteristic of it. While the conversation of some is severe and rather sad and of others pleas-

9

blanda sit elocutio atque ornata, illius inculta et aspera, atque alius
in loquendo prae se ferat urbis mores, alius vero ruris, est videri
qui velit facetus et comis, contra qui austerus et rigidus, qui maxime verus omnique a simulatione alienus, secus autem cui dissimulatio placeat aut ea quae Graece est *ironia*. Itaque loquendi genus
tum cuiusque naturam tum etiam mores sequi potissimum videtur.

2    Quid quod populi gentesque, sive natura ab ipsa sive ab institutione et usu quodque alia alibi magis probantur suntque in
pretio maiori, aliae taciturniores sunt, contra loquaciores aliae?
Magniloquentia delectat Hispanos; fucatus ac compositus sermo
Graecos. Romanorum gravis fuit oratio, Lacedaemoniorum brevis
et horrida, Atheniensium multa et studiosa, at Carthaginensium
Afrorumque callida et vafra, de natura illorum sic dicta. Quo fit ut
genus colloquendi alibi aliud magis probetur aut minus.

3    Cum igitur de fortitudine disseruerimus deque virtutibus iis
quae in pecunia versantur, quae quidem plures sunt ac diversae,
itemque de magnanimitate, prudentia deque fortuna ei contraria,
tentemus hoc in ocio, quod senectus nobis concessit visque etiam
hostilis, de iis item virtutibus praecepta tradere quae in verbis versantur quotidianoque in sermone, quique plerumque indicare
mores cuiusque consuevit ac vel laudem afferre vel reprehensionem, etsi, ut Horatius inquit, 'Oderunt hilarem tristes tristemque
iocosi.' Neque enim nos de laude sic nunc loquimur atque impro-
batione, ut qui ex aliorum iudiciis virtutes metiamur ac vitia, verum a ratione tantum atque a mediocritate, penes quam iudicium
est atque examen virtutum omnium.

ant and charming, this man's speech is flattering and ornate, and that man's unadorned and harsh, one reveals in speaking the manners of the city but another those of the country, one wishes to appear witty and affable but another austere and rigid, one who wishes to appear especially truthful and averse to all simulation but another who likes dissimulation or what is called "irony" in Greek.[6] And so the type of speaking is seen especially to follow each person's nature and character.

What about the fact that some peoples and countries, whether 2 by nature itself or by education and usage and because some things are more approved and held more valuable in one place than in another, are more taciturn, while others are more loquacious? Grandiloquence delights Spaniards; artificial and well-arranged speech, the Greeks. The speech of the Romans was grave, of the Spartans concise and rough, of the Athenians copious and studied, but of the Carthaginians and Africans clever and cunning, their speech so called from their nature.[7] So it happens that one type of speech is more approved in one place and less in another.

Therefore, since I have treated of courage and of those virtues 3 concerned with money, which indeed are many and diverse, and likewise of magnanimity, prudence, and of fortune which acts contrary to prudence, in this leisure that old age and, also, enemy forces have granted me, let me try likewise to hand down precepts about those virtues concerned with words and daily conversation, which usually reveals each person's character and brings praise or blame, although, as Horace says, "The sad hate the cheerful and the humorous hate the sad."[8] For I am not now talking of praise and blame as one who measures virtues and vices from the judgments of others but only from reason and the mean, in whose power is the judging and weighing of all the virtues.[9]

: 5 :

*Etiam in oratione servandam esse mediocritatem.*

1 Censemus igitur rerum nostrarum omnium, non in agendo solum
verum etiam in loquendo explicandisque in sententiis ac consiliis
mentis denique atque animi conceptis sive seriis sive iocosis, mediocritatem esse iudicem, quam qui sequantur ii et in dicendo et in
agendo cum delectu rationem retineant ipsaque cum ratione modum ac mensuram, sive sermo ipse gravis sit atque austerus sive
iucundus et comis aut in festivitatem deflectat aut in severitatem.
De quibus singillatim distincteque ordine quidem dicemus ac pro
natura virtutis cuiusque sua.

2 Verum quoniam virtutum earum quae in loquendo versantur
oratio materia est quasi quaedam eaque ipsa nobis a natura tradita,
id videndum est, dum aut faceti videri volumus aut graves, ne adversus naturam ipsi propriam contentionem moliamur aliquam,
neve velimus universa illi acie ire obviam, quod est non modo difficile ac laboris plenum, verum etiam reprehendi iure solet a sa-
pientibus viris, cum (ut proverbio etiam monemur) nihil invita sit
agendum Minerva, hoc est natura repugnante. Nec nisi etiam sa-
pientissime est a Cicerone praeceptum, ut, quibus ipsi apti rebus
3 sumus, in iis potissimum occupemur. Nam etsi concessum est aliquando, propria relicta natura, alienae se accommodare, tamen
adversus universam ut suscipiatur certamen, nullo id pacto videtur
committendum, quando praestari id cum laude ac dignitate vix
omnino queat, idque si ad breve fortasse tempus, natura tamen
ipsa ad id quod est proprium ac suum tandem recurrit. Qua e re
argui solet atque haud iniuria accusari vitae inconstantia ac morum levitas.

∷ 5 ∷

*Even in speech the mean must be observed.*

I am firmly of the opinion that the mean is the judge of all our  1
affairs, not only in acting but also in speaking and in explaining
our thoughts, the deliberations of our mind, and lastly the con-
cepts of our intellect, whether serious or joking. Those who follow
with discrimination the mean in both speaking and acting hold
fast to reason and to limit and measure with it, whether their
conversation is grave and austere or pleasant and affable or turns
toward mirth or severity. I will speak about these things singly
and distinctly, in order and in accordance with the nature of each
quality.

But since language is the material, as it were, of all the qualities  2
that occur in speaking and has been given to us by nature, we
must see to it, when we want to appear witty or grave, that we do
not quarrel with our own nature and that we do not wish to go up
against it with the whole battle line. This is not only difficult and
laborious but also is usually and justly censured by wise men,
since, as the proverb also admonishes us, nothing must be done
when Minerva is unwilling, that is when nature is opposed.[10] Nor
has it been less wisely taught by Cicero that we should occupy
ourselves above all with those things for which we are suited.[11] For  3
although it has occasionally been granted to adapt oneself to another's nature, having abandoned one's own, nevertheless it seems
not at all right that one should engage in a struggle against the
whole of one's nature. One can hardly do this with praise and
dignity, and if by chance one can for a short time, nature itself
nevertheless comes back at last to what is peculiarly its own. On
this account inconstancy of life and levity of character are usually
and not wrongfully blamed and accused.

: 6 :

*A natura inesse homini cupiditatem quietis ac recreationis.*

1 Principio, quod hominum vita tum corporis tum animi laborum
plena est ac molestiarum, iccirco post labores cessatio quaeritur, in
qua recreetur animus, atque inter molestias iocus. Natura enim
2 duce ad requietem trahimur ac voluptatem. Nam et a regibus et
bene constitutis populis et a Romanis praecipue, gentium dominis, ludi fuere diversi etiam generis instituti, quibus spectandis
tum populus universus tum magistratus ipsi relaxarentur quotidianis a laboribus negociisque susceptis et privatim et publice, quando
et fossores et qui caedendis exercentur lapidibus et ioca inter se
funditant oblectandi gratia et, illa ubi defuerint, cantu laborem
mulcent leniuntque erumnas. Unde et recte et naturaliter ab equite
Romano eodemque poeta suavissimo dictum est, 'Crura sonant
ferro sed canit inter opus.'

: 7 :

*Urbanitatem ac veritatem merito laudari.*

1 Merito igitur laudatur urbanitas expetiturque a plerisque urbano-
rum ac facetorum hominum consuetudo ac familiaritas. Et quia
tractandis rebus atque administrandis ratio recta praesidet, cuius
maxime amica est veritas, proinde, a quibus ea colitur, ii et com-
2 mendantur ab omnibus et summo habentur in pretio. Ad hoc autem tum veri tum iucundi studium motusque circa ea animorum
atque affectus moderatio ubi accesserit eaque quae mediocritas dicitur, existent illico quae et viris bonis et civibus ingenuis dignae,

: 6 :

*Nature has given man a desire for repose and restoration.*

First of all, since the life of men is full of labors and troubles of 1
both body and mind, after labor we desire rest, in which the mind
is restored, and, among troubles, we desire jokes. For we are drawn
by nature as our guide toward repose and pleasure. For kings, 2
well-regulated peoples, and especially the Romans, masters of the
world, instituted games of various kinds, so that by viewing them
the whole populace and the magistrates themselves might relax
from their daily labors and private and public business. Diggers
and stonecutters hurl jokes at one another for amusement, and, in
the absence of jokes, soothe their labor and lighten their cares
with song. Thus a Roman equestrian and a very pleasant poet
rightly and naturally said, "His leg irons resound, but he sings at
his work."[12]

: 7 :

*Urbanity and truth are deservedly praised.*

Therefore urbanity is deservedly praised, and many seek inter- 1
course and intimacy with urbane and witty men. And because
right reason presides over the handling and administering of affairs and is the special friend of truth, so those who cultivate truth
are commended by all and held most valuable. When moderation 2
and what is called the mean are added to this pursuit of the true
and the pleasant and to the motions and affections of the mind
toward these things, there will directly emerge virtues worthy of

et suo etiam utraque nomine vocata est virtus: altera quidem quae susceptorum laborum honestum sit levamen relaxatioque maxime laudabilis a curis ac molestiis, altera vero quae hominem ipsum ita constituat, ut per eam constet humana conciliatio vigeatque in civitate fides, penes quam actionum nostrarum omnium ac negociationum vinculum existat ac promissorum dictorumque observatio. Quod ita esse nobis innuit Christus et deus idem et homo, cum veritatem se se esse professus est.

3    Verum cum ipsis e virtutibus aliae versentur aut in eroganda pecunia aut in obeundis periculis, aliae in moderandis voluptatibus aut in reddendo quod suum est cuique, aliisque atque aliis aliae, nomineque singulae appellentur suo, hae quidem duae quae tum veritatem in dicendo tum leporem sequuntur circa orationem tantum operam suam conferunt verbaque sibi perinde ac materiam subministrant. Et alteri quidem, quae relaxationem quaeritat ab laboribus ac molestiis, maiores nostri nomen fecere urbanitati et, qui ea praeditus esset, nunc urbanum dixere, nunc vero aut facetum aut comem.

: 8 :

*Unde urbani dicti sunt ac faceti.*

1    Et urbanos quidem vocavere, quod ii oratione uterentur et cive et eo qui in urbe conversaretur digna, cum viventium in agris et vita esset agrestior et sermo etiam qui rus referret rusticanaeque consuetudinis tum mores tum etiam locutionem ac gestus, facetos vero, quod in congressionibus collocutionibusque domesticis, familiaribus item ac popularibus in sermonibus, verba cum iucundi-
2    tate facerent cumque audientium voluptate ac recreatione. Etenim

good men and freeborn citizens, and each of the two virtues has been designated with its own name.[13] One is the honorable alleviation of labors undertaken and a praiseworthy relaxation from cares and troubles, but the other constitutes man so that human union lasts and in the city flourishes trust, in whose power lie the bond of all our actions and affairs and the observing of promises and one's word. That such is the case Christ, both God and man, intimated when he declared himself to be the truth.[14]

But since some virtues involve paying money or confronting 3 dangers, others moderating pleasures or giving each man his due, others other things, and each is called by its own name, these two that follow from truthfulness and charm in speaking do their work only in speech and provide themselves with words as their material. And to the one that seeks relaxation from labors and troubles our ancestors gave the name urbanity, and they called the man endowed with it sometimes urbane but at others witty or affable.

: 8 :

*Why men have been called urbane and witty.*

And they called them urbane because they used language worthy 1 of a citizen and of one who lived in a city, since the life of those living in the fields was more rustic and their conversation too, recalled the country and the customs, pronunciation, and gestures of country intercourse. But they called men witty [*facetos*] because in gatherings and domestic colloquies and likewise in familiar and public conversation they spoke [*verba . . . facerent*] agreeably and pleased and restored their listeners.[15] For among the ancients the 2

apud priscos illos verbum *facio* maxima in usurpatione fuit loquendi, quando et 'foedus facere' et 'pacem' et 'bellum' et 'insidias' et
'ludos' et 'delicias' et 'iocos' et 'verba facere' dicebant aliaque etiam
plurima diversi quoque generis; et qui eleganter ac copiose, 'facundos,' et tum 'facundiam' tum 'facunditatem' dicendi vim: quibus in
vocibus temporis illius poetae, quantitati uti consulerent, tertiam
literam geminarunt. Nam, ne a *fatu* dictus sit *facundus*, tertia re-
3   pugnat litera; neve a *fando*, plura simul obstant. Itaque, qui verba
facerent serendis in sermonibus cum audientium oblectatione ac
dicendi lepore, facetos eos dixere et comes, ad haec et festivos et
lepidos nec minus libenter etiam salsos.

∶ 9 ∶

*De lepidis, festivis et salsis.*

1   Quanquam autem hi ipsi quos nominavimus eodem continentur
genere suntque inter se cognati et familiae pene eiusdem, differunt
tamen inter se. Quocirca ostendendum videtur in quo ab alio alius
iudicetur differre; neque indigna sane neque inutilis inquisitio,
cum sit omnino nihil tam fugiendum in disserendo ratiocinan-
doque quam ne confusio incertitudoque exoriatur e verbis aliqua,
neque aliud magis sequendum quam ut distinctio adhibeatur se-
2   lectioque et verborum et rerum. Tentabimus igitur, quoad fieri
poterit et res ipsa tulerit, secernere eos inter se ut quid commune
invicem habeant, quid item disiunctum, aperte intelligatur. Ac
materia quidem ipsa communis est, oratio scilicet ac verba, et item
finis ac propositum. Quaeritur enim pariter ex dictis oblectatio ac

word *make* was used very much in speaking, since they would say "make a treaty" and "peace" and "war" and "an ambush" and "game of" and "sport of" and "jokes" and "make words" and also many other things of a different sort. They would call those who spoke eloquently and copiously "fluent" and the ability of speaking, "fluency" and "eloquence," in which words the poets of that time, paying attention to quantity, doubled the third letter. For the third letter is inconsistent with the derivation of *facundus* from *fatum*, and many things stand in the way of the derivation from *fāri*.[16] And so those who spoke and engaged in conversation to the delight of their listeners and with charm of speech were called witty and affable, as well as mirthful and charming, and, no less gladly, pungent.[17]

:  9  :

*On the charming, mirthful, and pungent.*

Although these people whom we have just mentioned belong to 1 the same class and are related and almost of the same family, they nevertheless differ among themselves. So it seems right to show how one is judged to differ from another. Nor indeed is this an unworthy or useless investigation, since in discussing and reasoning nothing must be more entirely avoided than any confusion and uncertainty arising from words, and nothing is more to be sought than distinction and selection of words and things. Therefore I 2 will try, as much as may be and as the subject will allow, to distinguish them one from the other so that it may be clearly understood what they have in common and likewise how they differ. And indeed their matter is the same, namely speech and words, and likewise their end and intent. For delight and pleasure are

3 voluptas. Nanque, ut in carminibus nostris adolescentes lusimus, *lepos* levando est ab labore dictus, partim mutatis partim contractis literis. Itaque lepidus is videtur qui suavitate dicendi teneritudineque quasi quadam delectat et verborum et rerum, ut apud Terentium:

> Aedepol te, mea Antiphila, laudo et fortunatam iudico
> dum huic formae studuisti mores ut essent consimiles.

Omnia ibi in gratiam puellae et cum lepore dicuntur; et apud Plautum:

> Cum ego antehac te amavi et mihi amicam esse crevi,
> mea Gymnasium, et matrem tuam, tum id mihi hodie
> aperuistis, tuque atque haec: soror si mea esses,
> qui magis potueritis honorem ire habitum,
> nescio, ut meus est animus fieri non posse arbitror;
> ita, omnibus relictis rebus, mihi frequentem operam dedistis
> et eo vos amo et eo magnam a me iniistis gratiam.

Tantopere autem dicendi olim lepos datus est laudi, ut inde primus ille qui post idem genti cognomen reliquit cognominatus sit Lepidus.

4 Atque ut inter sapores suaves quidam tantum sunt, quidam et suaves simul et salsi, sic etiam et dicta alia tantum lepida, alia lepida pariter ac salsa, quemadmodum ratio ipsa fert aut dicendi aut respondendi, ut cum Pompeius, Ciceronem illudens, quanquam vultu fortasse hilariore dixisset, interrogans, 'Gener ubi est tuus?,' ibi Cicero, qui amarum atque aculeatum inesse quiddam verbis illius intelligeret, reddidit illi in respondendo par, 'Ubi et socer est tuus.' Erat enim Caesar belli suscepti et dux et auctor, quem Dolabella sequebatur. Itaque et qui aderant suavitate eos atque extemporalitate responsi affecit et suavitati salem adiunxit, ut ipse

equally sought from witticisms. For, as I playfully wrote in my   3
poems when a young man, *lepos* is derived from "levare laborem,"
partially by changing, partially by contracting letters.[18] And so the
charming person is seen to be the one who delights with a sweet-
ness of speaking and, as it were, a tenderness of words and subject
matter, as in Terence:

> By Pollux, my Antiphila, I praise you and judge you fortu-
> nate for having striven to make your character entirely like
> your beauty.[19]

All of this is charmingly said to please the girl. And in Plautus:

> Although I previously loved you and considered you and
> your mother my friends, my Gymnasium, you and she have
> proved it to me today. If you were my sister, I don't know
> how you could have held me in more esteem — in fact, I
> firmly think it impossible. Abandoning all your own con-
> cerns, you have bestowed such constant care on me. For this
> reason I love you and feel so greatly obligated to you.[20]

And long ago charm in speaking was praised so much that the first
man who was given the cognomen, "Lepidus," afterward left it to
his family.

And just as some tastes are only sweet, others both sweet and   4
salty, so also some witticisms are only charming, others pungent as
well as charming, as the manner of speaking and responding requires. For example, when Pompey, mocking Cicero, although
perhaps with a cheerful expression, asked, "Where is your son-in-
law?," Cicero, as he realized that there was something bitter and
pointed in Pompey's words, responded in kind, "Right where your
father-in-law is."[21] For Caesar was the leader and initiator of the
war that had been undertaken, and Dolabella was following him.
Thus Cicero affected those present with the pleasantness and
spontaneity of his response and added pungency to pleasantness

quidem arbitrer utrumque, et Ciceronem et Pompeium, ex eo in risum conversos. Atque eiusmodi quidem dicta dicuntur salsa et
5 qui iis utuntur ipsi quoque salsi. Lepidis itaque suavitas tantum inest dictis, salsis etiam acumen, quando salsus sapor est ipse quidem acutior. Inesse autem eiusmodi dictis acrimoniam docet etiam apud Terentium illud ipsum de quo gloriatur ille, 'Eon, Strato, es ferox quia imperium in belluis habes?' Illud autem, etsi salsum admodum, non caret tamen oscenitate, 'Lepus tute es et pulpamentum quaeris.' Plautinum vero hoc et salsum et lepidum et cive etiam ingenuo dignum:

> Speravi ego istam tibi parituram filium,
> verum non est puero gravida sed insania.

6 Veniamus ad festivos, qui mihi videntur a fando dicti, vetustate temporum immutante literas. Festis enim diebus mos fuit et benigne hilariterque affari populum et in ludis, qui in honorem deorum fiebant, oblectare eos qui divinas ad res convenerant, blande eos appellando atque accipiendo comiter. Quanto autem studio diebus iis festis oblectamenta quaererentur, indicio sunt et ludi et tibiae et tubae et cantus et choreae et lectisternia et templorum apparatus ac theatrorum et porticuum et viarum et ipsa etiam fercula ut, qui illis in ludis, sacrificiis, pompis, ferculis in popularium ac convenarum gratiam iucunde se haberent eaque et excogitarent et loquerentur quae ad iucunditatem facerent ac laetitiam
7 merito ii festivi vocarentur. Adhibent praeterea festivi in iocando aeque ac ludendo dicendoque varietatem permultam, quae sermones maxime condiat, ut quae in cessationibus animorumque relaxatione praecipue exigatur. Ludi enim ac festi dies, etsi in honorem deorum, cessationis tamen gratia potissimum fuere inventi. Indicio sunt apud Graecos nostrosque actiones, sive comoediarum

so that, in my opinion, both of them, Cicero and Pompey, were moved to laughter. And witticisms of this sort are called pungent and those who make use of them are too. And so in charming wit- 5 ticisms there is only pleasantness; in pungent ones there is also sharpness, since a pungent taste is itself sharper. The following line in Terence, on which the speaker prides himself, shows that there is something biting in witticisms of this kind, "So, Strato, you're fierce because you rule over wild beasts?"[22] The following, though very pungent, is not without obscenity, "You're a hare and you're looking for delicacies."[23] But these lines of Plautus are pungent, charming, and also worthy of a freeborn citizen:

I hoped that she would bear you a son, but she's pregnant not with a child but with madness.[24]

Let's come to the mirthful [*festivos*], whose name, it seems to 6 me, is derived from *fari* [to speak], a long period of time having changed the letters. For in festivals it was customary to address [*affari*] the people kindly and cheerfully and to delight with spectacles in honor of the gods those who had assembled for the sacred rites, calling upon them pleasantly and receiving them affably. And an indication of the diligence with which amusements were sought in those festivals is the games, pipes, trumpets, songs, dances, feasts of the gods, decoration of temples, of theaters, of porticoes, and of streets, and even the carrying frames themselves. So in these games, sacrifices, processions, and frames, the people who showed themselves to be pleasant, gratifying countrymen and strangers, and who contrived and said things suited to pleasantness and joy, were deservedly called mirthful. Moreover, in joking, 7 as well as in playing and speaking, the mirthful use a great deal of variety, especially to enliven conversation, since it is particularly required for rest and relaxation of our minds. For spectacles and festivals, although in honor of the gods, nevertheless were primarily invented for rest. The performances of comedies and tragedies,

sive tragoediarum: in iis enim et histriones mimique et musici et gladiatores exhiberi soliti, venationes item et pugnae navales. Itaque festivi varietatem admiscent plurimam in dicendo, ludendo, delectando.

: 10 :

## De comibus.

1 Iam vero comis viri studium eo etiam spectat, dicendo ut delectet pariatque audienti iucunditatem; eius tamen consilium est, quae a se dicantur, non ut delectent modo, verum etiam ut sint grata, nec solum verba, verum etiam res ipsae quae dicuntur, quippe cuius 2 studium sit gratificari atque in gratiam loqui audientium. Itaque et ornatum rebus adiungit praestatque quod Terentianus ille desiderat, 'Ornato munus verbis quantum potes,' et in eo est maxime, ut verba etiam ipsa resque quae a se dicantur gratiam prae se ferant; itaque a comendo, hoc est ornando, dictus. Puellae nanque placere ornatu praesertim amatoribus student illisque ex eo gratiores fieri. Vide, quaeso, quibus verbis quam etiam comptis, quam gratis item sententiis Aeneam alloquatur apud Virgilium Evandrus:

Aude, hospes, contemnere opes et te quoque dignum
finge deo rebusque veni non asper egenis.

Non dubitavit Livius post sermonem illum a Marcello habitum adversum Nolanum Bancium, qua in collocutione multa in commendationem, multa de beneficentia populi Romani dixerat deque futura benevolentia et opera in illum sua, non dubitavit, inquam, haec dicere: 'Ea verborum comitate devinxisse sibi iuvenem.'

by the Greeks and by us, are an indication. For in them actors, mimes, musicians, and gladiators were customarily exhibited, and likewise hunts and naval battles. And so the mirthful stir the greatest variety into speaking, playing, and delighting.

: 10 :

## On the affable.

Now the affable man also endeavors in speaking to delight and create pleasure for the listener. Nevertheless, he intends that what he says will not only delight but also be gratifying, not just the words but the subject under discussion, since his endeavor is to gratify and speak gratifyingly to his audience. And so he adorns his subject and accomplishes what the character in Terence desires, "Adorn my gift with words as much as you can."[25] The principal thing the affable man seeks is that the words and the subject spoken by him be gratifying, and thus his name derives from *como* ("make elegant"), that is from adorning.[26] For girls are especially eager to please their lovers with their adornment and thus to be more gratifying to them. Look, please, how Vergil's Evander addresses Aeneas with such elegant words and such gratifying sentiments:

> Guest, dare to scorn riches, make yourself, too, worthy of the god, and do not come unkindly to our poverty.[27]

Livy did not hesitate, after the conversation Marcellus had with Bantius of Nola, a colloquy in which he said much in praise of the Roman people and much about their beneficence, their future goodwill, and their exertions for Bantius — Livy did not hesitate, I say, to say this: "He bound the young man to himself with the

Comitatem appellavit quod undequaque in gratiam illius Marcellus esset locutus.

3    An non, quod in convivio coenisque grata omnia convivis esse debeant ac praesertim sermones, translatum est verbum etiam ipsum ad coenas, ut comiter accepti et convivio et hospitio dicantur, quod et verba admodum grata sermonesque et frons etiam serena

4    epulis accesserit? Omnino vero comis viri oratio, quo grata sit atque iucunda et lepida, versatur magna e parte in fabellis referendis; in iis enim et oblectationi maxime amplus conceditur locus et verborum ornatui; suntque omnino comitate praediti enarratores iucundissimi et in conviviis et in circulis collocutionibusque sive inter paucos sive multos. Qua quidem e re Ioannes Boccatius maximam sibi laudem, apud doctos pariter atque indoctos homines, comparavit centum illis conscribendis fabulis, quae hodie in hominum versantur manibus. Hoc idem Graece conatus est Lucianus. Innuere autem hoc ipsum quod dicimus Plautus videtur, cum ait in Milite glorioso:

> Mihi ad enarrandum hoc argumentum est comitas,
> si ad auscultandum vestra erit benignitas.

Quae autem et qualis sit comitas, Ovidius in commutationibus illis formarum explicandis plurimis in locis ostendit, praecipue vero locus is declarat, qui est de Vertunni conversione in aniculam. Cuius hic particulam inserere placuit, idque voluptatis tantum gratia varietatisque ostendendae:

> Rege sub hoc Pomona fuit, qua nulla Latinas
> inter Hamadryadas coluit studiosius hortos,
> nec fuit arborei studiosior altera foetus;
> unde tenet nomen: non silvas illa nec amnes,
> rus amat et ramos felicia poma ferentes.
> Nec iaculo gravis est, sed adunca dextera falce
> qua modo luxuriem premit et spatiantia passim

affability of his words."[28] He called it affability because Marcellus had spoken to gratify him in every way.

Wasn't the word *affable* [*comis*] also transferred to dinners [*coenas*] because at banquets and dinners everything, especially the conversation, ought to gratify the guests, so that they might be said to have been affably received at a banquet and an entertainment because gratifying words and conversation and also a cheerful countenance accompanied the dishes? But in general the speech of an affable man, to be gratifying and pleasant and charming, consists in great part in telling stories, for in them the greatest scope is given to delighting and to adorning words, and in general the pleasantest storytellers in banquets, companies, and colloquies, whether among few people or many, have been endowed with affability. For this reason Giovanni Boccaccio has obtained the greatest praise, equally among the learned and unlearned, by writing those hundred stories that today are in everyone's hands. In Greek Lucian tried the same thing. And Plautus appears to mean the same thing that I'm saying when he says in *The Braggart Soldier*:

> I'll have the affability to recount the argument of the play if
> you'll have the kindness to listen attentively.[29]

Ovid shows the nature of affability in many passages while setting forth those changes of forms, but especially in that passage on the conversion of Vertumnus into a little old woman. I've decided to insert here a bit of it solely for pleasure and variety:

> Under this king lived Pomona, who cultivated gardens more
> devotedly than any of the Latin wood nymphs. No other
> was more devoted to the fruit of the tree; from this she takes
> her name. She doesn't love forests or rivers but the country-
> side and branches bearing fertile fruit. Her right hand does
> not hold a javelin but a curved pruning hook, with which she
> sometimes checks the luxuriant growth and restrains the

brachia compescit, fixa modo cortice lignum
inserit et succos alieno praestat alumno;
nec sentire sitim patitur bibulaeque[6] recurvas
radicis fibras labentibus irrigat undis.

Quibus dictis haud multo post transit ad Vertunni amores atque
ait:

O quoties habitu duri messoris aristas
corbe tulit verique fuit messoris imago,
tempora saepe gerens freno religata recenti.

Hisque aliisque varie eleganterque explicatis, vertit illum in anum
et blande et illecebrose loquentem, quippe quae,

Innitens baculo, positis per tempora canis,
assimulavit anum, cultosque intravit in hortos,
pomaque mirata est 'Tantoque peritior,' inquit,
'omnibus es nymphis quas continet Albula ripis.
Salve, virginei flos intemerate pudoris'
paucaque laudatae dedit oscula, qualia nunquam
vera dedisset anus; glebaque incurva resedit,
suspiciens pandos autumni pondere ramos.
Ulmus erat contra speciosa nitentibus uvis,
quam socia postquam pariter cum vite probavit
'At, si staret,' ait, 'caelebs sine palmite truncus
nil praeter frondes, quare peteretur, haberet.
Haec quoque, quae iuncta vitis requiescit in ulmo,
si non iuncta foret, terrae acclinata iaceret.
Tu tamen exemplo non tangeris arboris huius?'

Vides quam et delectet et comiter ludat et variet rem ac dictionem
et verbis innitatur ornatis ac maxime suis. Verum de hac ipsa
comitate post huberius.

branches spreading in every direction, sometimes splits the bark and inserts a cutting and provides sap to the foreign nursling. Nor does she allow it to feel thirst; she irrigates the curving fibers of the thirsty root with flowing water.[30]

Soon after these words Ovid proceeds to Vertumnus' love and says:

O how many times in the guise of a rough reaper he brought ears of grain in a basket, and he was the image of a real reaper, his temples often bound with a new bridle.[31]

After setting forth these things with variety and elegance, Ovid turns Vertumnus into an old woman, who speaks flatteringly and enticingly:

Leaning on a staff, white hair about the temples, he assumed the likeness of an old woman. He entered the cultivated gardens, looked at the fruit, and said, "You are so much more skillful than all of the nymphs the Albula contains in its banks. Hail, pure flower of virginal modesty." He gave a kiss or two to the one he'd praised—kisses such as a real old woman never would have given—and sat bowed on the earth, looking up at the branches bent with the weight of autumn. There was an elm opposite, splendid with glistening grapes. After he commended the elm and its companion vine, he said, "If the trunk stood unmated without the vine shoot, it would have no reason to be sought besides its leaves. Also, if this vine, which rests joined to its elm, had not been joined, it would lie and lean on the earth. Yet you won't be touched by the example of this tree?"[32]

You see how he delights, plays affably, varies the subject and the diction, and relies on words that he has adorned and made completely his own. But later I will talk more fully about affability.

: II :

## De blandis.

1 Eorum vero qui blandi dicuntur, etsi eadem videtur esse materia, finis tamen ubique non est idem; nec sola delectatio ac iucunditas quaeritur, verum potius utilitas, quale illud est:

> Nunc obsecro te, Milphio, hanc per dexteram
> perque hanc sororem levam perque oculos tuos
> perque meos amores perque Adelphasium meam
> perque tuam libertatem;

alibi irae delinitio aut morositatis, alibi doloris indignationisque, alibi illectio ad turpem voluptatem atque in appetitiones proprias. Non pectinem eburneum Plautus, non caseum molliculum, non monedulam praetermisit inter blandiendum. Atque illa quidem
2 amantium sunt, non facetorum hominum. Itaque servi familiaresque iratis blandiuntur dominis, patribus filii, nutrices puerulis, captatores iis quibus nec liberi ulli nec legitimi sunt haeredes. Quocirca blandos in eorum numero qui oblectationem tantum quaerant urbanis ex allocutionibus habendos non esse Iuvenalis etiam docet. Proditum quoque est a scriptoribus Helvium Pertinacem Augustum blandum potius quam benignum fuisse habitum, quod verbis quidem alliceret homines essetque affabilis admodum, coeterum re ipsa non modo non liberalis, verum etiam sordidus.

: II :

## On flatterers.

Although the material of those who are called flatterers appears to be the same, they nevertheless do not always have the same aim. They seek not delight and pleasantness alone but rather advantage, as in the following:

> Now I beseech you, Milphio, by this right hand, by its sister, this left hand, by your eyes, by my beloved, by my Adelphasium, and by your liberty.[33]

In another place there is softening of anger or moroseness, in another, softening of pain or indignation, elsewhere allurement to shameful pleasure and one's own desires. While flattering, Plautus did not overlook "ivory comb," "sweet little cheese," or "jackdaw."[34] And these are expressions of lovers, not witty men. And so slaves and servants flatter their angry masters, children their fathers, nurses their little children, and legacy hunters those without children or legitimate heirs. For this reason Juvenal teaches that people who only seek to delight with their urbane conversation are not to be numbered among the flatterers. Authors have also related that Helvius Pertinax Augustus was considered a flatterer rather than a generous man in that he allured men with words and was very friendly but in reality was not only illiberal but also miserly.[35]

: 12 :

## De urbanis et facetis.

1 Reliquum est de urbanis ut dicamus ac facetis. Et quoniam urbanitas non ad iocos tantum ac festivitatem dicendique leporem pertinet, quod in ea quidem virtute potissimum laudatur, verum ad virtutes quoque alias quae et viro et cive ingenuo dignae sunt, videtur alia quaerenda virtus quae propria magis sit solumque id complectatur ac respectet quod ad iocos tantum animorumque re-
2 laxationem spectet. Nam et urbanus dictus est, quod urbis servet sciatque ac retineat mores, quando adversus illi est qui e contrario ruris sequatur, non urbis, institutiones; indeque agrestis vocatus ac vitium id a rure rusticitas, ut ab urbe urbanitas dicta. Nam et qui seniori assurgit praetereunti et qui magistratum ab domo deducit in curiam et qui praeteriens salutat urbanitate utitur. Facetus vero
3 ex eo nullo modo est dicendus. Video populariter atque a viris minime indoctis affabiles quosdam vocari qui et ipsi urbanitate quidem utantur. Nam et in accipiendis hospitibus et in adventu peregrinorum, in primis etiam congressibus ac salutationibus, et blande affantur ac comiter et hospitaliter alloquuntur; iidem amice quoque et salutant et compellant et summa cum iucunditate congrediuntur.

4 Sed nos eum quaerimus qui parte ex omni munus ipsum impleat; qui e iocis suavibusque e dictis oblectationem tantum quaerat ac recreationem post labores; qui et salem habeat in dicendo et quae ipse dicit tanquam illo condiat; qui leporem admisceat; qui verba apta idonea concinnata iocisque accommodata usurpet vultumque illis adiungat ubi opus est ac gestum; qui fabellis narrandis recitandisque iocosis ac ludicris rebus et curas sedet et deliniat molestias; qui non discedat urbanitatis e finibus aut e cive in

∶ 12 ∶

## *On the urbane and witty.*

It remains to talk about the urbane and witty. And since urbanity  1
does not only have to do with jokes, mirth, and charm of speaking, something especially praised in that virtue, but also with other
virtues that are worthy of a man and a freeborn citizen, it appears
that another virtue must be sought that is more appropriate and
includes and concerns only what relates to jokes and the relaxation
of our minds. For a man is called urbane because he observes,  2
knows, and retains the manners of the city, while his opposite is
the one who on the contrary follows the customs of the country,
not of the city, and thence is called agrestic and the vice, rusticity,
from *country* [*rus*], as *urbanity* comes from *city* [*urbs*]. For someone
who rises for an elder passing by, escorts a magistrate from home
to the court, or greets in passing acts with urbanity. But he ought
not on this account be called witty. I see that commonly and by  3
men not at all unlearned some are called friendly who also act
with urbanity. For in receiving guests, at the arrival of foreigners,
also at first meeting and greeting, they address flatteringly and
speak affably and hospitably; they also greet and address in a
friendly manner and meet with the greatest pleasantness.

But I am looking for the man who in every respect performs  4
this office; who seeks from jokes and pleasant witticisms only delight and restoration after labors; who has wit when he speaks and
seasons, as it were, what he says with it; who mixes in humor;
who uses words that are apt, suitable, appropriate, and well
adapted to making jokes, and adds to them, when necessary, gesture and facial expressions; who, by telling stories and reciting
jocular and ludicrous things, allays cares and soothes troubles;
who does not leave the bounds of urbanity or pass from being a

rusticum atque agrestem transeat ex ingenuo in servum aut servo
persimilem, ni forte res ipsa ita tulerit; qui minime volens offendat
dictis, nisi lacessitus, idque tamen urbane; qui et temporis et loci
et audientium et sui ipsius et quam gerit personae et aetatis et
negociorum et publicae privataeque letitiae habeat ac tristitiae
moerorisque rationem idque cum primis curet, in singulis ut retineat modum, ne et verba profundat et iocos; qui denique summo
id studio videat, ne, cum alios in risum provocat, ipse ab astantibus risui habeatur trivioque dignior iudicetur quam honestorum
atque ingenuorum hominum audientia ac consessu; demum etiam
qui intelligat, perinde ut cessatio omnis quiesque conceditur re-
laxandi gratia utque reditus ad labores ac negocia non sit gravis, sic
iocos, dicta, sales, lepores facetiasque concedi, ne vitam cogitatio-
nesque nostras omnis studiaque in iis collocasse aut in ocio desi-
diaque aut in marcescentia potius nos appareat. Hunc, ni fallor
(quando qui et qualis comis sit, qui etiam urbanus ac festivus, explicatum est), maiores nostri facetum vocavere.

5    Nam urbanus, ut diximus, plura quae urbanae consuetudinis
morumque civilium sunt complectitur, perinde ut etiam comis; at
festivus minime quidem omnia quae virtuti huic conveniant quaeque inesse ei debeant qui iocis dictisque iucundioribus usurus sit
cum mediocritate et gratia. Quam in opinionem propendere vide-
6    tur Cicero, cum ait duo esse genera facetiarum. Habemus igitur
nomen eius qui tali sit mediocritate ac virtute praeditus, coeterum
virtutis atque habitus ipsius nomen hactenus proditum est nullum
quod quidem sit proprium ac suis limitibus terminatum. Nam etsi
rerum scriptores et comitatem usurpant et urbanitatem, tamen, ut
dixi, parum sunt omnino propria. Quia vero cognata haec essent

citizen to a rustic or an agrestic or from a free man to a slave or
someone like a slave unless perhaps the business at hand requires
it; who is most unwilling to offend with his witticisms unless provoked, but if so, offends urbanely; who takes account of the time
and place, his listeners and himself, the role that he is playing, the
age, business, public and private joy, sadness and grief, and first of
all takes care in every single case to hold fast to the mean so that
he does not squander words and jokes; who, then, sees to it with
the greatest assiduity that, while he incites others to laughter, he
himself is not considered ridiculous by the bystanders and thought
more deserving of the street than the attention of an assembly of
honorable and free men; who, finally, also understands that just as
all rest and repose are granted for relaxation and so that return to
work and business may be not difficult, so jokes, witticisms, quips,
pleasantries, and funny stories are granted so that we do not appear to have placed our life and all our thoughts and pursuits in
these things or rather in leisure and laziness or in languor. This
man, unless I'm mistaken (since it has been explained who and
what sort of man is affable, and who urbane and mirthful) has
been called witty by our ancestors.

For the urbane man, as I said, encompasses many things that 5
belong to the customs of the city and civil manners, just as the affable man does; but the mirthful man by no means encompasses
all the things that suit this virtue and ought to be in the one who
is to use jokes and pleasanter witticisms gracefully and in accordance with the mean. Cicero seems to incline to this opinion when
he says there are two kinds of witticism.[36] So we have the name of 6
the person endowed with such a mean and virtue, but up to this
time no name has been provided for the virtue and quality itself
that is appropriate to it and confined within its limits. For although writers on these matters use both *affability* and *urbanity*,
nevertheless, as I've said, they are hardly appropriate.[37] But because they are related and joined by affinity, writers are seen to

7   et necessitudine sua coniuncta, iccirco illis usi videntur. Nos vero licet non absque rubore (neque enim licentiosi haberi volumus), tamen, quod in acie cum periculo versamur, tentabimus illud noviter deducere: quod in plurimis et Cicero e nostris aliique non pauci servavere et Aristoteles inter Graecos, etiam non quadam sine libertate, etsi maxima tamen cum utilitate legentium.

8   Ac primum quidem minime ut a modesto deducimus modestiam, sic a faceto facetiam, quando facetiae ipsae dicta quidem
9   sunt iucunda et lepida, nequaquam vero habitus aut virtus. Verum ut sanctitatem a sancto et ab honesto honestatem castitatemque a casto, sic a faceto facetitatem deducemus, ut facetitas ipsa sit virtus eademque faceti viri habitus: forsan non omnino etiam displicuerit facetudo, subducta syllaba, ut a sordido sorditudo, quae Plautina deductio est. Nam neque maiores illi nostri aut castitudinem reformidarunt aut moestitudinem. Quid si ut moestities, sic etiam
10  dicatur faceties? Sed nos haec ipsa ita tradimus ut qui nullo modo velimus regulam hac in parte praescribere. Sit enim sua cuique libertas usurpandi nominis; verum ideo hoc facimus, ut aperte magis intelligatur habitus ipse qui sit et quo etiam quis nomine ac proprio et tantum suo vocitandus. Constituimus itaque sive facetitatem, sive facetudinem facetiemve, habitum et, qui eo sit habitu ornatus, facetum. Sed ad alteram quoque partem verborum transeundum est, ut quae in ea versetur mediocritas, lucide etiam intelligatur.

have used them both. But not without blushing—for I do not  7
want to be considered presumptuous—since I am engaged in a
dangerous battle, I will try to derive a new term.[38] On a great
number of occasions Cicero and not a few others among our Latin
writers and also Aristotle among the Greeks have observed this
practice, not without a certain license although with the greatest
utility to their readers.

And first we do not at all derive *facetia* from *facetus* as we do  8
*modesty* from *modest*, since funny stories [*facetiae*] are indeed pleasant and charming expressions of wit but by no means a quality or
a virtue.[39] But I will derive *facetitas* from *facetus*, as *holiness* from  9
*holy*, *honor* from *honorable*, and *chastity* from *chaste*, so that *wittiness*
may be the virtue and likewise the quality of a witty man.[40] Perhaps *facetudo* will not entirely displease, stealing a syllable, as *sorditudo* from *sordidus*, which is Plautus' derivation.[41] In fact, our ancestors were not afraid of *castitudo* or *maestitudo*.[42] What if one
should even say *faceties*, like *moestities*?[43] But I propose these things  10
in this way since I by no means want to prescribe a rule in this
matter. For let everyone be free to use his own term; rather I do
this so that the quality itself may be more openly understood,
what it is and by which name, appropriate to him alone, such a
man ought to be called. And so I designate the quality (*wittiness*)
as *facetitas*, *facetudo*, or *faceties*, and the person furnished with the
quality, as *witty*. But we must also pass over to another branch of
words so that the mean that is involved in it may also be clearly
understood.

: 13 :

## De veracitate.

1 Quemadmodum autem virtutis huius, de qua pauca locuti sumus, sive comitatis urbanitatisve sive facetudinis, proprium munus est atque officium sedare molestias in cessationibusque ac in relaxatione a negociis iucundum aliquid quaerere ad reficiendos animos, sive in ipsis quoque laboribus ac negociis interque molestias reficere eos, quo vegetiores ipsi fiant longeque valentiores, sive pervincendis aut tolerandis laboribus difficultatibusque sive leniendis doloribus atque molestiis, qui finis ei virtuti est constitutus, sic, cum eadem ipsa oratio ac sermo vel praecipuum sit vinculum retinendae societatis, ad quam colendam nati atque educati sumus coetusque ipsius una sociati et ampliandi et conservandi, sic, inquam, alterius virtutis, cuius etiam initia quaerimus, proprium munus est veritatis studium ac cultus.

2 Loquimur autem de veritate hoc in loco, non illa quidem quae a physicis quaeritur aut mathematicis quaeve versetur circa certitudinem syllogismorum in ipsisque disputationibus quae sunt de rerum natura deque disciplinis atque scientiis hominum ac facultatibus, verum de veritate ea quae nihil in sermonibus atque in oratione, nihil etiam in moribus inesse fictum, fallax, fucatum indicet, nihil quod simulatum, adulatorium, mendax, gloriosum, vanum quodque supra vires appareat supraque facultates ipsas aut veri fines excedat captusve nostri terminos; quam assecuti qui sint retineantque et in dicendo et in tractandis rebus domesticisque in consuetudinibus, ii veri dicuntur, et virtus ipsa veritas, ni fortasse proprie magis veraces illi, virtus autem ipsa veracitas, ut veritas sit rei ipsius, veracitas vero ea utentis habitus. Ac nihilominus et verum fuisse hominem Catonem dicimus et quod summa etiam in

*On truthfulness.*

Now just as the proper function and task of this virtue of which I have spoken a little, whether it be affability, urbanity, or wittiness, is to assuage troubles and, in periods of rest and relaxation from business, to seek something pleasant to restore our minds or, also, in work, business, and troubles, to restore them so that they become more vigorous and much stronger, either by conquering and tolerating labors and difficulties or alleviating sorrows and troubles, which has been established as the aim of this virtue, so, since speech itself and conversation are the most important bond holding society together, which we have been born and raised to care for and whose assemblies, once joined together, must be increased and preserved, so, I say, the proper function of this other virtue, whose principles I am also seeking, is the pursuit and observance of truth.

But in this place I am speaking not about that truth sought by natural philosophers or mathematicians or involved with the certainty of syllogisms, and in those disputations about the nature of things and the disciplines, sciences, and faculties of men, but about that truth which reveals nothing fictitious, fallacious, or falsified in conversation, speech, or also in character, nothing pretended, adulatory, lying, boastful, or false, and which appears beyond our ability and faculties or exceeds the limits of truth and the boundaries of our capacities. Those who have attained this truth and retain it in speaking and managing business and domestic intercourse are called *true* and the virtue itself *truth*, unless perhaps they would more properly be called *truthful* and the virtue *truthfulness*, so that truth is of the thing itself but truthfulness the quality of someone practicing it. But nonetheless we say that Cato

eo inesset veritas, Sibyllas quoque veras et vates etiam atque ha-
ruspices veros. Haec vero a nobis eo consilio dicta sunt, quo distinctius intelligatur quaenam res ipsae sint et quales.

3    Tertia quoque quaedam virtus, si Aristoteli credimus, in eadem
hac versatur materia quae amicitia ab illo dicitur, de qua quoniam
his in libris dicendum nihil decrevimus, de duabus his virtutibus,
et facetitate et veritate, tantum disseremus ac primo quidem de
veritate deque oppositis ei vitiis.

: 14 :

*De adulatoribus.*

1    Admodum autem veritati adversatur lucri studium atque habendi
cupiditas; itaque huiusmodi hominum una est cura totique in eo
ipsi sunt, quo adulando rei suae consulant familiari; et, quasi verborum mercaturam faciant, oratione ubique utuntur secunda et
blanda; hocque sibi vitae genus delegerunt ad ampliandam rem
domesticam: periculosa sane ac maxime pestilens hominum consuetudo ac familiaritas, quorum quia primatum virorum princi-
pumque ac regum praecipue plenae sunt aulae, inde adulatores
dicti; qui dum placere et gratificari tantum student, veritati apud
dominos aures obstrudunt atque ad illorum vultum libidinemque
servilem in modum omnia loquuntur, nam et *dulos* Graece servus
est; iidem alio sunt nomine assentatores ab assentiendo dicti, quod
eorum cogitationes atque consilia in id solum intendant, id ipsi
tantum agant, sibi ipsis ut prosint, secuti Terentianum illud, 'Ais,
2    aio; negas, nego.' Quibus hominibus quod plerunque solis qui res

was a true man and also that the greatest truth was in him and that the Sibyls were also true as well as the prophets and soothsayers. But I have said this with the intention that it may be more distinctly understood what the things themselves are and of what sort.

If we believe Aristotle, some third virtue is also involved in this 3 same matter, and he calls it friendship.[44] Since in these books I have decided not to say anything about it, I will only discuss those two virtues — wittiness and truth — and first truth and the vices which oppose it.

## : 14 :

## *On adulators.*

Now the pursuit of profit and the desire of possessing are greatly 1 opposed to the truth. And so men of this sort have only one concern and are totally devoted to looking after their private property by adulation. Everywhere they speak subserviently and flatteringly, as if they were trafficking in words, and they have chosen this kind of life to increase their own wealth. The companionship and familiarity of these men are truly dangerous and very noxious, and they are called *adulators* because the courts of noble men, princes, and kings are especially full of them. While they strive only to please and to gratify, they make their masters' ears deaf to the truth and say everything according to how their masters look and what they desire, as slaves do, for *doulos* means *slave* in Greek.[45] They are called by another name, *yes-men*, from their saying yes, because their thoughts and plans only intend one thing and they only do it to profit themselves, following this line from Terence, "You say yes, I say yes; you say no, I say no."[46] Since the governors of states 2

moderantur publicas suas patefaciunt aures, hinc et videmus et audimus et legimus eorum res frequentissime in praeceps rapi turbarique ac misceri repente principatus ac regna. Quae res nostris quoque temporibus clariores sunt quam ut exemplis indigeant.

3    Huius autem generis hominum plures quidem sunt species; nesciam tamen sintne omnes adulatorum in numero habendi, quando, ut Aristoteles queri etiam videtur, singulis, sive virtutibus sive vitiis, certa neutique propriaque insunt nomina. Itaque et lucri
4    et compendiorum tantum gratia adulantur non pauci; quidam captandae solum aurae ac favoris in populo atque inter cives; alii quod ita a natura comparati sint usuque etiam confirmati ut ipsa tantum blanditione capiantur eaque, avicularum in modum, se se oblectent, quam vel maximam etiam voluptatem vel solam potius statuant.

: 15 :

*De captatoribus.*

1    Eorum igitur qui pecuniarium secunda ex oratione sibi quaestum constituerint duplex cum sit genus, et illorum qui tum captatores dicuntur, in quibus late quidem regnat ambitio et levitas, tum qui adulatores communi tamen nomine vocitantur, captatorum quidem ipsorum studium est, non dictis modo sed conferendis muneribus, captare animos ac voluntates illorum, praesertim quibus aut certi minime sint haeredes aut eorum eiiciendorum ex haereditate spes adest. Quod genus late diffunditur non maximis inhiantium
2    modo fortunis verum patrimoniis etiam minimis. Dicti igitur a captando, quo in verbo et fraus inest et maius etiam habendi studium, quippe cum ipsi non verbis modo verum etiam donis conviviisque grassentur, aucupum morem atque allectationes secuti.

generally open their ears only to these men, we see, hear, and read that their affairs are very frequently drawn into crises and their dominions and kingdoms suddenly disturbed and confused. In our days, too, these things are too clear to require examples.

Furthermore, there are several species of this class of men, but  3 I do not know whether they are all to be considered adulators, since, as Aristotle also seems to complain, fixed and proper names for individual virtues and vices are completely lacking.[47] Thus not  4 a few flatter simply for profit and gain; some only for winning approval and favor among the people and citizens; others because they were formed that way by nature and also confirmed by experience, so that they are only captured with flattering and, like little birds, divert themselves with what they hold to be either the greatest or rather the only pleasure.

: 15 :

## On the grasping.

Therefore, since there are two classes of people who have resolved  1 upon seeking money from subservient speech — those who are called grasping and in whom ambition and frivolity rule widely, and those who are commonly named adulators — the endeavor of these grasping men is to capture, not only with words but by conferring services, the minds and wills, especially of those whose heirs are undetermined or those they can hope to drive out of their inheritance.[48] This class is widespread, coveting not only the greatest fortunes but also the smallest patrimonies. They thus take  2 their name from *grasping*, a word that includes fraud as well as eagerness to have more, since they go to work not only with words but also with gifts and banquets, following the manner and

Eorum enim captiosa sunt omnino obsequia fraudisque atque insi-
diarum plena, adversum quos merito et dentes acuunt et gladios
stringunt satyrarum scriptores. Sed nobis hac satis in parte fuerit
vitii genus innuisse. Quantopere autem veritati horum obsit hominum oratio atque obsequium abunde quidem manifestum est.

3    Sunt quoque quos ambitio honorisque studium, minime vero
pecuniae cupiditas, trahat ad assentandum, levitate quadam tantum duce, dum videri quam esse ipsi malunt, solaque populari et
capiuntur et pascuntur aura: qua in re seque suasque res omnis
videntur collocasse, plebeiorum etiam ad hominum opinionem
omnia referentes. Ac superius quidem vitium captatio, et qui ea
utuntur captatores; huius autem proprium ac maxime suum nomen existit nullum, levitas tamen est ac vanitas sane maxima et
homines ipsi perquam leves ac vani, dum umbra capiuntur rerum
magisquam rebus ipsis. Atque hoc quidem vitium potest ratione
alia ad ambitionem referri, qua de re alibi quoque a nobis dictum
4    est. Quod si captationem ipsam duplicem fecerimus, et eorum
quos cupiditas habendi trahit et quos popularis aurae atque ambi-
tionis studium, ut alteri pecuniae, alteri popularis aurae captatores
dicantur, fortasse non male distribuisse iudicabimur, quando etiam
sunt qui inter loquendem disserendumque etiam verba captent,
qui quidem ipsi dicantur captiosi et fraus ipsa captiuncula.

5    Verum ad adulatores redeamus, quique iidem assentatores sunt,
neque alio quidem nomine inter se discernuntur. Coeterum studium id eorum est ex adulationibus rem facere ac peculium ut,
dum verbis opsequuntur, dum oratione secunda primatum ac
principum res consiliaque extollunt, dum eorum admirantur facta,
dicta, consilia, mores, gestus, et, ut Iuvenalis inquit, ubi 'Trulla

allurements of bird catchers. For their complaisance is wholly captious and full of fraud and deceit. The satirists deservedly sharpen their teeth and draw their swords against them. But in this part it will be enough for me to hint about the character of the vice. It is abundantly clear, however, to what extent the speech and complaisance of these men oppose the truth.

There are also those whom ambition and pursuit of honor, 3 rather than any greed for money, draw toward flattering assent, only led on by levity, since they prefer appearance to reality and are caught by and feed only on popular favor, in whose service they seem to have placed themselves and all their substance, relating everything to the opinion of men, even plebeians. And the former vice is grasping and those who practice it, grasping men, but there exists no proper and particular name for the latter, although it is frivolity and the very greatest vanity, and the men themselves very frivolous and vain, since they are caught by the shadow of things more than the things themselves. And indeed this vice can for another reason be referred to ambition, on which subject I've spoken elsewhere, too.[49] But if I have divided grasping into two classes — 4 some people are drawn on by greed to possess and others by the pursuit of popular favor and ambition, so that the former are said to grasp for money, the latter for popular favor — perhaps I will not be judged to have distinguished poorly, since there are also those who, while speaking and discoursing, quibble with words, and who indeed are called captious and the offense itself, captiousness.[50]

But let's return to adulators, who are the same as yes-men; they 5 are not distinguished one from the other by a different name. Moreover, their endeavor is to make money and acquire a *peculium* by means of adulation.[51] While they speak obsequiously, while they extol with subservient speech the possessions and plans of nobles and princes, while they admire their deeds, witticisms, plans, manners, and gestures, and, as Juvenal says, when "his

inverso crepitum dedit aurea fundo,' domesticam rem adaugeant
amplificentque patrimonium. Quorum hominum studiis dominantium, ut dixi, aures plerunque oppletae sunt, dum iis se se re-
6 gendos permittunt. Quo efficitur ut veritas videri possit eorum
inimica, praesertim ubi qui rerum potiuntur adolescentes ipsi fue-
7 rint vel aetate annisque vel etiam moribus ac rerum usu. Horum
igitur omnium studium est atque propositum, adulando atque in
gratiam loquendo rebus ipsos suis consulere hisque artibus atque
consiliis rei familiari prospicere. Quod dum consequantur, non
modo nulla e parte molesti esse volunt, verum singula laudant
dictisque et factis quibusque assurgunt; quin, quae maxime fortasse ridenda sint, et admirantur illa et in coelum ferunt verbis
quoque ipsis, oris gestum adiungentes et corporis totius habitum.
'Regem aliquem capies,' inquit ille apud Iuvenalem ad magni illius
rhombi aspectum,

> aut de temone Britanno
> excidet Arviragus: peregrina est bellua, cernis
> erectas in terga sudes?

8 Itaque, quid in maioribus illi ipsi assentatores facturi essent negociis consultationibusque, coniicere ex his facile quidem possumus.
His accedit maxime vanum genus hominum, quorum studium
tantum est loquendi in aliorum gratiam atque ad illorum ipsorum
vultum atque opinionem orationem suam seque ipsos componere,
iisdemque in omnibus morem gerere seque suaque dicta sermonesque ad haec ipsa tantum instituere. Quorum quidem consilium
Terentianum quoque est illud et meta quasi quaedam ad quam se
ipsos instruunt, 'Obsequium amicos, veritas odium parit.' Quod
dictum quanquam latius fortasse patet, tamen maxime ad eos referendum qui voluptatem solam suis e dictis quaeritant, quam ad
adipiscendam se se omni arte instituunt ac dicendi studio solumque eorum est propositum dominantibus, ut placeant et,

golden cup, turned upside down, gave forth a fart," they are increasing their private wealth and amplifying their patrimony.[52] As I said, the ears of rulers are generally full of the endeavors of these men, while they allow themselves to be ruled by them. From 6 which it follows that the truth may seem to be their enemy, especially when those in power are adolescents either by age and years or also by character and experience. Therefore their whole en- 7 deavor and intention is to look after their own interests by adulation and ingratiating speech, and to provide for their family wealth with these arts and plans. While seeking this they want to avoid causing any annoyance, but rather they praise everything and stand up respectfully at whatever is done and said. Why, they admire things that are especially ridiculous and praise them to the skies with their words, adding the right facial expression and posture of the whole body. "You will capture some king," says that man in Juvenal at the sight of the huge turbot,

> or Arviragus will fall from his British chariot pole. It's a
> foreign beast. Do you see the spikes erect on its back?[53]

And so from these things we can easily conjecture what these yes- 8 men will do in more important affairs and deliberations.

To these people one can add the falsest kind of men, whose only endeavor in speaking is to please others, to compose themselves and their speech to accord with the expressions of others and with their opinions, to indulge them in everything, and to arrange their witticisms and conversation only with these objects in view. Indeed, their intention is also the well-known saying of Terence's and, as it were, the goal toward which they prepare themselves, "Obsequiousness begets friends but truth begets hatred."[54] Although this saying perhaps has a wider application, nevertheless it especially refers to those who seek only pleasure from what they say. To obtain it they prepare themselves with every art and with studied speech. Their only design is to please those in power and

quibuscum versantur, eos ut delectent, iis blandiantur, et illorum
arte ut omni aures demulceant voluptatis gratia, demum omnia.
Hicque illorum est finis ac propositum.

: 16 :

*De lascivis.*[7]

1 Qua in re quoniam nec modum nec mensuram tenent ullam, las-
civire eos necesse est, ut qui neque in iocando neque in oblectando
delectum habeant aut rationem aliquam, verum qui et verbis et
iocis et fabellis referendis nimium ipsi serpant atque inter iocandum explicandumque dilabantur alio atque alio. Quocirca lascivi
sunt vocati et vitium ipsum lascivia; nimis enim profundunt se se
ad ioca dictaque omnia, ad quae dilapsi nec lasciviunt tantum nimiique in illis sunt, verum petulantes, osceni et (quod turpissi-
2 mum est) impuri. Minime autem verebimur hoc ipsum genus
partiri eorum qui ad voluptatem tantum atque in gratiam loquantur comparandae tantum voluptatis causa. Sunt enim qui ipsi quidem minime lasciviant serventque in iocando delectum atque in
dicendo, verum in hoc a recto atque honesto abeunt quod voluptatem sibi proposuerunt, vile sane pretium, pro quo tamen asse-
quendo et veritati obstant et ab hominis recedunt dignitate, siquidem, quo instrumento quaque naturae dote praediti sumus cum
excellentia animalium coeterorum, eo ipsi pro re maxime sordida
3 belluarumque magisquam hominum propria abutuntur. Neque
enim finis eorum est in laborum requiete molestiarumque relaxatione, ut iucunditatem aut quaerant aut afferant, quo et tran-
quillent audientium animos ac suos et refocillent eos a praeteritis
defatigationibus viresque renovent ad easdem rursus obeundas,

to delight those with whom they associate, to flatter them, and soothe their ears with every art to please — in short, whatever it takes. This is their end and design.

: 16 :

### On the unrestrained.

Since they hold to no limit or measure in this,[55] they necessarily 1 run riot, as they have no discrimination or rule in joking and pleasing but rather twist about too much when speaking their words and telling their jokes and stories, and between joking and explaining they lose themselves in this and that. For this reason they are called unrestrained and the vice, lack of restraint. For they pour themselves too much into jokes and all sorts of witticisms, and, once they've lost themselves, they not only run riot and are excessive in these things, but they are also impudent, indecent, and (what is most shameful) filthy. I will not hesitate at all, moreover, 2 to divide this category of those who speak only for pleasure and those who speak only with the motive of providing pleasure for gratification. For some do not run riot at all and maintain discrimination in joking and speaking. But they depart from what is right and honorable in making pleasure their goal, certainly a vile reward, yet to obtain it they oppose truth and depart from human dignity, since they abuse that instrument and gift of nature with which we have been endowed to excel the other animals for something especially sordid and more suited to beasts than men. For 3 their end in view is not to seek and bring delight in rest from labors and relaxation from troubles, and thereby to calm the minds of their listeners and their own, to revivify them from past fatigues and to renew their strength for confronting them again, but,

verum, quod a natura atque ab habitu ita quidem instituti ad ea
ipsa sunt, ut neque ab desidia ignaviaque longius absint. Atque
haec quidem videntur esse assentatorum genera.

: 17 :

*De insulsis et profusis.*

1 Sunt ex hoc etiam numero qui, dum oblectare student, maxime
aures audientium offendant, tum insulse loquendo tum profun-
dendo et res et verba, nec delectu habito nec modo aut mensura
2 adhibitis. Itaque taedii genus hoc ac molestiarum veteres dicebant
hominem occidere, cum eiusmodi homines in cunctis et multi essent et insulsi ineptique ac cum primis importuni, ut non inconve-
nienter a ranarum similitudine sint qui eos coaxatores vocitent,
quod coaxare eos quam loqui magis existiment, ut qui non modo
non mulceant aures, verum ad impatientiam usque obtundant.

: 18 :

*De contentiosis.*

1 Adulatorum studiis maxime adversi videntur contentiosi quidam
homines, quorum ea est natura, id etiam studium, ut, non modo
non loquantur in aliorum gratiam neque gratificentur ipsi aliis, sed
contra ut adversentur et ubique et in quibusque neminemque ve-
reantur dicendo offendere; quin et serant ipsi sponte studioseque
contentiones et ab aliis satas accipiant laetenturque iis et fovendis

because they have been formed to these things by nature and habit, not to be too far from inactivity and idleness. And these appear to be the classes of yes-men.

: 17 :

## *On the insipid and prolix.*

Some of this class, while eager to delight, very greatly offend the ears of their listeners, sometimes speaking tastelessly, sometimes pouring out words and matter without discrimination, limit, or measure. And so the ancients used to say that this kind of tedium and bother killed a man, since men of this sort were on all occasions numerous, tasteless, inappropriate, and, especially, annoying. So some people aptly call them croakers from their resemblance to frogs, since they suppose them to croak rather than speak, not only not soothing the ears but pounding them beyond all endurance.

: 18 :

## *On the contentious.*

The complete opposite of adulators in their endeavors appear certain contentious men, whose nature and also endeavor are not only not to speak to please or gratify others, but on the contrary to oppose them and, nowhere or in any situation, to fear to offend anyone by speaking. Indeed, they both sow disputes willingly and eagerly take up ones sown by others and rejoice in fostering and

et exercendis; quibus etiam vita ipsa vel molesta futura sit, ni in
cunctis vel dentes imprimant vel infigant aculeos ut ad contentiones, dissidia rixasque atque altercationes nati prorsus videantur.
Et quam alii a natura concessam elocutionem exercent in conser-
vanda hominum societate, in conciliandis amicitiis, in solandis
demulcendisque molestiis, laboribus ac moeroribus aliorum, ea
ipsi in adversum utantur vel abutantur potius ad odia contrahenda
litesque excitandas ac serenda discordiarum semina. Hos et con-
2  tentiosos vocavere et rixatores et alio atque alio nomine. Vitium
autem, etsi est fortasse innominatum, quid tamen prohibeat rixationem appellare ac contentiositatem, ut contentionem rerum esse
dicamus ac rixam, vitium vero ipsum perversumque illum habitum
tum rixationis appellatione tum contentiositatis designemus? Odi-
osum sane genus hominum et muscarum maxime simile, ut nati hi
omnino videantur ad turbas, vexationes, inquietudinem vitaeque
ad universae turbationem ac taedia, quod Plautus indicavit in servi
illius persona:

> decretum est mihi
> quasi umbra, quoquo ibis tu, te persequi;
> quin, adepol, si in crucem vis pergere,
> sequi decretum est.

3  Horum duplex mihi videtur esse partitio: eorum una qui id
student, ut commoda utilitatemque inde sibi comparent; illorum
altera qui voluptatis tantum gratia utque invidentissimae suae naturae ac perversissimis cogitationibus morem gerant. Eorum autem utrum genus longe sit perversius, iudicatu difficile videri iure
4  quidem potest; utrumque tamen perversissimum. Montium adolescens ipse novi Branchatium qui, generis ac familiae contempta
vel repudiata potius dignitate, totum litibus se se tradiderit; ac satis scio lites quasdam ab actoribus destitutas, sive ob inopiam rei
familiaris ad eas prosequendas seu quod male essent coeptae,

keeping them going. For some life itself would even be a burden unless on all occasions they sank in their teeth or thrust in their stings; they seem to have been born entirely for contentions, disputes, quarrels, and altercations. And the eloquence granted by nature, which others employ to preserve the society of men, to bring about friendship, to console and soothe the troubles, labors, and sorrows of others, the contentious use or rather abuse in the opposite way, to produce hatred, excite quarrels, and sow the seeds of discord. They have been called contentious, quarrelsome, and various other names. But what prevents calling the vice, although    2
nameless by chance, quarrelsomeness and contentiousness, so that we may say that there is a contention or quarrel over things but designate the perverse habit by the term quarrelsomeness or contentiousness? An absolutely odious kind of men and most like flies, so that they appear completely born for turmoils, vexations, agitation, and for the disturbance and annoyance of all of life, a fact that Plautus indicated in the character of that well-known slave:

> I've decided to follow you wherever you go, like a shadow; indeed, by Pollux, if you want to mount the cross, I've decided to follow.[56]

It seems to me that the contentious can be divided into two    3
classes: some strive to furnish themselves with good and useful things; others, solely for pleasure, indulge their utterly envious nature and their most perverse thoughts. But it can justly seem difficult to judge which of them is more perverse; nevertheless, each is very perverse. When I was a young man, I was acquainted    4
with Monte Brancaccio, who despised or rather repudiated the dignity of his ancestry and family and gave himself entirely to law suits.[57] I know well that after paying the price agreed upon he bought some suits which had been abandoned by the plaintiffs, either on account of lack of funds to proceed with them or because

pretio mercatum, quo, uti convenerat, exoluto, prosecutum sump-
tibus suis litigia: in hocque vitam suam egisse omnem. Ex eadem
item familia alterum mirifice controversiis assuetum, quin omnino
illis addictum, ut, cum aliquando ab Antonio Panhormita, iucun-
dissimo homine, per risum interrogaretur, 'Quo nam modo cum
causis?,' responderit bene sibi atque e sententia in omnibus succes-
sisse easdemque in rem suam terminatas, duas tamen aut tris in
longum a se se ea ratione protrahi, quod aliter ocio immarcesceret
illasque eo a se studio reservatas, ut haberet in quo oblectaretur
pasceretque animum. Vide hominis ingenium, qui litigia contro-
versiasque sibi voluptatem statuerit!

5      Sed nobis hac in parte loquendum neutique est iudicialibus de
contentionibus; tantum studia volumus contentiosorum quorundam hominum ostendere. Itaque hos ipsos litigiosos seu litigato-
rios potius quis vocaverit et controversos. Nam litigiosas res proprie magis dicimus. Contentiosos autem illos volumus qui maxime
adversentur adulatoribus et, quantum hi loquuntur in omnium
gratiam, tantum illi nemini parcant studeantque prorsus offendere;
quos siquis inciviles vocaverit, ne ille mea sententia vera ab appellatione recesserit. Quando autem res ipsa intelligitur, nolumus de
verbo nimio plus esse soliciti.

6      Laurentinus Vallensis in grammaticis, rhetoricis dialecticisque
ita et scripsit et disputare est solitus, ut minime videretur velle
praecipere, nec appareret tam contendere illum de veritate proprie-
tateque aut docere velle quam maledicere obiectareque vetustis
scriptoribus atque obloqui; itaque Ciceronem vellicabat, Aristote-
lem carpebat, Virgilio subsannabat, quippe qui propalam sit asseverare ausus, sive Pindarus quispiam auctor is nomine suo fuerit sive alio (de hoc enim ambigitur) qui Homericae libros
omnis Iliados non multos admodum in versus contractos Latine

they had begun badly, and proceeded with them at his own expense. He spent his whole life this way. Moreover, I knew another member of this family who was wonderfully accustomed to disputes, or rather so completely addicted to them that once when he was asked with a laugh by Antonio Panormita,[58] the most delightful of men, "How are your suits going?," he replied that they were going well and that they had turned out in all points as he wished and had finished to his profit, but that he was dragging out two or three because otherwise he would waste away in leisure and he was reserving them with the intent of having something in which to delight and to nourish his mind. See the character of the man, who held law suits and disputes a pleasure!

But in this part I need by no means speak of judicial disputes;   5
I only want to show the pursuits of some contentious men. And so someone might call these men *litigiosus* or rather litigious and disputatious. For we more properly talk about things as subjects of lawsuits.[59] By the *contentious*, however, I mean those most opposed to adulators. As much as the latter speak to please everyone, so much do the former spare no one and endeavor to offend completely. If anyone calls them uncivil, in my judgment he does not stray from the true appellation. But since this thing is understood, I do not want to worry too much about the word.

Lorenzo Valla wrote and was accustomed to dispute on gram-   6
matical, rhetorical, and dialectical subjects in such a way that he apparently had no wish to instruct and clearly did not want to dispute about truth and appropriateness or to teach so much as to abuse, reproach, and contradict the ancient writers. And so he would rail at Cicero, carp at Aristotle, deride Vergil.[60] In fact, he dared to assert in public that, whether some Pindar was the author, under his own name or another's (for there is a dispute about this), who translated all the books of Homer's *Iliad*, condensed

convertit, qui propalam sit, inquam, asseverare ausus Pindarum eum Virgilio anteferendeum. Est autem carminis illius principium:

Iram pande mihi Pelidae, diva, superbi,
tristia qui miseris iniecit funera Graiis.

Tali igitur iudicio hominem ingenioque tam sive retroverso sive praepostero (quippe qui maximis quibusque ringeret auctoribus, uni tantum Epicuro assurgeret) quam ob communem utilitatem contendere aut cognitionem dicas atque altercari? qui nec aliud velit, curet, studeat quam ut detrahat quibus minime par est ac maledicat? quando, qui cum Laurentio familiarius vixerunt, affirmant illum eo nequaquam consilio in grammaticis scripsisse ac dialecticis, quo doceret disciplinasque ab ignoratione vendicaret atque a sorde, verum ut malediceret obloquendoque detraheret de fama atque auctoritate rerum scriptoribus, tum illis qui exemplo sunt ad scribendum aliis propter antiquitatem maiestatemque dicendi ac praecipiendi, tum illis ipsis qui tunc viverent, qui ne dubitaverit ipse quidem dicere profiteriqui palam habere se quoque in Christum spicula.

Sed nobis propositum minime est detrahendi homini maxime studioso, quem senem adolescens ipse noverim, cumque e Roma se Neapolim contulisset ad Alfonsum regem, et inviserim etiam reverenter pro illius meaque aetate et plures post congressiones maxime familiares, ita ab eo discesserim uti ex eo de me nisi pleno
7   atque amico ore locutus fuerit nunquam. Sunt ex his igitur quos non tam contentiosos dicas quam insectatores cum singulorum tum etiam humani generis, quod de Timone traditur, neque veritatis ipsius cultu et gratia, sed quod ita quidem sint a natura instituti atque ab assuetudine confirmati et moribus.

into not very many verses — he dared to assert in public, I say, that this Pindar was to be placed before Vergil. Here, however, is the beginning of that poem:

Reveal to me, goddess, the wrath of the proud son of Peleus,
who hurled many sad deaths upon the wretched Greeks.[61]

On account of what common utility or understanding would you say that a man with such judgment and a nature so backward and preposterous — a man, in fact, who would snarl at all the greatest authors and stand up respectfully only for Epicurus — would dispute and wrangle?[62] Who wants, takes care, endeavors for nothing other than to detract from and speak ill of those least deserving it? For those who lived in some intimacy with Lorenzo affirm that he did not at all write with the intention, in his grammatical and dialectical works, of teaching or freeing those disciplines from ignorance and squalor but of speaking ill and detracting by contradiction from the fame and authority of writers, both those who serve as an example of writing to others owing to their antiquity and their majesty of speaking and teaching, and also those who were his contemporaries, and that he did not even hesitate to say and profess publicly that he also had some barbs against Christ.[63]

But it is by no means my intention to detract from a most learned man, whom I myself, a young man, knew as an old man, since he had come from Rome to the court of King Alfonso at Naples.[64] I also visited him, showing the respect befitting his age and mine, and after many very friendly meetings I took leave of him in such a way that from that time he never spoke of me except with cordiality and friendliness. There are then some whom you 7 would not so much call contentious as persecutors of both individuals and even of the human race, as is related of Timon, and not for love or cultivation of the truth itself but because they were made that way by nature and confirmed in it by custom and habits.[65]

: 19 :

## De verbosis.

1 Praeter hos in utroque genere quos peccare dicimus delabique in excessum sive adulando sive contendendo rixandoque, sunt qui verbosi dicuntur vitiumque ipsum verbositas. Hi, dum placere student et grati esse, minime quidem aut placent aut voluptatem afferunt; quin molestiam potius ac taedium pariunt defatigationis ac satietatis plenum, decepti iudicio rerumque simul ac verborum acervationibus ut nescias, ex eo quod aures vel offendunt vel exatiant, sint ne contentiosis potius quam insulsis annumerandi.

2 Verum contentiosi id agunt, ut nemini parcant parumque omnino offensitare alios aut curent aut caveant. Verbosis vero propositum est ac consilium oblectandi, modum tamen dum minime retinent, dum delectum adhibent nullum, in castra transeunt adversariorum apparentque transfugis similiores. Itaque verbosi et initio et inter dicendum subinde delectant, nec odio ipsi habentur, sed recusantur eorum sermones magisquam fugitantur. At contentiosi ubique offendunt et odio eos boni omnes prosequuntur ab illisque abhorrent audiundis, quos et maledictis quoque insectantur.

: 20 :

## De loquacibus.

1 Sunt qui vitium hoc loquacitatem dici malint et illos ipsos loquaces, in quo non est cur eos impediamus; tamen loquaces nos a verbosis differre hoc ipso volumus quod verbosi versentur in iis

: 19 :

## On the verbose.

In addition to those of each class who, I say, are at fault and fall    1
into excess, either by adulating or by contending and quarreling,
are those who are called verbose, and the vice itself verbosity.
These men, while they strive to please and gratify, do not at all
please or give delight. In fact, instead, deceived by their judgment,
they produce annoyance and tedium full of weariness and satiety
by heaping up matter as well as words so that you would not know
from their offending and sating your ears whether they are to be
numbered among the contentious rather than the insipid. But the    2
contentious act in such a way that they spare no one, and not a
whit do they care or guard against offending others. The verbose,
however, intend and plan to delight. Nevertheless, by observing no
limit and making no distinction they pass into the camp of their
enemies and seem more like deserters. And so the verbose please,
both at the beginning and from time to time while speaking, nor
are they held in aversion; rather, their conversation is refused more
than fled. But the contentious always offend, and all good men
send them on their way with aversion, shrink from hearing them,
and even attack them with curses.

: 20 :

## On the loquacious.

Some people prefer to call this vice loquacity and the men loqua-    1
cious, and there's no reason to keep them from doing so. Nevertheless, I want to make this distinction between the loquacious

quae iucunditatem prae se ferant inque illis ipsis in quibus locum
2 habeat facetudo et comitas. At loquaces eos esse contendimus quorum studium minime sit quale est aut facetorum urbanorumque
aut contentiosorum ac molestorum hominum, quippe cum et dicendi infinitate capiantur et, dum loquantur dumque exultent
campo equisque, ut dici solet, ac viris, aliud nihil aut quaerant aut
curent aut sibi propositum habeant, quibus quidem servandis in
diversa etiam vitia incurrant.

: 21 :

*De nugatoribus.*

1 His ipsis haud multum etiam videntur differre nugatores, quorum
narrationes inopes quidem rerum sint, 'nugaeque,' ut Horatius inquit, 'canorae.' Coeterum vanitate illi verborum atque aggestione
magis peccant, hi rerum; uterque tamen et confunduntur in dicendo et nimii sunt, nullum cum delectum adhibeant; indeque
maxime etiam molesti uterque, quando uterque inepti sunt max-
2 imeque inconsiderati. Horum haud multum dissimiles sunt qui
garruli dicuntur, quorum sermo et molestus est et nimius. Obtun-
dunt autem tum vanitate rerum tum inanitate verborum, quibus in
omnibus et nimii sunt et importuni valdeque indecentes. Vitium
autem ipsum garrulitas ab avibus ductum, neque enim cessant et
in iisdem assiduo versantur vel potius interstrepitant. Verum atti-
gisse haec satis fortasse hoc in loco fuerit, cum ea sive vitia sive
virtutes minime sint aut ad veritatem de qua dicturi sumus aut ad
3 comitatem urbanitatemve referenda. Loquaces enim videri magis
possunt taciturnis adversari, taciturnitasque ipsa loquacitati. De
quibus dicere his in libris minime propositum est nostrum.

and verbose: the verbose busy themselves with things that bring forth delight and in which wittiness and affability have a place. But I contend that the loquacious are the ones whose endeavor is not at all like that either of the witty and urbane or of the contentious and annoying men. Indeed, when the loquacious are caught up in endless speaking, while they talk and frisk about on the field with all their forces, as the proverb has it, they seek for, care for, and intend nothing else.[66] In fact, keeping up these things they also run into diverse vices. 2

: 21 :

*On the triflers.*

From these the triflers do not appear to differ much; their stories are poor in matter, "sonorous trifles," as Horace says.[67] But the loquacious are more at fault for the emptiness and heaping up of their words; the triflers, of their matter. Yet both are confused and excessive in speaking, since they make no distinction, and so both are annoying because inept and thoughtless. Not very different from them are the ones who are called garrulous, whose conversation is both annoying and excessive. Moreover, they pound away with the vanity of their matter and the inanity of their words, in all of which they are excessive, importunate, and most unbecoming. This vice, garrulity, takes its name from the birds, for the garrulous do not stop and constantly deal with the same things or rather interrupt with a loud noise.[68] But to have touched on these things in this place will perhaps suffice, since, whether vices or virtues, they have very little to do with the truth about which we are to speak or with affability or urbanity. In fact, the loquacious may appear more opposite to the taciturn, and taciturnity itself, to loquacity. I do not intend to discuss them in these books. 1

2

3

: 22 :

## De taciturnis.

1 Illud tamen non praetermittemus, taciturnitatem mediocritatem esse quandam, loquacitatem excessum; parte vero ex altera, qui tacendo excedant, eos esse sine nomine; neque enim aut ubi aut quantum aut quomodo aut quid oporteat, dum tamen taceant, pensi quicquam habent, et siquid quandoque, musitant potius 2 quam loquuntur. Sed musitatio ex ore innutuque constat ac superciliis non minus quam verbis et plerumque occulta est gigniturque interdum e metu aut reverentia, non nunquam pudore aut stupore, non raro simulatione, ut eorum adversarii videantur qui obganniunt potiusquam qui loquaces sunt. Sed quaerere haec ipsa distinctius hoc, ut dictum est, loco nostri non est propositi.

Quam ob rem qui mediocritatem hac ipsa in re de qua disputa-3 tio est sequantur quique ipsi sint, perquiramus. Cum enim contentiosi atque assentatores e regione pene sint constituendi atque ex adverso collocari debeant, medium quidem inter hos ipsos perquirendum est, etsi nomen mediocritatis eius minime est proditum, et contentiositatem et adulationem extrema verius dicimus 4 quam opposita, quippe quae a medio recedant. Itaque mediocritas ipsa quaerenda[8] nobis est. Aristoteles vero, quanquam innominatam Graece tradat, putat tamen illam et retinere quae[9] utrinque oporteat ac servare et ratione eadem reiicere quae et ubi et quomodo opus fuerit atque omnino repellere, ut etiam existimet hanc ipsam mediocritatem amicitiae maxime esse similem. Qua in parte si aliquantum fortasse immorabimur veritatis ac rei ipsius indagandae gratia, sat confidimus te, quod humanitatis est tuae proprium, vitio id minime esse daturum.[10]

: 22 :

## *On the taciturn.*

Nevertheless, I shall not pass over the fact that taciturnity is a    1
kind of mean, and loquacity, an excess, but, on the other hand,
that those who are excessively silent have no name. For they do
not care where, how much, in what way, or what is necessary to
keep silent, provided that they do keep silent, and if they do care
at some time, they mutter rather than speak. But muttering relies    2
on the face, nodding, and the eyebrows no less than on words.
Usually it is hidden and sometimes is caused by fear and reverence, occasionally by modesty or astonishment, not infrequently
by simulation, so that their opposites seem the ones who speak
with a snarl rather than those who are loquacious. But to inquire
here into these things more precisely, as has been said, is not my
intention.

So let us investigate which people observe the mean in this
matter under discussion and who they are. For since the conten-    3
tious and the yes-men are to be stationed almost directly against
each other and ought to be placed in opposition, a mean between
them must be sought, even though the name of this mean has not
been handed down and it is more accurate to call contentiousness
and adulation extremes than opposites since they recede from the
mean. And so we must seek this mean. Moreover, although Aris-    4
totle teaches that it is nameless in Greek, nevertheless he thinks
that it retains and preserves what is necessary from each extreme
and in the same way rejects and completely repels what is necessary, whenever and however it must. As a result, he judges that
this mean is most like friendship.[69] If perhaps I have tarried a
while in this part to investigate the truth of this matter, I am
pretty confident that you will be too kind to count it a vice at all.

: 23 :

## De delectu, qui et qualis sit.

1    Et poetae et scriptores rerum, tum humanarum tum naturae,
voces rebus ipsis adiiciunt, unde dictae sunt adiectivae, quibus
proprietates appellationesque et declarant explicantque et etiam
finiunt. Nam hominem cum dicunt animalem esse et rationalem
et mortalem, hominem ipsum finiunt et quae substantia sit eius
declarant. Quid cum poetae et placidam dicunt quietem et arma
horrentia et fertilem Ausoniam, nonne et armorum et quietis et
agrorum qualitatem indicant? Et cum humilem Italiam et campos
iacentes et colles supinos, an non situm innuunt ac posituram? Et
ubi ingentis artus mariaque patentia, quid nisi amplitudinem
signare volunt ac magnitudinem et membrorum et pelagi?

2    Eadem ratione qui de moribus scribunt, oportet ut vocibus
adiectis actiones nostras, quae mores ac virtutes constituunt, ter-
minent. Terminantur autem actiones ipsae perficiunturque, si qui
agunt et sicuti oportet et quando oportet quantumque etiam oportet agant modumque in cunctis retineant neve aut nimia sit eorum
opera aut remissior minimaque, utque et loci meminerint et personarum ac rerum etiam ipsarum. Quae qui servant, hi dicuntur

3    agendis rebus delectum adhibere. Delectu enim illa continentur
omnia quibus actiones ipsae virtutesque perficiuntur. Etenim
quemadmodum consultationem ipsam sequitur electio confirma-
tumque consilium ac propositum, sic, postquam elegimus incipere
suscepimusque agendum aliquid, sequitur e vestigio delectus, hoc
est ut deligamus, inter ea quae ad agendum offeruntur, et tempus
quod sit opportunum actioni susceptoque negocio et locum
idoneum et viam quae tenenda sit, cum plures offerri soleant.

: 23 :

## On discrimination, what it is and what kind of thing it is.

Both poets and writers about things human and natural add ex- 1
pressions to things, and from this adding the words are called
"adjectives," and with them they declare, explain, and even define
properties and terms. For when they say that man is a rational,
mortal animal, they define man himself and declare what his substance is.[70] What about when poets speak of "peaceful rest," "bris-
tling arms," and "fertile Ausonia" — aren't they indicating the quality of arms and rest and fields?[71] And when they speak of
"low-lying Italy," "extending fields," and "sloping hills," aren't they
intimating the situation and position?[72] And where they speak of
"huge limbs" and "wide seas," what do they wish to designate if not
the amplitude of the members and the magnitude of the sea?[73]

In the same way those who write about character need to define 2
our actions, which constitute character and virtues, by adding
words. But actions are defined and perfected if the actors act in a
way that is necessary, when necessary, and as much as necessary,
and if they observe moderation in all things so that their labor is
neither excessive nor too relaxed and minimal and they remember
the place, persons, and things themselves. Those who observe
these things are said to exhibit discrimination in action. For dis- 3
crimination contains all those things by which actions themselves
and virtues are accomplished. And indeed, just as choice follows
deliberation and a confirmed plan and intention, so, after we have
chosen to begin and have undertaken to do something, discrimination follows instantly. That is, we choose from those things
presented for action the opportune moment for the action and for
the business undertaken, the appropriate place, and the way that
must be taken, since several usually are presented.

4     Ad haec multi cum indigeant, ut de liberalitate exemplum pro-
ponamus, deligendum est quibus potissimum daturi simus; cumque non universa sit pecunia eroganda, ne fons ipse liberalitatis
exareat dandoque aliis plurima liberis desimus, parentibus, uxori
nepotibusque, quantum etiam iis ipsis quibus daturi sumus singillatim sit erogandum. Quo in delectu praecipue etiam videndum
est rationem uti habeamus et negocii et eius ipsius quicum habenda res est et urbis et civilium tum legum tum consuetudinum
ac propriae praesertim personae quaeque alia recta ipsa ratio tenenda monstraverit, ne in aliquo agentes peccemus. Neque enim
tantummodo a nobis peccabitur, si aut nimii erimus aut astric-
tiores in erogando, ut in quo coepimus exemplo persistamus,
verum etiam si liberales in eos fuerimus qui minime digni sunt
liberalitate, aut si quibus conferenda praesens est pecunia, quod
domestica extremaque laborent egestate, equestri eos praerogativa
exornaverimus, aut si quibus opus est opera eos verbis iuverimus
persequemurque consiliis ac monitis.

5     Igitur haec ipsa mediocritas de qua nunc disserimus versatur
potissimum in habendo delectu ne aut ad nimiam declinemus verborum gratificationem, quae levis sit ac vana, ubi forte opus esset
commonitione oporteretque verbis gravioribus maximeque accommodatis retrahere amicum vel acrius etiam obiurgare, aut, ubi in-
dulgentius fortasse agendum esset, ut in nuptiis atque in publicis
ludis, afferre in mensam atque ad choreas supercilium et publicam
laetitiam velle aut sermone minus suavi aut fronte obducta contris-
tare hilaritatemque inficere iurgiis atque contentionibus. 'Quid,'
inquit ille, 'in theatrum, Cato severe, venisti?' Intelligebat enim
alium hilaritudinis locum esse debere, alium severitatis, 'Non hoc
ista sibi tempus spectacula poscit.' Diversa omnino haec est persona; monet enim, omissa rerum inanium picturaeque inspectione,

Moreover, to set forth an example concerning liberality, since 4 many people are needy, we must choose whom above all others we will give to. And since we must not spend all our money, lest the fount of liberality dry up and by giving most things to others we fail our children, parents, wife, and grandchildren, we must choose how much also to give individually to those to whom we will give.[74] In making this discrimination we must also especially see that we take account of the affair and of the person with whom we are dealing, of the city, the civil laws and customs, and particularly of our own person, and of what other things right reason shows us ought to be taken into account, so that we are not at fault in something when we act. For we will not only be at fault if we are excessive or too stingy in paying, to continue with the example with which I began, but also if we are liberal toward those who by no means are deserving of liberality, or if we bestow the privileges of knighthood on those to whom we ought to give ready money because they labor under extreme poverty at home, or if we help with words and follow up with counsels and admonitions those who need our exertions.

Therefore, this very mean which I am now discussing is con- 5 cerned most of all with making a discrimination so that we do not slide into an excessive, light, and empty verbal gratification when perhaps an admonition is required and it is necessary to drag back a friend with graver and pointedly appropriate words or even to rebuke him more harshly. Nor should we bring a frown to table or dances and wish to sadden public joy with unpleasant conversation or contracted brow, and spoil cheerfulness with quarrels and contentions when we ought perhaps to act more indulgently, as at weddings and public recreations.[75] "Why," said that famous man, "did you come to the theater, severe Cato?"[76] For he understood there should be one place for cheerfulness, another for severity, "This is no time for you to be looking at that."[77] This person is completely different, for she warns that he must stop inspecting a

rei maxime seriae quae instaret praevertendum esse. Quem locum animadvertens Cicero, 'Turpe esse,' dixit, 'valdeque vitiosum in re seria convivio dignum aut delicatum aliquem inferre sermonem.'

: 24 :

*Ad consequendam mediocritatem opus esse delectu.*

1 Qui igitur mediocritati huic daturus est operam ne aut in gratiam loquens recedat a medio profundatque se se in assentationem atque obsequium aut, dum seria sequitur, delabatur in adversum acerbasque ad contentiones, modo refragatoris personam, modo rixatoris induens, huic delectus cum primis habendus est et rerum et temporum et locorum et personarum, quo virtutem maxime laudabilem ac publice privatimque et apud cives peregrinosque

2 aeque spectatam consequatur. Ex hoc itaque Aristoteles mediocritatem eam amicitiae perquam similem esse putat, quando qui eiusmodi virtute est praeditus et cives amplectatur et exteros et aequales atque inferiores et quibuscum vivendi consuetudinem frequentat et quibus nulla prorsus necessitudine est coniunctus; quin eodem quoque erga eos afficietur studio qui in honoribus constituti sunt ac magistratibus primumque in populis locum optinent.

picture of vanities and turn his attention to a most serious and urgent matter. Considering this subject, Cicero said, "It is unseemly and very blameworthy to introduce in serious business conversation that is wanton or appropriate to a dinner party."[78]

: 24 :

*Discrimination is needed for achieving the mean.*

Therefore, a man who is to pay attention to this mean — so that he neither recedes from the middle state by speaking to please and plunges himself into yes-manship and obsequiousness, nor, while he is pursuing serious things, slides into the opposite and into bitter contentions, now assuming the role of the opponent, now of the wrangler — must especially discriminate among things, times, places, and persons so that he may achieve a virtue praiseworthy in public and private and equally respected among citizens and foreigners. And so, as a result of this, Aristotle thinks this mean extremely similar to friendship, since a man endowed with a virtue of this kind welcomes citizens and foreigners and equals and inferiors and those with whom he lives on close terms and those to whom he is joined by no connection at all.[79] In fact, he will also be moved by the same goodwill toward those who are established in official posts and magistracies and obtain the first place among the populace.

: 25 :

## De mensura servanda in gratificando et commonendo.

1   Hoc autem tale est ut, cum opus fuerit, gratum se se illis exhibeat
in sermonibus conversationibusque in eisdemque appellandis atque invisendis, in salutationibus, deductionibus reductionibusque
atque assurrectionibus; denique ut omni e parte gratus esse illis
studeat et, quantum par est, in illorum gratiam ac commendationem loqui ac modo res eorum laudare proque loco ac tempore
commendare dicta, probare consilia, sententias, actiones, studia,
opera, vitae genus efferre — eaque cuncta cum delectu ac ratione.

2   Contra haec, ubi labi aliquem viderit, peccare, decipi, parum prudenter rebus suis consulere aut nimium sibi ipsi tribuere, disceden-
tem ab honesto delabentemque ad ostentationem ac vana consilia
captantemque popularis auras et, ut Severus Alexander usurpabat,
vendentem fumos, et loco suo et tempore et verbis maxime accommodatis commonefaciet illum, etiam auctore Christo optimo
maximo, studebitque ab inceptis aut inutilibus aut parum honestis
retrahere iis verbis, exemplis, consiliis, ut monitoris recti, viri boni,
civis benevolentis, reprehensoris quandoque lenis, blanditoris non
nunquam comis, consiliarii ubique prudentis et integri, institutoris
interdum et probi et sapientis personam suscipiat. Forsitan et locus et tempus et res ipsa aliquando tulerit, ut increpatoris etiam
acerbi aut inclamatoris agrestis, non ut molestiam afferat, verum
ut, ubi retinere suavioribus illum verbis nequit aut dictis exemplis-
que aut probabilibus suasoriisque rationibus, deterreat inclamando
austerius, proponendo etiam turpitudinem, infamiam periculaque
tum rerum honorisque tum vitae quoque ipsius.

## : 25 :

*On observing due measure in gratifying and advising.*

Moreover, this goodwill is such that, when necessary, he will show    1
himself agreeable to others in conversation and intercourse and in
addressing and visiting them, in greeting, escorting to and from
home, and rising deferentially. In short, he should endeavor in every respect to be agreeable to them and, as far as is proper, speak
to please and commend them and to praise their affairs with moderation and to commend what they say as suits the moment and
place, to approve their plans, opinions, actions, pursuits, works, to
exalt their way of life — and all this with discrimination and reason. On the contrary, when he sees that someone is slipping, sin-    2
ning, being deceived, looking after his affairs with too little care or
thinking too well of himself, departing from honor and sliding
into ostentation and vainglorious plans, grasping for popular favor,
and, as Severus Alexander was wont to say, selling smoke, he will
admonish him at the appropriate time and place with the best
suited words, even by the authority of Christ, the best and greatest.[80] And he will endeavor to hold him back from useless or
hardly honorable undertakings by words, examples, and advice, as
he assumes the role of a righteous admonisher, a good man, a be-
nevolent citizen, sometimes a mild reproacher, sometimes a kind
flatterer, always a prudent and virtuous adviser, sometimes an upright and wise teacher. Perhaps sometimes the place, time, and the
matter itself will even require the role of a harsh chider or a rude
reviler, not to annoy but, when he cannot hold him back with
more pleasing words or witticisms and examples, or more probable
and persuasive reasons, to deter him by rebuking him more se-
verely, setting forth also the disgrace, infamy, and dangers both to
property and honor and even to life itself.

3    Videamus quibus dictis Hannibalem, etiam efferatis moribus ducem, Maharbal verberet, 'Nimirum, o Hannibal, non omnia tibi dii dedere: vincere scis; victoria uti nescis.' Forsan autem haec ipsa increpatio acerbitasque hunc ipsum de quo disputamus minime decuerit; nihilominus eiusmodi esse debet ut, dum prodesse possit, dum iuvare dictis suis atque commonitionibus, sibi proponat potius recte admonendo prudenterque consulendo in molestiam esse aliquam incidendum quam tacendo aut loquendo in gratiam assentandoque in turpitudinem honorisque iacturam ac famae pati amicum, familiarem, civem, hospitem, addam et peregrinum, incurrere. Itaque Terentianum illum dictum, 'Nihil humani a me alienum puto,' nequaquam videtur ab hoc ipso quem adumbramus alienum.

4    Est apud Sallustium commonefaciens Iugurtam Micipsa rex gravissima hac vel paterna potius oratione:

> Parvum te, Iugurta, amisso patre, sine spe, sine opibus in meum regnum accepi, existimans non minus me tibi quam liberis, si geniussem, ob beneficia carum fore. Neque ea spes falsum me habuit. Nam, ut alia magna et egregia tua facta omittam, novissime rediens Numantia meque regnumque meum gloria honoravisti tuaque virtute nobis Romanos ex amicis amicissmos fecisti. In Hispania nomen familiae nostrae renovatum est. Postremo, quod difficillimum inter mortales est, gloria invidiam vicisti. Nunc quoniam mihi natura finem vitae facit, per hanc dexteram, per regni fidem moneo obtestorque te, ut hos, qui tibi genere propinqui, beneficio meo fratres sunt, caros habeas neu malis alienos adiungere

Let us look at the words with which Maharbal lashed Hanni-   3
bal, a general strongly disposed to ferocious habits, "Clearly,
Hannibal, the gods didn't give you everything: you know how to
conquer; you don't know how to make use of victory."[81] But perhaps this chiding and harshness are not at all becoming to the man
we are discussing. Nonetheless, he must be the kind of person to
determine that, provided he can do some good, provided he can
help with his words and admonitions, it is better to annoy by
rightly admonishing and prudently advising someone than to allow a friend, family member, citizen, guest — I'll even add a foreigner — to encounter disgrace and loss of honor and reputation by
keeping quiet or by seeking to gratify and flatter him. And so that
saying of Terence's, "I count nothing human foreign to me," appears not at all foreign to that man whom we are sketching.[82]

In Sallust the king Micipsa admonishes Jugurtha with this very   4
serious, or rather, paternal speech:

> I received you, Jugurtha, into my kingdom when you were
> small, had lost your father, and had no hope or resources,
> judging that I, owing to this kindness, would be no less dear
> to you than to my own children, should I have any. Nor has
> this hope deceived me. For, to omit your other great and
> outstanding deeds, recently upon returning from Numantia
> you have honored both me and my kingdom with glory, and
> by your valor you have made our friends the Romans most
> friendly to us. In Spain the name of our family has been re-
> stored. Finally, a thing most difficult among mortals, you
> have defeated envy with your glory. Now, since nature is put-
> ting an end to my life, by this right hand, by the loyalty
> owed to the kingdom, I exhort and conjure you that you
> hold these dear, who are related to you by birth and are your
> brothers by my kindness, and that you do not desire to at-
> tach to yourself foreigners rather than retain those joined to

quam sanguine coniunctos retinere. Non exercitus neque
thesauri praesidia regni sunt verum amici, quos neque armis
cogere neque auro parare queas: officio et fide pariuntur.
Quis autem amicior quam frater fratri, aut quem alienum
fidum invenias, si tuis hostis fueris? Equidem ego vobis regnum trado firmum, si boni eritis, sin mali, inbecillum. Nam
concordia parvae res crescunt; discordia maximae dilabuntur.
Coeterum te his, Iugurta, qui aetate et sapientia prior es, ne
aliter quid eveniat, providere decet. Nam in omni certamine
qui opulentior est, etiam si accipit iniuriam, quod plus potest, facere videtur. Vos autem, Adherbal et Hiempsal, colite
et observate talem hunc virum. Imitamini virtutem et eniti-
mini ne ego meliores liberos sumpsisse videar quam genuisse.

Quales igitur admonitiones in eiusmodi rebus ac negociis esse debeant locus hic Sallustii nos docet.

5    Nec minus docet apud Livium Scipio in maxime amica et
sapienti illa ad Masinissam allocutione, qua nihil gravius, nihil
amicius ac, si rem ipsam introspicias, nihil accommodatius; neve
aliqua in parte dignitati aut suae aut Masinissae deesset post So-
phronisbae interitum, nunc solatur illum, nunc leviter castigat;
post, etiam advocata concione, regem appellat eximiisque ornatum
laudibus aurea corona, aurea patera, sella curuli, scipione eburneo,
toga item picta palmataque tunica donat additque et verbis ho-
6    norem. Quamvis autem, ut decoro reique praesertim ipsi satisfiat,
severior non nunquam assumenda videatur persona, quid tamen

you by blood. Armies and treasures are not the defense of the kingdom but friends, whom you cannot force with arms or buy with gold: they are acquired by service and loyalty. And who is more friendly than a brother to a brother, or what foreigner would you find loyal if you were an enemy to your own people? For my part I hand over a strong kingdom to you all if you are good, but a weak one if you are wicked. For in concord small states increase; in discord the greatest collapse. For the rest, it is right that you, Jugurtha, who are older and wiser than they are, take care that it not turn out otherwise. For in every dispute the man with more resources, even if he suffers injury, seems to commit it because he is more powerful. But you, Adherbal and Hiempsal, honor and respect this great man. Imitate his virtue and strive that I may be seen not to have adopted better children than I have begotten.[83]

So this passage in Sallust teaches us what kind of admonitions there ought to be in matters and affairs of this sort.

Nor in Livy is Scipio less instructive in the very friendly and   5 wise address to Masinissa, than which there is nothing more grave, nothing more friendly, and, if you look into the situation, nothing more appropriate. And so as not in any degree to neglect his own dignity or Masinissa's, after the death of Sophronisba, at one moment he consoles him, at another he lightly reproves him. Afterward, having also called an assembly, he addresses him as king, extols him with extraordinary praise, and gives him a golden crown, a golden bowl, a chair of state, an ivory staff, also a varicolored toga and a tunic embroidered with palm branches, and he adds honor with his words.[84] Although sometimes it seems neces-   6 sary to take on a more severe role to satisfy decorum and especially the situation itself, Plautus, nevertheless, in the character of

comem deceat in commonefaciendo Plautus docet in Philoxeni
illius persona:

> Eia, Lyde, leniter qui saeviunt sapiunt magis.
> Minus mirandum est illec aetas si quid illorum facit
> quam si non faciat. Feci ego istec itidem in adolescentia.

7      Igitur quoniam hic ipse vir circa voluptates versatur ac molestias
quae inter conversandum usuveniunt, illud omnino praestabit,
hinc molestus ne sit, illinc ut oblectet probetque probanda modeste et graviter pro re ac loco sitque in alloquendo gratus atque
periucundus, non tamen ut aut omnem refugiat molestiae respectum vereaturque ne, recte monendo ac suadendo honesta, parum
forte placeat, aut undecunque gratiam ut inire velit assentando
impudenter; quin eum se se geret utrunque ut referat tum ad
honestatem tum ad utilitatem, quae tamen honestate non sit va-
8      cua. Et quod meretriculae servare audent in re impudica, non servabit in re maxime honesta et utili vir qui sibi proposuit ubique
gratus esse seque in omni vita hominumque consuetudine mediocritatem velle sequi, tum in commendando ac loquendo in gratiam, tum in continendo ab iis quae parum laudanda videantur aut
in iis improbandis retinendo modum ac mensuram? Nam quanquam eius studium est, ut sit maxime gratus atque etiam utilis,
negliget tamen leviorem interdum offensiunculam quae posset ex
commonefactione proficisci dum prosit multum. 'Satis nunc,' inquit apud Plautum,

> credo, soror, ornatam te tibi viderier;
> sed ubi exempla conferentur meretricum aliarum, ibi tibi
> erit cordolium, si quam ornatam melius forte aspexeris.

Philoxenus, teaches what becomes an affable person while admonishing:

> Whoa, Lydus, those who rage mildly are wiser. It's less a
> wonder if that time of life does that sort of thing than if it
> doesn't. I myself did things like that in my youth.[85]

So then, since this man we are discussing is involved with the 7
pleasures and annoyances occurring in conversation, he will absolutely take care on the one hand not to annoy, on the other to delight, to approve what ought to be approved decorously, gravely, and in accordance with the matter and the place, and to be pleasant and gratifying in his speech. Nevertheless, he should not avoid any thought of annoying and fear that he might perhaps please too little by advising what is right and urging what is honorable; nor should he wish to curry favor through impudent yes-manship from any source whatever. Instead, in each case he will comport himself so that he has recourse to both honor and utility, which nevertheless should not be void of honor. And will a man not ob- 8
serve in highly honorable and beneficial affairs what prostitutes venture to observe in a shameful ones? Shall he not decide to be pleasing everywhere and to wish to follow the mean in every kind of life and every gathering of men, both while commending and gratifying, and while restraining others from things which seem hardly praiseworthy or reproving them within due measure? For although he endeavors to be most pleasing and also most useful, nevertheless he occasionally disregards a small offense that might arise from an admonition, provided that he may do much good. "I believe, sister," someone in Plautus says,

> that you think yourself well enough dressed now, but when
> comparisons with other prostitutes are made, then you'll be
> sorry if you happen to catch sight of someone better
> dressed.[86]

Non verita est illa sororem paulisper offendere, dum ei prodesset multum ad cultum atque ornatum utque inter alias excelleret quae pariter quaestum facerent.

9 Novimus ipsi et temperantem et mediocritatis huius studiosum hominem qui, cum sermo aliquis allatus esset in quo retineri a se modum posse diffideret, sensim e concilio se subtraheret sub ali-

10 quam honestam causam. Quoniam autem nullum hic aspernatur genus hominum, quod ita sit a natura usuque institutus, quippe cuius studium sit gratificandi notis ignotisque, summis atque infimis, meminisse eum oportet aliam cum cive, aliam cum hospite aut peregrino rationem a se sequendam esse, cum amico quam cum ignoto, cum ignobili quam cum eo qui sit honesto loco natus educatusque maxime liberaliter. Qua in re delectum eum adhibebit, ut cuique quantum sat est tribuat, seu in gratiam loquatur ac commendationem seu, dum commonefaciendo prosit, in molestiam ut incurrat aliquam, quanquam studium eius illud est praecipuum gratiam ut verbis ineat, offendat vero in conversando neminem; atque ut in illud maximum omnino studium confert adiungitque operam, ita ab altero praecipue cavebit, quantum ta-

11 men honestas simul utilitasque dictabit. Qua quidem ratione ab utroque, et assentatore et contentioso, mutuabitur sibi quantum satis est, atque ut oportet et decet; quaeque parum decuerint neque honesta erunt minimeque[11] conducibilia, ea pro loco ac tem-

12 pore repudiabit. Et res tamen et locus ac tempus ipsum, non nunquam etiam persona, illud exigent, ut peregrino quam civi, plebeio quam nobili, plusculum sit aliquid tribuendum. Cavendum tamen ubique ne, dum in gratiam alterius loqui volumus, alterum in iram atque odium provocemus.

She was not afraid to offend her sister for a little while as long as she could much improve her dress and adornment, and so that she might excel other women engaged in the same profession.

I myself knew a restrained man who pursued this mean. When 9 some subject of conversation was introduced in which he was not confident that he could remain moderate, he would gradually withdraw from the company under some respectable pretext. But 10 since this man whom we are discussing disdains no kind of men because he is made that way by nature and habit and endeavors to gratify people whom he knows and does not know, the high and the low, he must remember that he should follow one mode of conduct with a citizen, another with a guest or foreigner, a different mode with a friend than a stranger, a different mode with one of low birth than with someone born in an honorable position and liberally educated. In this he will use discrimination, so that he gives as much as is enough to each person, whether he speaks to please or to commend. He will risk making a nuisance of himself provided that he does some good with his reprimand, although his principal endeavor is to talk pleasantly while not offending anyone with his conversation. And as he brings his greatest effort to the former and directs his exertion to it, so he will especially avoid the latter as much as honor and utility will dictate. For this reason he 11 will borrow as much as he needs from each, both the yes-man and the contentious man, as is necessary and appropriate. He will reject, as time and place allow, those things which are inappropriate, dishonorable, and not at all expedient. Nevertheless, the matter, 12 place, and time itself, sometimes also the person, require that a little bit more must be given to the foreigner than the citizen, the plebeian than the noble. One must always take care, while we wish to speak to gratify one person, that we do not provoke another to wrath and hatred.

: 26 :

*Virtutem eam non esse amicitiam sed aliam quampiam sine nomine.*[12]

1 Virtutem vero hanc non esse amicitiam, quamvis sit ei non parum similis, illud docet quod amici officium est in amicum, quodque mutuus inter amicos est amor, mutuum etiam studium, mutua utilitatum collatio expetitioque gratificandi, quodque amicus est
2 alter ego, ut omnes consentiunt. At hic ipse, quem suo sine nomine esse dicimus, non movetur in peregrinum, advenam, summum vel infimum civem, notum ignotumve benevolentiae atque amoris mutuique ipsius gratia, sed naturali quadam commotione, quodque ita suapte natura institutus sit eumque se se ipse assuescendo comparaverit, ut qui gratus esse omnibus velit, molestus vero nulli aut impudenter contentioseque adversari; quin ut assentari minime vult recusatque altercari ac rixas serere, sic media inter utrumque officia inter omnes exercere nititur, humanitatis praecipue memor generisque hominum studiosus eorumque societatis et
3 insiti a natura officii. Quo fit idem bonus ut sit vir, civis probus, homo hominis amicus, gratus ac iucundus et simul cunctis publice et privatim singulis, molestus vero nemini, quique in conversationibus vitaque sociabili eum se se geret, ut lenibus pariter gratus sit ac severis, iucundis aeque ac tristibus, mansuetis item ac duriusculis, praestabitque adversum singulos id quod Horatius praecipit:

> Sed pater ut gnatis, sic nos debemus amicis,
> siquod inest vitium non fastidire: strabonem
> appellat poetum blandus pater.

80

: 26 :

## This virtue is not friendship but some other without a name.[87]

Moreover, that this virtue is not friendship, although it is very like 1
it, is demonstrated by the facts that a friend's duty is to his friend,
that the love between friends is mutual, their devotion mutual,
their conferring of benefits and seeking to please mutual, and that
a friend is an another self, as all agree.[88] But this man, who we say 2
has no name, is not inclined toward the foreigner, stranger, highest
or lowest citizen, known or unknown person by benevolence and
this mutual love but by some natural inclination and because he
has been made so by his own nature and has prepared himself via
habituation, since he wishes to please everyone but not to oppose
anyone impudently or contentiously. Instead, as he by no means
wishes to be a yes-man and refuses to dispute and sow quarrels, so
he strives to perform the duties midway between these extremes
with everyone, particularly mindful of kindness and the nature of
men, devoted to their society and the duty instilled by nature.
And so he is at the same time a good man, an upright citizen, a 3
friendly man, pleasing and pleasant both to everyone in public and
to individuals in private but annoying to no one, and a man who
comports himself in conversation and social life so as to be equally
pleasing to the mild and the severe, the pleasant and the sad, the
gentle and likewise the harsh. He will do with individuals what
Horace teaches:

> But as a father with his sons, so with our friends we must
> not be disgusted if they have some defect; a flattering father
> calls a squinter "Squinty."[89]

: 27 :

*Quae ad habitum hunc innominatum pertineant.*

1 Omnino igitur huiusmodi habitu qui est praeditus ita loquetur in gratiam, ut in impudentiam aliquam nullo modo incidat aut pa-
2 rum modestam commendationem ac laudem. Quod si quandoque deflectendum sit a linea, illud servabit quod ii qui rapida ac maiora tranant flumina, in obliquum trahi se tantisper ut sinant, dum ea ratione ad alteram ferantur ripam, cum velle adversum ire contentius sit non modo difficile verum etiam temerarium longeque perculosissimum; de quo idem illud iure dici poterit, quod de Empedocle ridet Horatius; rursusque ita aliquando adversus contendet eaque modestia et lenitate aut refragabitur aut parum aliquid probabit, ut exemplo illorum qui dirigere virgulam aut flagellum incurvum volunt et sensim et molliter retorquendo dirigere illud studeant ne, maiorem dum afferre vim volunt, flagellum ipsum frangant. Quid enim imprudentius quam, dum studes bene facere, id agas ut obsis?

3 Adversatio enim immodesta et parum prudens iram nunc occultam parit atque indignationem, nunc manifestum odium, saepe etiam repentinum excitat impetum; id quod incivilis et parum experti est hominis, quod quantopere sit evitandum Antisthenis factum docet. Illud itaque praecipue Iuvenalis attendendum est dictum:

> Venit et Crispi iucunda senectus,
> cuius erant mores qualis facundia, mite
> ingenium. Maria ac terras populosque regenti
> quis comes utilior, si clade et peste sub illa
> saevitiam damnare et honestum ferre liceret

: 27 :

*What pertains to this condition without a name.*

Therefore, in general a person endowed with this condition will 1 speak to please so as not to fall in any way into impudence or immodest commendation or praise. But if sometimes he has to deviate from the line, he will act like those who swim across broad and rapid rivers. They allow themselves to be borne sideways for a while until in this way they are carried to the other bank, since wishing to go straight on more vigorously is not only difficult but also rash and extremely dangerous—about this one might justly say the same thing that Horace said mockingly of Empedocles.[90] On the contrary, sometimes he will argue against and either will oppose with moderation and gentleness or will approve only a little, following the example of those who want to straighten a rod or a bent flail and endeavor gradually and gently to straighten it by twisting it back, to avoid breaking the flail in their eagerness to apply greater force. For what is more imprudent than doing harm while endeavoring to do good?

For immoderate and imprudent opposition sometimes breeds 3 hidden anger and indignation, sometimes manifest hatred, often even excites sudden attack. This is the behavior of an uncivil and unskilled man, and how much it is to be avoided the act of Antisthenes teaches.[91] And so one must pay particular attention to what Juvenal said:

> Pleasant old Crispus came also, a gentle nature, whose character was like his eloquence. Who would have been a more useful companion to the ruler of seas, lands, and peoples if he had been allowed to give honorable advice and to condemn savagery under that destruction and plague? But what

consilium? Sed quid violentius aure tyranni,
cum quo de pluviis aut aestibus aut nimboso
vere locuturi fatum pendebat amici?
Ille igitur numquam direxit brachia contra
torrentem.

Itaque hic ipse Crispus, maximus et civis et senator, in ipso adver-
sandi atque in gratiam loquendi genere sic quidem continuit, ut a
rapiditate fluminis illius trahi se in obliquum pro re ac tempore
permiserit, quod servans saevissimi monstri rabiem, etsi difficulter,
praeteriit tamen.

4    Sed desinamus iam in hac ipsa mediocritate indaganda hube-
riores velle videri aut acutiores, cum et in gratificando et in obsequendo aut commonefaciendo ac tum modeste adversando tum
obsequendo pudenter, satis illud fuerit, delectus si adhibeatur, de
5  quo abunde admodum dictum est. Vides iam quae mediocritas
haec ipsa sit et qualis; quodque apud Graecos est ignominis, ut
minus mirum videri possit, si sua apud Latinos appellatione careat,
quando qui de iis Latine scripserit, perscrutando ea et quae ac
quales virtutes ipsae sint, indagando Aristoteleo praesertim more,
aut nullus in hunc usque diem extitit aut eius scripta ad nostra
haec tempora parum pervenere.

:  28  :

## De comitate.

1  Coeterum recte inquirenti ac perscrutanti acutius quae virtutis
huius partes sint ac munera apparebit fortasse eam esse comitatem, de qua non pauca haud multo ante dicta sunt a nobis,
quando comitas ipsa communis est ad omnes non ad paucos, ad

was more violent than the ear of the tyrant on whom depended the fate of a friend about to talk about rain, heat, or cloudy spring? Therefore he never struck out against the torrent.[92]

Thus this Crispus, a very great citizen and senator, in this kind of opposing and of speaking to please, restrained himself so as to allow himself, in accordance with the matter and the time, to be carried sideways by the rapidity of the stream. By doing so he escaped, although with difficulty, the rage of that most savage monster.

But let us now stop wishing to seem too copious and acute in 4 investigating this mean, since in gratifying and indulging or in admonishing and then moderately opposing or indulging modestly, it will be enough if discrimination is used, about which I have said quite a lot. Now you see what this mean is and what its nature is. 5 Since it has no name among the Greeks, it can hardly appear surprising if it lacks its own appellation among the Latins, since there is no one to this day has who has written in Latin about these matters — or else his writings have not survived to our time — inquiring into what these virtues are and their nature, in particular investigating them in the manner of Aristotle.

: 28 :

*On affability.*

Moreover, to one inquiring in the right way and examining more 1 acutely what the parts and functions of this virtue are it will perhaps appear to be affability, about which I have spoken quite a bit not very long ago.[93] For affability is courteous to everyone, not just

exteros ignotosque non tantum ad cives et cognitos ac familiares, neque modo ad aequales atque eiusdem ordinis verum ad ignobiles atque in excelso gradu constitutos; versaturque in verbis ac collocutionibus, studetque oblectare atque in gratiam loqui minimeque
2 molestiam afferre, neque ab honesto recedit atque utili. Livius quoque, alios ut praeteream scriptores, satis aperte pluribus in locis nobis ostendit comem virum suavem esse in consuetudinibus ac familiaritatibus et facilem admodum ac lenem dantemque operam ut, quibuscum familiaritatem exercet atque consuetudinem, gratiam sibi eorum sic conciliet ut tanquam influat in ipsorum animos.

3     Itaque videamus, obsecro, quid hic ipse Livius de Marco Valerio Corvino loquatur:

> Non alius militi familiarior dux fuit omnia inter infimos militum haud gravate munia obeundo. In ludo praeterea militari, cum velocitatis viriumque aequales certamina ineunt, comiter facilis; vincere aut vinci vultu eodem nec quenquam aspernari parem qui se offerret.

Agnosce facilitatem eius ad cedendum minimeque esse contentiosum vultum insuper, qui indicio esse potest quibus etiam uteretur verbis. Ad haec et communitatem tantam illam quidem, ut dux ipse militem non aspernaretur quenquam concertatorem in iaculando, equitando, in cursu se exercendo. Praeterea consideremus
4 eiusdem etiam auctoris verba de Lucio Papirio Cursore: 'Sensit peritus dux quae res victoriae obstaret: severitatem miscendam comitate.' Atqui proprium est et comis et eius cuius appellationem quaerimus reiicere a se austeritatem, retinere lenitudinem, et obsequi potius quam repugnare, et cedere magis quam in contentionem prorumpere aut iurgia.

to a few, to foreigners and strangers, not only to citizens, acquaintances, and family members, and not only to equals and people of the same rank but to the lowborn and those placed in a high position. It is involved with words and conversations, endeavors to delight and to speak pleasingly and at least not to cause annoyance, and does not depart from the honorable and useful. Livy 2 also, to pass over other writers, shows openly enough in many places that the affable man is pleasant in social and familiar intercourse and very easy and mild, and makes an effort to gain the affection of those with whom he is in social and familiar intercourse so that he may influence their minds.

And so let us look, I pray, at what Livy himself says of Marcus 3 Valerius Corvinus:

> No other general was more familiar with the soldiers, performing all the duties ungrudgingly among the lowest of them. Besides, in military exercises, when contemporaries compete in speed and strength, he was affably easygoing; his countenance remained the same winning or losing, and he did not disdain anyone who presented himself as a competitor.[94]

Note his ease in yielding as well as his agreeable expression, which can be an indicator of the words he would use. In addition, his sense of fellowship was so great that, although a general himself, he would not disdain any rival in throwing the javelin, in riding, in running a race. Let us also consider the words of the same author 4 about Lucius Papirius Cursor: "The skillful general sensed what was preventing victory: he had to blend his severity with affability."[95] Nevertheless, it is characteristic of the affable man and of the one whose appellation we are seeking to reject harshness, to remain gentle, to comply with rather than oppose, and to yield rather than burst forth into contention and quarrels.

5    Animadvertamus quoque quae et de Volumnio idem dicit:

Volumnium provinciae haud poenituit, multa secunda prelia
fecit, aliquot urbes hostium vi cepit, praedae erat largitor et
benignitatem per se gratam comitate adiuvabat.

Hoc illud est quod paulo ante retulimus verbis honorem addere,
quo videlicet maiorem inde gratiam sibi a militibus compararet,
6    quod quidem virtutis est huius proprium quaerere. Sed nec illud
negligamus quod de Quinto Fabio tradit: inita illum cum Samni-
tibus pugna, vocasse ad se Maximum filium et Marcum Valerium
tribunos nominatimque utrumque pari comitate nunc laudibus
nunc promissis honerasse. Quid magis consentiens ad gratiam
ineundam, quod mediocritas haec nostra quaeritat?

7    Nam et de Marco Marcello, ut diximus, refert accitum ad se
Bancium Nolanum benigne appellasse. Cuius enim virtutis, nisi
huius, benignae sunt appellationes? Militaria ei facinora retulisse,
quae a civibus ob invidiam sibi minime indicata erant. Quid accommodatius ineundam ad benevolentiam? Non posse tamen ob-
scura esse quae Romanis in castris fortiter gererentur; adiisse illum
et multa et gravia pericula pro dignitate populi Romani; Cannensi
in pugna non ante abstitisse prelio quam prope exanguem, ruina
oppressum superincidentium virorum, equorum, armorum. Et
honesta et gravia allectamenta ad demerendam gratiam, ad contra-
hendam benevolentiam ex commemoratione rerum strenue gestarum. Postque assurgentem illum Bancii fortitudini rebusque ab eo
egregie gestis, 'Macte virtute esto,' cum dixisset, hortatum refert
secum inde ut esset frequentius: futurum ei apud se omnem honorem atque omne pretium cum dignitate atque emolumento.
Credendum est his dictis et vultum et totius corporis gestum

Let us also pay attention to what the same author says about    5
Volumnius:

> Volumnius did not at all regret his assignment, he waged
> many successful battles, he captured some enemy cities by
> force, he was a bestower of booty, and he enhanced his liber-
> ality, pleasing in itself, with affability.[96]

This is what I mentioned a little while ago[97] — to add honor by
means of words — by which he clearly won greater favor for himself from the soldiers, which indeed it is characteristic of this virtue to seek. But let us not neglect what Livy relates of Quintus    6
Fabius. Having begun the war with the Samnites, he summoned
the tribunes, his son Maximus and Marcus Valerius, and by name,
with equal affability, he loaded each now with praise, now with
promises.[98] What is more consonant with entering someone's
good graces, which is what this mean of ours seeks?

For, as I have said, Livy relates that Marcus Marcellus sum-    7
moned Bantius of Nola and addressed him kindly.[99] To which
virtue, indeed, if not to this one, belong kind addresses? Marcellus
related Bantius' own military deeds to him, which the citizens out
of envy had mostly concealed from him. What could be more
suited to procuring goodwill? Nevertheless, deeds courageously
performed in the Roman camps could not be obscure; Bantius had
confronted many grave dangers for the honor of the Roman people; at the battle of Cannae he had not withdrawn from the fight
until he was weak from loss of blood and had been crushed by
men, horses, and arms falling on him. These were honorable and
weighty enticements to earn favor, to produce goodwill by recalling things done with spirit. And later, Livy relates, after Marcellus,
rising to honor Bantius' courage and the outstanding deeds done
by him, had said, "Well done!," he urged him to be with him more
often: with him Bantius would have every honor and reward, with
rank and advantage.[100] It must be believed that he added the

convenientem accessisse. Nam cum primis gestus gratiam sibi
conciliat, et, quod ingeniossimus poeta inquit, 'Super omnia vul-
tus/accessere boni.'

8    Quocirca haec ipsa omnia cum ad comitatem Livius referat
cumque propria sint mediocritatis huius de qua tam multa diximus, quis dubitet comitatem eam appellare, cum ex omni parte
comitas ea complectatur ac sibi vendicet quae mediocritatis huius
propria esse dicimus, quando et in gratiam loquitur et commendat
et laudat et hortatur et mulcet et monet et amice consulit om-
niaque cum delectu, neque ab honestate recedit, neque utilitatis
eius obliviscitur quicum orationem habet et cuius inire studet gratiam, idque hac solum ratione ac via?

9    Eadem quoque, ut est summe facilis, benigna, lepida, accom-
modans se se omnibus et civibus et exteris, sic omni studio cavet
ne offendat, ne molesta sit, ne in contentionem incidat, altercationes, iurgia, tantum denique in gratiam intenta et in eorum tum
iucunditatem tum commoda cum quibus ipsa versatur; non ita
tamen ut refugiat molestiam aliquando subire sive aurium sive
animi, pudenter tamen ac permodeste, dum prosit, dum, quod
impetrare ipsa nititur, retrahat ab inhonesto ac parum utili aut
etiam damnoso maleque tum dignitati tum rei domesticae condu-
centi. Itaque et moderanter at accommodate apud Plautum agit
cum domino servus:

> Numquid tu quod te aut genere indignum sit tuo
> facis aut inceptas facinus facere, Phedrome?
> Num tu pudicae cuipiam insidias locas
> aut quam pudicam esse oporteat?
> Ita tuum conferto amorem semper, si sapis,
> ne, id quod amas populus si sciat, sit probro.
> Semper curato ne sis intestabilis.

appropriate countenance and bearing of his whole body to these words. For such a bearing especially procures favor, and, as the most talented poet says, "In addition to all this were added kindly faces."[101]

Wherefore, since Livy relates all these things to affability and 8 they are particular to this mean about which I have spoken so much, who would hesitate to call it affability, since affability completely includes and lays claim to all those things that we say are particular to this mean, because it speaks to please and commends and praises and exhorts and soothes and warns and gives friendly advice — and all these things with discrimination — and does not hesitate to honor, and does not forget the utility of the person with whom it is speaking and whose good graces it is trying to acquire, and does this only by this way and means?

Likewise affability also, as it is most easygoing, kind, charming, 9 accommodating itself to all, both citizens and foreigners, takes care with every effort not to offend, to annoy, to fall into contention, altercations, quarrels; in short, it is only intent on pleasing and on the delight and advantage of those with whom it is involved. But it does not do so in such a way as to run away from sometimes troubling ears and mind, yet it does so with modesty and great moderation, provided that it does good, provided that — and this is what it strives to obtain — it draws away from what is dishonorable and useless or even harmful and ill-suited either to social rank or domestic prosperity. And so in Plautus a slave speaks moderately and appropriately with his master:

> You're not doing anything unworthy of yourself or your family or preparing to commit a crime, are you, Phaedromus? You're not setting a trap for some chaste woman or one who ought to be chaste? If you have any sense, always bestow your love so that it won't be shameful if people know the object of your love. Always take care lest you be disqualified

Quod amas ama testibus praesentibus.

Nemo ire quenquam publica prohibet via.

10   Quid quod et comitatis et mediocritatis huius materia et
quidam quasi campus in quo versentur eadem ipsa est atque
una: collocutiones videlicet, appellationes, congressiones, sermones, consuetudines, conversationes, salutationes, visitationes,
confabulationes conventionesque in coenis, in nuptiis, in ludis, in
rebus tum iocosis tum ad vires refocillandas ac repellenda taedia?

11   Sed maluerint fortasse aliqui mediocritatem hanc innominatam
iacere; nos vero nequaquam ii sumus qui, cum contentionem ac
rixationem vitium esse censeamus, velimus hac praesertim in parte
contentiosi videri atque altercatores; satisque fuerit virtutem hanc
ipsam, etiam innominatam, quae et qualis sit, ostendisse.

: 29 :

*De popularitate.*

1   Illud vero praetereundum non est, popularitatem vocari hanc ipsam mediocritatem quosdam malle, quando popularitas comitatem[13] quandam erga populares facilitatemque prae se fert, ut videatur virtus esse illorum potius qui in alto sunt gradu constituti
quique adversum inferiores se se faciles admodum gerant exhi-
beantque affabiles, quam fuisse in Augusto principe traditum est.
Sed ea fortasse non minus perspicitur in actionibus, favore, suffra-
giis, quam in oratione ac verbis, quanquam et popularitas comitate

2   condienda est. Ad haec popularitas studium habet populi ac mul-
titudinis multique ob eam populares dicti ac factiosi habiti, ut
videri possit adversari eidem contrarium erga nobilitatem studium:

from calling witnesses. Love what you love in the presence of your witnesses. No one prevents anyone from going on a public road.[102]

What about the fact that the material of affability and of this   10
mean and, as it were, the field in which they dwell are one and the same? Namely, colloquies, addresses, gatherings, speeches, social intercourse, conversations, salutations, visits, chats, and meetings at meals, at weddings, at games, at pleasant affairs, both to restore strength and drive away tedium. But perhaps some will prefer this   11
mean to remain unnamed. I, however, am by no means the sort of person to wish, especially in this part, to appear contentious and a disputant, since I think contention and quarreling a vice. Let it suffice to have shown what this virtue is, even if nameless, and what kind of thing it is.

: 29 :

*On popularity.*

It must not be overlooked, however, that some prefer to call this   1
mean popularity, since popularity exhibits a certain kind of affability and ease toward the people, so that it appears to be the virtue of those who are placed in high rank and bear themselves very easily toward their inferiors and show themselves friendly—a virtue said to have been present in the emperor Augustus. But perhaps it is no less perceived in actions, favor, and influence than in speech and words, although popularity also must be seasoned with affability. In addition, popularity is devoted to the people and the   2
multitude, and on account of it many men were called supporters of the people and held to be factious, so that the contrary devotion to the nobility can be seen to oppose popularity—which was the

quod in Appio Claudio fuit, ut de Mario taceamus ac Sylla con-
trariisque utriusque studiis. Habet praeterea popularitas applica-
tionem illam suam erga populum popularesque atque illorum res
3  tantummodo. At comitas, delectu adhibito, eadem quoque est adversus exteros atque alieni generis homines, et natura et habitu et
ratione ita dictante.

: 30 :

## De humanitate.

1  Nec desunt qui humanitatem eam dici malint. Verum nec humanitas adversatur contentionis ac rixarum studio, nec qui humanus
est contentioso ac rixatori est adversus; est tamen comis vir etiam
perhumanus, etsi non pauci humani quidem ipsi sunt nequaquam
tamen comes. Nemo tamen comis quin idem ipse sit humanus.
2  Agit comiter familiaris meus Antonius Galateus, dum, quod ingenium est eius quique etiam habitus, quoscumque habet obviam,
gratificari iis studet salutando perhumane, appellando benigne,
congrediendo hilariter, iocando urbane, arridendo familiariter, of-
ferendo grate operam suam et facilem et minime importunam.
Quo fit ut, quemadmodum maximam in congressu affert iucunditatem ac delinimentum, sic post digressum maximum quoque
relinquat sui desiderium delinitionemque animi quandam cum requiete ac voluptate: quod suaves praestare sorbillationes consuevere, uti os ac buccam, quod hodie dicunt, suavem relinquant, satietate omni prorsus repulsa et epularum et coenae.
3  Exhibet se quacumque in actione ac vitae genere humanum
Ioannes Pardus, quod et philosophiae studium, quod in eo summum est, exigit et natura eius exposcit; nihil superbe agit, nihil
arroganter. In incessu, in sermone, in consuetudine aequalem se

case with Appius Claudius, not to mention Marius and Sulla and the opposing endeavors of each.[103] Moreover, popularity applies only to the people, supporters of the people, and their affairs. But affability, used with discrimination, is also the same with foreigners and men of a different race, as nature, custom, and reason dictate.

: 30 :

*On humanity.*

Nor are those lacking who prefer to call it humanity. But humanity is not opposed to pursuing contention and quarrels, nor is the humane man opposed to the contentious man or quarreler. Nevertheless, the affable man is also very humane, even if not a few humane men are by no means affable. Yet no one is affable who is not also humane. My close friend Antonio Galateo, in accordance with his nature and habit, behaves affably in that he endeavors to please anyone he meets by greeting them very humanely, addressing them kindly, meeting them cheerfully, joking with them urbanely, smiling on them like a friend, freely offering them his easygoing and accommodating services.[104] So it happens that just as he brings the greatest delight and charm to a meeting, so after his departure he also leaves behind the greatest longing for himself and a soothing of the mind with peace and pleasure — the sensation sweet sips customarily offer, in order to leave the mouth and the *bucca* (as they say today) sweet, thus completely driving out the sensation of satiety after banquets and dinners.[105]

Giovanni Pardo shows himself to be humane in every action and mode of life, as devotion to philosophy, which is very great in him, requires and his nature demands; he does nothing proudly, nothing arrogantly.[106] In his manner of walking, his speech, and

cunctis exhibet; aegre fert ubi in quempiam agi viderit insolentius; fert gravate et amicorum et civium adversos casus; solatur moerentes; laborantibus qua potest succurrit, adest, opitulatur, operam suam confert; astat ubique comes ei mansuetudo ac facilitas; studium tamen loquendi in gratiam vix ullum; nulla obsequendi, quemadmodum nec contendendi, proclivitas; oratio eius suavis et placida, quae tamen nullum prae se ferat studium ineundae gratiae propriique compendii; abstinet autem sic a gratiloquentia, ut maledicentiam prorsus detestetur ac contentiones.

4      Quocirca a comitate non uno modo differt humanitas. Etenim qui aliorum moveatur damnis, incommodis, captivitate, orbitate, inopia, exilio malisque aliis, humanum hunc dicimus, nequaquam in hoc tamen comem. Itaque aliud est comis viri officium, aliud humani. Inest tamen utrique quaedam quasi communitas vivendi quacumque in actione ac negocio, sive eam facilitatem vocare volu-

5      mus sive tractabilitatem. Non desunt tamen qui, quam comitatem ipsi vocari non iniuria fortasse dicimus, civilitatem eam appellari malint, quod virtus ea sit maxime honesto cive digna; ac tametsi adversum peregrinos exterosque ius extendat suum, tamen ducere potiore a re appellationem volunt. Qua ratione qui eam assecuti sint, civiles et ii dicantur. Quorum opinioni minime quidem adversaremur, si civiles ipsi non minus in actionibus rebusque versarentur aliis quae civiles et dicuntur et habentur quam in verbis congressionibusque atque in gratiam conserendo sermones suos.

6      Igitur cum et qui et quales adulatores sint atque assentatores abunde explicaverimus, qui item contentiosi ac rixatores, mediusque inter utrosque habitus qui sit et qualis ostenderimus, ad veraces transeamus et ad eam verborum partem quae aut veritatis studiosa est unius aut contra mendacii, de qua insequenti libro disseremus.[14]

his conversation he shows himself an equal with everyone. He takes it ill whenever he sees anyone treated insolently; he is oppressed by the adversities both of friends and of citizens. He consoles the grieving and succors, assists, helps, and works for the afflicted as much as he can. Always gentleness and ease stand by him as companions, but hardly ever does he endeavor to ingratiate himself; he has no inclination to flatter nor to contend. His speech is sweet and calm but exhibits no eagerness to enter someone's good graces or for his own gain. Moreover, he so abstains from ingratiation that he completely detests ill-speaking and contentions.

So humanity differs from affability in more than one way. For 4 we call humane whoever is moved by others' losses, troubles, captivity, bereavement, poverty, exile, and other evils, but nevertheless we by no means call him affable for this. And so the duty of an affable man is one thing, of a humane man, another. But in each there is a kind of fellowship of living, as it were, in every action and business, whether we wish to call it good nature or tractability. Nevertheless, some prefer to give the name civility to what I, 5 perhaps not unjustly, call affability, on the grounds that that virtue is most worthy of an honorable citizen, and although it extends its jurisdiction to strangers and foreigners, they still wish to derive its name from the principal thing. For which reason those who have achieved this virtue should also be called civil. I would not disagree if civil men themselves were not less involved in actions and other affairs both called, and held to be, civil than in words and meetings and in engaging in conversations for pleasure.

Therefore, since I have abundantly explained who and of what 6 kind both adulators and yes-men are, and likewise who the contentious and quarrelers are, and I have shown what and of what kind is the middle state between them, let us proceed to truthful men and that part of language devoted to the truth alone, or on the contrary to lying. I will treat this in the following book.

# LIBER SECUNDUS

*De ostentatione et simulatione.*

1 Veritati autem huic quae in sermone versatur civilique in consuetudine atque in hominum vita illinc adversa obsistit fronte ostentatio, nequaquam ex aequo seque resque suas metiens, cum aut affingat sibi maiora quam quae re ipsa sint et quam ingenium ferat
ac facultates, aut falsa omnino de se praedicet aliaque quam sint
eaque praeclara admodum magisque ac magis narratu atque hono-
ratu digna — vitium sane levissimorum hominum seque ipsos deci-
pientium idque etiam conantium, ut alii quoque decipiantur. Quid
enim est aliud simulare quam sub veritatis specie velle decipere?
2 Hinc vero adversatur dissimulatio, utque illa supra verum et loquitur et se se effert, sic huius est studium aut dissimulare quae in-
3 sunt aut deiicere ea infraque verum elevare ac deprimere. Itaque ut
veritati mendacium, sic mendax adversatur veraci veracitatique
mendacitas. Sed verax unus ipse quidem dumtaxat est et simplex,
mendax vero duplex. Nam e numero mendacium alii, ut dictum
est, ostentatores sunt ac simulatores, alii dissimulatores; de quibus
post.

# BOOK TWO

: 1 :

*On ostentation and simulation.*

Ostentation sets itself head on against this truth which is involved 1
with conversation, civil intercourse, and the life of men. By no
means does it fairly measure itself or its own affairs, since either it
makes them greater than they really are and than its natural capacity and faculties allow or it proclaims about itself things that are
completely false and other than they are, as things very brilliant
and very worthy of narration and honor. This is, of course, the
vice of the most insignificant men, who deceive themselves and try
to deceive others, too. For what else is simulation than wishing to
deceive under the appearance of truth? But dissimulation is op- 2
posed to this, and as the former speaks and elevates itself above
the truth, so the latter endeavors either to dissimulate what is in it
or to throw it out and diminish and depress it below the truth.
Thus, as truth is opposed to falsehood, so the truthful person to 3
the liar and mendacity to truthfulness. But the truthful man is
indeed only one, single in nature, while the liar is double. For, as
has been said, of the class of liars some are ostentatious and simulators, others dissimulators. I will speak about these later.

: 2 :

## De veracibus.

1 Nunc de veracibus, quos nihil refert si veros aliquando vocaverimus, tametsi verax ab habitu ac consuetudine suoque ab instituto veritatem profitetur eamque ubique sequitur estque moribus ac sermone, hoc est factis dictisque, ita constitutus, cum tamen verus dici quis possit ex aliquo dicto sententiaque qui tamen mentiri ple-
2 rumque sit solitus. In actione igitur omni vitaque universa cum laudetur veritas vituperetur mendacium, efficitur ut veracitas virtus sit, mendacitas vero vitium, siquidem improbatur vitium, commendatur e contrario virtus. Nec vero veritatis studium inesse cuiquam potest absque summa etiam probitate, perinde ut nec sine improbitate mendacitas. Igitur qui veraces iidem et viri et cives probi sunt; ex adverso mendaces improbi.
3 Saneque non maximis tantum aut mediocribus in actionibus inque minus gravibus sive sermonibus sive congressionibus ac sive seriis sive iocosis in rebus veracitatis elucescit studium ac vis, verum etiam in minimis quibusque, ut veritatis studiosi et tanquam professores de minutissimis quibusque ac maxime levibus non aliter sint soliciti quam pudicissimae matronae de honestatis ac pudicitiae fama, nec de continentia tantum pudorisque commendatione deque motibus ac verbis singulis, verum etiam de levissima oculorum inflexione deque incessu qui forte mollior iudicari posset
4 aut de manuum agitationibus atque oris habitu liberiore. Et vero alia ratione nequaquam praestare illud poterit ut, quod Aristoteles dicit, et vita et sermone verax sit; quod necesse est assuetudo praestet habitusque ita comparatus, ut veritas ipsa, et ubicumque

: 2 :

## *On the truthful.*

Now for truthful men: it doesn't matter if on some occasion we  1
have called them true.[1] Notwithstanding that, the truthful person
declares the truth from habit, custom, and his own mode of life,
follows it everywhere, and is so constituted in character and conversation, that is, in deeds and words, whereas someone nevertheless can be called true on the basis of some saying and opinion,
even if he is a habitual liar. Therefore, since truth is praised and  2
lying is censured in every action and the whole of life, it follows
that truthfulness is a virtue but mendacity a vice, since vice is condemned, virtue on the contrary commended. Nor can anyone be
devoted to truth without also having the highest integrity, just as
there is no lying with integrity. Therefore those who are truthful
are also honorable men and citizens; liars, on the other side, are
dishonorable.

Of course, devotion to truthfulness and its power shine out not  3
only in the greatest or in moderate actions, in less grave conversations and meetings, and in serious or joking matters, but also in
some of the smallest. So the devotees and, as it were, professors of
truth are just as anxious about some of the most minute and most
trivial things as the most modest matrons are about their reputation for honor and modesty, and not only about their continence
and excellence in modesty, about particular movements and words,
but also about the slightest glance of the eyes or a way of walking
that might perhaps be judged too sensual or about movements of
the hands and too free a facial expression. And truly in no other  4
way can one accomplish this than to be truthful both in life and in
speech, as Aristotle says.[2] Custom and an acquired habit are necessary to accomplish this so that truth itself, whenever needed and

opus est et quocumque in sermone minimaque quaque in actione, oculis semper obversetur eius, neque aliud aut studiosius medite- tur aut potius esse censeat magisque perpetuum aut constitutum habeat quam nullo pacto veritatis e via deflectere deque veri delabi curriculo. Sequitur igitur veritatis studium virtus ea quae suo no- mine est veridicentia et qui ea utuntur veridici, unde et qui vera vaticinantur, sive vates sive harioli, dicti sunt veridici pariter ac veriloqui.

5     Quanquam autem in iis quae supra sunt a nobis dicta satis praefati sumus — hac nos in parte hocque in tractatu minime loqui ea de veritate quae in inquirendis versatur rerum ac naturae causis aut de iure iniuriaque ac sive forensibus in negociis sive physicis mathematicisque inquisitionibus — tamen id ipsum iterum testa-
6    tum volumus. Itaque illiusmodi quidem vero falsum opponi dici- mus, huic autem mendacium potius. Qui enim sua in opinone fallitur ac sententia non statim ipse mendax est aut id agit ut deci- piat, et qui mentiendi studio tantum peccat vanus magisquam fal-
7    lax est aut deceptor. Sequitur praeterea veridicentiam benedicen- tia, cum sit probi viri benedicere sitque veridicus et ipse maxime probus ac bonus et vir et civis. Nec profecto, si detrahendum ali- quando flagitio fuerit, verax ipse parcet veritati, ita tamen ut ne maledicendi aut detrahendi studio id agere videatur, verum ut honestas vigeat in civitate ipsaque simul libertas, commune civium omnium bonum, proculque repellatur flagitium atque improbitas.

8     Contra vero mentientium hominum comes esse consuevit male- dicentia, quando mendaces existunt plerumque maledici pariter ac nugatores. Nanque ut lucrentur, ut vanitatem patefaciant suam, necesse est perperam multa ut dicant et fingant atque, ut comici

in whatever speech or however small an action, always hovers before his eyes and so that he reflects on nothing more eagerly or considers more important or holds more lasting and fixed than not diverging, under any circumstances, from the path of truth and falling from the chariot of truth. Therefore, that virtue which is named truth-telling follows devotion to the truth, and those who practice it, truth-tellers, whence those who prophesy truly, whether seers or soothsayers, are also called truth-telling and likewise truth-saying.

Although in those things that I said above I said enough in 5 advance so that in this part and in this treatise I am not at all speaking about the truth involved in inquiring into the causes of things and of nature, or about right and wrong, or legal business or physical and mathematical investigations, nevertheless I want it declared again.[3] And so we say indeed that falsehood is opposed to 6 that kind of truth but instead that lying is opposed to the truth under discussion. For a man who is mistaken in his opinion and judgment is not immediately a liar or does it to deceive, and a man who sins only in his zeal for fabrication is insincere rather than deceptive or a deceiver. Moreover, speaking well follows from 7 speaking the truth, since an honorable man speaks well of and speaks the truth and is himself very honorable and both a good man and a good citizen. And assuredly, if sometimes it is necessary to censure a disgraceful action, the truthful man will not abstain from the truth, yet in such a way that he does not appear to act out of eagerness to speak ill or to censure but rather so that honor may thrive in the city and at the same time liberty, the common good of all citizens, and disgraceful action and wickedness may be driven far away.

But conversely, speaking ill is usually the companion of lying 8 men, since for the most part liars are slanderers and triflers at the same time. For in order to make a profit and to expose their insincerity they have to say and make up many falsehoods, and, as the

inquiunt, garrulose deblatterent; quorum sunt e numero nebulones, nugigeruli, blatterones, veteratores et id genus vanissimo-
9 rum hominum ac maxime servilium. Veri igitur ipsius studiosus et
tanquam professor, in vita omni et in actione quacumque ac sermone, qualis est veritas, talem ipse personam assumet, quippe qui
etiam in iis, in quibus forte nihil referret, ne vel tantulum quidem
e via deflexerit, nedum ut a linea digrediatur veri; maioribus in
rebus ac negociis quin tenorem ubique suum servabit rectaque ad
metam proficiscetur, ut qui mendacium, nugas veterationesque
ubique fugiat detesteturque perinde ut rem maxime turpem summeque indignam recto et bono viro. Etenim prima veracium cura
est recti atque honesti. Itaque et a turpitudine, quae honestati adversatur, et ab insinuatione atque obliquitate, quae a rectitudine
10 est aliena, abhorreat necesse est. Quando autem virtus omnis gra-
tuita est ac per se expetitur veracitasque ipsa est cum primis etiam
laudabilis ac percommoda et retinendae et amplificandae hominum societati, nimirum veraces ipsi propter solam veritatem veri
sunt ipsius studiosi eamque tum propter se ipsam colunt, tum
quod vinculum eam humanae societatis vel maxime tenax esse intelligunt, ad quam colendam natos se esse sciunt.

11    Quia vero de veritate nunc illa loquimur quae potissimum in
sermone versatur atque oratione ac tum in laudando deque se atque de aliis praedicando, tum in improbandis ac reprehendendis
turpibus, veracis viri officium est vera et cognita de se nequaquam
dissimulanter sed libere atque aperte, ubi opus fuerit, loqui nihilque supra quam suum est sibi aut arcessite affingere aut subductim
detrahere — modeste tamen omnia. Evitabit insinuationes flexus-
que verborum, non detorquebit iter a linea, nihil simulanter dicet
aut dissimulanter, aperte quidem cuncta sineque iniuria. Erit autem sermo eius nequaquam aut affectatus aut lubricus, neque

comic poets say, babble nonsensically; this group includes the good-for-nothings, the trumpery-peddlers, the babblers, the old cheats, and very insincere and servile men of this sort. Therefore 9 the man devoted to and, as it were, a professor of the true itself, in all his life and in whatever action or speech, will assume such a role as belongs to truth, since he, even in things that perhaps do not matter, would not deviate even a little out of the path, much less stray from the line of the true. Yes, and in greater things and affairs he will always hold his course and head straight for the goal, since he always detests and flees lying, trifles, and tricks as things utterly base and to the highest degree unworthy of an upright and good man. For the first concern of truthful men is for the right and honorable. And so he must shrink from both baseness, which is opposed to honor, and from insinuation and deviousness, which are foreign to rectitude. Since, however, all virtue is disinterested 10 and is sought for itself, and truthfulness itself is especially praise-worthy and most suited to preserving and increasing the society of men, of course truthful men are themselves devoted to the true solely on account of truth. They cherish it both for its own sake and because they understand that it is the firmest bond of human society and know that they were born to cherish it.

But since I am now speaking of that truth which is particularly 11 involved in speech and conversation and both in praising and commending oneself and others and in blaming and censuring the base, the duty of a truthful man is to say, when necessary, true and acknowledged things about himself with absolutely no dissimulation but freely and openly, and to say nothing more than what is his due and not to make up anything far-fetched or secretly remove anything—and yet everything with moderation. He will avoid insinuations and shifts with words, he will not turn aside from the straight line, and he will say nothing with simulation or dissimulation but everything openly and without injury. Moreover, his conversation will by no means be either affected or slippery,

rancescet ille quidem, neque spurcabitur prorsusque alienus erit a fuco, infractione, effoeminatione, mollitia, talis denique, qualem serenitatem esse nocturnam requirimus, in qua nihil turbidum, nihil ventosum, neque quod vel aestum afferat vel gelu, qualis profecto serenitas est verna, quae nullo modo cum offendat — quod suavissimum tamen est — rorem effundit ad omnem germinationem quam maxime utilem ac felicem. Qui igitur talis erit ut de se rebusque suis vera tantum et qualia sunt praedicet nimirum idem hic non erit a se ipso alienus ac diversus in explicandis ac referendis aliorum rebus, quas ita referet atque explicabit in circulis, in conciliis, in coenis conventibusque, ut minime in gratiam loqui videatur atque inservire auribus sed veritatis unius studio et causa.

12    Ac nescio etiam quomodo videtur hic ipse veridicus, de se dum dicit, si quippiam sibi rebusque suis subduxerit, dum ne dissimulandi gratia, de modestia vel merito laudandus; quin, modo tamen modeste, siquid laudandis ac referendis aliorum rebus ornatus addiderit, ut virtutis laudatori, ut recte factorum commendatori videtur assurgendum. In quo naturam imitatur ipsam, quae ornatus

13    quoque ac cultus nunquam videtur oblita. Namque ut in enarrandis suis, ubi fuerit parcior, dum ne id fiat cum dissimulatione, commendatur ut modestus, sic videndum est ne, si disserendis alienis fuerit constrictior, detur id invidentiae.

14    Optat Cicero, ut laudum expetentissimus, exornari res suas a Luceio, videlicet cupit illas amplificari adiungique iisdem ornatum ac nitorem. Quis accusaverit Ciceronem, si idem cupiat quod natura nobis ipsa exemplo est cupere ut debeamus? Tamen verecundius cum Luceio suo cumque rebus a se gestis egisset, si illum ita

nor indeed will it stink or be foul, and it will be completely free
from artificial embellishment, effeteness, effeminacy, or softness.
In short, it will be like the fair weather we seek at night, in which
there is nothing cloudy, nothing windy, and nothing that brings
either heat or cold; indeed, such as fair weather in spring, which,
although it does not harm in any way — which is still the pleasantest thing — pours forth dew as useful and fruitful as possible for
every bud. Therefore, someone who declares only true things, just
as they are, about himself and his affairs will not, of course, be
different from or contrary to himself in explaining and relating the
affairs of others. He will so explain and relate them in companies,
in councils, in dinners and meetings that he will not at all appear
to speak to ingratiate and to flatter the ears but only on account of
and in devotion to the truth.

Also, it somehow appears that this truthful man must even be 12
deservedly praised for moderation if he takes something away
from himself and his affairs when he speaks about himself, provided that he does not do so to dissimulate. In fact, if he adds ornaments while praising and relating the affairs of others, provided
that he does so with moderation, it seems that one must rise in
respect for him as a praiser of virtue, a commender of things well
done. In this he imitates nature itself, which seems never to forget
ornaments and adornments. For truly, as he is commended as 13
moderate when he is more sparing in detailing his own affairs,
provided that he does not do so with dissimulation, so he must
make sure not to be thought envious if he is too concise in discussing the affairs of others.

Cicero, a man very eager for praise, wants his deeds to be glori- 14
fied by Lucceius, that is, he wishes them to be amplified and to
have ornament and splendor added to them.[4] Who would blame
Cicero for wanting the same thing that nature shows us we ought
to want? Nevertheless, he would have behaved more modestly
with his friend Lucceius and with his own deeds if he had asked

rogasset, ut historici officio fungi vellet naturaeque ipsius exem-
15 plum sequi illique inhaerere. Sanctus fuit vir Hieronymus et per-
beatus ut Christianus et deo maxime carus, Rufinus tamen pati
illum minime potuit cum ut Ciceronianum male se habitum referret. Quis autem non vel magnam eloquentiae laudem Hieronymo
etiam indulgentissime concesserit? Tamen a Ciceroniano dicendi
genere, si ob hoc ipsum male fuit habitus, et a simplicitate illa
Attica Ciceronis amica tantum abest, ut oratio quidem Hieronymi
appareat conquisitior nimioque elaborata studio, id quod non
solum verba verum etiam ductus ipse orationis prae se ferat.

16 Quintus Fabius ille cunctator ex iis quae apud Livium ei re-
spondentur a Scipione fuit fortasse nimius iis edisserendis quae
adversus opinionem transferendi ex Italia in Africam belli facere
videbantur, itaque iudicatus a quibusdam ob invidentiam magisquam ob veritatem ipsam ea disseruisse — quod, ne iudicari de se
17 possit, verax omni studio vir cavebit. Alexander Augustus parce
admodum ac breviter de rebus a se contra Parthos gestis in senatu
retulit et, quamvis summam victoriae non dissimulanter expressis-
set, datum tamen est illi modestiae, quod diceret minime opus
esse referendis illis magniloquentia. Non pepercit veritati Alexan-
18 der hic, consuluit tamen modestiae imperatoriae. Caesar in terrore
illo formidabili adventantium Germanorum forsan infra verum,
minime tamen praeter tempus de hostium virtute locutus est, eam
deprimendo apud milites, pluraque de legione decima sibi persuadere ostendit quam re ipsa sibi persuadebat. Nequaquam itaque
aut se ipsum decepit aut milites, verum imperatoriae satisfecit
prudentiae. Quo fit ut veritas ipsa — quod pudicis etiam matronis
concessum est, quod etiam sacerdotibus in publica laetitia sa-
crisque solennibus — patiatur aliquando sibi cultum adiici, decen-
tem tamen, quamvis nequaquam perpetuum sed pro tempore.

him to fulfill the duty of a historian, to follow and stick to the
example of nature itself. Jerome was a saintly man, very holy since   15
he was a Christian and especially dear to God, yet Rufinus found
him unbearable when he told how he was mistreated as a Ciceronian.[5] But who would not be indulgent enough to concede even
great praise to Jerome for his eloquence? Nevertheless, he is so far
from Cicero's manner of speaking, if that is why he was mistreated, and from that Attic simplicity dear to Cicero, that in fact
Jerome's style appears too recherché and too studied, as not only
the words but also the structure of his periods reveals.

To judge from Scipio's reply to him in Livy, Quintus Fabius   16
Maximus, that famous delayer, was perhaps excessive in expound-
ing those things which appeared to argue against the idea of trans-
ferring the war from Italy to Africa. And so he was judged by
some to have discussed those things more because of envy than
because of the truth itself—a judgment against which a truthful
man will guard with every effort.[6] Alexander Augustus related in   17
the senate his deeds against the Parthians very succinctly and
briefly, and, although he did not express the main point of the
battle with dissimulation, nevertheless it was attributed to his
modesty that he said there was no need to relate those things
grandiloquently.[7] This Alexander did no injury to the truth but
respected the modesty of a general. In that formidable terror of   18
the advancing Germans, Caesar spoke perhaps less than the truth
but by no means inopportunely about the valor of the enemy, de-
preciating it to his soldiers. He put on a show of being more con-
vinced about the Tenth Legion than he actually was.[8] Thus he by
no means deceived himself or his soldiers but acted in accordance
with a general's prudence. So it happens that truth itself—this has
also been conceded to modest matrons and priests in public rejoic-
ing and solemn rites—sometimes allows some additional adornment, a fitting adornment nevertheless and by no means constant
but suited to the circumstances.

19     Omnino igitur veracis viri proprium est non simulate aut dissimulate de se ipso loqui, non obscure aut insinuanter minimeque
oblique, verum aperte, palam, directe, liberaliter, quod etiam est
maganimi, nihilque quod sibi non insit aut rebus suis adiungere
aut quod ex parte desit per simulationem affingere. Eritque oratio
eius ut ab omni iactatione vacua, sic nullo pacto nimia quaeve satietatem audienti afferat; careat supercilio, sit tamen severa et gravis atque ita tamen gravis, ut veritati ac gravitati suo loco sit
adiuncta comitas; sit dispositio et ordo ipse compositus accom-
modataque explicatio. Nanque, ut sit ea sive arcessita sive fucata,
nihil est quod tam veritatem ipsam inficiat; rerum denique ampli-
ficatio ita temperata, ut appareat cupere se extolli eam ab auditoribus magisquam ut ipse velit esse rerum suarum praedicator atque,
ut hodie usurpant, praeco. Praecipue vero erit in dicendo brevis et
candidus quique disposite atque ordinate prosequatur quae di-
cenda suscepit.

20     At in laudandis alienis, dum ne id fiat inserviendo auribus magisquam ut veritatem sequatur eamque ut approbet, et maior erit
atque huberior et oratio eius ornatior magisque magnifica et plena,
quo et virtus operae accipiat suae pretium et coeteri incitentur
exemplo. Summa tamen cura videndum erit ne, dum habenis utitur laxioribus, metam transiliat, quo vitio infecti sunt panagyrico-
rum maxime scriptores, qui pleraque arcessita partimque non vera
aut ficta afferunt, ut erubescendum etiam videatur sive lectoribus
illorum sive auditoribus.

21     Quando autem tenerrima quaedam res est veritas, eius ipsius
professor illum in cunctis quae ad eam explicandam spectaverint
modum retinebit, ut neque apud quosque neque quocunque aut

Therefore, it is altogether characteristic of a truthful man not to speak of himself with simulation or dissimulation, not obscurely or insinuatingly and by no means covertly, but openly, plainly, directly, liberally, which is also characteristic of a magnanimous man, and to add nothing which is not in him or his doings or to make up by simulation something partially lacking. And as his speech will be free from all boasting, so it will be in no way excessive or sate his listener. It will lack haughtiness but still be severe and grave and yet grave in such a way that affability is joined to truth and gravity in its proper place. The arrangement and sequence of his speech will be orderly and his exposition appropriate. For truly there is nothing that harms the truth so much as when speech is far-fetched or counterfeit. Finally, the amplification of deeds should be so measured that he appears to wish it to be increased by his listeners rather than wishing to be the publisher of his own deeds and, as people are accustomed to say these days, their herald. But he will be especially brief and clear in speaking and the sort of man who proceeds in a well-arranged and orderly manner with what he has undertaken to say.

But in praising others' deeds, provided it is not done to flatter the ears but rather to follow and establish the truth, he will be lengthier and more copious, and his speech more ornate, more magnificent and full, so that both virtue will receive the reward for its pains and others will be stimulated by example. Nevertheless, he must take the greatest care not to shoot past the goal while using the reins more slackly. Writers of panegyrics have been especially infected with this vice; they bring out many far-fetched things, some not true or fictional, so that it appears that even their readers or listeners ought to blush.

Since truth is a very delicate thing, however, in everything that pertains to setting it forth its professor will maintain such moderation that he will not think he is allowed to converse about it or to maintain the same method with everyone or in every place or time,

loco aut tempore aut in circulo neque quoque in conventu, concilio, coetu, neque iisdem ubique verbis aut vultu eodem putet sibi licere de ea habere sermonem aut eandem retinere rationem, cum aut locus aut tempus aut rerum status eiusmodi esse possit, ut tacere aut magis conducat aut contra obsit de se rebusque suis aut alienis loqui liberius oreque magis pleno, sitque non nunquam confugiendum ad exprobrationem collatorum beneficiorum, minime tamen exprobrandi gratia, sed quod necessitas ita ferat — quod imperatores servare solent, dum aut fugam sistere volunt militum aut minus eos obedientes seu parum promptos habent ad imperata facienda atque ad obeunda munia, aut dum decumare illos aut aliis suppliciis afficere aut ignominia volunt.

22     Quaeri potest hac in parte, an veraci huic sit permissum aut verum quandoque subticere aut aliquid quod nequaquam ita se habeat subsimulare atque effingere. Magna est vis temporis ac rerum,
23   non minor personae ipsius quam quis gerit. Fingunt nunc multa, nunc contra celant in adversis ac periculosis casibus sapientes, tum rerum publicarum temperatores, tum duces exercituum, multa peritissimi medici periculosissimis in morbis, non pauca sacerdotes quique praedicatores dicuntur, quo rebus adiungant auctoritatem; nec tamen illi ex eo aut mendaces habentur aut minus veridici, quando neque propositum eorum est aut mentiri aut fallere, verum et prodesse ea ratione et pericula avertere: quod omnino prudentium est hominum munus atque officium. Nesciam tamen quomodo perpetuitas illa veritatis retinendae maximum in mentibus atque in voluntatibus ipsis hominum locum obtinet in omni actione et causa.

24     Tribuit hoc nobis Innocentius Octavus Pontifex Maximus in componenda dissensione inter ipsum et Ferdinandum regem Neapolitanorum. Nam commonefacientibus quibusdam eum cardinalibus cavendum esse, ne a Ferdinando, quod esset, ut ipsi

in every company, assembly, gathering, or crowd, or everywhere with the same words and countenance, since the time, place, or state of affairs might be such that being silent is more profitable or, on the other hand, that talking too freely and heartily about oneself or one's own or others' affairs is harmful; and sometimes one must take refuge in reproaching men on account of the benefits conferred on them, yet not just for the sake of reproach but because necessity requires. Generals are accustomed to observe this method when they want to stop the flight of their soldiers or have ones less obedient or little prepared for carrying out orders and fulfilling their duties or when they want to decimate them or to inflict other punishments or ignominy.

At this point one may inquire whether it is permitted to this 22 truthful man either sometimes to pass over the truth in silence or to simulate and feign something which is by no means the case. The power of the moment and of circumstances is great, and that of the role one assumes is not less. In adverse and dangerous situ- 23 ations wise men, both governors of public affairs and leaders of armies, now feign many things, now on the contrary conceal them, as many times the most expert physicians do when dealing with dangerous diseases and not a few times priests and those who are called preachers do in order to add authority to their case. Nevertheless, on account of this they are not held to be liars or less truthful, since it is not their intent to lie nor to deceive but in this way to do good and to avert dangers, which is doubtless the task and duty of prudent men. Yet somehow that persistence in maintaining the truth obtains the greatest place in the minds and wills of men in every action and situation.

Pope Innocent VIII, in settling the discord between himself 24 and Ferdinando, king of Naples, attributed this to me.[9] For when some cardinals were admonishing him to take care, once matters had been settled, not to be deceived by Ferdinando, who in their

volebant, parum firma fide, compositis post rebus, frustra haberetur: 'At,' inquit, 'neutique falsos nos habuerit Iovianus Pontanus
quicum de corcordia agitur; neque enim eum veritas destituet ac
25   fides, qui ipse nunquam veritatem deseruerit aut fidem.' Sed a
nobis hac ipsa de re abunde admodum disputatum est iis in libris
quos de obedientia scripsimus. Quam ob rem, his de veracitate
veracibusque explicatis, hoc est de mediocritate ipsa, ad extrema
quaeque contraria ei sunt dicunturque vitia transeamus.

: 3 :

*De mendacibus.*[1]

1   Adversatur igitur mediocritati huic quam veracitatem appellare
placuit mendacitas, cuius et excessus existit quidam et defectus,
atque excessus quidem ipse suo nomine est ostentatio, quod iam
diximus. Sunt tamen qui iactantiam malint, alii qui arrogantiam.
2   Sed haec ipsa arrogantia magis versatur circa honorum nimiam
munerumque civilium affectationem quam in veri dictione atque
usu, quippe cum arrogantes, per vim praeterque quam suae ipsorum ita partes ferant, arrogent sibi supra merita ultraque natales
suos atque actiones ac vitae genus; neque enim captus sui rationem
habent. Itaque arrogantes ipsi quidem violenti sunt; qui vero sibi
plus in dicendo de se suisque de rebus tribuunt atque assumunt
quam quod re est vera atque ex merito assumendum, hi nequaquam violenti habendi aut impotentes, verum mendaces, vani, fu-
3   tiles, leves. Quocirca arrogantia accedit ad superbiam atque elationem, ostentatio ad vanitatem potius inanemque quandam rerum
suarum sive persuasionem sive ascriptionem, quando verbum ipsum *arrogo*, unde *arrogantia* deducitur, violentiae quidem est atque

opinion was not to be trusted, he said, "But Gioviano Pontano, with whom peace is being negotiated, will by no means deceive us. For truth and trustworthiness will never abandon him since he has never himself abandoned truth and trustworthiness." But I have 25 abundantly discussed this in the books that I wrote on obedience.[10] So, having explained these things about truthful men and truthfulness, that is, about the mean itself, let us pass on to those extremes opposed to it that are called vices.

## : 3 :

### *On liars.*

Therefore to the mean that I have decided to call truthfulness is 1 opposed mendacity, of which both an excess and a deficiency exist, and indeed this excess is named ostentation, as I have already said. Nevertheless, there are some who prefer *boasting* and others, *arrogance*. But arrogance itself is more concerned with excessive striv- 2 ing after civic honors and offices than with speaking and using the truth, since the arrogant, by force and beyond what their role allows, arrogate such things to themselves above their merits, birth, actions, and kind of life. For they do not take account of their own ability. And so these arrogant people are indeed violent. But the ones who apportion more to themselves while talking about themselves and their affairs and claim more than can be truly and deservedly claimed, are by no means to be considered violent or out of control but rather lying, insincere, futile, and light. Therefore, 3 arrogance resembles haughtiness and pride, but ostentation resembles insincerity and a kind of empty conviction about or allotment to one's own affairs. For the very word *arrogate*, from which *arrogance* is derived, is a word of violence and pride, but *to be*

elationis, *ostento* autem vanitatis atque inanis cuiusdam umbrae dictio, quasi videri sibi inesse velit quod nullo modo insit; et arrogans quidem hoc agit conaturque, ut re ipsa talis sit, qualis videri vult; ostentator vero, tantum ut videatur atque appareat.

: 4 :

*De iactatoribus et ostentatoribus.*

1 Nam qui iactantiam excessum hunc potius dici atque esse volunt in eo labuntur, quod, ostentatio cum plerunque vana sit, iactantia ipsa ad superbiam ubique est aut ad stoliditatem referenda; in levitate vero parum omnino differunt; et ostentatio quidem affingit sibi aut quae nulla prorsus e parte insunt aut maiora ea quam sint 2 facit. At iactator etiam in iis quae vera sunt referendis atque extollendis est nimius peccatque in eo vehementer, quod nec modum servat nec mensuram nimisque fastidit et gestu et verbis, et con- 3 tentione est immoderatior. Quo in toto fere genere Aiax peccat apud Ovidium, quando et quae dicit vera illa ipsa sunt atque adeo quidem magna, ut magnificari affingendo eis aliquid nullo modo necesse esset, et singula quidem erant notissima Graecorum ducibus ac senatui; tamen quod insolentius ea ab illo dicantur, quod nimis indignanter dictum videatur, 'Agimus, pro Iuppiter,' inquit / 'ante rates causam, et mecum confertur Ulixes,' quodque et ore et manibus et toto corpore, ut mos est indignantium, insolenter iactabatur, potest iactantiae iure ipso argui atque accusari, nequaquam tamen aut ostentationis aut fortasse arrogantiae. 4 Quo fit ut iactator ipse nimius sit aut immoderatus sive vera dicat

*ostentatious* is an expression of insincerity and a kind of empty shadow, as if it wishes something to appear in it that in no way is there. And indeed the arrogant person acts and strives to appear to be truly such as he wishes to appear, but the ostentatious one, only that he seem and appear.

: 4 :

*On the boastful and ostentatious.*

For those who hold that this excess should be called and actually  1
is boasting are mistaken in that while ostentation usually is insincere, boasting itself is always to be related to pride or stupidity. But in levity they hardly differ at all, and indeed ostentation either invents for itself things which belong to it in no way whatsoever or makes them greater than they are. But the boaster is excessive even  2
while relating and extolling things that are true and violently offends because he does not preserve either moderation or measure, is haughty in gesture and words, and is too immoderate in argument. In almost all of which Ovid's Ajax offends, since all the  3
things he says are true and in fact so great that it is by no means necessary to magnify them by adding anything, and indeed the particulars were very well known to the leaders and senate of the Greeks. Nevertheless, since these things are said too unrestrainedly by him, since it appears too indignantly spoken, "Oh Jupiter," he said, "we plead our cause before the ships, and Ulysses is compared with me,"[11] and since, as is the custom of the indignant, his face, hands, and whole body were shaking unrestrainedly, he can rightly be charged and accused of boasting, yet by no means of ostentation or perhaps arrogance. So it happens that the boaster himself  4

sive parum vera atque arcessita, cum ostentator nequaquam sit ipse iactatu nimius sed parum omnino dictis verus atque ex eo vanus magisquam aut superbus aut arrogator. Haec autem dicuntur a nobis non detrahendi recentioribus quibusdam scriptoribus verum docendi studio, cum praesertim de veritate ipsa sit quaestio.

: 5 :

*Plura esse mendacium genera.*

1 Mendaces igitur, cum eorum propositum sit mentiri, alii quidem honoris mentiuntur adipiscendi gratia, alii vero comparandae pecuniae. Sunt quibus mendacium ipsum pretium est ipsaque mentiendi voluptas perquam suavis est eorum fructus: quod genus maxime vanum iudicandum est. Videntur autem huiusmodi homines ab illo ipso ad quod geniti a natura sunt quam longissime discessisse, cum ad gravitatem geniti simus et ad constantiam ac firmitatem omnes nec, ut Cicero ait, quicquam sit turpius vanitate.

2 Iure igitur vani appellati sunt, cum eorum cogitationes ac voluntates prorsus inanes sint fluxaque consilia, vitium vero ipsum vanitas, quando propositum ipsum futile est, leve, inane, vacuum, quae omnia vanitatem et quidem summam indicant. Quam autem ridicula haec ipsa sit vanitas, ea fingens quae nusquam sint et mentiens quae fieri aut esse nequeant, Umber noster comicus docuit in milite illo ostentante victorias suas:

> Sexaginta hominum millia uno die
> evolaticorum manibus occidi meis;

et, quo sermo eius vanior appareret, subdit:

is excessive or immoderate whether he speaks true things or ones not true and farfetched, while the ostentatious man is by no means excessive in boasting but not at all true with his words and for this reason untruthful rather than proud or arrogant. But I do not say these things from any inclination to detract from some recent writers but to teach, especially since this inquiry is about the truth.

: 5 :

## There are several classes of liars.

Some liars, therefore, when they intend to lie, lie to acquire honor   1
but others to obtain money. For some the lie itself is the reward, and the very sweet pleasure of lying is itself what they enjoy; this class of liar must be judged to be especially untruthful. Moreover, men of this type appear to depart as far as possible from what they were naturally born for, since we have all been born for serious-ness, constancy, and firmness, and, as Cicero says, nothing is more shameful than untruthfulness.[12] Therefore they have rightly been   2
called untruthful, since their thoughts and intentions are com-pletely empty and their counsels inconstant, but the vice itself is called untruthfulness, since its intention is futile, light, empty, and vacuous, all of which indeed indicate the highest untruthfulness. Moreover, in that soldier boasting of his victories our Umbrian comic poet has taught how ridiculous this untruthfulness is, feign-ing things that never were and lying about ones that cannot be or come into being:

> With my own hands I killed sixty thousand fleeing men in one day;

and, to make his speech appear more untruthful, he adds:

Viscum legioni dedi
fundisque eos prosternebant ut folia farfari.
Quid multa? quos visco offenderant
tam crebri ad terram accidebant quasi pira.
Ut quisque ceciderat, eum necabam, indita
per cerebrum pinnula, sic quasi turturem.

Quid his evanidum magis?

3    Quam igitur vani per se ipsi sint mendaces huiusmodi, quam
4   ridiculi et contemptibiles, quis non videt? Atque hac quidem ratione poetas omnis ridiculos ac despicabiles forte quis dixerit. Non
esse autem despiciendos, verum admirandos potius, illud docet
quod Aristoteles et Homeri et aliorum poetarum auctoritate in
maximis quibusque rebus utitur et poetarum dicta pleraque habita
sunt pro oraculis, cum mendaces ipsi atque ostentatores nugentur
ac garriant magisquam fingant sitque fabula ipsa inventa non vanitatis gratia verum ut arte ea homines vel deterrerentur a vitiis, ut
cum Lycaonem in lupum fingunt ob crudelitatem maxime effera-
tam conversum, vel incitarentur ad virtutes, cum Castorem, Pollu-
cem, Herculem in coelum translatos decantitant. Aesopi fabula
exemplum vitae esse potest illis praesertim quos contigit obscu-
riore in loco aut nasci aut educari et vivere. At Homeri poema
virtutem esse sanctissimus vir Basilius iudicat. Nihil enim poeta
ille neglexit quod tum heroicas tum civiles ad virtutes pertineat.

5    Quid porro ad pietatem, religionem, tolerantiam, fortitudinem,
quid item ad declarandam rerum humanarum inconstantiam
fortunaeque varietatem, quod non Aeneae Virgiliani res declarent,
ut etiam illorum qui diem obiere quae praemia sint cuique pro
meritis constituta aut rursus poenae liceat apud illum plane nos-
cere? Et Horatius ait de Homero:

I gave birdlime to the legion, and they threw them down with their slings, like leaves of coltsfoot. What need of many words? The ones they hit with the birdlime fell to the ground as thick as pears. As each one fell, I would kill him by inserting a little feather through his brain, just like a turtledove.[13]

What could be more insubstantial than this?

Who does not see, therefore, how untruthful liars of this type 3 are, how ridiculous and contemptible? And indeed for this reason 4 someone might say that all poets are ridiculous and despicable. But the fact that Aristotle uses the authority of Homer and other poets in the most important subjects and that many sayings of the poets are considered oracles teaches us that they are not to be despised but rather to be admired, while liars and the ostentatious trifle and chatter more than invent. And the fable itself was devised not for its falseness but so that by its art men might be either deterred from vices, as when the poets feign that Lycaon was changed into a wolf on account of his savage cruelty, or incited to virtues, when they sing over and over that Castor, Pollux, and Hercules were translated to heaven. The fable of Aesop can provide a model for life, especially for those who happen to have been born or raised and live in an obscure position.[14] Moreover, the most saintly of men, Basil, judges that Homer's poem is virtue.[15] For that famous poet neglects nothing that pertains both to heroic and civil virtues.

Furthermore, what is there pertaining to piety, religion, toler- 5 ance, courage, and likewise the inconstancy of human affairs and the variety of fortune, that the deeds of Vergil's Aeneas does not reveal? One may even come clearly to learn in his work what rewards or punishments are appointed to each of those who have died according to his deserts. And Horace says of Homer:

Qui, quid sit pulcrum, quid turpe, quid utile, quid non,
plenius ac melius Chrysippo et Crantore dicit.

6  Itaque mendaces hi quidem inanes sunt ac vani, quando eorum finis ac propositum est vanitas et quidem moralis eaque apertissima
vanitas. At poetae habiti sunt admirabiles divinique. Delectando
enim et per blanditias in animos hominum influendo, conati sunt
eos ad generosissima quaeque ab maxime foedis ferisque atque a
belluarum oppido quam similibus moribus retrahere abducereque
7  a silvis. Quocirca ob hoc ipsum studium putatus est Orpheus sil-
vas cantu traxisse post se animaliaque illas incolentia, et Amphion
rupes ac saxa. Quid igitur inter fictiones intersit publicae utilitatis
atque humani generis instituendi gratia susceptas et eas quae solam ob vanitatem, non modo vetustissimi poetae docent, verum
etiam praedicatores huius nostri temporis, quibus familiare quidem est prudentissime excogitata quaedam et ficta in exemplum
adducere. Verum de hac ipsa mendacitate satis. Quantum enim
veritas ipsa laudatur estque in pretio, tanto est magis ridicula
ostentandi vanitas fallaxque ementiendi studium.

: 6 :

## Quid Aristoteles hac de re sentiat.

1  Totum autem hoc genus, de quo suscepta nobis disputatio est,
Aristoteles tradit in sermonibus versari atque in actionibus, ad
haec, quod ostentatores simulanter affingant sibi quae ipsis nequaquam insint aut maiora quam re ipsa illa sint, etiam in fictionibus
2  arcessitisque fucationibus. Hos ipsos autem homines ostentatores

Who says, more clearly and fully than Chrysippus and Cran-
tor, what is honorable, what shameful, what useful, what is
not.[16]

And so these liars are indeed empty and untruthful, since their    6
aim and goal is untruthfulness, indeed a moral and most evident
untruthfulness. But the poets have been considered admirable and
divine. For by delighting and influencing the minds of men with
allurements they have tried to lead them toward the noblest things
and away from the foulest and wildest behavior, entirely similar to
that of the beasts, and draw them out of the forests. So on ac-    7
count of this endeavor, Orpheus was thought to have drawn after
him with his song the forests and the animals inhabiting them,
and Amphion the rocks and stones.[17] Thus not only do the oldest
poets teach the difference between fictions undertaken for public
utility and instructing the human race, and those undertaken only
out of insincerity, but also the preachers of our time, with whom
it is indeed customary to adduce things very prudently devised and
feigned as examples. But enough of this kind of mendacity. For
the more truth itself is praised and valued, the more ridiculous the
vanity of boasting and the deceitful pursuit of fabrication.

: 6 :

*What Aristotle thinks about this subject.*[18]

Moreover, Aristotle teaches that this whole class that I have begun    1
to discuss is involved in speeches and actions, and what is more,
that the ostentatious feign and devise for themselves things that
are by no means in them or are greater than they actually are, even
in fictions and farfetched counterfeits. He says that these men are    2

esse ait proprioque nomine 'alazonas,'[2] qui apud Plautum sunt gloriosi; at quos 'irones' vocat, eos aut inficiari aut dissimulare quae ipsis insint, aut ex iis sibi multum detrahere eaque quae vera sunt dissimulando minuere; horum medium 'alitheuticon,' hoc est, et vita et sermone veracem esse, quaeque et quanto sibi insint profiteri illisque nihil aut fando demere aut adiicere rebus suis; atque haec quidem ipsa consuesse fieri aut nullius aut alicuius rei gratia. Esse autem unumquemque perinde ac sunt eius dicta factaque ac vita omnis, praeterquam si rei cuiuspiam dimoveatur gratia. Mendacium vero ipsum per se et turpe esse et opprobriosum, secus autem verum ipsum et honestum et laudabile.

3    Itaque veracem hominem, quod medium teneat, quasi aequipensatorem quendam merito laudari; contra mendaces utrosque, et qui ostentatores sint et qui ironici, vituperabiles, ostentatores tamen amplius. Esse igitur veracem qui et vita et sermone, hoc est factis dictisque, veritatem tueatur et colat talisque habitu existat ac consuetudine; exque eo probum illum virum esse utpote veritatis oppido quam studiosum etiam in minimis quibusque, atque hoc etiam magis in maximis iisdemque seriis rebus, quippe qui abhorreat a mendacio ducatque illud quidem per se ipsum fugiendum; quod etsi commendatione dignum est ac laude, tamen, quae veracis hominis modestia est, suapte eum natura propensiorem putat ad subducendum de veritate quippiam, cum superlationem omnem atque immoderantiam invidiosam existimet atque odio dignam. Ac de verace quidem haec ab illo traduntur.

4    E mendacibus vero qui, nullius rei gratia sed ob ipsam tantum mendacii voluptatem, maiora quam quae sunt sibi per simulationem rebusque affingat suis, pravum illum quidem suapte natura esse atque a probitate alienum, quae veracium hominum comes sit;

the ostentatious, their proper name *alazones*, who are called vain-glorious in Plautus.[19] But Aristotle calls *eirones* those who deny or dissimulate what is in them, or take away much of it from themselves and diminish by dissimulation those things that are true. The mean between these he calls the *aletheutikos*, that is, the person who is truthful both in life and in speech, who admits what is in him and to what extent and does not by speaking take away from or add to his doings; and this habitually happens, for a particular reason or for none. Moreover, he says that each person is just like his sayings, doings, and his whole life except when he is diverted for a particular reason. On the other hand, a lie by itself is base and shameful, while the truth itself is both honorable and praiseworthy.

And so the truthful man, because he keeps to the mean, is de- 3 servedly praised, as it were, as someone who weighs what is just; on the contrary, both classes of liars, the ostentatious and the self-deprecators, are blameworthy, but the ostentatious to a greater extent. Therefore a man is truthful who preserves and cares for the truth both in his life and in his speech, that is, in his deeds and words, and is such a person by character and custom. For this reason this man is upright, since he is completely devoted to truth even in the smallest things and even more in the greatest and most serious, for he shrinks from a lie and considers that it must be shunned in itself. Even though this deserves commendation and praise, nevertheless, such being the modesty of the truthful man, Aristotle thinks him more inclined by nature to subtract something from the truth, since he believes that all exaggeration and lack of moderation are odious and worthy of hatred. And this is what he has to say about the truthful man.

But the liar who, for no particular reason but only for the plea- 4 sure of lying itself, devises by simulation for himself and his affairs things that are greater than they are is indeed depraved by nature and a stranger to uprightness, which is the companion of truthful

ni enim ita esset, mendacio nequaquam gauderet; coeterum vanum potius videri quam malum. At qui, honoris gloriae ve ac famae gratia, ostentandis rebus suis iisque falso ac simulanter arcessendis, veri fines egrediatur adiiciatque supra quam res ipsae se se habeant, illum non ita quidem vituperatione dignum; at qui pe-
5 cunia captus ementiatur, hunc procul dubio turpiorem. Mendaces enim omnes ab electione existere atque ab habitu: et qui ostentatores ut vani mendacio laetentur, et qui honore et gloria capiantur velintque inter alios videri excellere, quique item pecuniis inhient
6 reique domesticae compendiis utque sibi prosint ac suis. Consuesse autem ea sibi affingere quae latere quidem posse eaque haud palam fieri arbitrentur, ut qui, cum e medicina aut divinatione aliquid modo attigerint, et medendi tamen et divinandi maximam se peritiam assecutos gloriantur profitenturque ea se tenere quae sint earum artium abditissima deque se ipsis magna cum ostentatione ac iactantia praedicant.

: 7 :

### De ironicis.

1 De ironicis vero ac dissimulatoribus haec sentit. Esse ex iis qui minora de se rebusque suis dicant aut ea prorsus inficientur ac dissimulent, in quibus iidem ipsi praestent sintque ea praeclara admodum ac magis magisque nobilitata, nullo modo tamen emolumenti causa aut pecuniae, verum ut insolentiam devitent ac tumo-
2 rem, cuiusmodi fuisse Socratem refert. Esse item alios qui parva ac

men. For if this were not the case, he would by no means take pleasure in lying. In addition, this man appears to Aristotle vain rather than evil. On the other hand, the liar who for honor, glory, or fame passes the bounds of truth and the actual state of affairs by vaunting his deeds and increasing them with falsehood and simulation is not so deserving of blame, but the one who lies because he is captive to money is without any doubt baser. For all 5 liars come into existence by choice and character: the ones who in vain ostentation delight in lying; those who are captured by honor and glory and wish to appear to stand out from others; and those likewise who long for money and to profit from their domestic affairs so that they can be useful to themselves and their families. Moreover, they habitually invent things about themselves which 6 they think can remain hidden and not become public — for example, men who have only a slight knowledge of medicine or divination yet boast that they have acquired the greatest skill in healing and divining and profess that they possess the most hidden secrets of those arts and extol themselves for these things with great ostentation and boasting.

∶ 7 ∶

*On self-deprecators.*

But he thinks the following about the self-deprecators and dis- 1 simulators.[20] Some of them say less about themselves and their affairs, or completely deny and conceal them, things in which they themselves excel and which are very notable and more and more renowned, yet in no way for profit or money but to avoid arrogance and pride. He says that Socrates was this kind of man. Likewise there are others who conceal some small, trivial, yet 2

minuta quaedam, ea tamen plane cognita, dissimulantes, dum minimis quibusdam e rebus, sive elevandis sive dissimulandis, laudem aucupantur; ex eo contemptibiles fieri esseque despiciendos. Quin etiam hanc ipsam interdum ironiam ostentationem prorsus esse quandam iudicat, qualem fuisse Lacedaemoniorum vestitum dicit; etenim ut excedentem arrogationem, sic attenuationem nimiam ad ostentationem esse referendam.

3    Itaque modeste qui utantur ironia in iis ipsis quae manifesta sint atque in promptu urbanos eos videri gratiamque quandam inter cives promereri indeque iucundos esse atque admodum gra-

4    tos. Quod autem ostentatio ipsa turpior per se sit ac viro probo indignior, inde ostentatores; quique ea simulant quae nullo modo insint, idque contendunt, ut inesse credi ea velint, atque ultra verum seque resque verbis magnificant atque extollunt suas quam qui ironici sunt suaque dissimulanter inficiantur aut ea deducunt veracibus utique magis adversari. Atque haec quidem in hanc traduntur sententiam a peripateticae sectae constitutore.

5    Nos vero, institutum nostrum secuti, in his iisdem diffusius versabimur magisque aliquanto explorate. Et aliud esse simulare dicimus, aliud dissimulare. Simulamus enim quae nullo modo vera sunt, quaeque ipsi nec fecerimus nec dixerimus, quaeque nec servare in animo habeamus; contra dissimulamus quae ipsa quidem dicta aut facta sint perinde ac nec dicta fuerint nec facta aut non quemadmodum quoque animo consilio ve aut fecerimus aut dix-

6    erimus. Qua ratione Sallustius Catilinam cuiusque rei simulatorem esse dixit ac dissimulatorem, cum tamen et simulare et dissimulare non nunquam prudenti vero sit permissum, ut qui 'Spem vultu simulat, premit altum corde dolorem.' Singula enim ad finem sunt ipsum referenda. Sed hac nos in parte de simulatione ac dissimulatione illa loquimur quae mendacium respectat utque ementiendo fallat recedatque a veritate profitenda.

well-known things if only they might hunt for praise by elevating or disguising certain insignificant things; hence they become contemptible and are to be despised. And he even judges that sometimes this self-deprecation is totally a form of ostentation, as he says the dress of the Spartans was, for excessive plainness, just as exceeding arrogance, must be ascribed to ostentation.[21]

And so those who use self-deprecation modestly in matters 3 which are manifest and public appear urbane, deserve some esteem among the citizens, and as a result are pleasant and very agreeable. However, ostentation is baser in itself and more unworthy of an 4 upright man; hence the ostentatious are baser and more unworthy. Those who simulate things which in no way are in them and strive to have these things believed to be in them, and with words magnify and extol beyond the truth themselves and their affairs are certainly more opposed to the truthful than those who are self-deprecators and disguise their affairs or downplay them. And indeed these things are taught in this sense by the founder of the Peripatetic school.

But I, following my plan, will engage these matters more expan- 5 sively and a bit more searchingly. And I say that simulating is one thing, dissimulating another. For we simulate things that are in no way true, that we ourselves have neither done nor said, and that we have no intention of maintaining. On the contrary, we dissimulate things that have in fact been said or done, just as if they were not said or done, or not in the way we intended or planned to have done or said them. This is why Sallust said that Catiline would 6 simulate and dissimulate anything, although both simulating and dissimulating are sometimes permitted to a prudent man, as one who "simulates hope with his expression but presses sorrow deep in his heart."[22] For individual cases must be referred to the end itself. But in this part I am speaking about the simulation and dissimulation that concern lying, both to deceive by lying and to depart from openly professing the truth.

7    Itaque simulatores ostentatorum necessarii sunt atque affines, dissimulatores ironicorum. Simulant nanque ostentatores. Dissimulant ironici. Alteri affingunt, ementiuntur, arcessunt quae non sunt simulantes; alteri subtrahunt, minuunt, inficiantur verum ipsum dissimulantes. Utcumque tamen se res habeat, diversum est utrisque consilium. Illi enim quod quaerunt ea id ratione assequi volunt, ut fingant et vultum et verba et consilia et res ipsas, non nunquam tristitiam, dolorem, lacrimas, aut contra hilaritatem, laetitiam, voluptatem; hi quae vera sunt, ut aut omnino inficientur aut plurimum illis demant.[3]

: 8 :

*De quatuor generibus ostentatorum.*

1    Triplex est igitur ostentatorum, ut dictum est, genus qui in simulationibus versantur: alii enim sunt quibus mendacium sit ipsum mentiendi auctoramentum, quo in vitio plane regnat vanitas; alii quibus ea e re proposita sit honoris famae ve consecutio, ostentant enim seque et sua quo honores, magistratus, dignitates, sacerdotia assequantur, quod studium non vacat ambitione. Sunt qui ampliandae rei familiari hac ratione dent operam, quod vitium ab avaritia ducit ortum.

2    Sed nec verebimur quartum quoddam iis genus adiicere hominum illorum qui, cum dissentionibus gaudeant ac discordiis, partim affingendo veris falsa partim subtrahendo, ac nunc demendo nunc accumulando, aut dicta factaque ipsa interpretando perperam, id agunt ut cives inter se committant serantque odia atque inimicitias: qui morbus ad naturae pravitatem morumque perversitatem est omnino referendus. Quae enim civili in congregatione

Therefore simulators are relations and relatives of the ostenta- 7
tious, dissimulators of the self-deprecators. For the ostentatious
simulate. Self-deprecators dissimulate. The first by simulation invent, lie, and speculate improbably about things that are not; the
second by dissimulation subtract from, diminish, and deny the
truth itself. However the matter stands, the intention of each is
different. For the first wish to obtain what they seek in this way:
they falsify their expression, words, plans, and the things themselves, sometimes feigning sadness, sorrow, tears, or on the contrary cheerfulness, joy, pleasure. The second either completely
deny true things or take much away from them.


: 8 :

*On the four classes of ostentatious men.*


Therefore, as has been said, there are three classes of ostentatious 1
men who engage in simulations. For there are some for whom the
lie itself is the reward for lying; vanity clearly rules in this vice.
Others have intended to acquire honor or fame in this way, for
they show off themselves and their affairs to obtain high offices,
magistracies, civic and ecclesiastical positions; this pursuit does
not lack ambition. Others by this means strive to increase the
wealth of their family; this vice arises from avarice.

But I am not afraid to add a fourth class to these: those men 2
who, since they delight in dissensions and discords, in part by
adding false things to true, in part by subtracting them, and now
taking away, now accumulating, or wrongly interpreting the sayings and doings themselves, cause citizens to commit crimes
against one another and sow hatred and hostility. This disease
must entirely be ascribed to depravity of nature and perversity of
character. For what greater plague can occur in a civil community

hominumque societate maior accidere pestis potest, quando, ad eam colendam cum instituti a natura simus, contra ad evertendam arte hac fingendique ac fallendi studiis innitimur? Hos commissores Latino et suo verbo vocare possumus vitiumque ipsum com-

3 missionem. Quin horum quidem e numero aliis propositum est hac via atque his artibus magnos se se ac potentes aliorum e contentionibus ac dissidiis facere, dum et miscent et interturbant omnia. Quod malum Romae latius se se diffudit Pompeii maxime ac Caesaris, item Antonii atque Octavii tempestatibus. Aliis vero nullum omnino propositum est ampliandae dignitatis locique in civitate maioris assequendi: tantum id curant, student, meditantur, contentiones ut exuscitent ac dissidia, perversitate quadam naturae ducti, quippe qui seditionibus tantum laetentur civiumque inquiete ac turbulentia.

: 9 :

*De susurronibus.*

1 His accedant, si placet, et susurrones, quibus etsi eadem haec voluptas est, nihilo tamen minus auribus quoque et ipsi inserviunt, quo aliquod inde emolumentum et coenas saltem et vultus bonos, ut dici solet, reportent—servile sane genus hoc hominum, nec depravatis modo verum etiam sordentissimis moribus. Utque prioribus illis magna praeclaraque observantur ante oculos, ita poste-

2 rioribus his minuta quaedam ac sordida. Nec vero inficias ibimus et virtutes et vitia ita quidem misceri inter se atque confundi, ut quaedam nunc ad hoc nunc ad illud vitium, quaedam tum ad hanc tum ad illam referri virtutem possint. Nam et insimulatores et falsi accusatores, de quibus nihil est dictum, mendaces quidem ipsi sunt: mentiuntur enim. Iidem tamen ipsi alia quidem ratione

and society of men, when, although trained by nature to preserve it, we on the contrary strive to overthrow it by this art of feigning and the pursuit of deception? We can call these men, with their own Latin word, subversives and the vice itself, subversion.[23] And in fact some of this number have intended in this way and by these arts to make themselves great rulers from the contentions and disagreements of others while they embroil and disturb everything. This evil was very widespread in Rome, especially in the times of Pompey and Caesar and also of Antony and Octavius. But others have no intention whatsoever of increasing their dignity and obtaining a greater position in the state. They only care, strive, and purpose to stir up contentions and disagreements; led by some perversity of nature, since they delight only in seditions and the agitation and disturbance of the citizens.

## : 9 :

### On murmurers.

To these may also be added, if you will, the murmurers. Although they take the same pleasure, yet nonetheless they also flatter the ears to obtain some profit, at least dinners and favorable looks, as is customarily said — truly a servile kind of men, and of a character not only depraved but also very sordid. And as the former keep great and glorious things in view, so the latter, trivial and sordid ones.[24] But I will not deny that virtues and vices are indeed so mixed and confused with each other that some things can be ascribed now to this, now to that vice, and others to this and that virtue. For both allegers and false accusers, about whom nothing has been said, are indeed themselves liars: for they do lie. Yet these men must be considered to be unjust for one reason but envious

iniusti habendi sunt, alia vero invidentes atque avari, dum et no-
cere aliis student, etiam quibus minime debeant, et illorum quieti
ac divitiis invident indeque conantur ipsi locupletiores fieri.

3    Nero ac Domitianus, Augusti, simulationes suas fictosque vultus ac verba composita ad crudelitatem plerunque convertere. Ferdinandus,[4] Neapolitanorum rex, magnus et ipse fuit artifex et
vultus componendi et orationis in quem ipse usum vellet. Nam
aetatis nostrae Pontifices Maximi fingendis vultibus ac verbis vel
histriones ipsos anteveniunt. Ptolemaeus ille qui postea in Nilo
periit a Caesare ita discessit, ut etiam lacrimaretur ostentans se
desiderium absentis eius vix esse passurum; qui tamen, ubi ad
exercitum atque ad suos transiit, bellum e vestigio multo acerri-
mum excitavit. Itaque non temere nostris a maioribus Alexandrini
habiti sunt aptissimi atque in primis solertes ad simulandum atque
fallendum.[5]

: 10 :

*De fucatis et illecebrosis lenocinatoribus.*

1    Et quoniam hanc, ut diximus, partem diffusius prosequimur, ex
hoc etiam sunt ordine qui fucata oratione utuntur, quos tamen
videas non tam mentiri velle quam veritatem ipsam artificio quodam verborum aut obtegere aut illi ipsi loquendi artificio ornatum
quasi quendam adiungere, sive ut vitium aliquod contegant sive ut
2    fucum illinant veritati. Fucatae nanque orationis non una est ratio,
et alii aliam ob causam fuco ipso utuntur orationis. Sunt enim ex
iis qui lenocinentur ut illiciant, quod est lenonum, inducantque
quos captant ad ea quae ipsi cupiant verborum lenociniis, hoc est
3    oratione ficta et illecebrosa admodum. Itaque eiusmodi homines

and avaricious for another. They endeavor to harm others, even those whom they should not, and envy their quiet and riches and so try to become richer themselves.

The emperors Nero and Domitian very often turned their sim- 3 ulations, contrived expressions, and feigned words to cruelty. Ferdinando, king of Naples, was also a great artist, a master at composing his expression and speech for whatever use he wished. Certainly, the popes of our day surpass even actors in contriving their expressions and words. That Ptolemy who afterward died in the Nile took leave of Caesar in such a way that he even wept, ostentatiously showing that he would hardly be able to endure the grief of his absence. Yet when he went over to his army and men, he immediately incited the bitterest war.[25] And so not without reason did our ancestors consider the Alexandrians the most able and among the most skillful in simulating and deceiving.[26]

<br>

### : 10 :

### On artificers and seductive enticers.[27]

And since, as I have said, I am pursuing this part more expan- 1 sively, in this class there are also those who use counterfeit speech. Yet you may see that they do not wish to lie as much as to cover up the truth with a certain artifice of words or to add to this artifice of speech a sort of ornament, either to conceal some vice or to smear some dye over the truth. Indeed there is not just one reason 2 for counterfeit speech, and different people use it for different reasons. For some entice in order to seduce, which is what pimps do, and with the enticements of their words, that is with fictitious and very seductive speech, they lead those whom they entrap to what they themselves desire. And so we call men of this sort seductive 3

illecebrosos dicimus magisquam fucatos, quamvis illecebrositas
non careat fuco. Quando omnem verborum compositionem, quae
ex eo adhibetur, quo aut verum occulat aut fictum quippiam vero
adiiciat aut tanquam comat quod dicitur ac res et verba lenit, fu-
4   cum dicimus. Nam et fuco puellae utuntur, quo aut formosae magis appareant aut ut quod inest deformitatis aut omnino tegant aut
ex parte minuant. Itaque ut sermo horum illecebrosus, sic fucatus
illorum. Quae vitia a simulatione proficiscuntur omnia atque a
dissimulatione.

: II :

## De proditoribus.

Perniciosissimum autem simulatorum genus itemque dissimulatorum sunt proditores, quippe qui simul et simulant et dissimulant,
tametsi neque simulatores habendi sunt aut dissimulatores magis
quam supremum in modum infidi, iniusti, impii, immanes, trucu-
lenti: societatum, amicitiarum, rerum publicarum, populorm, re-
gnorum omnisque probitatis, iuris item divini atque humani ever-
sores profligatoresque virtutum omnium: per quos nequaquam
stat, quo minus humana consortio funditus tollatur atque intereat.

: 12 :

## De fallacibus.

1   Hi tamen simul omnes fallacium comprehenduntur numero,
quippe cum mendaces sint omnes. Nemo autem mendax quin
idem sit fallax, ac si non qui ob vanitatem mentiuntur, et hi se se

rather than artificers, although seductiveness is not without artifice. Since we call artifice every arrangement of words that is employed either to hide the truth or to add something fictive to it or to adorn, so to speak, what is said and soften the things and the words. For girls use cosmetics either to appear more beautiful or 4 to conceal completely or partially diminish whatever deformity is in them. And so just as the conversation of the latter is enticing, that of the former is counterfeit. All these vices proceed from simulation and dissimulation.

: 11 :

## On traitors.

But traitors are the most pernicious kind of simulators and dissimulators, seeing that they both simulate and dissimulate, although they are to be considered neither simulators nor dissimulators but rather to the highest degree treacherous, unjust, impious, monstrous, savage. They overthrow societies, friendships, states, peoples, kingdoms, all honesty, divine and also human law; they destroy all the virtues. It is no thanks to them that human society is not utterly uprooted and destroyed.

: 12 :

## On the deceitful.

Yet all these are at the same time included in the number of the 1 deceitful, seeing that they are all liars. Moreover, no one is a liar without also being deceitful, as if those who lie on account of van-

2 ipsos praecipue fallant. Cum primis autem hoc ipso ex ordine accusandi sunt illi quidem qui, cum maxime, ut Cicero ait, fallunt, id tamen agunt, ut viri boni esse videantur. De quibus merito dicitur quod est apud Plautum: 'Lupus et homo homini, non homo.'

3 Horum non modo ficti vultus verbaque verum etiam vestitus, incessus, capitis ac cervicis tum demissio tum inflexio, oculorum deiectio in humum atque infixio, summum silentium, rarissima in publicum proditio. Iidem quaeritant solitudines, versantur in locis potissimum sacris, quin etiam oris colorem arte deformant. Nullum est autem vitae aut genus aut ordo in quo vel non paucos eiusmodi invenias. E sacerdotibus tamen illisque quos hodie religiosos dicimus plurimi hoc vitio infecti sunt; quo morbo affectos etiam philosophos insectatur Iuvenalis.

: 13 :

## De hypocritis.

1 Quibus quidem omnibus Christiani, Graecos secuti scriptores, fecere nomen hypocritis. Eorum autem omnium idem est propositum, ut quod ipsi minime sint id habeantur atque appareant. E quibus alii in id intendunt, ut lucrentur victumque inde sibi huberiorem parent maioremque reverentiam, utque habeantur in honore vendicentque sibi apud populum sanctitatis opinionem, existimenturque deorum frui colloquiis ac praesentia. De quibus tamen parcius loquar ne, dum vitium ac simulationem insector, velle videar religioni detrahere. Itaque huic parti finem facio, si rem tamen maxime ridiculam prius retulero.

ity do not also deceive themselves especially. But in this class those   2
are chiefly to be blamed who, as Cicero says, when they are being
most deceitful, yet act so as to appear to be good men.[28] The line
in Plautus is deservedly said about them: "Man is a wolf and not a
man to man."[29] Not only are their faces and words false but also   3
their clothing, gait, the lowering and bending of their heads and
necks, the casting down and fixing of their eyes on the ground,
their absolute silence, and their very infrequent appearance in public. They seek out lonely places and especially resort to sacred
ones; they even artfully fashion the color of their faces. Moreover,
there is no kind or class of life in which you will not find not a few
of this sort. But most of the priests and those whom today we call
the religious have been infected with this vice. Juvenal attacks even
philosophers affected by this disease.[30]

: 13 :

*On hypocrites.*

Christians, following the Greek writers, have given the name *hypo-*   1
*crite* to all these people. All of them have the same intention: to be
considered and appear to be what in no way they are. Some of
them strive to make a profit and thereby obtain a richer way of life
and greater reverence, to be held in honor and to claim for themselves with the people a reputation for sanctity, and to be thought
to enjoy the conversation and presence of the gods.[31] Nevertheless,
I will speak more sparingly of them lest I appear to wish to detract
from religion while attacking vice and simulation. And so I make
an end of this part, although first I will relate an especially ridiculous story.

2    Adolescentibus nobis, puer haud malae indolis a patre missus
est literarium in ludum. Is, quo patri appareret literis deditior
sensimque patrem diverteret ab incoepto, dum veretur ne vehe-
mentiorem ob operam in aegritudinem filius ipse incideret, e fabae
polline tenuissimum in modum contritae coepit mane sibi vultum
afflatim inspergere, magna arte adhibita. Quod dum aliquot a filio
continuatur diebus, animadvertit pater os eius subflavescere atque,
illi metuens, an bene se, an satis valide haberet, sciscitatur; re-
spondet ille et bene et valide; ac tum vehementius multo quam
ante literis incumbit, multum noctu vigilat, matutinus e lecto sur-
git, totumque se se ad libros convertit ac nihilominus singulis diebus plusculum e polline in faciem insufflat atque non ita multo
post languere se simulat. Quo cognito, pater vetuit illum ex eo ad
grammaticum proficisci: malle enim filium sibi illiteratum vivere
quam, ob causam literarum, in tenera eum aetate amittere. Quod
puer igitur simulando effecit, an non efficiet et religiosus et senex,
praesertim sub speciem bonitatis ac sanctimoniae?

3    Videas quosdam, cum nulla non parte corporis contaminati
sint, prae se ferre summam continentiam; alios qui, cum sint lan-
gori ac desidiae dediti, fortitudinem et quandam quasi vivendi
rusticitatem simulent; hos mirificam integritatem, cum sint cor-
ruptissimi; illos eximium in deum cultum, cum ab omni clam ab-
horreant pietate; nonnullos lacrimari, cum in miserabilem aliquem
inciderint ac miserari eum hacque arte occulere animi saevitiam
nefariasque cogitationes; haud paucos, quorum avaritiam atque
occultas foenerationes abscondat simulata liberalitas erogataeque

4    inter mendicantes atque in triviis stipes. Plurimorum perversa
consilia artisque dolosissimas obvelat templorum quotidiana frequentatio, aut obtegit nequissimas insusurrationes vivendi humili-
tas quaedam, aut multum in circulis silentium, aut coram ficta

When I was a young man, a boy of no mean ability was sent by 2
his father to an elementary school. To appear to his father more
dedicated to his letters and gradually to divert him from his project by making him fear that his son might fall ill from working too
hard, the boy began very artfully powdering his face in the morning with fine-ground bean flour. When his son had continued this
for several days, the father noticed that his face was becoming a bit
yellow and, fearing for him, inquired whether he was well and
quite healthy. He replied that he was well and quite healthy, and
then much more eagerly than before he fell to his letters, stayed up
very late at night, rose from bed early in the morning, completely
applied himself to his books, and nonetheless every day blew a bit
more pollen onto his face and not much later pretended to lan-
guish. When his father learned this, he forbade him on this account to go to the grammarian, for he preferred his son to live
uneducated than to lose him at a tender age on account of his
letters. So will an old man in a religious order not accomplish
what the boy accomplished by simulation, especially under an appearance of goodness and holiness?

You might see some who, although every part of their body is 3
contaminated, display the greatest continence; others who, although given over to languor and idleness, simulate strength and,
as it were, a rustic way of life; some a marvelous integrity although
they are most corrupt; others an extraordinary worship of God
although secretly averse from all piety; some weep when they happen upon a miserable person and show pity for him, and by this
art hide the cruelty of their minds and their wicked thoughts; not
a few, whose simulated liberality and alms distributed among beggars and in the crossroads hide their avarice and concealed usury.
Daily attendance at church veils the perverse plans and utterly 4
deceitful arts of many, or a humble way of life, much silence in
company, or a pretense of speaking well in public about individuals

quaedam de singulis benedicentia. Itaque rarissimi illi quidem sunt
ad quos non penetret simulatio.

5   Quodque flagitiosissimum est, ad permulta verisimilius simu-
landa nunc religionis adhibent vincula nunc affinitatis amicitiae ve.
Quae si persequar, an erit aliud quam velle iras hominum in me ac
malevolentiam provocare? Itaque satis nobis esse potest haec atti-
gisse, quae et inquirenda diligentius et accusanda liberius sacerdotibus relinquimus, qui ea ab confitentibus quotidie intelligunt, ac
praedicatoribus, quorum est officium coram atque in templis de iis
liberius disserere maioreque cum licentia.

6   Nec tamen hoc in loco fabella nobis deerit eaque divulgatis-
sima: fuisse in parte Italiae Iannem quendam, proavorum nostro-
rum temporibus, qui inter pastores assiduus agrestisque alios
diversaretur; eum autem consuesse die, cum aut aries feroculus
offerretur aut vitulus, vitabundum fugitare eum contremiscereque
ad illius aspectum; atque hac ratione ridiculum se se inter pastores
facere; noctu vero profundissimos saltus ingredi ausum atque ex
armentis vegetum quemque, sive bovem sive taurum, apprehen-
sum cornibus resteque illigatum secum trahere tractumque sociis
tradere deducendum ad fora mercatusque, ubi eum venalem facerent. Iure igitur ⟨ ⟩[6] meus mihique pernecessarius Marinus Tomacellus, vir ⟨ ⟩,[7] usurpare consuevit: nec Aquinatem Thomam nec
Ioannem Scotum plures reliquisse auditores doctrinaeque suae
sectatores quam Iannes hic, cui factum sit agnomen a vitellis, imitatores reliquit ac discipulos.

conceals the vilest insinuations. And so there are very few who are not shot through with simulation.

And what is most disgraceful, to simulate many things with a 5 greater appearance of truth, they use the bonds, now of religion, now of kinship or friendship. If I were to pursue this subject, would it not be tantamount to wishing to provoke the wrath and malevolence of men against me? And so it can be enough for me to have just touched on these things. I leave a more diligent investigation and a freer censure of them to the priests, who perceive them daily from those making their confessions, and to the preachers, whose duty it is publicly and in churches to discourse about them more freely and with greater license.

And yet in this place I will not neglect this widely-known story. 6 In the days of our great-grandfathers there was in some part of Italy a certain Gianni, who constantly lodged with herdsmen and other country people. On a day when a rather fierce ram or calf was exhibited, he was accustomed to shun and flee it and to tremble at the sight of it; and in this way he would make himself ridiculous among the herdsmen. But at night he dared to enter the densest pasturelands and to seize from the herds a strong ox or bull by the horns, bind it with a rope, drag it away, and hand it over to his companions to be led to the fairs and markets, where they would sell it. Therefore Marino Tomacelli, my ⟨ ⟩ and very close friend, a ⟨ ⟩ man, was accustomed to say that neither Thomas Aquinas nor Duns Scotus had left more scholars and followers of his doctrine than this Gianni, who having received a nickname from calves, left imitators and disciples.[32]

: 14 :

## De mercatoribus.

1 Transeamus ad mercatores, quorum non pauci sunt quos parum iuvet lucrari; nec multum ipsi possint proficere, nisi, ut Cicero ait, admodum mentiantur; quin et mendacio addunt iurisiurandi religionem, nec verbis solum verum etiam scriptis annotationibusque dum, qui pannus Italicus est aut Hispanus, Gallicum eum ementiuntur aut Britannicum, quoties genus panni aliquod maiori est in
2 pretio; idem in linteis servant ac sericis. Qui equorum, qui mularum mercaturam exercent, compungunt et equos et mulas eius generis notis, de quo maxima est opinio. Itaque vix aliquod genus est mercis in quo non primum sibi locum mendacium pepererit; potissimaque apud mercatores laus est scire et multum et caute fingere. Quo effectum est, ut fides mercatoria, quae antea maxime habebatur integra, nunc fluxa sit admodum ac fragilis.
3 Hannibal insidiis maxime ac fraude grassatus[8] est. Quotusque est hodie praesertim dux imperatorque exercitus qui non fraude nitatur insidiosisque consiliis? Caesar, cum in Africam venisset, dicitur cunctatior factus ad conserendas manus propter dolos
4 Afrorum hominum.[9] Itaque simulatio rerum verborumque atque consiliorum in omni artium genere ac negociorum facultatumque praecipue regnat, quasi non etiam in disciplinis: quod sophismata ipsa docent, ut iam veritas non in abdito atque in puteo delitescat, ut Democritus dictitabat, verum sophistarum laqueis praepedita
5 ac fallaciis prodire in lucem atque in libertatem nequeat. Iam vero pontificum, regum, dominorum ac principum hominum aulae ac domus, utque hodie dicuntur, curiae simulationibus ac fallaciis mendacissimisque susurrationibus iisdemque nocentissimis infectae sunt, ut videatur veritas ab illorum regiis exterminata; neque

: 14 :

## On merchants.

Let us pass on to the merchants, of whom there are not a few for    1
whom earning is not enough; and they can't make a great deal of
profit unless, as Cicero says, they lie a lot.[33] And in fact they add
their sworn faith to the lie, not only in words but also in writings
and advertisements, while they pretend that Italian or Spanish
cloth is French or English, whenever one kind of cloth is higher in
price. They do the same with linen and silk. Those who trade in    2
horses and mules brand them with signs of the breed that is most
esteemed. And so there is hardly any kind of merchandise in
which lying has not created the first place for itself, and the chief
ground of praise among merchants is knowing how to falsify a lot
without risk. As a result, trust in merchants, which formerly was
held to be absolute, is now very weak and fragile.

Hannibal was able to run riot most of all through treachery and    3
fraud. And particularly today, how many leaders and generals of
armies do not rely upon fraud and treacherous plans? When Caesar came to Africa, he is said to have become slower to join battle
on account of the wiles of the Africans.[34] And so the simulation of    4
things, words, and plans preeminently rules in all kinds of arts,
businesses, and faculties—as if it did not also rule in the disciplines. Sophistries show this: truth does not lurk in a hidden place
or a well, as Democritus maintained, but, fettered by the snares
and fallacies of sophists, it is not able to come forth into light and
liberty.[35] Now, in truth, the halls, homes, and the courts (as is said    5
today) of popes, kings, rulers, and princes have been infected by
simulations, fallacies, and most mendacious and likewise most
harmful insinuations, so that it appears that truth has been expelled from their palaces and that no one is considered a good

bonus quisquam habeatur curialis atque aulicus, nisi qui et mentiri admodum et pro loco ac tempore vultum fingere ac lenocinari scierit. Quo effectum est ut quae maximorum virorum domus est sit eadem simulationis ac mendacii.

: 15 :

## De dissimulatoribus.

1  Dissimulatorum studium longe ab his diversum est moresque item alii. Hi enim quae insunt quaeque dicta aut facta sunt aut parte ex omni inficiantur aut de iis multum detrahunt deque vero, quantum possunt, deducunt. Itaque quam illi dant operam ut veris ficta affingant ac falsa, tam hi ex adverso in id intendunt ut vel prorsus abnegent quae vera sunt, quod dissimulatoris est proprium, aut vehementius imminuta ut elevent.

2  Nesciam tamen quomodo saepenumero qui dissimulator est sit item diversa tamen ratione simulator. Nam et Iunius Brutus sapientiam dissimulavit et, cum minime esset stultus, eum se se gessit moresque eos induit, ut 'brutus' a civibus vocaretur proindeque idem hic et simulator dici et dissimulator potest. Illud tamen interest quod hic inficiatur, ille affingit. Sunt igitur dissimu-
3  latores quidem huiusmodi. Alexander, postquam ab Hammone rediit, Iovis se se esse filium voluit: quid hac ostentatione insolentius? Scipio, cum audiret Iovis quoque se et haberi et dici filium, iis dictis aures ea cum modestia adhibere est solitus, ut inficiari id nullo modo videri aut posset aut vellet.

courtier or palace attendant unless he knows how to lie a lot, to disguise his expression, and to pander as the time and place demand. So it has come about that the house of the greatest men is also one of simulation and lying.

: 15 :

## On dissimulators.

The aim of dissimulators diverges greatly from that of those men, 1 and their characters are also different. For these men deny completely what is in them and what they have done or said, or they greatly discount these and subtract from the truth as much as they can. And so just as the former take pains to add feigned and false things to the true, the latter, on the contrary, aim either to deny totally what is true, which is characteristic of the dissimulator, or to elevate what little there is with great vigor.

Yet somehow a man who is a dissimulator is often also a simu- 2 lator for a different reason. For Junius Brutus both dissimulated his wisdom and, although he was by no means a fool, bore himself and put on a character so that he was called "stupid" by the citizens; and so the same person can be called both a simulator and a dissimulator.[36] Nevertheless, there is this difference: that one denies, the other adds falsely. So there are dissimulators of this kind. After Alexander returned from the oracle of Ammon, he main- 3 tained that he was the son of Jupiter. What is more arrogant than this boasting?[37] When Scipio heard that he also was considered and said to be the son of Jupiter, he used to turn his ears to these words with such modesty that he either was able or wished in no way to appear to deny it.[38]

4    Audio de maioribus natu sacerdotes quosdam quique ab ordine
Fratres dicuntur quique post obitum inter sanctos relati fuere decreto Romanorum pontificum, cum viverent, interrogatos an vera
essent quae de ipsis ferrentur miracula, solitos respondere deum
esse qui et ipse miracula faceret et bonis viris eorundem faciendo-
5  rum vim infunderet. Quae, cum modestia quaedam potius quam
inficiatio dici possit, videtur dissimulationis quaedam species, ad
virtutem tamen referenda, cum modestiae sit civilisque cuiusdam
sive urbanitatis sive tractabilitatis plena; qua Socratem praecipue
fuisse usum legimus. Qua e re eiuscemodi homines a maioribus
nostris dicti sunt ironici; effectumque est ut ironia species quaedam sit virtutis, de qua post dicemus.


: 16 :

*Dissimulatorum plura esse genera.*

1  Sunt autem dissimulatorum genera quaedam eaque perniciosis-
sima in civitatibus ac populis, cum alios videas qui sub liberalitatis
speciem ipsi quidem sint largitiosi hacque ratione studeant cliente-
lis quibus cives alios opprimant seque efficiant quam potentis-
simos; alios qui, dum publica negocia resque civitatis maxime difficiles atque erumnosas diligentissime pariter ac fortissime obeunt
maximisque pro patria se se obiectant periculis, clam regno studeant; illos qui suscipiendis miserorum patrociniis ac popularium
causis factionibus clanculum dent operam; hos, eroganda inter
pauperrimos atque egentissimos quosdam stipe, qui[10] sub speciem
minutissimae ac vulgatissimae erogationis foenus occulant ac cives,
advenas, peregrinos clam excarnificent.

I hear from my elders that when some priests who are called 4
friars by their order and who after their death were canonized by
decree of the Roman pontiffs were asked while alive whether the
miracles attributed to them were true, they were accustomed to
reply that it was God himself who made the miracles and infused
the power of making them into good men. This, although it might 5
be said to be a kind of modesty rather than a denial, appears a
species of dissimulation, yet it is related to virtue, since it is full of
modesty and a certain courteous quality, whether urbanity or ame-
nability. We read that Socrates especially made use of it. This is
why men of this kind were called self-deprecators by our ancestors; consequently, self-deprecation has a kind of outward appearance of virtue, about which I will speak later.


: 16 :

*There are many classes of dissimulators.*

There are, however, certain classes of dissimulators that are most 1
pernicious in states and peoples. For you will see some who under
the appearance of liberality are indeed very lavish and in this way
favor clients with whom they oppress other citizens and make
themselves as powerful as possible; others who, while with great
diligence and bravery alike they attend to public business, and especially to difficult and troublesome matters of state, and subject
themselves to the greatest dangers for their fatherland, secretly
seek to rule; some who, by taking up the defense of the poor and
causes of the common people, secretly support factions; others
who, disbursing alms among some of the very poor and indigent,
conceal their usury and secretly fleece citizens, foreigners, and
strangers under the cover of a very small and well-advertised dis-
bursement.

2    Disserentem Mediolani de religione deque hominum moribus Bernardinum, quem merita ipsa inter divos retulerunt, adibat saepius hortabaturque mercator quidam, ut multus esset in abominando foenore: laborare enim urbem ipsam nimio plus eo morbo. Itaque dum Bernardinus mores vitamque exquirit hominis, comperit perditissimum eum esse foeneratorum omnium illudque agere quo, coeteris deterritis, liberior ipsi uni foenerandi relinqueretur provincia. Horum igitur omnium perinde ut turpe est admodum ac perniciosum urbibus genus, sic etiam multiplex est ac diversum.

3    'Videre etiam licet,' ut inquit Cicero, 'plerosque non tam natura liberales quam quadam gloria ductos, ut benefice videantur facere multa quae proficisci ab ostentatione magis quam a voluntate videantur. Talis autem simulatio vanitati coniunctior quam aut liberalitati aut honestati.'

4    Quod idem dicere de iis liceat qui appetitum voluptatis occultant honorumque dissimulant cupiditatem, quippe qui ostentatores videantur magis quam temperati ac continentes. Cognitum ipsi habemus hominem iurisconsultum iure iniuriaque corradentem undique summaque pressum avaritia deque deo ac religione Christiana male omnino qui sentiat; diebus tamen fere singulis, sive pro templo sive pro domus suae foribus, mane mendicantibus compluribus de manu numulum singulatim praebere, qua ratione et avaritiam celet et animum a religione prorsus alienum. Qua cogitatione ac facto quid perditius dicas ac perversius? Sub sanctitatis autem ac continentiae opinione, quantum mali foveret frater Hieronymus Ferrariensis, ex ordine beatissimi ac maxime sancti viri Dominici, declaravit nuper populus ipse, quem subduxerat, Florentinus, cuius decreto morte, et quidem acerbissima, atrocissimisque cruciatibus excarnificatus est.

When Bernardino, whose merits placed him among the saints, 2
was discoursing in Milan about religion and morality, a certain
merchant often approached and urged him to be assiduous in
abominating usury, for the city was far too afflicted by that disease. And so when Bernardino inquired about the life and character of the man, he discovered that he was the most incorrigible of
all usurers and was doing this so that, once the others were scared
off, a freer field for usury would be left to him alone.[39] So just as
the class of all these men is very shameful and pernicious for cities,
so also is it manifold and diverse. "It is also possible to see," as Cic- 3
ero says, "that most men are not so much liberal by nature as
drawn by some kind of glory, so that they may be seen to do many
beneficent actions that seem to arise from ostentation rather than
goodwill. But this simulation is closer to falsity than to either liberality or the pursuit of honor."[40]

One may say the same thing about those who hide their desire 4
for pleasure and dissimulate their longing for honors, inasmuch as
they appear ostentatious rather than temperate and continent. I
myself have known a lawyer who justly or unjustly scrapes together money from every source, is oppressed by the greatest avarice, and thinks very ill of God and the Christian religion. Nevertheless, almost every day, either in front of the church or the doors
of his house, in the morning he offers with his own hand a small
coin to many beggars individually in order to conceal in this way
both his avarice and his mind, which is completely alien to religion. What would you call more corrupt and perverted than this
thought and action? How much evil Girolamo of Ferrara, friar of
the order of the most blessed and holy Dominic, fomented under
a reputation of holiness and continence has recently been made
plain by the Florentine people, whom he had led astray and by
whose decree he was tormented with the bitterest death and most
atrocious tortures.[41]

5    Itaque vitium hoc dissimulationis late quidem patens est ac perpauci quidem sunt, quemcumque sive civium ordinem sive sacerdotum aut principum inspicias, in quo non invenire Suffenum possis, ne Valerii Catulli sive scomma sive maledictum aspernari videamur. Qui igitur dissimulatorum sint conatus, studia, proposita, iam videtis.

6    Sub Ferdinando Neapolitanorum rege agebat Caietae in coenobio Gerardus quidam, qui septimum in diem cibo abstinere consuevisset ac potu, indeque sanctus habebatur ac deo carus. Venerabatur illum populus, utque eum adorarent, frequentes ad eum finitimis conveniebant ex oppidis; tantam hanc hominum opinionem coenobitae adaugebant propter munera quae templo offerebantur. Misit ad eam rem perspicendam Ferdinandus Masium Aquosam, et perspicacem et abunde expertum virum, cuius etiam fides esset quam perspectissima. Is dies noctisque cum illo septem eodem simul in cubiculo cum egisset summa cum vigilantia et cura, comperit tandem et capitis illum et stomachi pituita laborare nimiaque de humectatione, quo e vitio appetendi cibi vis illa consopita iaceret ac pene extincta; esseque sive ieiunium illud sive abstinentiam ad morbum malumque corporis habitum referendam, vanosque illos esse rerumque religionis ostentatores, qui persuadere conarentur genios, hoc est Angelos, victum ad illum quotidianum ferre ciboque divino pascere.

7    Sub Alfonso rege, Ferdinandi huius patre, eandem hanc abstinentiam cum ostentaret alius quidam, cuius nomen e memoria excidit, adhibitaque esset cura, ne quid esculenti potusque ad illum inferretur, compertum postea est sub speciem nocturni luminis, erat enim hibernum tempus, victitare interim illum e candelis nocturni luminis causa sumministratis, quae e succaro cinnamoque constarent atque e gallinarum pectoribus minutissime contusis, sevo tamen super illito.

And so this vice of dissimulation is indeed evident far and wide, 5
and there are indeed very few — whichever class of citizens, priests,
or princes you inspect — among which you cannot find a Suffenus
(I wouldn't want to appear to disdain the scoff or curse of Valerius
Catullus).[42] So now you see what the efforts, endeavors, and intentions of the dissimulators are.

In the reign of Ferdinando, king of Naples, there lived in the 6
monastery at Gaeta a certain Gerardo, who was accustomed to
abstain from food and drink for seven days and thus was considered to be saintly and dear to God. The people venerated him and
would come in great numbers from the neighboring cities to adore
him. The monks magnified this great reputation on account of the
gifts that were offered to the church. To examine this thing Ferdinando sent Masio Aquosa, an acute and most experienced man,
whose trustworthiness was also completely proven.[43] After he had
spent seven days and nights with him in the same cell with the
greatest vigilance and care, he finally discovered that Gerardo was
suffering from catarrh of both the head and stomach and from
excessive humectation. From this defect his capacity for desiring
food lay dormant and almost extinguished. This fasting or abstinence was to be attributed to disease and the ill state of his body,
and the people who were trying to persuade that geniuses, that is
angels, were bringing daily nourishment to him and feeding him
with divine food were false boasters about religious matters.

In the reign of Alfonso, the father of this Ferdinando, when 7
someone whose name has slipped my mind displayed this same
abstinence, and care had been taken that no food or drink was
brought to him, it was later discovered that, under the pretext of a
night-light (for it was winter), he would sometimes eat from the
candles supplied as a night-light, which consisted of sugar, cinna-
mon, and chicken breasts finely pounded but smeared over with
tallow.[44]

: 17 :

*Dissimulationem aliquando esse ostentationem.*

1 Quid quod interdum dissimulatio et ipsa quidem ostentatio quaedam est cuiusmodi esse generis Aristoteles Laconicum arbitratur
vestitum? Sub illa nanque modicitate delitescere elationem ac su-
2 perbos spiritus. Qua de re parcius loquor propter sanctissimos
heremitas patresque illos et tanquam fundatores Christianae religionis, Paulum, Antonium, Malchum, Sabam, Onofrium aliosque
post hos innumerabiles, in iisque tot post seculis Franciscum,
quorum paupertas, continentia, simplicitas, sanctitas, vita omnis
denique visa est nobilitasse hominum imbecillitatem maximeque
languescentis eorum roborasse conatus.

3     Tali igitur sub modicitate ac vestitus sorde non pauci olim philosophiae professores pessima quaedam exempla prodiderunt. Utque de aliis taceam, Neronis Augusti temporibus, Publius Egnatius Stoicam professus est sectam, quo maiorem sibi fidem in
accusandis tum civibus aliis tum etiam senatoribus compararet.
Utinam ne aetate etiam nostra sub hac quoque specie atque habitu
turpiora magisque profana admitterentur!

4     Videas hodie quosdam minutissima ac sordidissima quaedam
vel obstinate dissimulare, quod ea ad virtutem ipsi, ut sunt animo
imbecillo admodum atque abiecto, referant publicamque ad commendationem. Quocirca dissimulant ea, dum e dissimulatione ac
reticentia magis magisque commendatum iri ea existimant; qui
meo quidem iudicio non degeneres modo atque abiecti verum nullius esse videantur pretii deque coetu prorsus hominum eiiciendi.

: 17 :

*Sometimes dissimulation is ostentation.*

What about the fact that dissimulation is occasionally a kind of    1
ostentation of the kind that Aristotle reckoned Spartan dress to
be?[45] For under that modesty lay hidden pride and arrogance. I    2
speak more sparingly about this matter on account of those most
saintly hermits, fathers, and founders, so to speak, of the Christian religion — Paul, Anthony, Malchus, Sabbas, Onofrius and innumerable others after them and among them, after so many cen-
turies, Francis.[46] Their poverty, continence, simplicity, sanctity, in
short their whole way of life, have been seen to have ennobled the
weakness of mankind and to have strengthened its faltering efforts.

Accordingly, under such modesty and squalor of dress in for-    3
mer times not a few professors of philosophy furnished some of
the worst examples. Not to mention others, in the time of the
emperor Nero, Publius Egnatius professed the Stoic doctrine to
win greater credibility for accusing both other citizens and even
senators.[47] If only even in our days too more shameful and more
impious things, clothed in this appearance, were not permitted!

Today you might see some men, even to the point of obstinacy,    4
dissimulating some very small and sordid things because, as their
minds are very weak and base, they associate them with virtue and
public commendation. For this reason they dissimulate these
things as long as they think that by dissimulation and reticence
the things will be more and more commended. At least in my
judgment they seem not only degenerate and base but worthless
as well, and deserving of complete expulsion from the company
of men.

5      Commendabatur religiosis ex his quidam quod ieiunia traduce-
ret ternis tantum cariculis ac nucibus aquaeque ciathulo, cumque
antistes id ex eo sciscitaretur, sat ipsi scimus tantum hoc illum respondisse, demisso vultu, voce quam maxime depressa et languida
miserum se peccatorem esse. Quid dissimulantius, imo quid ina-
nius atque, apud recte sentientes, contemptibilius? Risit antistes
hominis inanem ostentationem et, ut aliam insisteret viam quae ad
coelum ferret, commonuit.

6      Iacobus Zanes negociator Venetus, multa amplaque negocia
Neapoli cum administraret cerneretque Gasparem Ravennianum
singulis diebus sub matutinum tempus visitare templa, interesse
rebus divinis, sacraque dum celebrarentur, intentissimum illum
esse legendis Daviticis psalmis, captus imo deceptus, ut res ipsa
docuit, viri moribus, non parvam illi pecuniae summam credidit
administrandam, de qua post, ratione habita, lucrum compen-
diaque partirentur, ut mercatorum mos esset. Gaspar, accepta pecunia, cum advenisset reddendae rationis tempus, risui Iacobum
habuit, quippe qui non pecuniam modo abnegaverit verum igno-
rare se illum dixerit, cumque Iacobus mercatoribus ab aliis accusaretur: 'Non me,' inquit, 'Gaspar decepit, sed Gasparis libellus lectioque illius suspiriosa.'

7      Itaque vix aliqua vitae species est ad quam se se dissimulatio
non insinuet, quod non ita multis post annis frater Franciscus
Hispanus docuit. Is quamvis rudis atque indoctus, tractus tamen
audacia atque ambitione, pulpitum ascendere est ausus tantoque
sive fastu sive temeritate, palam ut asseveraret praedicare se de religione Christianisque de rebus, docente ac dictante angelo, cuius
admonitu et futura quaedam praediceret et, qui cum divis in coelo
e mortuis agerent, qui rursus apud inferos cruciarentur, sciret ac
proferret. Denique cum Ferdinando persuadere arte nulla aut

One of these religious was commended because he would get 5 through his fasts with only three little figs and nuts, and a small cup of water, and when his superior asked him about this, I know well that, with downcast face and voice as low and faint as possible, he only replied that he was a miserable sinner. What is more dissimulating, rather what is emptier and, to the right-minded, more contemptible? The superior laughed at the empty ostentation of the man and warned him to follow another path that would lead to heaven.

When Iacopo Zane, a Venetian trader, was managing many 6 great affairs at Naples and saw Gaspare of Ravenna attend church every day in the morning, take part in the divine services, and, while the sacred rites were being celebrated, read most intently the psalms of David, he was captivated — or rather deceived, as the event itself showed — by the manners of the man and entrusted to him no small sum of money to manage, from which later, after the accounting, they would share the profit and gain, as is the custom of merchants. Having accepted the money, Gaspare, when the time for rendering the account had arrived, mocked Iacopo in that he not only refused him the money but also said he did not know him. When Iacopo was blamed by the other merchants, he said, "It wasn't Gaspare that deceived me but Gaspare's little psalter and his sigh-filled reading."

And so there is hardly any kind of life that dissimulation does 7 not steal into, as not many years later friar Francisco the Spaniard showed.[48] Although uncultivated and unlearned, yet induced by his audacity and ambition, he dared to ascend the pulpit with such arrogance or rashness that he asserted publicly that he would preach about religion and Christianity with an angel teaching and dictating to him, at whose instruction he would both predict some things in the future and know and pronounce which of the dead were living with the saints in heaven and which, on the contrary, were being tortured in hell. Finally, when he could persuade Ferdi-

ratione posset ut Iudaeorum gentem exterminaret[11] e regni finibus, exemplo Ferdinandi patruelis Hispaniarum regis, Tarenti cum ipse ageret, commentum hoc iniit: e plumbo tabulam, divi Cataldi nomine clanculum a se inscriptam, haud Tarento procul in sacello semidiruto sub parietem occuluit; quam triennio post eruendam curavit, corrupto sacerdote qui diceret in somnis astitisse sibi Cataldum, monstrantem quo in loco tabella esset abdita commonentemque uti cum populo supplice collegioque sacerdotum iret ad effodiendam illam; quam effossam curaret ad regem deferendam, communicandam ab eo uni tantum viro, quem e suis optimum nosceret ac maxime fidum; deum enim iratum illi futurum clademque ac calamitatem immissurum, ni, quod in tabula scriptum esset, et cautum a rege praestaretur. Scriptum vero ipsum per ambages quasdam ac latebricosa verba eo spectabat uti Iudaeorum exterminatio indicaretur. Rex, accepta tabula, deprehendit fraudem; qua deprehensa, minime Franciscum ad eam legendam secum adhibuit, arbitratus eum interpretaturum verba in eam sententiam; dissimulavitque rem ipsam summa cum taciturnitate ac prudentia. At Franciscus, re cognita, furore percitus quod tantum commentum falsum eum habuisset, non populo, non regi, vix ipsi Cataldo publicis pepercit in praedicationibus; in tantumque excanduit ut Italia ferme omnis ipseque in primis Romanus pontifex de tabulae huius fuerit inventione solicitus atque anxius. Itaque vitii huius vis adeo culta et potens est, neque omnino animadversa, ut non modo interdum in ostentationem se se convertat verum etiam in spiritus superbissimos execrabilemque animorum impotentiam.

8     Quanquam autem Aristoteles recte putat veraci ostentatorem magis adversari longiusque ab illo digredi utpote deteriorem, non minus tamen difficile est ab his ipsis cavere, cum eorum morbus

nando by no artifice or reason to expel the Jewish people from the territory of the kingdom following the example of his cousin, Ferdinando king of Spain, he contrived this fabrication when he was at Taranto. He hid a tablet made of lead, secretly written by himself under the name of Saint Cataldus, not far from Taranto, under a wall in a half-destroyed chapel. He took care for it to be dug up three years later, having bribed a priest to say that Cataldus had stood beside him in a dream, showing in what place the tablet had been hidden and warning him to go with the suppliant people and college of priests to dig it up. Once it had been dug up, he should take care to have it delivered to the king and shared by him only with the one man whom he knew to be the best and most faithful of his men. For God would be angry with him and would send destruction and calamity unless the king decreed what had been written on the tablet. Of course the writing itself via certain ambiguities and obscure words aimed at proclaiming the expulsion of the Jews. Having accepted the tablet, the king detected the fraud, and, once it was detected, he by no means summoned Francisco to read it with him, judging that he would interpret the words in that way. He dissimulated the thing with the greatest silence and prudence. But once Francisco learned this, he was shaken with rage that his great imposture had been judged a fake; in his public sermons he did not spare the people, the king, even Cataldus himself. He burned so hot in anger that practically all of Italy and the Roman pope himself above all were worried and anxious about the finding of this tablet.[49] And so the force of this vice is so practiced and potent, and at the same time not fully recognized, that it not only sometimes turns into ostentation but also into the proudest arrogance and detestable fury.

Moreover, although Aristotle rightly thinks that the ostentatious man is more contrary to the truthful and departs further from him [than the dissimulator], being the worse man,[50] yet it is not less difficult to guard against dissimulators, since their vice is

8

vix appareat, ostentatio vero ipsa se se patefaciat, id quod nomen etiam ipsum declarat. Velle autem haec ulterius prosequi nec utile esse ducimus nec necessarium viderique abunde satis potest plane nos ostendisse quot et quae genera sint species ve eorum omnium atque in quibus versentur differant ve aut conveniant quique sit tum mendaces tum veri simulatoresque ac dissimulatores. Nam de ironicis alibi expressius[12] disputabitur.

9     Quoniam autem prudentia dux est ac magistra actionum humanarum omnium moraliumque virtutum, illud non videtur praetereundum prudentiam ipsam pro loco, tempore, negociis, administrationibus, periculis proque persona quam geremus, tum exigere tum etiam praecipere, uti nunc simulemus, contra nunc dissimulemus, nunc veritatem occulamus, nunc quae vera nullo modo sunt et fingamus et asseveremus. Quae res efficit ut fingere interdum, simulare, dissimulare, inficiari, celare, ostentare, demere, accumulare, dum tamen prudentia id exigat, dandum sit virtuti.

10     Sunt et actiones ipsae ad finem referendae: nam et Solon publicae rei gratia furorem simulavit et Brutus, de quo diximus, stultitiam; et sapientissimi rerum publicarum administratores in maxime periculosis casibus hilaritatem fingunt; quae autem adversa, celant, quae ficta et laeta, efferenda in publicum curant. Nec medici sanandis aegris, quo illos habeant obtemperantiores magisque abstinentes, non et ipsi multa se se dubitare aut eventura praeter opinionem fingunt, aut contra vel optimam illis pollicentur spem, licet ipsi de illorum salute nullam prorsus spem habeant, praesertim in pestilentibus ac desperatis morbis. Denique nullo ab hominum genere, nullis ab administratoribus plura aut simulantur aut dissimulantur quam ab exercituum ducibus rerumque administratoribus bellicarum. Quarum rerum tum Latinae Graecaeque historiae tum barbarae repletae sunt exemplis.[13]

scarcely apparent, while ostentation reveals itself, as the name it-self also declares. But I do not think it either useful or necessary to pursue these matters further, and it may be seen amply enough that I have shown plainly how many and what classes and species there are of all these men, in what things they are involved or in what they differ or agree, and who the liars, the simulators of truth, and the dissimulators are. For the self-deprecators will be discussed more distinctly elsewhere.[51]

Since prudence, however, is the leader and teacher of all human 9 actions and moral virtues, it seems that one should not omit to say that prudence, in accordance with the place, time, business, duties, dangers, and the role that we bear, both requires and also advises us now to simulate, now on the contrary to dissimulate, now to hide the truth, now to feign and maintain things that are by no means true. Consequently, sometimes feigning, simulating, dis-simulating, denying, concealing, revealing, removing, increasing, provided that prudence requires it, must be imputed a virtue.

And actions themselves must be referred to their end. For So- 10 lon simulated insanity for the state, and Brutus, of whom I have spoken, stupidity.[52] And the wisest administrators of states feign cheerfulness in especially dangerous situations; they conceal, more-over, unfavorable and take care that happy, fictive facts are pre-sented to the public. And doctors, while curing the sick, to make them more compliant and more abstinent, pretend to fear many things or ones that might happen beyond their expectation, or, on the contrary, promise them the very greatest hope, although they themselves have absolutely no hope for their survival, especially in plagues and desperate diseases. Finally, no class of men, no admin-istrators, simulate or dissimulate more than the leaders of armies and administrators of wars.[53] Latin and Greek histories, as well as foreign, are full of examples of these things.

# LIBER TERTIUS

## : I :

*Unde ductae sint* facetiae *ac* facetudo.

1 De facetudine igitur dicturi, quam mediocritatem esse quandam primo[1] libro ostendimus, ne a nobis ipsis desciisse videamur, ab
2 origine quidem ipsa nominisque exordiemur deductione. Verbum ipsum *facio*, unde *facetiae* ductae sunt, apud priscos illos et Latinos et Romanos homines in maxima fuit frequentissimaque usurpatione. Itaque et 'pacem' et 'bellum' et 'foedus' et 'inducias facere' dixerunt et 'delicias' et 'ludos' et 'nuptias' et 'convivia' et 'abortum' et 'domum' et 'templa' et 'porticum' et 'nomina' et id genus pene innumerabilia; in his autem et 'verba facere' et 'versus' et 'orationem' et
3 'iocos.' Indeque qui in comitiis, in consultationibus, in senatu, in concionibus verba cum gravitate facerent cumque dignitate et copia 'facundos' dixere et virtutem eam 'facundiam,' ut iam diximus, quam Plautus, quo Romanam locupletaret linguam, etiam 'facunditatem' appellavit a faciunda videlicet oratione. Qui vero in circulis, congressionibus, conviviis communibusque in sermonibus ac consuetudinibus ad iocunditatem solum animorumque recreationem cum moderatione et gratia, 'facetos,' quin etiam dicta ipsa appellavere 'facetias'; habitum vero reliquere innominatum, quem nobis appellare tum 'facetudinem' ac 'facetiem' placuit tum etiam 'facetitatem.'

# BOOK THREE

: I :

*The derivation of* witticisms *and* wittiness.

Therefore, since I am about to speak about wittiness, which I 1
showed to be a kind of mean in the first book, I will begin with
the origin and derivation of the word so as not to appear to seem
inconsistent.¹ The word *facio*, from which *facetiae* is derived, was 2
used with great frequency by the ancient Latins and Romans.
Thus they said "make peace" and "war" and "a treaty" and "a truce"
and "sport of" and "a game of" and "a marriage" and "a meal together" and "an abortion" and "a house" and "a temple" and "a portico" and "account entries" and almost innumerable others of this
kind, including "make words" and "verses" and "a speech" and
"jokes." And so they called those who made words with gravity, 3
dignity, and copiousness in assemblies, in consultations, in the
senate, in meetings "fluent" (*facundus*) and the virtue "fluency" (*fa-
cundia*), as I have said, which Plautus, to enrich the Roman language, also called "eloquence" (*facunditas*), evidently from making a
speech.² But they called those who spoke solely to be delightful
and to restore men's spirits with restraint and grace in companies,
gatherings, banquets and in common conversation and intercourse
"witty"(*faceti*) and furthermore the witty remarks themselves "witticisms" (*facetiae*). They left the quality unnamed, however, which
I have decided to call *wittiness* (*facetudo*) and *faceties* and even *facetitas*.³

: 2 :

*Facetudinem virtutem esse.*

1 Virtutem autem hanc esse illud praecipue docet, quod in sermonibus congressionibusque ineundis, in habenda item oratione sive
ad multos sive ad paucos popularibusque in concionibus, et
laudamur, ubi mediocritatem servaverimus, et vituperamur, cum
secus. Quod si mediocritas ea est, ut quidem est, inter duo uti
extrema constituatur oportet; quae igitur ea sint, quaerendum est
diligentius.

2 Nec mutus igitur opponetur faceto, quippe cum mutus non
solum non facetus esse, verum minime queat fari. Qua e re nequaquam etiam opponi ei potest qui aetate sit infans, cum hic ipse
infans non sit locutione cassus verum adhuc inhabilis ad bene
exacteque loquendum. Itaque neque infantia adversabitur facetu-
3 dini. Parte ex alia multo ei minus adversa erit loquacitas, de qua
supra est dictum. Quod vitium in sermone ipso ipsaque in
loquendi serie generalem quendam locum habet magis quam in
iocis ac dicteriis. Labitur enim in excessum non iocandi verum
implicandi sermonis blacterandaeque orationis gratia.

4 Cum igitur circa iocos sermonisque iucunditatem ac leporem
circaque urbanitatem ac comitatem versari facetum dicamus, si
rusticitatem ei opposuerimus, parum fortasse rei ipsius significan-
tiam adimplebimus, cum rusticitas ipsa rectius opponatur urbanitati ipsaque urbanitas sit facetudinis sive pars quaedam sive species; sin illepiditatem, idem erit peccatum, quod illepiditas adversa
tantum est lepori, qui dictorum comes est ac facetiarum; multo
etiam minus opponenda illi est insuavitas, quippe cum suavitas
ipsa in saporibus quoque versetur inque attactu et risu et gusta-
tione, et a nobis libris quidem superioribus non pauca dicta sint e

: 2 :

## *Wittiness is a virtue.*

Moreover, that this is a virtue is shown principally by the fact that, 1
while taking part in conversations and interviews, likewise while
giving a speech either to many or to few people and in popular
meetings, we are praised when we observe the mean and are
blamed otherwise. But if it is a mean, as indeed it is, it must be
placed between two extremes. Therefore one must seek diligently
what these are.

So the mute is not opposed to the witty man, since the mute is 2
unable not only to be witty but even to speak at all. So one too
young to speak can not be his opposite, since this speechless one is
not deprived of speech but incapable as yet of speaking well and
exactly. And so speechlessness is not the opposite of wittiness. On 3
the other hand, loquacity, which has been spoken of above, is
much less its opposite.[4] This vice applies generally to conversation
as such and to the very sequence of speaking rather than to jokes
and witty sayings. For it slips into excess not from joking but from
complicated and babbling speech.

Since I say, therefore, that the witty man is involved with jokes, 4
delight and charm in conversation, urbanity, and affability, if I oppose rusticity to it, I will perhaps not give the full sense of the
thing itself, since rusticity is more correctly opposed to urbanity,
and urbanity is a certain kind or species of wittiness. But if I oppose lack of charm, it will be the same mistake, since lack of
charm is only the opposite of charm, which is the companion of
bon mots and witticisms. Still less must one oppose unpleasant-
ness, seeing that pleasantness is also involved in tastes and in
touch, laughter, and tasting, and in the preceding books I have
said not a few things from which it may be judged what and what

quibus iudicari possit et quid quaeratur et quale. Quaerimus enim (cum ad laborem hinc nati simus illinc ad relaxationem cumque iucunda sint nobis amica, tristia vero inimica ac permolesta) et requietem inter labores ac cessationem et a molestiis curisque gravioribus relaxationem, quandamque quasi vacuitatem.

5    Cum igitur qui sint urbani, qui comes lepidique, qui item aut blandi aut festivi sit a nobis abunde ostensum, et quid et quantum et qua etiam via differant inter se, nimirum genus aliquod esse oportet quod ab his ipsis constituatur, ut quemadmodum contingit in avaritia, plures enim avarorum sunt species, quod cum de liberalitate ageremus plane aperuimus, sic illorum quoque non una est consideratio qui iocis utuntur delectanturque verborum iucunditate ac lenociniis.

6    Itaque qui omnes iocandi partes cum mediocritate fuerit consecutus, hunc quidem, ut ab omni parte in hoc ipso genere absolutum, facetum esse volumus, ut qui omnem complexus sit avaritiam, avarum, quanquam et avaros et facetos etiam dicimus qui partem fuerint aliquam assecuti sive facetudinis sive avaritiae, quippe cum et species insit generi et genus mutuo in species distribuatur. Quocirca habitum ipsum, quamvis novo quidem non improprio tamen nomine, uti superius explicatum est, appellandum ducimus. His autem hunc in modum expositis, pro nostra consuetudine institutoque, ab ipsis tanquam incunabulis facetum instituemus, nihil omittentes eorum quae conducere remque ad ipsam explanandam magis magisque facere intelligantur.

kind of thing is being sought. For we seek (since on the one hand we are born for labor and on the other for relaxation, and since delightful things are pleasing to us but sad ones unpleasing and troublesome) repose and rest among labors and relaxation from troubling and more serious cares, a kind of vacation, so to speak.

Therefore, since I have abundantly shown who are the urbane, 5 who the affable and the delightful, and likewise the flattering or mirthful and how, how much, and also in what way they differ among themselves, clearly there must be some class that is constituted by them, as happens with avarice, for there are many species of misers, which I clearly explained when I was discussing liberality.[5] So also there is not only one way to consider those who use jokes and delight in the pleasantness and enticements of words.

And so I define the witty man as one who has achieved the 6 mean in all parts of joking, perfect in all parts of this class, just as I define the one who embraces all of avarice a miser, although we also call misers and witty men those who have attained some part either of wittiness or of avarice, seeing that the species is in the class and in return the class is distributed into species. For this reason we consider that the quality itself ought to be called by a name, a name which though admittedly new is yet nevertheless not improper, as has been explained above. Having then set forth the foregoing in this way, following my custom and practice, I will rear up the witty man from the cradle, as it were, omitting nothing understood to be appropriate and effective for making the virtue ever more intelligible.

: 3 :

*De principiis et causis virtutis huius.*

1   Principio res nostrae omnes positae sunt in motu. Motus autem ipse trahit nos ad agendum. Actio vero suapte natura est laboriosa. Causae vero quae ad agendum nos trahunt et utiles sunt et voluptatem prae se ferunt: naturaliter enim et utilia appetuntur et iucunda. Itaque et utilia et iucunda appetitionibus proposita sunt nostris. Et utilia quidem ipsa vix assequimur sine labore atque in-

2 sudatione. Labor vero actioque omnis cum non sit absque defatigatione, tum cessationem requirit refocillationemque quasi quandam inter agendum, tum requietem postquam ad finem perventum fuerit. Itaque et in progressione rerum recreatio quaeritur et in exitu quies.

3   Recreationes autem ipsae ac refocillationes quietesque tum e rebus constant, ut cum eventus ipsi rerum felices sunt atque e sententia, tum e verbis dictisque, cum ea iucunditatem afferunt ac delinitionem et dicendo et audiendo; contra molestiam, tristitiam, moestitudinem, ubi et acerba fuerint et erumnosa animumque ipsum conficientia. Quocirca non e rebus solum verum etiam e dictis tum utilia manant tum etiam iucunda. Manant autem e rebus utilia ac iucunda, ut cum res ipsae fructum nobis afferunt et cum profectu pariter iucunditatem, aut cum voluptatem tantummodo. Manant item e dictis pariter, ut cum apud praetorem amicus nobis adest, in causa apud iudicem, patrocinioque suo causam tuetur paritque ex ea tum utile tum iucundum. Quid enim victoria iucundius?

4   Sed nos hac in parte de iis tantum dictis ac verbis rationem habemus quae communi in consuetudine animorum relaxationem quaerunt atque ab labore remissionem ipsisque a molestiis.

5 Quocirca dictiones huiusmodi nostrae quae in contrahenda vita

: 3 :

*On the principles and causes of this virtue.*

In the first place all of our acts depend upon motion, and motion 1
itself leads us to act, but action by its very nature is laborious. But
the causes that lead us to act both are useful and bring pleasure
along with them, for both useful and delightful things are naturally striven for. And so both useful and delightful things have
been set before our appetites. And we hardly attain useful things
without labor and exertion. But since all labor and action are not 2
without fatigue, so now they require repose and almost a kind of
restoration while acting, now rest after the end has been reached.
And so in the course of our affairs recreation is sought for and, in
the end, rest.

Moreover, recreation, restoration, and rest depend both on 3
things, as when events themselves are fortunate and to one's liking,
and on words and witticisms, when these bring delight and comfort through speaking and hearing. On the contrary, they bring
annoyance, gloom, and sorrow when they are bitter and troublesome and wear out the mind. Therefore, both useful and delightful results flow not only from things but also from witty words.
Useful and delightful effects flow from things when the things
themselves bring us profit, advantage and delight together, or
merely pleasure. Likewise they flow from witticisms, as when a
friend is on our side before a magistrate, in a case before a judge,
and defends our case by his advocacy and brings something both
useful and delightful out of it. For what is more delightful than
victory?

But in this part I am taking account only of those witticisms 4
and words that seek relaxation of mind in common intercourse
and rest from labor and troubles. Hence our funny remarks of the 5

hominumque versantur societate aut rigidae ipsae sunt, rusticanae, acerbae nimisque agrestes animosque ipsos et perturbant et gravius etiam afficiunt, nedum ut recreationi adversentur quae naturaliter et sponte nostra quaeritur, aut cum delectare illae quidem student, id potius agunt ut, iocandi mediocritate relicta, aut turpe oscenumque aliquid aut parum consideratum atque ingratum eorum qui audiunt auribus infunditant, quod ruborem afferat aut stomachum moveat, aut nos ad eius qui dicit ac dictorum eius irrisionem ac contemptum inducant.

Utrumque sane vitiosum, quippe cum agrestis ille ac rigidus naturae ipsi adversetur quae, cum relaxationem a labore quaerat, ipse contra molestiis eam praegravet. Hic scurrilis atque oscenus, cum honestas a natura rationeque ab ipsa proposita nobis sit, et illam dictis suis foedet et se, dum iucundum exhibere debet ac gratum, ridiculum potius apud audientes efficiat ac contemptibilem cogatque auditorem, civilibus praeditum moribus atque ingenuum, ad demittendum os atque oculos in humum ad auresque avertendas ob dictorum oscenitatem dicentisque ipsius aut convitiationem aut impudentiam garrulitatemque. Utrinque enim ita peccatur, ut alter mediocritatem defugiat, alter illam praegrediatur
6   cum indecentia atque astantium irrisione. Et hunc, qui de moribus scripsere, scurram vocitant, qui Graece est *bomolochus*, habitumque scurrilitatem; illum vero alterum rusticum, nam Graece est *agrios* defectumque ipsum rusticitatem.

De quibus deque habitu medio antequam dicimus, non temere pauca quaedam praefabimur quae cognitu digna quidem sunt atque in ipso explicandi ingressu iure suo edisserenda.

kind involved in the conduct of life and human society either are rough, rustic, bitter, and too rude and perturb our minds and even afflict them more seriously — not to mention that they oppose the recreation that we naturally and freely seek — or, although they endeavor to delight, to be sure, they instead have abandoned the mean of joking and manage to pour something base and obscene or inconsiderate and unpleasing into the ears of their auditors, so that it raises a blush, turns the stomach, or leads us to deride and scorn the speaker and what he says.

Each is certainly vicious. The rough and rude man opposes nature itself, since it seeks relaxation from labor, while he on the contrary burdens it with vexation. The buffoonish and obscene man, although decency has been set before us by nature and reason itself, befouls that decency with his talk, and, while he ought to show himself delightful and pleasing, he instead makes himself ridiculous and contemptible to his audience, and forces a freeborn listener endowed with civil manners to cast down his face and eyes to the ground and to avert his ears on account of the obscenity of his speech and the insult, impudence, and garrulity of the speaker. For there is a fault on both sides, as one shuns the mean, the other surpasses it with his indecency and his mockery of bystanders. And writers on ethics call this man a buffoon, which is *bomolochus* 6 in Greek, and the quality, buffoonery, but they call the other one a rustic, since in Greek it is *agrios* and the deficiency, rusticity.[6]

Before I speak about these things and the intermediate quality, it is reasonable for me to preface a few things worth knowing and relating in their own right at the beginning of this explanation.

: 4 :

*Conciliabula inter cives fieri aut utilis aut iucundi gratia.*

1 Quod homines igitur natura sunt ipsa sociabiles atque in unum
conveniunt tuendae rei tum publicae tum privatae gratia, hinc
quoque, tametsi de utilitate minime agitur, congregantur tamen
una nunc pauci admodum nunc complures, tum ut naturae ipsi
morem gerant ac rerum necessitati, tum ut susceptorum delinitio-
2 nem laborum inveniant ac molestiarum. Itaque conciliabula ipsa
conventusque alias utilitatis, alias relaxationis tantum fiunt gratia,
quibus in ipsis ridicularia utique quaeritantur sedationesque animorum ac vitae difficilioris recreatio, quin etiam defatigationum
ipsarum sive intermissio sive soporatio quasi quaedam. His itaque
sive conventibus ac conciliabulis civiumque sive paucorum sive
multorum communioni et coetui sive etiam convictui atque consess-
sioni propter refocillationem ioca proposita sunt verborumque re-
laxamenta et privata quaedam, ut ita dixerim, spectacula dicte-
3 riaque theatralia. Omnem autem et colloquendi et congrediendi et
dicendi sive affabilitatem festivitatemque atque urbanitatem sive
comitatem, leporem iucunditatemque, quae in iis exerceatur deque
iisdem manet profluatque ex dicendo, ad ioca prorsus dictaque io-
cularia atque ad facetias identidem referenda ducimus.

: 4 :

*Meetings of citizens occur for either utility or delight.*

Therefore, since men by nature itself are sociable and come to- 1
gether to protect both public and private interest, they also nevertheless, even in matters of minimal utility, congregate in smaller or
greater numbers both to comply with their natural inclinations
and the necessity of affairs and also to find comfort amid the labors they have undertaken and amid troubles. And so meetings 2
and assemblies sometimes occur for utility, sometimes only for relaxation. In them jests are especially sought after, and mental seda-
tives and relief from life's difficulties—yes, and even an intermis-
sion or, as it were, a kind of putting to sleep of fatigue. So in these
assemblies and little councils, or in the association and coming
together of citizens, whether a few or many, or even in a banquet
or a meeting, jests and relaxing words and some private spectacles
and theatrical performances of witty sayings, so to speak, are produced for the sake of recreation. Moreover, I have consistently 3
maintained that all friendliness, mirth, urbanity or affability,
charm and delight, whether of conversing or addressing each other
or speaking, that is practiced in such meetings and spreads and
flows from speaking in them, must be entirely ascribed to jokes,
witty sayings, and to witticisms.

: 5 :

*Triplex esse iocandi genus.*

1 Iocandi autem in eiusmodi tum conciliationibus tum coronis triplex genus statuimus: et quod servile maximeque degenerans est, quales servorum sunt ioci, qualis etiam affabilitas eo hominum genere digna, ut 'Gymnasium flagri, salveto,' 'Quid ais, custos carceris?,' 'O catenarum colone,' 'O virgarum lascivia.' Et 'Num me illuc ducis ubi lapis lapidem terit? Ubi vivos homines mortui incursitant boves?' Et 'Ut miser est homo qui amat! — Imo vero, hercle, qui pendet multo miserior.' Et 'Noctem tuam et vini cadum.' Quorum quidem dictorum et Graecae et Latinae comoediae sunt perplenae; et quod inter rusticos versatur urbanisque a moribus alienos homines, siquidem horum iocis ac dictis ut alibi ruditas quaedam inest atque ineptitudo, sic alibi illiberalitas ingenuo viro nullo modo digna, utque ex Casina Plauti depromantur exempla:

'Dum gladium quaero, ne habeat, arripio capulum.
Sed cum cogito, non habuit gladium, nam esset frigidus.'
'Eloquere.' 'At pudet.' 'Num radix fuit?' 'Non fuit.' 'Num cucumis?'
'Profecto hercle non fuit quicquam holerum,
nisi, quicquid erat, calamitas profecto attigerat nunquam.
Ita, quidquid erat, grande erat.'

Singula dicta rus olent et in ore villici et in ore item matronae, quae et ipsa rusticabatur iocandi gratia.

2 At quod sequitur non caret illiberalitate:

: 5 :

*The class of joking is threefold.*

I hold then that the class of joking in gatherings and assemblies of 1
this kind is threefold. One is servile and altogether degenerate, like
the jokes of slaves and the repartee befitting that sort of men, such
as "Hello, you exercise-ground for the whip," "What are you saying, you filthy screw?," "Hey, you chain-farmer," "Hey, you whip-
lover."[7] And "You're not leading me where stone grinds stone, are
you? Where dead oxen attack living men?"[8] And "How wretched
is the man who loves! — But surely, by Hercules, the man who
hangs is much more wretched."[9] And "A night with you and a jar
of wine."[10] Greek and Latin comedies are full of these witticisms.
Another class obtains among rustics and men not versed in urban
manners, since in one place there is a certain rudeness and inept-
ness in their jokes and funny remarks, in another a vulgarity completely unbecoming a free man. To take examples from Plautus'
*Casina*:

> "While I'm checking that she doesn't have a sword, I get
> hold of a hilt. But when I think about it, it's not a sword she
> has, that would have been cold." "Speak, out with it!" "But
> I'm ashamed." "Was it a radish?" "It wasn't." "A cucumber?"
> "By Hercules it wasn't any vegetable except that, whatever it
> was, I'm sure no blight had ever touched it. Whatever it was,
> it was so huge."[11]

Each expression smells of the country, both in the mouth of the
steward and likewise in the mouth of the matron, who also talks
like a rustic for the sake of humor.

And what follows is not without vulgarity: 2

Illa haud verbum facit et saepit veste id qui estis.
Ubi illum saltum video opsaeptum, rogo ut alterum sinat
adire.

Quod dictum, quamvis illiberale, haud tamen illiberaliter expressum sed verbis quidem suis ac rusticanis. Quale etiam et illud, 'Fundum alienum arat; familiarem incultum deserit.' Tertio autem generi liberalitas inest ac suavitas illa, honestae iucunditatis comes, tantumque ab rusticitate remota quantum rusticanis a moribus urbani absunt, tantumque ab servilitate aliena quantum ab ingenuitate atque a libertate servitus. Et huiusmodi quidem ioci materia sunt in qua tum facetudo versatur ut genus tum ut species eiusdem: festivitas, lepos, comitas, urbanitas, cuique ab affandi suavitate nomen est affabilitati.

: 6 :

*In iocando adhibendum esse delectum.*

1 Ipsa autem ioca nimirum alia senum sunt, alia iuvenum, alia eorum qui magistratum gerunt pretioque dignam personam, alia privatorum; habentque haec ipsa, ut fructus pomaque, sua quoque tempora, sua etiam loca; nec carent auditorum consideratione ac considentium: nequaquam enim omnia omni aut tempore aut loco
2 aut quacunque in audientia ac consessu decent. Itaque non digna solum esse debent dictu verum etiam auditu, quaeque neutique aut ridiculum faciant dicentem aut contemptibilem aut quae molestia afficiant auditorem, cum ex iocis relaxatio quaeratur, minime

She didn't speak a word and covered with her clothes that thing by which you are [a woman]. When I saw that that path was closed up, I asked her to allow me to enter the other.[12]

This expression, although vulgar, nevertheless is not expressed in a vulgar way but in fact with appropriate, rustic words. The following is also of that sort: "He plows another's farm; he leaves his family's uncultivated."[13] There is in the third class, however, courtesy and pleasantness, the companion of honorable delight, as far from rusticity as the urbane are from rustic manners and as alien to servility as slavery to good birth and liberty. And indeed jokes of this kind are the material in which wittiness is involved both as a class and as its species: mirth, charm, affability, urbanity, and friendliness [*affabilitati*],which takes its name from pleasantness in speaking [*affandi*].

## : 6 :

### *Discrimination must be used in joking.*

There is no doubt, moreover, that the jokes of old men are of one kind, those of young men another; those of men who hold magistracies or who represent something of value are of one kind, those of private men another; they also have, like crops and fruits, their own times and places. Nor will jokes overlook consideration of those listening and assembling, for no joke suits every time, place, audience, or assembly. And so jokes should be fit not only to be spoken but also to be heard, and by no means should they either make the speaker ridiculous or contemptible or inflict annoyance on the listener, since relaxation is sought from jokes but not

vero taedium aut molestia, siquidem ipsis in consessionibus ac
circulis hominumque congregatione quae ad recreationem animorum familiaremque ad affabilitatem sit et loqui consessores ipsos
usu venit et audire per vices quasi quasdam. Is igitur a dicente
delectus iocorum dictorumque habendus est ut et suam tueatur et
astantium personam, nec non et aetatis et temporis et loci et rerum ipsarum ipsiusque civilitatis.

3    In primis vero honesti decorique ratio habeatur ut, quod in
epulis exigitur, nec insulsa sint ioca nec nimis salsa, quaeque nec
ieiuna sint ac macrescentia neque crassa nimis stomachoque prorsus ingrata, nanque ut ea conviciis careant ac maledicentia abhor-
reantque ab invehendo, hoc quoque civilibus et legibus et institutis
cautum est vindicaturque nunc suppliciis nunc mulcta. Quod quid
est aliud quam abuti velle iocis? Qui cum inventi sint ad refocillationem, eos quis, obsecro, convertat, nisi rixator quispiam, ad odia,
4    simultates, contentiones ac tumultus? Quae quidem ipsa et tenenda et sequenda sunt faceto, perinde ut recta dictat ratio eius-
que alumna prudentia, ut et quid et quantum decet, et quomodo,
et quo tempore, quoque item loco, et apud quos, quaeque item alia
delectum comitantur ad hamussim, ut dici solet, cuncta perpendat
dirigatque ad normam.

∶ 7 ∶

*De altero extremo, id est rusticitate.*

1    His itaque explicatis, primo de iis dicendum videtur quae in
defectu versantur, quem habitum rerum scriptores moralium

disgust and annoyance, seeing that in assemblies, circles, and con-
gregations of men that aim at recreation of mind and congeniality,
the practice is for those assembled to speak and listen by turns.
Therefore the speaker must use this discrimination in jokes and
witticisms so that he may preserve his role and that of those present, and also take account of age, time, place, the subjects themselves, and civility itself.

But first of all one must take account of what is respectable and 3
decorous so that, as is required at feasts, the jokes are neither insipid nor too pungent, and they aren't dry and lean, or too heavy
and completely unpleasing to the stomach. For that they be without insults and abuse and avoid invective has also been decreed by
civil laws and regulations, and such things are punished now by
penalties, now by fines. What is the latter if not an intention to
abuse jokes? Since jokes were invented for recreation, who on
earth would ever use them to incite hatred, enmity, contention,
and tumult except a quarrelsome person? The witty man ought to 4
hold and follow these things just as right reason and her pupil,
prudence, dictate so that he may weigh and direct everything according to the norm: what is fitting and how much, in what way,
at what time, likewise at what place, with whom, and likewise
other things which go along with discrimination, precisely according to rule, as they say.

: 7 :

*On the other extreme, that is, rusticity.*

After the foregoing explanations, it now seems necessary to speak 1
first about those things involved with the deficiency [of wit].
Writers on morality were pleased to call this disposition rusticity,

rusticitatem libenter appellavere, neque improprie sane neque inconsiderate, cum teneritas ipsa iocandi civilis admodum res sit; contra rusticorum hominum sive rigiditas sive iocandi fuga atque horror inhumanus ille quidem ab omnique iucunditate aversus.

2 Nam et homo ad risum sponte sua instinctus est atque ad iocum refocillationis gratia, perinde atque agendi gratia ad severitatem et laborem. Neque enim a philosophantibus non et apte et secundum naturam homo risibile animal est dictus, quemadmodum et equus

3 hinnibile, mugibile autem bos. Ad haec quota laborum est suscep-tio quae non et quietem respectet et, antequam ad exitum, qui ipse finis quidam est, pervenerit, et recreationem desideret et intermis-sionem quandam, per quam post ad laborem ipsum susceptumque ad opus resurgat robustior novatorque quasi quidam coeptam iam resumat actionem?

: 8 :

*Agrestitatem potius quam rusticitatem opponendam esse facetudini.*

1 Sed nesciam quomodo rusticitas vim ipsam parum omnino implet eaque convenientius urbanitati opponitur, quae species quaedam est, quam facetudini, quae genus ipsum repraesentat; ipsaque rus-ticitas in iocis versari potius rusticanis videtur, perinde ut in urba-

2 nis urbanitas, quam ut facetiei sit opponenda. Neminem tamen ab opinione sua suaque a sententia deterremus, dum tamen aequo patiatur animo facetudini nos agrestitudinem opponere ac faceto agrestem, id quod Aristotelicum fortasse verbum magis innuit et Horatius e nostris cum ait, 'rusticitas agrestis et inconcinna gra-visque.' Ad rusticitatem enim addidit et agrestem et inconcinnam

and the word is surely proper and well-considered, since the delicacy of jokes is very much a matter of civility. On the contrary, the roughness of the rustics' joking or their avoidance of it and their brutish severity are opposed to all delight. For man is naturally 2 impelled to laughter and joking for the sake of recreation, just as he is to seriousness and labor for the sake of action. Indeed philosophers have aptly and naturally called man an animal capable of laughter, as they have called the horse the animal capable of neighing and the cow the animal capable of mooing.[14] In addition, how 3 few are the labors we undertake that do not look toward repose and, before they reach their end, which is itself a certain goal, do not need refreshment and some respite thanks to which we rise up again stronger to our labors and to the task undertaken and, renewed, resume an action already begun?

: 8 :

*Agresticity rather than rusticity should be opposed to wittiness.*[15]

But somehow rusticity does not completely express the sense and 1 is more appropriately opposed to urbanity, which is a species, than to wittiness, which represents the class itself. The essence of rusticity seems rather to be concerned with rustic jokes, just as urbanity is concerned with urbane ones, than it is to be opposed to wittiness. Nevertheless, I do not discourage anyone from his opinion 2 and judgment, provided that he does not mind my opposing agresticity to wittiness and the agrestic to the witty man. Aristotle's word perhaps signifies this better and Horace among our Latin writers when he says, "an agrestic rusticity, awkward and oppressive."[16] For to rusticity he added agrestic, awkward, and

et gravem ut, agrestem dicens, rigiditatis vim rusticitati adiungeret
et, incultam ac gravem agrestitudinem vocans, declararet qualis
ipsa esset.

3    Itaque ut a forti fortitudo est deducta, sic, ab agresti agrestitudinem deducentes, hanc ipsam facetudini opponemus, qua ratione
id efficitur ut *agrestitudo* ipsa et rustica sit admodum et inconcinna
perque quam gravis ac molesta, perinde ut e regione facetudo est
urbana admodum et undique concinnata eademque perquam
suavis et grata. Quis enim inficias eat rura qui inhabitent et colant
4    rusticos appellandos, perinde ut qui urbem incolant, urbanos? At
agri cum a cultu humano plerumque propter finium vastitatem
squalescant magisque a feris frequententur quam ab hominibus,
inde agrestitas ipsa feris similior quam hominibus, et feras res
Graeci 'agrias' vocant. Quocirca agrestitudinem, vel si fortasse magis te agrestitas delectaverit, extremum alterum facetudinis esse
volumus.


: 9 :

*De agresti et agrestitudine.*


1    Agrestis autem proprium est viri, tum abhorrere a dicendis facetiis
atque a iocando, tum etiam ab audiendis quae cum iucunditate
dicantur. Quam ob rem huiusmodi hominum consuetudines difficiles sunt et parum gratae vitaque eorum tristior nec omnino so-
ciabilis, ut videantur cum natura ipsa parum consentire, quae, ut
somnum dedit animalibus ad recreationem sensuum omnium, sic
tribuit homini et locutionem, non ad utilitatem modo conciliatio-
nis atque ad eam conservandam verum etiam ad recreationem laborum ac molestiarum, quae plurimae contingunt in vita agenda
atque in gerendis rebus.

oppressive, so that by saying agrestic he could join the sense of rigidity to rusticity and, by calling agresticity uncultivated and oppressive, he could declare what its quality is.

And as *strength* is derived from *strong*, so by deriving *agresticity*    3
from *agrestic*, I will oppose it to wittiness. Thus it transpires that the essence of agresticity is to be exceedingly rustic, awkward, solemn and troublesome, just as wittiness, on the contrary, is consummately urbane, neat, and likewise very pleasant and agreeable. For who would deny that those who inhabit and dwell in the country must be called rustics, just as those who dwell in the city, urbane? But when the fields lie barren, uncultivated by men mostly    4
on account of the devastation of the territory, and are more frequented by wild beasts than men, then this agresticity is more similar to wild beasts than men. And the Greeks call wild things *agrios*. For this reason I define *agrestitudo*, or perhaps *agrestitas* if that pleases you more, as the other extreme of wittiness.

∶ 9 ∶

*On the agrestic and agresticity.*

Moreover, it is characteristic of the agrestic to shrink both from    1
witticisms and from joking and also from hearing things which are delightfully said. So intercourse with men of this sort is difficult and disagreeable, and their lifestyle is rather grim and not at all sociable so that they appear not to accord with nature itself, which, as it gave sleep to animals for the restoration of all the senses, so it also endowed man with speech not only for the utility of gaining and preserving favor but also for recreation from labors and troubles, which happen in great number in living and conducting business.

2      Est autem agrestitatis ipsius comes ruditas quaedam incivilis ac
male accepta, nec minus et morositas. Eiusmodi enim homines
non modo circa iocos et dicta verum etiam circa consuetudines ac
facta difficiles sunt parumque omnino accommodantes aliis aut
indulgentes: duri ipsi quidem, acerbi, inconditi, atque ab omni
genere urbanitatis alieni, ut ex omni fere vitae parte agrestes sint
iudicandi. Qui siquando in dictum prorumpant aliquod — homines enim sunt quibus natura nec risum negavit nec iocum,
tametsi hac in parte manci prorsus sunt ac deficientes —, eorum
tamen dicta aut rusticana quidem erunt, incondita, rudia, aut
maledica, conviciosa et tanquam a morositate profecta, quaeque
aut lacessant aut mordicent aut ita sordescant, ut risui habeantur
atque contemptui.

: 10 :

*De fatuis, insulsis et inconditis.*[2]

1  Horum quoque sunt e numero qui tum fatui dicuntur tum insulsi,
quorum quidem dicta non modo salem non habeant verum in eo
deficiant, ut risum nullo modo pariant, quem ubi forte pepererint,
id accidet non e dicendi suavitate verum ab insulsitate potius ipsa
2  quae ridiculos illos reddat ac despicabiles. Insulsi autem ac fatui
pene iidem sunt; differunt tamen quod insulsorum sale quidem
ioci careant, cum salsi tamen ipsi esse cupiant; fatuis vero natura
ab ipsa parum concessum sit id ipsum assequi posse, perinde ut
holeribus quibusdam quibus negatum est condimentum accipere,
quod quamvis non nunquam accipiant, nihilominus incondita tunc
quoque appareant, unde et iidem inconditi dicuntur, quando incondita atque insulsa absque sapore sunt.

A certain uncivil and unwelcome rudeness, as well as morose- 2
ness, is the companion of this agresticity. For men of this sort are
tiresome not only in jokes and witticisms but also in their intercourse and acts, and they are not at all accommodating to others
or indulgent. Indeed, they are hard, bitter, uncouth, and averse to
every kind of urbanity so that they are to be judged agrestic in almost every part of life. If ever they burst out with some witticism—for they are men and nature has not denied laughter or
joking to them, although they are very imperfect and deficient in
this department—, nevertheless their funny remarks will be rustic,
uncouth, rude, or abusive, hurtful and as though proceeding from
peevishness; and they will irritate, sting, or be so sordid that they
will be held in laughter and contempt.

: 10 :

*On the fatuous, insipid, and unseasoned.*

Both those men who are called fatuous and those called insipid are 1
also included in this group. Indeed, their witticisms not only have
no wit but also fail to produce laughter in any way. If by chance
they do produce it, this happens not from any pleasantness of
speech but rather from an insipidity that makes them ridiculous
and despicable. Moreover, the insipid and the fatuous are almost 2
the same. Yet they differ in that the jokes of the insipid lack wit,
although they themselves want to be witty, but nature has not allowed the fatuous to be able to strive for that, just as it has been
denied to certain vegetables to be seasoned. Although sometimes
they are seasoned, they still seem unseasoned afterward. Just so
these men are also called unseasoned, since things unseasoned and
insipid are tasteless.

: 11 :

## De ineptis.[3]

1  His adiungas licet etiam ineptos quosdam, quorum tamen dicta forsan ipsa per se delectarent, sunt tamen parum apte inconcinniterque aut sine delectu pronuntiata. Sed inepti nomen ad multa ac diversa pertinet, nam et risus et gestus et vestitus ineptus dicitur,
2  nedum ut ineptus aut sermo dicatur aut iocus. Hi autem ipsi, quod neque in dicendo neque in iocando aut tempus aut locum aut dignitatem servant suam, inepti inde vocati; ex eo etiam inepti pictores, poetae item inepti, qui dignitatem minime suam retineant in pingendo ac describendo. Itaque ineptitudo neutique dictorum est ac iocorum tantum verum ad plura refertur ac diversa.
3  Quo fit ut, in utendis quoque iocis ridicularibusque, qui a dignitate discedunt ac persona ipsoque ab decoro ac tum a rerum ac temporum tum vero a locorum atque audientium delectu observationeque, et ipsi inepti dicantur: quid enim vetat rem eandem alias ob causas aliam atque aliam habere rationem?

: 12 :

## De trivialitate.

1  Nam neque ruditas solum in hoc versatur vitio neque tantum rigiditas, fatuitas insulsitasque sed trivialitas quoque quaedam, eaque non in ridicularibus modo verum etiam in seriis ac gravibus rebus. Existit autem trivialitas circa popularia, et pervulgata quaedam

## : 11 :

## *On the inept.*

To these you might also add certain inept persons. Although some [1]
of their witticisms might perhaps please in and of themselves, yet
they are pronounced inappropriately and awkwardly or without
discrimination. But the word *inept* applies to many different things,
for laughter, gesture, and clothing are called inept, not to mention
conversations and jokes that may be called inept. Moreover, these [2]
men have been called inept because, both in speaking and joking,
they do not observe the time, the place, or their own dignity.[17]
Hence painters and likewise poets who lose all dignity in painting
and writing are also called inept. And so ineptitude is by no means
only a matter of funny sayings and jokes but also refers to many
different things. So it happens that, also in using jokes and jests, [3]
those men are called inept who depart from their rank, their
proper role, and decorum itself and do not discriminate and respect their subjects, times, places, and hearers. For why shouldn't
the same thing have a different rationale in different circumstances?

## : 12 :

## *On triviality.*

Now crudeness is not only involved in this vice, nor only rigidity, [1]
fatuity, and insipidity, but also a certain triviality, and not only in
jests but also in serious and grave matters. There is, however, a
certain very common, and also sordid, triviality that has to do

eaque etiam sordida. Itaque et apud doctos homines et versatos inter urbis atque aulae mores ridiculo, qui eiusmodi sunt, habentur ac despicatui. Sunt enim eorum dicta non modo frigida sententiaeque pene aniles verum etiam rancentes et, pene dixerim,

2   marcidae. Sunt ex his quoque qui, dum iocari student, ruptare eos verba potius dicas foetereque illorum dicta ac confabulationes — quod tamen vitium nunc ad rusticitatem quidem referre possis nunc vero ad scurrilitatem.

3       Sed scurrae id ipsum et quaeritant et affectant, ut videmus histriones in comoediis; labuntur enim volentes ad excessum, cum rustici quandoque studeant ipsi quidem velle iocari verum ita in hoc deficiunt, ut ruptare eos dicas magis quam iocare; habent tamen et hi aliquando auditores sui studiosos. Quocirca Horatius propter tempora, ut arbitror, et aulam illam Augusti ridet quaedam apud Plautum quae frigida tunc haberentur forsan et ruptatilia. Sed nos, dum vitia defectusque hac in parte diligentius exquirimus, nimii fortasse sumus. Quocirca qualis hic ipse habitus sit, quales qui eo sint praediti hactenus explicatum sit. Hinc ad diversum et huic contrarium vitium, quod de excessu profluit, transeamus.

: 13 :

*De altero extremo, hoc est scurrilitate.*

1   Scurrilitatem eam maiores nostri, ut dictum est, vocavere et, qui ita sit affectus, scurram; atque hic quidem nequaquam accusandus videatur, quia delectare dictis suis ac iocis consessores studeat et tanquam recreare a curis ac solicitudinibus verum ex eo quod nec

with popular things. And so men of this sort are held in ridicule and contempt by those who are learned and versed in the affairs of city and court. For their witticisms are not only feeble and their opinions almost old womanish but also rancid and, I might almost say, rotten. There are also some of them who, while they are eager 2 to joke, belch out their words instead, you might say, and their witticisms and stories have a foul smell. Yet you might attribute this vice now to rusticity, now to buffoonery.

But buffoons both seek and strive for the same thing we see the 3 actors in comedies doing. For they willingly slip into excess, while rustics sometimes strive to wish to make jokes themselves but are so deficient in this that you might say they belch rather than joke. Nevertheless, even these men sometimes have listeners devoted to them. For this reason Horace, on account of the times, I think, and that famous court of Augustus, laughs at some things in Plautus that were perhaps considered at that time feeble and belchable.[18] But when I investigate vices and defects in this department with great care, I am perhaps being excessive. So this is a sufficient explanation of what this quality is and what kind of men are endowed with it. After this let me proceed to a different vice, contrary to this one, that issues from the excess.

: 13 :

*On the other extreme, that is, buffoonery.*

This extreme, as has been said, our ancestors called buffoonery 1 and the person so inclined, a buffoon. And it appears that this person should by no means be blamed because he endeavors to delight his companions with witticisms and jokes and, as it were, to restore them from cares and anxieties but because he retains no

modum in iis retinet nec mensuram; dumque iocari queat ac risum movere, hinc honestatis modestiaeque digreditur e via, illinc
vellicat astantes ac molestia afficit et perturbat potius quam delectet aut recreet, ut finis eius nequaquam sit refocillare facetiis ac
iucundis dictis sed quovis modo risum movere; dumque delectet,
2 parum omnino curat alios lacessere ac suggillare. Itaque facetudinis e curriculo digressus ac decori ipsius delectusque, de quo paulo
est ante dictum, oblitus, delabitur ad oscenitatem, dicacitatem,
spurcitiam. Siquidem scurrarum ipsorum non una est species, de
quibus singillatim ordineque dicemus suo.

3     Cum enim ipsi a iocandi ac dicendi excessu rapiantur, huic uni
tantum student; et alii quidem, relicta prorsus mediocritate, decorique ipsius ac temporis locique et item personae immemores id
tantum quaerunt, ut et videantur et iudicentur faceti, in quo, ut
dixi, nihil omnino pensi habentes, vanitate quadam ducti, nomen
vix ipsi suum ac certum habent; alii qui videri velint tum oblectare
tum etiam vellicare ac mordicus petere, sive ultioni studentes sive
ut maledicant molestiamque ingenerent, cum natura sint ab ipsa
incommodantes, sive ut inde timeantur lucrumque ex eo referant,
et hi quidem dicaces vitiumque ipsum dicacitas; alii vero qui nequaquam molesti videri aut mordaces velint, nec quo oblectent per
se, verum, dum placent, fructum ut inde aliquem referant hique
arrisores appellari fortasse possunt, cum vultu quam verbis ut placeant magis dent operam, vitium autem ipsum arrisio; alii contra,
his ut displiceant, illis ut placeant, aliis ut gratificentur, alios ut
derideant summo contendunt studio, hique derisores, et habitus
ipse derisio iure suo vocabitur.

restraint and measure in them. Provided that he can joke and move to laughter, he sometimes strays from the path of honor and modesty, while at other times he taunts, bothers, and disturbs the bystanders rather than delighting or restoring them, so that his goal is not at all to revive with witticisms and pleasant talk but to raise a laugh by any means possible. Provided that he can amuse, he doesn't care at all about irritating and mistreating others. And so departing from the course of wittiness and forgetting decorum and discrimination, which has been discussed a little earlier, he slips into obscenity, raillery, and filth. Since in fact there is more than one species of buffoon, I will speak about them individually and in turn.

For since they are carried away by an excess of joking and speaking, they strive only for this one thing. Some indeed, completely abandoning the mean, disregarding decorum itself, time, place, and also their own position, seek only to appear and to be judged witty; this type of character, as I've said, unscrupulous and motivated by vanity, has hardly any fixed and proper name. There are others who wish to appear both to delight and also to irritate and attack with their teeth, either because they are seeking to avenge themselves or to revile and to produce annoyance, since they are natural troublemakers; or because they want to be feared or to obtain some profit from their acts, and these men are railers and the vice itself, raillery. There are others who have no intention of seeming annoying or mordant nor of providing amusement for its own sake but provide pleasure in order to obtain some gain from it, and they perhaps may be called fawners, since they work harder to please with their face than their words, but the vice itself may be called fawning. On the other hand, others strive with the greatest eagerness to displease some and please others, to gratify some and deride others, and they will rightly be called deriders, and the quality itself, derision.

Sunt quibus curae sit oscenitas, hoc est dicta parum modesta eaque nec verecunda nec proba quaeque impudentiam prae se ferant et a modestis auditoribus non sine rubore audiantur oculorumque demissione, cum verba ipsa sint oscena ac res ipsae saepenumero osceniores—quod vitium ab Oscis, id est antiquisissimis Campaniae populis, manasse volunt, unde hodie quoque vindemiarum temporibus hoc ipsum vitium ipsaque oscenitas regnare apud Campanos videtur. Quosdam non tantum oscena verum etiam spurca capiunt estque eorum studium spurcari, hoc est impuris et iocis et dictis diffluere, ut non iucunditas eos moveat sed turpitudo potius ipsa, tum rerum tum verborum intemperata ac deformis explicatio; ipsi spurci vocati vitiumque ipsum spurcitia.

4

His accedunt maligni quidam, naturaque etiam ab ipsa ad maledicendum proclives, ad detrahendumque habitu atque exercitatione confirmati, quorum dicta non pungant modo verum et urant et pustulas inducant atque carcinomata nec careant aut veneno aut aperta petulantia morsibusque viperinis. Videbuntur autem hi ipsi duplici fortasse appellatione usurpandi: alterique petulantes, alteri vero ampullosi, ut petulantes magis declinent ad oscenitatem atque intemperantiam, ampullosi ad maledicentiam ac detractionem, quorum dicta vetusti ampullas nominarunt. Erit autem alterius habitus petulantia, alterius nomen ampullositas, utrumque a natura ipsa rei ductum.

5

6

Haec autem fere scurrarum videntur esse genera, quorum deformatissimi quidem sunt qui apud principum mensas inque dominantium aulis versantur, non modo rei familiaris ampliandae gratia, quod tolerabilius quidem videatur, verum ut ventri satisfaciant atque ebrietati; hique facile quidem in omnem turpitudinem

7

There are those to whom obscenity is dear, that is, they are immodest in their language, neither restrained nor honorable, and
this irreverent and wicked talk puts their shamelessness on show
and is heard by modest listeners not without blushing and casting
down of eyes, since the words themselves are obscene and the
things themselves often more obscene. It is thought that this vice
emanates from the Oscans, that is, from the most ancient peoples
in Campania, so even today at vintage time this vice and obscenity
are seen to reign among the Campanians.[19] Some people are capti-   4
vated not only by obscene but also by filthy things, and they endeavor to become filthy, that is, to put out a stream of dirty jokes
and witticisms, so that delight does not motivate them but rather
baseness and the unrestrained, foul expression now of subjects,
now of words. These men have been called filthy and the vice itself, filth.

To these one can add certain malignant men, inclined to speak-   5
ing ill even by nature itself, and confirmed in this by their character and practice of detraction. Their witticisms not only sting but
also burn and cause blisters and ulcers and do not lack poison,
undisguised impudence, and viperish bites. Moreover, it will ap-   6
pear perhaps that these men ought to be called with a dual appellation: some impudent but others bombastic; as the impudent fall
more into obscenity and intemperance, the bombastic tend toward
speaking ill and detraction, and the ancients called their talk bombast. Moreover, the quality of the former is impudence, the name
of the latter, bombast, each derived from the nature of the thing.

These then appear to be most of the classes of buffoon. The   7
foulest of them are the ones who resort to the tables of princes
and the halls of rulers, not only to increase their property, which
might seem more tolerable, but to satisfy their belly and drunkenness. And they may quite easily slide into baseness in pursuit of

dilabantur gulae ac ventris studio; Graeco nomine nunc 'parasiti'
vocati nunc 'sicophantae,' vitium ipsum 'parasitatio' ac 'sicophantia.'

: 14 :

*Longius distare a medio agrestem quam scurram.*

1 Abest autem agrestis a mediocritate multo quidem quam scurra
longius, quod huic modus tantum deest ac mensura, illa quidem
quae mediocritatem gignit, quam ubi sectari voluerit atque ad illam regredi, facile ipse quidem facetus erit. At agrestis ex omni
profecto parte adeo deficiens est ut nullo pacto accedere ad mediocritatem queat aut illam assequi, quippe cui omnia simul de-
2 sint. Inter haec igitur vitia virtus ipsa de qua loquimur sic constituta est ut alterum illum qui agrestis dicitur ab se repellat tanquam
fugientem a medio quique revocari ad illud aut nullo modo possit
aut sit omnino difficillimum, alterum vero ut scurram, oscenum,
spurcum ad se se revocet perinde ut longius a signis digressum
ipsaque ab mediocritate, quam circa virtutem quidem omnem versari moralem, vel mediocritatem ipsam potius virtutem esse, satis
inter omnes constat qui recte quidem philosophati sunt.

filling their throats and bellies. In Greek they are sometimes called "parasites," sometimes "sycophants," and the vice itself, "parasitism" and "sycophancy."[20]

: 14 :

*The agrestic is further from the mean than the buffoon.*

The agrestic, however, is much further from the mean than the 1 buffoon because the latter only lacks moderation and measure— that which produces the mean—and when he wants to follow and return to it, it will be easy for him to be witty. But the agrestic is so deficient in absolutely every respect that he can in no way approach the mean or reach it, seeing that he lacks everything at the same time. So this virtue I am talking about has been so estab- 2 lished between these vices that it thrusts from itself the one called agrestic as if he is fleeing the mean and can in no way or only with the greatest difficulty be called back to it, but does call back to itself the other, the buffoon, the obscene man, the filthy man, like one who has strayed too far from the battle standards and from the mean itself. Indeed, that every moral virtue has to do with the mean, or rather that the mean itself is a virtue, is quite agreed upon by all who have correctly studied philosophy.

: 15 :

## De facetis.[4]

1 Est igitur faceti hominis proprium in dictis factisque, in seriis ac iocis, in dicendo atque audiendo quae ad recreationem spectent animorumque relaxationem, in convictibus consessionibusque atque in congressibus ipsisque in circulis atque hominum coronis collocutionibusque, mediocritatem sequi; e qua id assequitur ut facetus ipse iure suo et sit et habeatur eoque se se vestiat habitu quam facetudinem vocari dicimus; quo de habitu ipse sibi nomen desumat, ut qui sub Caesare, sive eques sive pedes, militarit, miles dictus est Caesarianus, qui sub Pompeio Pompeianus aut sub Ma-
2 rio Sylla ve sive Marianus sive Syllanus. Habitus enim ipse ipsaque insignia militem quidem ostendunt, cuius videlicet sit factionis, in agendo vero actiones ipsae civilem atque urbanum hominem; nam et ioculatio et dictorum familiaris iucundaque invicem usurpatio actiones quidem sunt, moresque et ipsae nostros determinant, ut a facetis dictis iocisque suavioribus dicamur faceti, a scurrilibus scurrae, ab agrestibus agrestes, perinde ut a nimio pecuniae studio atque habendi cupiditate avari, ab usu mediocri et recto liberales, ab diffluentia vero ac dissipatione diffluentes atque effusi.

3 Facetorum igitur hominum ea est mediocritas ut delectum, de quo diximus, cum primis servent. Servabunt autem illum, si personae propriae auditorumque loci item ac temporis dignitatem retinuerint, ut neque in dicendo iocandoque procaces fuerint, petulantes, immodici, intempestivi, osceni, spurci, ampullosi neque in audiendo aut detestabuntur iucunde ac concinne dicta aut aures avertent a lepide atque urbane pronuntiatis, utque, dum

: 15 :

## On the witty.

Thus it is characteristic of the witty man to follow the mean in his     1
witticisms and actions, in serious things and in jokes, in saying
and listening to what concerns the restoration and relaxation of
mind, in banquets and sitting together, in gatherings, companies,
assemblies, and colloquies of men. From this it follows that he
rightly both is and is considered a witty man and clothes himself
with the habit which I say is called wittiness. He takes his name
from this habit, as one who fought under Caesar, whether cavalry-
man or infantryman, was called a Caesarean soldier, one under
Pompey a Pompeian, or under Marius or Sulla, either a Marian or
a Sullan. For the habit and insignia reveal the soldier, namely     2
which faction he belongs to, but in acting the actions themselves
reveal the civil and urbane man. For both joking and the familiar
and mutually pleasant use of witticisms are actions in the full
sense and they too determine our character, so that we are called
witty from our witty remarks and more pleasing jokes, buffoons
from buffoonish ones, and agrestic from agrestic ones, just as we
are called misers from an excessive eagerness for money and a desire to possess, liberal from a moderate and correct use, but lavish
and prodigal from lavishness and dissipation.

Therefore, the mean of witty men is such that they observe     3
above all the discrimination of which I have spoken. Moreover,
they will observe it if they retain the dignity of their own position
and that of their listeners, and likewise of time and place, so that
in speaking and joking they are not shameless, impudent, immodest, inopportune, obscene, filthy, and bombastic, and in listening they will not deprecate things said pleasantly and fitly or avert
their ears from ones delivered with charm and urbanity so that,

mediocritatem assequi ipsam nequeunt, ne rusticentur ne ve efficiantur insulsi, rancidi, hircosi, quorum etiam dicta culinam oleant.

:  16  :

*De dictorum iocorumque diversitate.*

1   Ipsa autem dicta ac ioca quae ad relaxationem pertinent, ut generaliter de iis loquamur, nequaquam uniusmodi quidem sunt, licet ad refocillationem curarum spectent ac requietem. Siquidem alia sponte sua atque ex tempore profluunt, alia tanquam provocata atque excita extrinsecus in responsionibus sunt posita, ut cum Cneus Pompeius salse aculeateque, sicuti ante diximus, interrogavit, 'Ubi gener est tuus, Cicero?,' non minus argute ac morsiculate
2   ab illo responsum est, 'Ubi et socer est, Pompei, tuus.' Eiusdem est generis responsum ab homine redditum viatore — nec agreste nec illepidum, salsum tamen. Cum enim, offenso pede ad lapidem, crus fregisset imploraretque opem a praetereuntibus respondissetque ex illis maior natu quispiam, 'Deus tibi ipse et opem et suppetias ferat,' tum ille subdit, 'Nec dei nec coelitum cuiuspiam e numero auxilium peto; hominis tantum hac praetereuntis peto.'
3       Utriusque autem generis diversae admodum sunt species, quippe cum dicta ipsa alia sub increpationis speciem risum moveant, quale Plautinum illud: 'Iste quidem gradus subcretus est cribro pollinario'; itemque 'Vicistis cocleam tarditudine'; alia quae e difficultate peragendae rei ac frustratione deliniant auditorem, quale illud: 'Himbrem in cribrum geras.' Aut quae ex annominatione, ut ' — Ecquid is homo scitus est?  — Plebiscitum non aeque est scitum,' et 'Hic equus non in arcem verum in arcam faciet impetum.'[5]

while they can not obtain the mean itself, they do not talk like rustics or make themselves insipid, rancid, or goatish, whose witticisms smell of the kitchen.

: 16 :

*On the diversity of witticisms and jokes.*

Moreover, witticisms and jokes related to relaxation, to speak about them in general, by no means are of one kind, although they concern rest and restoration from cares. If some flow forth of their own accord and on the spur of the moment, others, as if provoked and excited externally, are put into replies, as when Gnaeus Pompeius asked pungently and stingingly, as I said earlier, "Where is your son-in-law, Cicero?," the other replied not less cleverly and bitingly, "Right where your father-in-law is."[21] A reply given by a traveler is of the same kind — neither agrestic nor lacking in charm, yet pungent. For when he struck his foot against a stone, broke his leg, implored aid from the passersby, and one of them, an older man, replied, "May God himself bring you aid and succor," he replied in turn, "I'm not asking for help from God or anyone in heaven; I'm asking it only from a man passing by this place."

Moreover, the species of each class are very different, since in fact some witticisms move to laughter while appearing to rebuke, as in this line from Plautus: "This slow pace of yours has certainly been sifted by a flour sieve"; likewise "You've beaten the snail in slowness."[22] Others that charm the listener come from the difficulty and frustration of achieving something, like "You should carry water in a sieve."[23] Or those which come from paronomasia, like " — Is this man judicious? — A judgment of the people isn't nearly so clever,"[24] and "This horse will not attack a castle but a casket."[25]

4    Sunt quae ab probrositate pariant iucunditatem, quale hoc:

Noctu in vigiliam quando ibat miles, tum tu ibas simul,
conveniebat ne in vaginam tuam machaera militis?

Aut a cavillatione, ut

— Cistella hic mihi, adolescens, evolavit.
— In cavea latam oportuit.

Aut ab illusione, ut cum ille dixisset, 'Vox ad auris advolavit'; tum
alter, 'Nae, ego infelix fui qui non alas intervelli: volucrem vocem
gestito.' Interdum ex perplexitate verborum, ut 'Non ex uxore
natam uxoris filiam.' Alibi ex retorsione maledicti, ut ' — Ve tibi!
— Hoc testamento servitus legat tibi'; et retorsit maledictum et
testatorum usus est similitudine ac verbis. Et

— Eos asinos praedicas
vetulos, claudos, quibus subtritae ad foemina iam erant
ungulae?
— Ipsos, qui tibi subvectabant rure virgas ulmeas.

Nonunquam ex verborum novitate, ut

Quid istae quae vesti quotannis nomina inveniunt nova?
Tunicam rallam, tunicam spissam, linteolum caesicium,
indusiatam, patagiatam, calthulam aut croculam,
supparum aut subminiam, ricam, basilicum aut exoticum,
cunatile aut plumatile, cerinum aut gerrinum — gerrae
maxumae!
Cani quoque ademptum est nomen: vocant Laconicum.

There are some which produce delight from infamy, like    4

> when the soldier was going to his watch at night and you
> went at the same time, did the soldier's sword fit your
> sheath?[26]

Or from quibbling, like

> — Young man, a little box has flown away from me here.
> — You should have put it in a cage.[27]

Or from mockery, as when one man said, "A voice has flown to my
ears"; then the other, "Truly I was unlucky not to have clipped its
wings: I have a flying voice."[28] Sometimes from the ambiguity of
words, like "His wife's daughter, who wasn't born from his wife."[29]
At another time from twisting a curse back on itself, like " — Bad
luck to you! — That's what slavery bequeaths you in her will"; he
both retorted to the curse and used a comparison and the words of
testators.[30] And

> — You're speaking of those old, lame asses whose hooves
> have already been worn to the thighs? — Exactly, those same
> ones that brought you elm scourges from the country.[31]

Sometimes from the novelty of the words, like

> What about those women who invent new names every year
> for their clothes? The thin tunic, the thick tunic, the little
> white linen, the outer tunic, the bordered dress, the marigold
> or saffron, the undergarment or light vermilion, the head
> veil, the queenly or foreign dress, the sea-colored or the
> feathery, the waxen or nonsensical — the greatest nonsense!
> A name has also been taken from a dog: they call it Spar-
> tan.[32]

Iucundissima sane tum effictio nominum tum innovatio mulie-
brium vestimentorum, ex ore praesertim servi subdoli ac veterato-
ris. Aliquando ex cautione, ut 'Cave, sis, cum filia mea copulari
hanc . . . divertunt mores virginis longe a lupae.' Aut ex contemptu
atque aspernatione, ut

> — Haec negat tuam esse matrem. — Ne fuat,
> si non vult: equidem, hac invita, tamen ero matris filia.

: 17 :

## De locis unde ducuntur dicta
## ac facetiae.

1   Habent igitur ridicularia quaeque dicta vocantur ac facetiae locos
suos unde deducantur, quemadmodum et argumenta apud dialec-
ticos, in quibus ostendendis si aliquantum versabimur — nam ut
omnia colligamus esset profecto laboris magis affectati quam necessarii — videbitur fortasse non omnino alienum, praesertim cum
a maioribus nostris pars haec non fuerit omnino neglecta.

2       Puer Florentinus et argutus et perurbanus, adductus ante sacerdotem cardinalem iocandi gratia, multa cum facete admodum nec
minus etiam scite dixisset sacerdosque ipse, ad amicum qui astabat
conversus, susurrasset huiusmodi pueros consuesse, ubi ad aetatem pervenissent robustiorem, ingenio subcrassescere, 'Nae,' inquit,
'o bone cardinalis, puerulum te oportuit scitum fuisse admodum.'

An utterly pleasant confection of names as well as an innovation in women's clothing, especially from the mouth of a tricky and crafty slave. Sometimes from cautioning, like "Take care, please, that girl doesn't associate with my daughter . . . the character of a virgin differs greatly from that of a whore."[33] Or from contempt and disdain, like

—This woman says she isn't your mother. —Let her not be, if she doesn't want to; even against her will I'll still be my mother's daughter.[34]

: 17 :

*On the places from which witticisms and funny stories are drawn.*[35]

Therefore jests and those things called witticisms and funny sto- 1
ries have their own places from which they are drawn, just as arguments do among the dialecticians. If I shall concern myself for some time with revealing these things—for collecting all of them would certainly be more an affectation than a necessary labor—it will perhaps not seem entirely foreign to my theme, especially since this portion of the subject was not entirely neglected by our ancestors.[36]

A Florentine boy, both quick-witted and thoroughly urbane, 2
was brought before a cardinal priest to make jokes. After he had made many witty and clever remarks, the priest turned to a friend who was standing nearby and whispered that boys of this sort, when they had attained a lustier age, usually became thick-witted. "Yeah, cardinal," said the boy, "you must have been really clever as

Dictum itaque in se puer in sacerdotem retorsit magna cum auditorum hilaritate et risu.

3    Est apud Plautum dictum et salsum et bene argutum:

Prodigum te fuisse oportet olim in adulescentia,
quia senecta aetate mendicas malum.

Locus hic ipse quidem in ipsa rerum natura constitutus est, siquidem initio qui sunt prodigi, necesse est eos, effusa prodigenter pecunia, tandem egere.

4    Antonius Panhormita, suavis admodum vir, interrogatus ad rem uxoriam iucunde concorditerque agendam quibus nam maxime opus esse duceret, sumpto argumento a frequentia molestiarum ac magnitudine quae in vita contingerent coniugali, duobus tantum opus esse respondit: vir ut aurium surditate teneretur, uxor vero ut oculis esset capta, ne altera videlicet inspiceret quae a marito intemperanter fierent plurima, alter ne audiret obgannientem assiduo domi uxorem.

5    Nicolaus Porcinarius, praetor admodum severus, tris cum torsisset eadem de causa reos adductusque esset quartus ad funem, interrogavit, quo is esset nomine; respondit illico reus sibi nomen esse Sextodecimo. Demiratus Nicolaus raritatem cum esset nominis, subdidit ille, 'A re ipsa reique ipsius eventu nomen mihi hoc optingit, praetor; nam cum tres illi quaternatim, hoc est duodecies, funiculo ante me contorti sint, nimirum sextadecima mihi tortura sortito obvenit.' Quo quidem dicto delectatus ille a supplicio temperavit. Et facete et extemporaliter sumptus est iocandi locus ab enumeratione torturarum, quae posset et animum movere et iram temperare.

6    Puella et modesta et catula, cum ab muliere quadam iracunda atque annosa non solum amaris verum etiam impudentibus incesseretur dictis, 'Quando,' inquit, 'ut video, abundas annis, mulier,

a little boy."[37] Thus the boy turned this saying against himself back on the priest, to the great hilarity and laughter of the listeners.

There is a pungent and very acute witticism in Plautus:                     3

You must have been prodigal back in your youth because in your old age you are begging for trouble.[38]

This place is in fact rooted in the very nature of things, since it is inevitable that those who are prodigal at the beginning will in the end be in want, after extravagantly squandering their money.

When Antonio Panormita, a very pleasant man, was asked    4
what he considered necessary for a pleasant and harmonious marriage, taking for his theme the frequency and magnitude of the annoyances that occur in married life, replied that only two things were necessary: the husband must be deaf, but the wife must be blind, in other words so that she would not see the numerous out-of-control things done by her husband and that he would not hear her continuous snarling at home.[39]

After Niccolò Porcinari, a very severe judge, had tortured three    5
men accused of the same crime and the fourth had been brought to the rope, he asked what his name was.[40] The accused immediately replied his name was Sixteenth. Since Niccolò was astonished at the extraordinary name, he added, "This name falls to my lot from this affair and its outcome, judge. For since these three before me have been tortured by the rope four times, that is twelve times, clearly the sixteenth torture has been assigned to me by fate." Delighted by this witticism, the judge refrained from punishing him. The place for joking was wittily and spontaneously drawn from enumeration of the tortures, which was able both to move the mind and to mitigate anger.

A modest and shrewd girl, when attacked not only with bitter    6
but also shameless words by an angry old woman, said, "Since, as I see, you have lots of years, woman, and are short on decency, my

pudorisque egena es admodum, te hortor ut huiusce sumas aliquid alicunde mutuum.' Locus sumptus a consuetudine eorum qui, cum pecuniae egeant, illam sumunt mutuam.

7      Homuncio et dicaculus ipse quidem et coronis assuetus, ingressus domum, conspicatur uxorem amatori implexam, cuius ex humeris nudata cruscula pedes autem calceolati dependerent. Tum ille, 'O mea,' inquit, 'uxorcula, ut benefacis, ut rei familiari utiliter consulis! hac enim ratione toto anno ne par quidem calceolorum ipsa conteres, nullique rei futura est tibi necessaria sutoris opera.' Et huius quidem ioci sedes in utilitate collocata est.

8      Cossentinus, civis callidus admodum ac versutus, questus est apud equitum praefectum subreptam sibi noctu fuisse equam, quam clam quidem praefectus ipse surripi iussisset. Responsum est illi a praefecto atque imperatum, ut in ea conquirenda nihil omitteretur diligentiae et operae; coeterum, quo illa clam extra oppidum incognita alio traduceretur, et freno instrui et phaleris ornari splendidioribus eam iussit; quae cum paulum modo extra portam processisset coenosumque incidisset in locum, corruit resupinato corpore cognitaque est a domino, qui illic forte observabat. Is itaque comparatis statim subligaculis, quas, ni fallor, hodie bracas vocant, statim ad praefectum rediens: 'Ego,' inquit, 'heri et precatoris personam apud te et supplicis gessi, hodie vero et adiutor advenio et consiliarius. Ecca tibi subligacula, quibus uti posthac tuto poteris ad equas a furtis vindicandas sexumque obtegendum.' Dicti huius sedem constitutam esse in instrumento et ornatu parum idoneo, quis non videt praetoriaque in turpitudine?

9      Ludovicus, Galliae rex, Caroli eius pater qui paucis ante annis regnum Neapolitanum armis occupavit, filiam collocaverat Aureliensi Ludovico. Ea cum deformis esset ac parum venusta atque

advice is to take out a loan of decency from some place or other." The place was taken from the custom of those who borrow when they need money.

A little man, both quick-tongued and used to an audience, 7 came home and saw his wife embracing a lover, her legs hanging naked off his shoulders but with her shoes still on her feet. Then he said, "O my dear little wife, well done!, what a thoughtful use you are making of our property! At this rate, you won't wear out even one pair of shoes in a whole year and won't need to employ a cobbler at all." And the source of this joke was located in utility.[41]

A man from Cosenza, a very resourceful and clever citizen, 8 complained to a commander of cavalry that during the night someone had stolen his mare, which, in fact, the commander himself had secretly ordered to be stolen. The commander answered him and gave the order to spare no efforts in searching for her. But he also ordered her to be provided with a bridle and adorned with very splendid trappings so that she might secretly be conveyed elsewhere outside the city without being recognized [as a mare]. When she had gone only a little beyond the gate and come upon a muddy place, she tumbled, turning upside down, and was recognized by her owner, who by chance was watching there. And so immediately after obtaining breeches (which, unless I am mistaken, are today called "trousers") and returning at once to the commander, he said, "Yesterday I played the role of petitioner and suppliant before you, but today I come as a helper and counselor. Here are some breeches for you, which you may hereafter safely use to protect mares from theft and to hide their sex." Who does not see that the source of this witticism was based on inappropriate equipage and adornment, and on the infamy of the commander?

Louis, king of France, father of that Charles who a few years 9 ago occupied with arms the kingdom of Naples, gave his daughter in marriage to Louis of Orléans. When in the presence of her

patre coram forma eius a viro praeter modum commendaretur, sensit socer inesse generi verbis spicula, quae quo retunderet, ab obliquo gladii aciem obiecit et: 'Hoc,' inquit, 'laudibus istis adiice:[6] uxorem tuam pudicissimae esse matris filiam.' Erat enim constans opinio Aureliensis matrem parum pudice se se habuisse, quippe quae, priore viro mortuo, familiari eius nupsisset, quicum vivo illo se se immiscuerat.

10    Meis e tribulibus quispiam abunde comis, cum hospes vociferantem diutius uxorem eius rixantemque cum ancillis parum aeque[7] ferret, conversus ipse ad hospitem: 'Ecquae,' inquit, 'amice, impatientia est tua? Duos et triginta annos huius clamores diesque ac noctes aequissime[8] ipse perfero, tu vero ne dieculae quidem sextantem ferre eam potes?' Quo dicto et hospitem leniit et uxorem ab ira ad risum convertit. Quae iocandi occasio ab incusatione sumpta est atque ab exemplo.

11    Diverterat aliquando familiaris quidam meus, peregre iter faciens, ad meritoriam; apposita est ei coena omni e parte holitoria; vinum item dilutissimum, omnia demum administrata parcissime. Postquam autem coenavit, iussit vocari ad se medicum ad mercedem capiendam; igitur caupo cum respondisset, 'Ecquid, malum, in viculo maxime agresti medicum requiris,' ibi ille, 'Num ne, o bone, te te ipsum ignoras? Quo sit igitur merces operae suae par, medici pretium accipe, non cauponis, quando ut aegrotum me pavisti in coenula.' Ab irrisione et contemptu deductum est dictum. Eiusdem est generis quod subiicio.

12    Homo Hispanus, vasto admodum nedum procero corpore, praetereuntem nanulum irridebat; conversus itaque ad eum nanulus, percontatur quo ipse esset nomine. Cum respondisset Rodoricillo sibi nomen parentes fecisse, tum ore quam maxime prompto

father her beauty was praised beyond measure by her husband, since she was in fact ugly and not beautiful at all, the father-in-law felt his son-in-law's words were barbed. To blunt them he presented sideways the blade of the sword and said, "You can add this to those praises of yours: your wife is the daughter of a most chaste mother." For there was a settled belief that Orléans' mother had conducted herself unchastely, since, on the death of her former husband she married a servant of his with whom she had been involved while her husband was alive.[42]

One of my kinsmen, an exceedingly affable man, when a guest 10 of his took umbrage with his wife's screaming for a long time and quarreling with the maids, turned to his guest and said, "Look here, my friend, why this impatience? I have been calmly putting up with her shouting for thirty-two years, day and night, but you can't put up with her for even the sixth of one little day?" With this witticism he soothed his guest and turned his wife from anger to laughter. The occasion for joking was drawn from accusation and example.

Once a friend of mine, journeying abroad, put up at an inn. A 11 dinner completely of vegetables was set before him; the wine was very diluted; in short, everything was served very sparingly. After he had dined, he called for the doctor so he could receive his fee. So when the innkeeper replied, "Why the devil do you demand a doctor in such a little, rustic village?," he said, "My good man, can it be that you don't know what you are yourself? A fee should correspond to the work done. So accept the pay of a doctor, not an innkeeper, since you fed me with a tiny dinner as though I'm a sick man." The witticism was drawn from derision and contempt. What follows is of the same kind.

A Spaniard, very broad as well as tall, was mocking a little 12 dwarf who was passing by. So the little dwarf turned toward him and asked what his name was. After he replied that his parents had given him the name of Little Rodrigo, the dwarf replied

nanulus: 'Atqui,' inquit, 'parentes istos tuos maxime omnium men-
dicos fuisse oportet, qui, in tanta nominum copia, in te appelli-
tando tanta inopia laboraverint.'

13    Subdiderim et aliud non iniucundum ex eodem fonte. Diverterat ad meritoriam Pyrrhiniculus Vasco atque, apposita mensa,
anaticulum versabat in lancibus perbelle unctum atque halliatum.
Ingreditur repente ad illum viator Hispanus, iniectisque in anaticulum oculis: 'Potes,' inquit, 'o amice, advenientem comiter amicum accipere?' Ibi tum Pyrrhiniculus, quo nomine ipse esset,
exquirit. Audenter ille ac iactabundus: 'Alopantius,' inquit, 'Au-
simarchides Hiberoneus Alorchides.' 'Pape,' tum Pyrrhiniculus,
'quatuor ne avicula haec heroibus et quidem Hispanis? Absit iniuria: ea Pyrrhiniculo satis est uni; minutos enim decent minuta.'

14    Idem hic, de quo dixi, familiaris, aliquando peregre proficiscens,
in cubile incidit ab cimicibus simul plurimoque a pulice insessum.
Itaque ubi paulum modo quievisset, excitatus ab illorum aculeatis-
simis demorsiunculis, evocato caupone, petiit falcem sibi ab eo
afferri. Cum ille, quam ad rem opus ea esset, percontaretur, 'Qua,'
inquit, 'excidam senticetum, quod mihi nocte hac excidendum lo-
casti.' Sentes et spinas ad cimices transtulit ac pulices, cubile autem ad senticetum.

15    Alfonsus, Hispaniae citerioris itemque Neapolitanorum rex, ve-
nationi cum esset admodum deditus percontareturque Antonium
Panhormitam sciscitabundus, qui Neapoli essent nobiles viri
venandi studiosi, siqui item scriptores de natura canum aliquid
prodidissent: 'Nae, tu,' inquit, 'rex ad latus habes rerum harum
omnium prudentissimum virum, ne aliunde quaerites, quippe qui
annos supra quadraginta cum hoc genere animalium sit ita conver-
satus, ut noctis quoque ipsas cum canicula cubitaverit. Hic tibi et
canum naturas describet et illorum instituendorum artes.' (Erat
autem is eques Neapolitanus, quem honoris gratia ne nomina-
verim.) Cumque his dictis surrisisset Antonius, indicavit sub
caniculae nomine uxorem illius significari, mulierum omnium

instantly, "Anyhow, those parents of yours must have been the poorest people in the world, since, with such an abundance of names, in naming you they suffered from such poverty."

I will also add something delightful from the same source. Pirrinicole, a Gascon, had put up at an inn and, once the table had been set, was turning over a duckling, beautifully seasoned with oil and garlic. Suddenly a Spanish traveler advanced toward him, cast his eyes on the duckling,[43] and said, "Friend, can you kindly entertain a friend who is arriving?" Then Pirrinicole asked what his name was. The other boldly and boastingly said, "Alopanzio Ausimarchide Iberoneo Alorchide." Then Pirrinicole, "Wow! This little bird for four heroes, and Spaniards to boot? No offense, it's only enough for Pirrinicole, for little things suit little men."

Journeying abroad one time, the same friend I spoke of came upon a bed infested with bedbugs and many fleas. After he had rested for just a little while, he was awakened by their sharp little bites, called the innkeeper, and asked him to bring him a scythe. When the other asked what it was needed for, he said, "To cut down the thornbush which you arranged for me to cut down tonight." He used the brambles and thorns as a metaphor for the bedbugs and fleas and the bed for a thornbush.

When Alfonso, king of Hispania Citerior[44] and Naples, who was very devoted to hunting, questioned Antonio Panormita, asking which noble men at Naples were fond of hunting and also if any writers had published something on the nature of dogs, he said, "Truly, king, you have by your side a man most experienced in all these things, so you need not seek elsewhere, since for over forty years he has kept such company with this kind of animal that even at night he has slept with a little bitch. He will describe to you both the natures of dogs and the arts of training them." (This was a Neapolitan cavalier, whom I will not name for the sake of his honor.) And after Antonio had smiled at the words, he indicated that under the name of little bitch he meant the wife of

clamosissimam pariter ac rabiosissimam. Quod dictum et Alfonsum et qui circum stabant omnes maximum in risum extemporalitate ipsa provocavit, ut illic per iocum ac festivitatem enarrata fuerit historia coniugalis sive vitae sive captivitatis.[9]

16     Obversabatur ante oculos Ludovico Pontano, sui temporis iurisconsultorum praestantissimo, litigator mirifice importunus, cui et nasus esset simior et barba admodum promissa et hispida. Cum hic igitur Ludovicum salutasset ac de more percontatus esset, ut valeret ipse ac familia, ut salvi essent quos amaret domestici, canes illi duos venaticos, egregie etiam phaleratos ac copulatim iunctos, dono dedit. Ad ea Ludovicus et recte valere suos omnes respondit et gratias egit de canibus ac statim ore quam maxime renidenti: 'Tu vero,' inquit, 'mi hirquicule, ut pacate, ut salubriter tuo cum grege, qui lupis illum, abductis canibus, incustoditum reliqueris?' Vides quam belle, quam urbane in barbam ac nares iocatus sit atque in gregem destitutum.

Federicus, rex Neapolitanorum, usus est magistro epistolarum, utque hodie dicunt secretario, Vitho Pisanello.[10] Is erat capillo crispo, qualis Aethiopibus esse solet. Forte inter Federicum et Prosperum Columnam, exercitus eius ducem, sermo inciderat de hominum applicationibus naturaeque ipsius signis quibusdam eorumque observatione. Cumque in referendis illis Federicus dixisset fieri vix posse, cui crispus erat capillus, quin idem aut musicus esset aut depravata ac parum constanti mente, tum Prosper: 'Per Christum,' inquit, 'o rex, Vithulus hic quidem tuus haudquaquam musicus est.' Argute admodum atque aculeate, namque ex adversatione sequebatur laborare illum mentis infirmitate ac perversitate animi.[11]

17     Valentinum scortillum efflictim cum amaretur ab adolescente parum pecunioso peteretque ille ab ea noctem praesensque deesset pecunia ac noctis pretium, de quo fidei suae tamen ut staret, rogabat in triduum persolvendo. Tum ea, nudato femore: 'An tibi,'

that man, the most clamorous and rabid of all women. With its spontaneity this witticism provoked Alfonso and his entourage to the greatest laughter, that the story of the man's conjugal life — or captivity — was told there by means of a good-natured joke.

A marvelously troublesome litigant, rather snub-nosed and with a long, shaggy beard, appeared before Ludovico Pontano, the most eminent jurist of his day.[45] When he had greeted Ludovico and asked, in the usual fashion, how he and his family were, and whether the servants he loved were in good health, he gave him two hunting dogs, excellently adorned with medals and joined as a pair. Ludovico replied to this that all his relatives were in good health, thanked him for the dogs, and instantly said, his face smiling as much as possible, "But you, my little goat, is your flock peaceful and healthy, which you've left unprotected from wolves by taking away the dogs?" You see how prettily, how urbanely, he joked at his beard, nose, and abandoned flock. 16

Federico, king of Naples, employed a master of letters, a secretary as they say today, Vito Pisanello.[46] He had curly hair, as Ethiopians usually do. A conversation between Federico and Prospero Colonna, the general of his army, happened to turn upon men's inclinations, natural signs, and their powers of observation.[47] And when they were talking of these things and Federico said that it could hardly happen that someone was curly haired without either being a musician or having a depraved and inconstant mind, Prospero said, "By Christ, king, this little Vito of yours is by no means a musician." It was a clever and pointed remark, for from his reply it followed that Vito suffered from weakness of mind and perversity of spirit.[48]

When an impecunious young man desperately loved a young prostitute from Valencia and was asking her for a night, lacking the ready money and the price of the night, he asked her nevertheless to credit him for it and he would pay in three days.[49] Then she bared her thigh and said, "Do you think this merchandise is only 17

inquit, 'mercimonium hoc videatur fidei tantum accredendum?' Ibi
adolescens, nudato e vagina sua capulo, confestim subdidit: 'Num
nam mercatori huic fides adhibenda non est sua?' Ioci huius sedes
in translatione collocata est, a mercatoribus sumpta, innititurque
consimilitudini.

18    Rodoricus Carrasius, ut sunt plerique Valentini cives, tum senes tum iuvenes, amoribus dediti ac deliciis, licet octogenarius iam
exercebat se se ad tibiam; praeteriens ante eius fores Rebolleta,
homo cum primis suavis ac facetus: 'Quis,' inquit, 'o pueri, hic ad
choreas instituitur?' Cum respondissent Rodoricum dare operam
choralistio: 'Nae,' inquit, 'Rodoricus nuntium ab Orco accepit ludos apud manes apparari ac festos dies.' Dicendi ac ridendi argu-
mentum omne ab annositate ductum.

Quibus igitur e locis dicta ipsa deducantur quibusque in se-
dibus collocata sint ex iis quae dicta sunt facile est intelligere.
19 Perinde autem ut natura ipsa terrae agrorumque diversitatem inge-
nerat succi ac saporum, sic locorum quoque positura nunc dicte-
riorum acumen gignit nunc salsitatem aut leporem; alias autem
alius atque alius tum iucunditatis condimentum tum iocandi voluptatem ac delicias, neque unius quidem aut generis aut modi.
'Iam dudum,' inquit ille apud Plautum, 'sputo sanguinem'; refertur
ei statim a collocutore, 'Resinam ex melle Aegyptiam vorato.' Item
alibi:

— Dic mihi: solent ne tibi oculi unquam duri fieri?
— Quid? tu locustam esse censes, homo ignavissime?

Quid his ridiculosius? Quid illo autem lepidius?

— Is odos demissis pedibus in coelum volat.
— Eum in odorem coenat Iupiter quotidie.

granted on credit?" Then the young man, having bared his sword from its sheath, added immediately, "Well, don't you think credit should be given to this merchant?" The source of this joke has been located in a metaphor, taken from merchants, and rests upon similarity.

Rodorico Carrasio, being like most citizens of Valencia both young and old devoted to love and pleasure, although eighty years old, still practiced the flute. Rebolleta, a man especially pleasant and witty, passing by his door, said, "Boys, who is learning how to dance here?" When they replied that Rodorico was working on his flute playing, he said, "Rodorico must have received a message from Orcus that games and festivals are being prepared among the spirits of the dead." The whole argument of the witticism was drawn from old age.

Therefore, it is easy to understand from what has been said which places these witticisms are derived from and in which sources they are located. But just as the nature of lands and fields engenders a diversity of flavor and tastes, so also their context produces now sharpness, pungency, or charm in witty remarks, while on other occasions it produces the spice of delight; at another the pleasure and enjoyment of joking, and not even in one kind or way. "For a while," says that man in Plautus, "I have been spitting blood"; at once the person he's talking to replies to him, "Swallow Egyptian resin with honey."[50] Likewise elsewhere:

—Tell me: are your eyes ever liable to become hard?
—What? Do you think I'm a lobster, you scoundrel?[51]

What is funnier than those words? And what is more charming than this?

—That smell flies to the sky with its feet hanging down.
—Jupiter dines on that smell every day.  — A smell with its

—Odor demissis pedibus?  —Peccavi insciens
quia demissis naribus volui dicere.

Quid hoc? quam est populare ac simplex!

—Hae oves volunt vos.
—Prodigium hoc quidem est, humana cum nos voce appellant
oves.

Contra quid illo argutius? '—Quin fles?  —Pumiceos oculos habeo.' Et alibi: 'Genus nostrum semper siccoculum fuit.' Non ne et
illud suavissimum?

—Hodie me in ludum recepi literarium;
ternas scio iam.  —Quid ternas?  —Amo.

Et illa quoque cum primis ad risum alliciunt:

—Quisquis homo huc venerit pugnos edat.
—Apage, non placet me hoc noctis esse: coenavi modo.

Et:

—Gestiunt pugni mihi.
—Si in me exerciturus, quaeso in parietem ut primum domes.

Item:

—Amphitruo, redire ad navem melius est nos.  —Qua gratia?
—Quia domi nemo daturus est prandium advenientibus.
—Qui tibi nunc istud in mentem venit?  —Quia enim sero
advenimus.
—Qui?  —Quod Alcmenam ante oculos stare saturam
intelligo.

Itaque pro natura locorum unde ducuntur dicteria ipsa qualitatem
sortiuntur ac saporem.

feet hanging down? —I stupidly made a mistake because I meant to say with its nose hanging down.[52]

What about this? how common and simple!

—These sheep want to speak with you. —This indeed is a prodigy, the sheep are addressing us with a human voice.[53]

On the other hand, what acuter than this? " — Why aren't you crying? —I have eyes of flint." And elsewhere: "Our family always was dry-eyed."[54] Isn't this also very pleasant?

—Today I returned to primary school; I already know three letters. —What do you mean, "three"? —A-m-o [I love].[55]

And these lines too especially make you laugh:

—Whoever comes here will eat fists. —Away with you, I don't like that at this time of night; I've already had dinner.[56]

And:

—My fists are itching. —If you're going to practice on me, please calm them down against the wall first.[57]

Likewise:

—Amphitruo, it's better for us to go back to the ship. —Why? —Because no one at home is going to give us lunch when we arrive. —Why did that come into your mind now? —Well, because we are arriving late. —Why is that? —Because I see plainly that Alcmena is standing there well-fed.[58]

And so in accordance with the nature of the places from which witty remarks are drawn they obtain their quality and taste.

20    Ipsae autem sedes constitutae sunt tum in rebus tum in verbis. In verbis, quale hoc:

> — Ut valentula est!
>
> Pene me exposuit cubito.  — Cubitum ergo ire vult.

Et:

> — Num medicus, quaeso, es?
>
> — Imo aedepol una litera plusquam medicus.

Et:

> — Advenisti, audaciae columen, consutis dolis.
> — Imo consutis tunicis huc advenio, non dolis.

In rebus, ut: ' — Si neque hic neque Acherunti sum, ubi sum? — Nusquam gentium.' Item:

> Ait se obligasse crus fractum Aesculapio,
> Apollini autem brachium. Nunc cogito
> utrum me dicam ducere medicum an fabrum.

Et: 'Non placet mi coena quae bilem movet.' Quid quod loci quidam constant ipsi quidem e rebus ac verbis una immistis, quale est hoc?

> Credo alium in aliam belluam hominem vortier.
> Ille in columbam, credo, leno vortitur,
> nam in collumbari collum haud multo post erit.

Pro locis igitur proque rebus ac verbis dicta ipsa succulenta sunt.

21    Hinc alia, ut dictum est, salem habent; alia leporem; alia aut mordicant aut vellicant; quaedam vero titillant; alia prima fronte risum movent; alia, diutius versata, relinquunt in animo sedationem quasi quandam. Sunt quae ruborem afferant, quae contra

Moreover, these sources are located sometimes in things, some- 20
times in words.[59] In words, like this:

—How strong the little woman is! She almost laid me out
with her elbow. — So she wants to get laid.[60]

And:

—Please tell me, are you a doctor? — No, by Pollux, more
than a doctor by one letter.[61]

And:

—You've arrived, summit of audacity, with your tricks
stitched together. — No, I arrive here with my tunic stitched
together, not with tricks stitched together.[62]

In things, like: "—If I'm not here or in Acheron, where am I?
— Nowhere in the world."[63] Likewise:

He says he bound Aesculapius' broken leg and Apollo's arm.
Now I'm asking myself whether I'm hiring a doctor or a
carpenter.[64]

And: "I don't like a dinner that stirs up my bile."[65] What about the
fact that some places consist of things and words mixed together,
like this?

I believe each man is turned into a different animal. That
pimp, I believe, is turning into a dove, for pretty soon his
neck will be in a dove collar.[66]

So these witticisms are juicy in accordance with the places, things,
and words.

Hence some, as has been said, have pungency; others, charm; 21
others either bite or pinch, while others tickle; others move to
laughter right away; others, after long reflection, leave almost a
kind of calm in the mind. There are some that bring a blush,

animum erigant aut moneant aut dehortentur. De quibus singulis velle minutatim disserere licet supervacaneum videatur, cum eorum admonuisse satis quidem videri possit, tamen, si aliquantum etiam in iis versabimur, nec tibi quidem nec, si qui forte alii rerum harum lectores futuri sunt, ingratum fore arbitramur.

22    Illud tamen satis liquet in verborum concinnitate ac vi plurimum quidem repositum esse, sive ad delectandum molestiasque lepore tantum ipso sedandas sive ad vulnerandum saleque illinendas plagas sive ad retorquenda iacula relinquendam ve suspitionem absconditi risus ac ioci notae ve pudendae, tum cicatrices inurendas tum mentis ipsius clam quidem cruciandae acerrimos morsus torturasque gravissimas.

: 18 :

*De Valerii Martialis poetae dictis.*

1    Valerius Martialis, artificiosissimus epigrammatum scriptor, ita in iis quidem iocatus est, ut frequentius carpat quam delectet, tametsi e demorsione ipsa delectatio quoque paritur. Adhaec dictis eius partim occultissima quaedam insunt spicula, partim verba quae non solum a faceto sint aliena verum aut oscena ipsa admodum scurrilia aut maxime ampullosa et acida, quod quidem Hispanicum est. Nam etsi Hispani cum primis sunt facetiarum studiosi,
2    tamen si populares respexeris ac plebeios gentis eius homines, invenies eorum iocos non tam propendere in lusum ac delicias quam in summorsiones magisque spectare in invectivas et subsannationes quam in risum voluptatemque e iucunditate conceptam,
3    quae in facetis viris tenerrima quidem est. Sunt tamen dicta eius

some, on the other hand, that encourage or warn or dissuade. Although wishing to discuss these things individually and in detail may seem superfluous, since it might seem sufficient just to remind you of them, nevertheless, if I concern myself with them even for a little time, I think I will displease neither you nor other future readers of these things, if there happen to be any.

Nevertheless, it is clear enough that very much indeed depends 22 on the elegant arrangement and force of the words, whether to delight and calm annoyances with charm alone, or to injure and rub wounds with salt, or to hurl back spears, or leave behind a suspicion of hidden laughter, joking, or a shameful reproach, sometimes to burn in scars, sometimes to subject a mind that should be secretly crucified to the sharpest bites and heaviest tortures.

: 18 :

*On the witticisms of the poet Valerius Martial.*

Valerius Martial, the most artistic writer of epigrams, has joked in 1 them in such a way that he carps more often than entertains, even though entertainment is also produced from this biting criticism. In addition, sometimes there are sharp points hidden in his witticisms, sometimes words not only foreign to a witty man but also obscene, very buffoonish, or bombastic and tart, which is very Spanish.[67] For although Spaniards particularly pursue witticisms, 2 nevertheless, if you look at the common and plebeian men of this race, you will find that their jokes do not incline to play and enjoyment as much as to secret gibes and that they tend to invective and derision more than to laughter and pleasure conceived from good humor, which in witty men is indeed very delicate. Never- 3

in universum arguta suptiliterque conquisita; abstrusae sententiae
eaedemque rarae, salsae, aculeatae; inventio vero maxime acuta;
verba autem praecipue accommodata quaeque non prima tantum
facie atque in ipso explicatu lectorem alliciant atque auditorem,
verum quae in eius animo relinquant tacitam quandam quasi sub-
titillationem.

4      Nihilo tamen minus in iis non pauca quidem animadvertas
quae digna prorsus sint facetis ac temperatis civibus retineantque
decorum illud quod virtutis huius de qua praecipimus maxime est
proprium, quale illud, quod et iucundum simul et salsum est ri-
sumque venuste pariter atque honeste movet ac vel in ore etiam
matronae non dedecet:

> Unguentum, fateor, bonum dedisti
> convivis here, sed nihil scidisti.
> Res salsa est bene olere et esurire.
> Qui non coenat et unguitur, Fabulle,
> hic vere mihi mortuus videtur.

Est et illud quoque eiusdem generis in Caecilianum:

> Quicquid ponitur hinc et inde verris:
> mammas suminis imbricemque porci
> communemque duobus attagenam
> mullum dimidium lupumque totum
> murenaeque latus femurque pulli
> stillantemque alica sua palumbum.
> Haec cum condita sunt madente mappa,
> traduntur puero domum ferenda;
> nos accumbimus ociosa turba.
> Ullus si pudor est, repone coenam:
> cras te, Caeciliane, non vocavi.

Itemque et aliud undique quidem et suave et bellum:

theless, his witticisms are generally acute and subtly chosen, his
opinions abstruse and also remarkable, pungent, and stinging. But
his invention is especially acute, and his words particularly appropriate. They not only allure the reader and listener at first sight
and as they unfold, but leave behind in his mind a certain, as it
were, silent, secret tickling.

Nonetheless, you may observe not a few of his witticisms that   4
are completely worthy of clever and temperate citizens and preserve the decorum particular to the virtue I am teaching, such as
the following epigram, which is delightful and at the same time
pungent, moves to laughter equally with charm and decency, and
is not unbecoming even on the lips of a matron:

> Yesterday you gave your guests, I confess, a good ointment,
> but you carved nothing. It's a witty thing to smell good yet
> go hungry. One who doesn't dine and is anointed, Fabullus,
> really seems to me to be dead.[68]

And this one against Caecilianus is also of the same kind:

> You sweep up whatever is served on each side: teats of a
> sow's udder, sparerib, a partridge for two people, half a mul-
> let, a whole pike, a side of eel, a chicken leg, a dove dripping
> in fish sauce. When these have been hidden in a dripping
> napkin, they're handed over to your slave to take home, but
> we recline, an idle crowd. If you have any shame, put back
> the dinner: I didn't invite you, Caecilianus, to dinner tomor-
> row.[69]

And likewise another one, in every part pleasant and pretty:

Quod fronte Selium nubila vides, Rufe,
quod ambulator porticum terit serus,
lugubre quiddam quod tacet piger voltus,
quod pene terram tangit indecens nasus,
et dextra pectus pulsat et comam vellit,
non ille amici fata luget aut fratris,
uterque natus vivit et precor vivat,
salva est et uxor sarcinaeque servique,
nihil colonus vilicusque decoxit.
Moeroris igitur causa quae est? Domi coenat.

5    Et hoc quoque quod subdam; licet admodum mordax, plenum tamen est venustatis ac leporis, quippe quod sive lectum sive au-
ditum mirifice delectat exhilaratque tum legentem tum etiam qui
audit:

Garris in aurem semper omnibus, Cinna,
garris et illud teste quod licet turba.
Rides in aurem, quereris, arguis, ploras,
cantas in aurem, iudicas, taces, clamas.
Adeo ne penitus sedit hic tibi morbus
ut saepe in aurem, Cinna, Caesarem laudes?

Summe autem urbanum hoc et lepidum:

Spectabat modo solus inter omnes
nigris munus Horatius lacernis,
cum plebs et minor ordo maximusque
sancto cum duce candidus sederet.
Toto nix cecidit repente caelo:
albis spectat Horatius lacernis.

6    Profluunt autem haec dictorum genera fonte ex eo qui non una
quidem et tenui manat scatebra verum huberiore quae decurrat ac
praeterlabatur rivo, nec paucis dictum ipsum constat verbis verum

Although, Rufus, you see Selius with a clouded brow, although he strolls about and treads the portico late in the day, although his sad face hides something mournful in silence, although his ugly nose almost touches the ground and he beats his breast and pulls his hair with his right hand, he is not mourning the death of friend or brother, both of his children live (and I pray that they keep on living), his wife, his belongings, and slaves are in good health, and his tenant farmer and steward have wasted nothing. So what is the cause of his sorrow? He dines at home.[70]

And I will also add this one. Although it is very mordant, yet it is  5 full of charm and grace, since either read or heard it is marvelously delightful and exhilarates both the reader and listener:

You're always chattering in everyone's ear, Cinna; even what's allowed for you to chatter before the witness of a crowd. You laugh in an ear, complain, blame, weep; you sing in an ear, pass judgment, are silent, shout. Is this disease so deep-seated in you, Cinna, that you often praise Caesar in an ear?[71]

And this one is supremely urbane and charming:

Horatius recently was watching the show in a black cloak, alone of those present while the common people and the lesser and greatest order were sitting in white with our venerable leader. Suddenly snow fell from the whole sky: Horatius watches in a white cloak.[72]

But these kinds of witticisms spring from a source that does  6 not flow with one, slight gush but with a more abundant stream that runs down and glides by. And this witticism does not consist

compluribus. At illud et breve et mordax et perquam salsum, oscenum tamen, nec conventu honestorum virorum dignum:

> Os et labra tibi lingit, Manuela, catellus:
> non miror, merdas si libet esse cani.

Quod dictum non tam res ipsae quam verba scurrile efficiunt atque degenerosum. Est et illud eiusdem generis, minus tamen oscenum:

> Quod fellas et aquam potas, nil, Lesbia, peccas.
> Qua tibi parte opus est, Lesbia, sumis aquam.

7 At illud neque oscenum neque honesta hominum consessione indignum:

> Formosam faciem nigro medicamine velas,
> sed non formoso corpore laedis aquas.
> Ipsam crede deam verbis tibi dicere nostris:
> 'Aut aperi faciem, vel tunicata lava.'

8 Sunt apud eundem poetam dicta, et quidem non pauca, quibus sub velo abscondita insint spicula eaque peracuta. Quale hoc:

> De nullo quereris, nulli maledicis, Apici;
> rumor ait linguae te tamen esse malae.

Itemque:

> Versiculos in me narratur scribere Cinna.
> Non scribit, cuius carmina nemo legit.

In hoc vero manifesta apparet se seque ostentat mordacitas:

of a few words but of several. But this one is short, mordant, and exceedingly pungent, yet obscene and not worthy of an assembly of honorable men:

> The puppy licks your mouth and lips, Manuela: no wonder the dog likes to eat shit.[73]

Not so much the things themselves but the words make that witticism buffoonish and degenerate. And this one is of the same kind, yet less obscene:

> You suck and drink water, Lesbia; you're making no mistake. You're taking water, Lesbia, for the part of you that needs it.[74]

But this one is neither obscene nor unworthy of a honorable gathering of men: 7

> You cover your lovely face with black makeup, but you offend the waters with your unlovely body. Believe that goddess herself is speaking to you with my words: "Either reveal your face or bathe in your tunic."[75]

In this same poet there are witticisms, and indeed not a few, in 8 which sharp points are hidden beneath a veil—very sharp points. Like this one:

> You complain of no one, you speak ill of no one, Apicius; yet rumor says you have an evil tongue.[76]

And likewise:

> It is said Cinna writes little verses against me. A person whose poems no one reads doesn't write.[77]

But in this one manifest mordancy appears and shows itself:

> Credi virgine castior pudica
> et frontis tenerae cupis videri,
> cum sis inprobior, Massilane,
> quam qui compositos metro Tibulli
> in Stellae recitat domo libellos.

Et in hoc item:

> Nulli, Thai, negas, sed si te non pudet istud,
>> hoc saltem pudeat, Thai, negare nihil.

Illa vero videri possunt fortasse etiam iure suo frigida:

> Omnis quas habuit, Fabiane, Lycoris amicas
>> extulit: uxori fiat amica meae.

Item:

> Millia misisti mihi sex bissena petenti;
>> ut bissena feram, bis duodena petam.

At hoc cum primis ridiculum, tametsi minime vacuum est oscenitate:

> Infantem secum semper tua Bassa, Fabulle,
>> collocat et lusus deliciasque vocat,
> et, quod mireris magis, infantaria non est.
>> Ergo quid in causa est? Paedere Bassa solet.

Illud vero, prima fronte quanquam est perfamiliare ac facetum, la-
tet in eo tamen etiam maledicentia accusatioque impotentiae:

> Hospes eras nostri semper, Matho, Tiburtini.
>> Hoc emis. Imposui: rus tibi vendo tuum.

You wish to be thought more chaste than a modest maiden and to appear all blushes, Massilanus, though you are more shameless than someone who recites at Stella's house little books composed in the meter of Tibullus.[78]

And likewise in this one:

You say no to no one, Thaïs, but if you're not ashamed of this, at least, Thaïs, you should be ashamed of saying no to nothing.[79]

But these may perhaps appear feeble even in their own right:

Fabianus, Lycoris has buried all the friends she's had: let her become my wife's friend.[80]

Likewise:

You sent me six thousand when I asked for twelve. To get twelve I'll ask for twenty-four.[81]

But this one is especially ridiculous, even though it by no means lacks obscenity:

Your friend Bassa, Fabullus, always puts a baby by her and calls it her plaything and darling, and, to make you marvel more, she's not a baby lover. So what's the reason? Bassa is constantly farting.[82]

But although at first blush this one is very friendly and witty, nevertheless it also conceals abuse and an accusation of lack of self-restraint:

You were perpetually a guest, Matho, at my estate in Tivoli. You're buying it. I've tricked you: I'm selling you your own villa.[83]

9   Eiusmodi sunt igitur Martialis dicta, ut pleraque multum habeant salis nec minus fellis atque ampullosi proque loco et iocen-
tur et delectent, interdum ruborem inducant magis quam risum;
alia vero quae non pruritum tantum exciant aut titillatum verum
etiam petulantiam prae se ferant lususque parum omnino modes-
tos. Persaepe autem verecundari ita nescit ut vel aperte scurretur,
nec solum invidere sicophantis videatur ac parasitis verum etiam
mimis. Adeo autem cuncta haec complexus est genera estque in iis
ita frequens et multus ut aliis in eiusmodi iocis ludendi praeri-
10  puisse videri velit materiam. A nobis autem cum mediocritas parte
in hac quaeratur defugianturque extrema, alia dictorum tum genera quaerenda sunt tum species quae facetorum sint omnino
11  propria. Utque Valeri huius dicta, parte quidem non exigua, insti-
tutioni huic nostrae parum consentiunt, sic et Marci Ciceronis
quaedam etiam explodenda, quippe quae oratori magis conveniant,
ad victoriam causae comparandam, quam ad eam animorum relaxationem, quae a nobis cum honestate ac dignitate quaeritur,
cuiusque insita est hominibus a natura appetitio. Itaque quid et
quomodo Cicero de iis sentiat, a nobis praetereundum non est.


: 19 :

*Duo esse secundum Ciceronem facetiarum genera.*

1   Legitur autem apud eum duo esse genera facetiarum: alterum ae-
quabiliter in omni sermone fusum, alterum peracutum et breve;
illamque cavillationem a veteribus appellatam, alteram vero hanc
dicacitatem; utramque tamen levem rem esse, quando leve prorsus
sit risum movere. Nihilo tamen minus in causis multum persaepe
2   lepore ac facetiis, Antonio auctore, profici. In neutra vero artem

Thus Martial's witticisms are of such a kind that many have a    9
lot of pungency and no less bile and bombast.[84] In the right place
they are humorous and entertaining; sometimes they induce a
blush more than a laugh. But some not only produce an itch or
tickle but also display impudence and jest shamelessly. Very often
he is so incapable of being ashamed that he even openly plays the
buffoon, appears to envy not only sycophants and parasites but
also mimes. Moreover, he has embraced all these classes to such an
extent and is so constant and abundant in them that he wishes to
appear to snatch the material for witty play from others in jokes of
this sort. But since I seek the mean in this part and avoid the ex-    10
tremes, I must seek out other classes and species of witticisms that
are entirely characteristic of witty men. And as the witticisms of    11
this Valerius, indeed in no small part, do not accord with my doctrine, so certain things in Marcus Cicero must also be rejected,
seeing that they are more appropriate to an orator trying to win a
lawsuit than to the kind of decent and dignified mental relaxation
we seek, the desire for which has been planted in mankind by nature. And so I must not pass over what and in what way Cicero
thinks about these matters.

: 19 :

*According to Cicero there are two kinds of witticisms.*[85]

One reads in him that there are two classes of witticisms. One is    1
spread equally over the whole speech, the other very sharp and
brief. The ancients called the former banter but the latter raillery,
yet each is a trifling thing, since raising laughs is entirely a trifling
thing. Nonetheless, according to Antonius, very often much can
be accomplished in lawsuits with charm and wit. In neither one    2

ipsam quippiam habere loci, quando in illo genere perpetuae festi-
3 vitatis ars non desideratur: naturam enim ipsam fingere homines
et creare imitatores et narratores facetos, et vultu adiuvante et voce
et ipso genere sermonis. In altero vero nihil prorsus artem habere
quod praestet, cum ante illud facete dictum emissum haerere deberet quam cogitari potuisse videatur sitque in celeritate positum
ac dicto.

: 20 :

*Circa dicta facetiasque inveniendas artem*
*plurimum valere.*

1 His igitur in hunc tenorem inter disserendum explicatis, res ipsa
nos hortatur et ostendere artem in dictis quoque ac facetiis multum habere loci et exercitationem studiumque plurimum in his
valere. Primum enim quod in omni actione ac virtute exigitur, id
quoque inter iocandum utendisque facetiis servandum esse, uti
delectus habeatur rerum, locorum, personarum, auditorum, temporum, fortunae item, atque eventuum: haec enim ad retinendam
2 atque assequendam mediocritatem cum primis exiguntur. Ipsa
vero mediocritas non virtutes solum constituit quae morales dicuntur verum etiam eloquentiam quaeque Graece est rhetorica
habuitque tam multos ac maximos auctores et Latine et Graece.
3    Igitur si elocutio, quae constat e verbis atque oratione, in praecepta redacta est habeturque de ea ratio, et facetudinis quoque ratio habenda est tradique de ea praecepta possunt—qua enim in re
versatur ratio, in ea quoque et institutio locum habet—cum et
oratores ipsi dicant et lusus iocique facetorum vocentur etiam, a

does art have any place, since in that kind of continuous pleasantry art is not desired. For nature itself fashions men and creates mim- 3 ics and witty storytellers with the help of expression, voice, and manner of speaking. But, in the other, art has nothing at all to offer, since a witty remark ought to be hurled and stick fast before it can appear premeditated, and its wit depends upon the rapidity of the retort.

: 20 :

*Art is highly effective for inventing witticisms and funny stories.*

Having thus explained and discussed the foregoing along these 1 lines, the subject itself urges me to show both that art also has a large place in witticisms and funny stories and that practice and application have great importance in them. For first of all, whatever is required in every action and virtue must also be preserved while joking and using witticisms, so that a choice is made of subjects, places, persons, listeners, times, and likewise of fortune and events, for these things are especially required for reaching and keeping to the mean. But this mean not only establishes the 2 virtues called moral, but also eloquence, which is "rhetoric" in Greek, and has had so many superlative authors in Latin and Greek.

Therefore, if speaking, which consists of words and discourse, 3 has been reduced to precepts and there is a reasoned account of it, there must also be a reasoned account of humor, and precepts about it can be handed down — for when reason is concerned in something, instruction also has a place in it — since orators themselves "say" and the jests and jokes of witty men are called "sayings"

dicendo, dicta cumque eloquenter etiam dicendi sive peritia sive
ars sive doctrina usu comparetur observationeque multaque et in
litibus controversiisque et in senatu popularibusque concionibus
4  exercitatione eaque maxime frequenti ac meditata. Quo fit ut facete quoque dicendi regula sit aliqua, quemadmodum et bene et
maledicendi, hoc est laudandi et vituperandi. Non ne autem si
dicta ipsa pleraque sunt in celeritate posita et ante quidem emittuntur quam cogitari potuisse videantur, non ne, inquam, contingit et hoc quoque in orandi exercitatione ac peritia? Principia enim
haec ipsa et loquendi oratorie et dicendi facete ac tum ridendi et
hilarescendi tum dolendi ac lacrimandi, in natura posita sunt ab
eaque proficiscuntur, quibus postea ratio ipsa modum quendam,
ac certum eum quidem, adhibet, ut, quod de amore Ovidius inquit, 'Et quae nunc ratio est, impetus ante fuit,' etiam ad haec ipsa
trasferri recte possit.

5    Nam et leges modum statuere funeribus et ludis simul ac conviviis, et conclamandis quidem funeribus praeficae praeponi consuevere, illis vero tum ludorum rationem qui haberent tum qui essent
convivendi periti. Quin convicia, obiurgia contentionesque immo-
deratae quaedam mulctis, quaedam suppliciis coercentur; famosis
6  quoque de libellis leges sunt editae ac plebei scita. Igitur et in facetudine utenda dictisque temperandis modus quoque si repertus
est, an id profecto mirum? An et de dicteriis ridiculariisque ac iocis praecepta tradi nullo modo poterunt? Neque ulla erit eorum
tradendorum sive ars sive doctrina quae mediocritatem et doceat
et ostendat, qua ea sit via et assequenda et retinenda, ut, si principia sunt naturae, modus tamen ac mensura ratione temperetur at-
7  que institutione? Nam et pedum incessus, civili quidem homine
dignus, regulam suam habet; est et sua quoque gestus temperatio
ac lex.

[*dicta*, i.e., witty remarks] from *say* and since the skill or art or knowledge of speaking eloquently is also acquired by use, observation, and much practice, repeated very frequently, in lawsuits and disputes, in the senate and popular assemblies. So it happens that 4 there is also a rule for speaking wittily, just as for speaking well and ill, that is for praising and blaming. And is it not the case that if most witty sayings depend on speed and are hurled before it appears that they could have been thought of, is it not so, I say, that this also happens in the practice and skill of oratory? For these principles of talking as an orator and speaking wittily, as well as laughing and becoming cheerful, grieving and crying, depend on and set out from nature. Afterward reason sets some limit to them, a fixed limit, so that what Ovid says of love, "And what was impulse before now has a reason," can also be rightly transferred to them.[86]

For laws have established a limit for funerals and games along 5 with banquets. Hired mourners have customarily been put in charge of funeral processions, but in the other two activities, those who understood the games and were skilled at banqueting were put in charge. In fact, some insults, reproaches, and immoderate disputes are restrained by fines, some by punishments; laws and plebiscites concerning notorious libels have also been promulgated.[87] Therefore if a limit has also been found in the use of wit 6 and in tempering speech, is this really astonishing? Will there be no way to hand down precepts for witty sayings, jests, and jokes? Will there be no art or doctrine for handing them down that shows and teaches the mean, which way it must be reached and preserved, since, if the principles are nature's, the limit and measure still are tempered by reason and instruction? For even the 7 movement of the feet, at least that worthy of a civil man, has its proper rule, and there is also a proper tempering and law of gesture.

8      Erit igitur et iocandi suus, atque ingenuo homine dignus, modus ac temperamentum. Nam si facetudo virtus est quaedam eaque mediocritas, ut probatum iam est, ea ut institutione constet ac
praeceptis necesse est, cum praesertim nos nequaquam oratoriam
quaeramus urbanitatem verum moralem quaeque ad animorum
9  refocillationem conducat eamque honestam ac laudabilem. Natura
quoque nos docet uti argumentationibus, quarum tamen permulta
extant praecepta. Estque illarum sive ars sive doctrina atque erudi-
tio et magistra et iudex illa quae logice dicitur, nostro autem no-
10  mine tum disserendi ratio tum disertiva. Ipsorum autem argumen-
torum ut sunt sedes, quae dicuntur loca eaque cognitio appellatur
tum localis ac de locis tum topica, Graeca appellatione, sic etiam
dictorum ac facetiarum propriae sedes sunt eaeque admodum cer-
tae, quas si, praeter quae dicta sunt, diligentius pervestigaverimus
inque formam, etsi non absolutam, aliquam tamen redegerimus,
non pigebit huius sive laboris sive studii. Nam et futuros vatici-
namur qui de iis sint suptilius atque enucleatius diserturi.

: 21 :

*Aliter oratoribus ac comicis, aliter ingenuis*
*civibus facetiarum locos quaerendos.*

1  Itaque nec ut Martiali aut Plauto nec ut Ciceroni quaerendae nobis sunt facetiae sive earum loci et quasi regiones. Mediocritatem
enim quaerimus quae habitum faceti constituit, non quo aut spectatoribus risus moveamus, aut aucupemur plausum carminisque
commendationem, aut quo iudices capiamus ac lepore facetiisque
in nostram trahamus sententiam, verum quo urbane ac festive

Therefore there will also be a moderation and tempering proper 8
to joking, one worthy of a freeborn man. For if wittiness is a kind
of virtue and a mean, as has already been proven, it must be based
on instruction and precepts, especially since I am not at all seeking
oratorical urbanity but a moral one that leads to a decent and
praiseworthy form of recreation for the mind. Nature also teaches 9
us to use arguments, for which however very many precepts exist.
And the teacher and judge of arguments is the art or doctrine and
instruction that is called logic in Greek but, as we call it in Latin,
the system of discourse or the discursive system.[88] But as these 10
arguments have sources that are called "places" and knowledge
about them is called sometimes "local knowledge" and "knowledge
of places," and sometimes by the Greek appellation "topics," so
there are proper sources for witty sayings and stories, very definite
ones. And if I examine them more diligently, in addition to what
has been said, and reduce them to some form, if not an absolute
one, this labor and endeavor will not displease. For I predict that
there will be men in the future who will discuss these things more
subtly and plainly.

: 21 :

*The places of witticisms must be sought in one way by orators
and comic poets, in another by free citizens.*

Thus I must seek witticisms or their places and, as it were, regions 1
in a way distinct from that of Martial or Plautus or Cicero.[89] For
I seek the mean that determines the quality of a witty man, not to
move spectators to laughter, or to hunt for applause and praise of
a poem, or to win over judges and lead them to my opinion with
charm and witticisms, but to relax the mind urbanely and mirth-

2   relaxemus animos. Inventa enim et constituta sunt concilia, conventus, circuli ac coronae tum ad utilitatem et communem et privatam, tum etiam ad iucunditatem relaxandosque ab labore ac

3   curis animos. Tametsi loci ipsi sunt communes et, quod Cicero dicit, quibus e locis ridicula ducuntur ex iisdem graves possunt duci sententiae, idem nos quoque sentimus posse deduci quoque et quae dicta in spurcitiam delabantur atque scurrilitatem et quae in leporem atque urbanitatem; alteri enim loci et rebus et verbis modum statuunt, alteri in risum propendent atque scurrilitatem. Modus igitur his accedere potest ac ratio quo scurrilitas omnis absit iocantibus. Quod officium delectus est proprium tum in rebus tum in verbis.

4   Verum oscenitas plerumque est in verbis, scurrilitas in utrisque potius, siquidem scurrile habetur quem minime debeas eum dictis lacessere, quando, ut est apud Ciceronem, quae cadere possunt in quos nolis, quamvis sint bella, sunt tamen ipso genere scurrilia. Nimis igitur salse dicta aculeataque atque in quos minime conve-

5   niat scurrilia et ipsa sunt. Possunt tamen et faceti homines in consessionibus coronisque—ut qui referant quidem dicta emissaque ab aliis, non ut qui ex se se dicant ingerantque in quempiam—quandoque et mordacia afferre in coetum, quasi ea in memoriam reducant idque exempli gratia, non tamen mordaciter, scurriliaque minime scurriliter, scilicet ut verbis parcatur et gestibus. Quod in referendis fabellis praecipue usuvenit, ut quae in illis insint turpia explicentur non turpiter, interdum vero innuantur potius quam dicantur.

fully. For councils, meetings, companies, and assemblies have been 2
established sometimes for common and private utility, sometimes
also for delight and relaxing the mind from labor and cares. Even 3
though these places are common and, as Cicero says, serious
thoughts can be drawn from the same places from which jests are
drawn, I also think the same thing about witticisms that slip into
filth and buffoonery and ones that incline to charm and urbanity.[90]
For some places set a limit to things and words; others lean toward
laughter and buffoonery. Therefore a limit and rule can be added
to these things so that all buffoonery may be absent from those
who joke. This is the particular duty of discrimination, both in
things and words.

But obscenity is for the most part in words, buffoonery rather 4
in both, since it is considered buffoonery to irritate with humorous remarks someone whom you should by no means irritate, seeing that, as Cicero says, those things which, although neat, can fall
on people you do not want to hit, are still by their very nature
buffoonish.[91] Therefore witticisms which are too pungent and
pointed and directed against inappropriate people are also buffoonish. Nevertheless, in assemblies and gatherings witty men— 5
the kind of men who relate things said and discharged by others,
not like men who are speaking for themselves and dumping them
on some other person—sometimes can also report biting remarks
in company, as if calling them to mind and as an example, yet not
in a biting way, and report buffoonish things without buffoonery,
that is to say, refraining from buffoonish words and gestures. This
especially happens in relating stories so that the shameful things
that are in them are unfolded in no shameful way, but sometimes
are intimated rather than said.

: 22 :

*Divisio in iocos, dicta, ridicula, fabellas.*

1 Quae quo expressius a nobis ostendantur, ea partiemur in iocos, in dicta, in ridicula ac fabellas. Totum autem ipsum genus est iocari.

2 Ioca vero et dictis constant et ridiculis et fabellis, ac dicta quidem alia lepida, alia salsa sunt, alia et salsa simul et lepida, alia oscena, dicacia eaque non unius generis, alia brevia atque ex uno tantum verbo, alia e pluribus constituta. Sunt contra inepta quaedam, insulsa, fatua, illepida, frigida; itaque multimoda ipsa quidem sunt.

3 Ridicula quoque non unius sunt naturae, alia enim faceta sunt, alia vero minime. Itaque species haec indagationi huic nostrae minus congruit, quippe qui relaxationem quaeramus, quae facetudinis est alumna.

4 Fabellae iucundissimae ipsae sunt atque ad omne facetiarum genus accommodatae locisque omnibus congruunt, si non fortasse temporibus, quanquam et temporibus et item personis, si delectus accesserit. Quarum duplex est genus: unum quod sumptum est a mutis animalibus in exemplum, quales Aesopicae fere sunt fabulae et earum similes, aut a rebus minime sentientibus ut ab herbis, arboribus, lapidibus, ut quae in senatum Romanum introducta fuit contentio ventris adversum coetera corporis membra, ut quae de Phocione refertur adversus exactores pecuniae viritim conferendae ad sacros quosdam ludos Athenis publice institutos, cum illi non tantum importune verum etiam cum clamore instarent ac comminationibus.

Ignavum olim militem, cum in militiam proficisceretur, a cornicibus deterritum quae circa ipsum clamitantes volitarent itaque, quod infaustum id duceret, arma humi posuisse neque ultra progredi ausum. Ibi tum cornices et volatum inhibuisse et cantum.

: 22 :

*Division into jokes, witticisms, jests, and fables.*

To show these things more distinctly I will divide them into jokes, 1
witticisms, jests, and fables. Jokes, however, are the class as a
whole.[92] Moreover, jokes consist of witticisms, jests, and fables. 2
And some witticisms are charming, others pungent, others pungent and at the same time charming, others obscene, railing. And
they aren't of one kind; some are brief and only of one word, others composed of several. On the other hand, some are inept, insipid, uncharming, feeble, and so they are indeed of many sorts.
Jests are also not of one nature, for some are witty but others not 3
at all. And so this species accords less with this investigation of
mine, since I'm seeking the relaxation that is the daughter of wit.

Fables themselves are most delightful, suited to every kind of 4
witticism, and accord with every place, if not perhaps with every
time, although they do accord with times and likewise with persons, if discrimination is used. There are two kinds of them. One
is taken from mute animals as an example, like most of Aesop's
fables and ones like them, or from wholly insentient things, such
as herbs, trees, stones, like the fable brought into the Roman senate about the contention of the belly against the other parts of the
body, or the one told by Phocion against collectors gathering
money from individuals for some sacred games publicly instituted
at Athens, when they set upon him not only rudely, but even with
shouts and threats.[93]

Once upon a time, he said, a cowardly soldier, setting out for
military service, was frightened by some crows that were clamoring
and flying around him. He took this as a bad omen, so he put his
arms on the ground and did not dare to advance farther. Thereupon the crows stopped flying and singing. But a little later the

Paulo autem post militem ipsum, cum rem animo agitasset, decrevisse iter prosequi; denuo tum cornices et cantum resumpsisse et volatum; ad easque conversum illum dixisse: 'Vos quidem pro arbitrio dirumpemini me vero . . .'[12]

Alterum quod, sive fictum sive verum, vel ut vetus tamen versatur in ore hominum vel ut novum refertur. His, ni forte displicuerit, addam quas aniles dicunt fabulas, quales sunt quae narrantur ad cunas atque infantulorum vigilias, nam et hae quoque, ubi res ipsa tulerit, afferre iucunditatem possunt. Ponenda quoque videntur in hoc ipso genere fabellarum carmina et quae amatoria sunt et quae sive ludunt ad citharam aut tibiam sive ad virtutem hortantur, afferunt enim quoquo modo delectationem auditoribus. Nam quid dicendum est de explicationibus historiarum? Qua enim e re maior voluptas afferri honeste potest quam e relatione rerum gestarum? Itaque persaepe etiam seria relaxationem in consessibus inducunt et laborum et curarum. Sed hoc fortasse ad facetudinem minime spectaverit, etiam si spectet ad recreationem. De quibus ipsis deinceps quidem dicemus, etiam exemplis propositis.

soldier, after revolving the matter in his mind, decided to continue his journey. Finally the crows resumed singing and flying. Turning toward them, he said, "You can sing till you burst, if you please, but you won't get a taste of me."[94]

The second kind of fable, whether fictional or true, either is still on men's lips as something old or is told as something new. To these I will add, unless perhaps it displeases, the so-called old wives' tales such as are told at cradles while little children are awake, for these also can bring delight in the right circumstances. It also appears that songs ought to be placed in this kind of fable, both those about love and those they play to cithara or pipe or that exhort to virtue, for they bring delight to the listeners in some way. But what must be said about the accounts in histories? For from what source can one honorably bring forth greater pleasure than from the relation of past actions? Thus very often even serious matters produce in gatherings relaxation from labors and cares. But perhaps this pertains very little to wit, even if it pertains to restoration. Next I will speak about these things themselves, also setting forth examples.

# LIBER QUARTUS[1]

## : I :

### [Sine titulo]

1 Ioci igitur suapte natura iucunditatem pariunt, ab eadem enim
ducuntur voce: sunt enim a iuvando detractis literis. Hi, ubi hila-
riusculi fuerint, remissiores tamen, et curas sedant et animos tran-
quillant; itaque astantes afficiunt suavitate, lepiditate, et ea, quae
proprie tum iucunditas dicitur, tum hilaritudo vocata est. Ubi vero
vehementiores fuerint, excitant etiam risum, qui alias ad hilaritatem quidem tantum spectat meramque animi refocillationem, alias
2 ad irrisionem atque contemptum. Irrisio vero ac despicientia
oriuntur tum a turpitudine aliqua deformitateque morum, corporis, disciplinae, habitus, consuetudinis, aut facti dicti ve cuiuspiam,
ac tum patriae tum maiorum, cognatorum, affinium, amicorum,
sodalium; nam quod et indignationem quandoque ac perturba-
tiones etiam intemperatiores afferre soleant, facetudini ac relaxa-
tioni videtur omnino contrarium; alias ab ineptitudine, insulsitate,
frigiditate despectum ingenerant.

3    Quod autem haec ipsa ioca dictis constant, versantur enim in
verbis ac rebus, hinc dicta ipsa alias brevia sunt atque unius interdum verbi, alias fusa verborum plurimorum magisque continuum
in tractum ducta quaeque; nec risum ubique moveant, tum quia
saepenumero e contrario pariunt admirationem, tum quia nec res
nec verba eiusmodi sunt virium, nec qui dicit idoneus est ad risum
4 excitandum. Quod autem collocutiones congressusque ipsi nostri
constant allocutoribus ac responsoribus ipsaeque allocutiones
plerunque sunt ab initio ignotae, iccirco partes respondentis, quod

# BOOK FOUR

## : I :

## [Untitled]

Thus jokes (*ioci*) by their nature create delight (*iucunditatem*), for 1
they are derived from the same word: for they are from the verb *to
delight* (*iuvo*), with some letters removed.[1] When these jokes are
quite cheerful yet relaxed, they assuage cares and calm minds; thus
they affect the bystanders with pleasure, charm, and what sometimes is properly called delight, sometimes cheerfulness. But when
they are more vigorous, they also excite laughter, which sometimes
aims only at cheerfulness and pure restoration of mind, sometimes
at derision and contempt. But derision and contempt arise from 2
some baseness and deformity of character, body, education, de-
meanor, habit, or of something done or said, and of country, ancestors, relatives, affines, friends, companions.[2] Indeed, the fact
that they also are accustomed sometimes to bring indignation and
even more immoderate disturbances does seem completely opposed to wit and relaxation. At other times they produce contempt from ineptitude, insipidity, feebleness.

Moreover, since jokes themselves consist of witty sayings, for 3
they are concerned with words and things, it follows that sometimes witty sayings are brief and occasionally consist of one word,
sometimes ample, of many words, and more drawn out over a
continuous extent; and they do not always provoke laughter because very often they rather excite surprise, and also because neither the things nor the words have that sort of force, and the
speaker is not the right person to excite laughter.[3] Moreover, since 4
our conversations and encounters consist of addressers and re-
sponders and the addresses are usually unknown at the beginning,

extemporales sunt, dum arguta sint responsa appareantque repentina et improvisa, pariunt etiam cum iucunditate admirationem ac
5  laudem dictisque ipsis addunt plurimum gratiae ac leporis. Induc-
tiones vero fabellarum atque relationes,[2] quod iis natura delecte-
tur, mirifice etiam sedant animum et tanquam defatigatum sor-
dentemque sudore in balneis lavant deterguntque lavatum. Est
enim magna in illis vis ad quancumque persuasionem actionemque,
nedum ad relaxationem sedandasque ad molestias ac curas.

6   Quod igitur in natura soli ac terrarum usuvenit, alia ut alibi et
nascantur et coalescant, idem in dictis quoque contingit ac ridiculis, ut diversis e locis diversa deducantur sive dicta sive ridicula.
Quo fit ut quoties naturae regionum sint cognitae sedesque e quibus deducuntur facetiae, materia ipsa praebita sit ac sumministrata
7  etiam affatim iocari volentibus. Itaque nec natura deerit arti nec
ingenium ab arte destituetur atque observatione, observatio enim
pedetentim in praecepta redigitur, ars autem praeceptis constat.
Quae si quibusdam in rebus ad summum atque absolutum non
pervenit nec penitus consumata[3] est, quod aut ipsarum rerum infi-
nitas quaedam est aut quod tum negligentia est in causa, tum rerum difficultas, tum etiam quia pervenisse ad aliquam cognitionem satis quidem videatur et movendi quidem risus peritia levior
videatur, perque satis sit oratori, qua orator, et urbano homini, qua
civis est, ex hac ipsa observatione tantum esse consecuto ut et
movere ex se pro loco ac tempore risum queat et animorum refocillationem parere hac ipsa via quam facetiae munierint ac lepores
solersque iocandi cognitio, non quae oratoris sit propria sed faceti,
qua de re libro hoc ipsi disserimus.

for that reason the role of the responder, because it is extemporaneous — provided that the responses are sharp and appear sudden and improvised — also produces admiration with delight and adds praise and much grace and charm to the witticisms themselves. But introducing and relating fables, because nature delights in  5 them, also wonderfully assuages the mind and, as it were, washes it in baths when it is exhausted and filthy with sweat and wipes it when washed. For fables have a great power in them to bring about any persuasion and action you like, not to mention their power to relax and to assuage annoyances and cares.

Therefore, the same thing that happens with the nature of soil  6 and lands, that different things are born and grow strong in different places, also occurs with witticisms and jests, that different ones, whether witticisms or jests, are derived from different places. So it happens that whenever the natures of regions and the sources from which witticisms are derived are known, sufficient material is also offered and furnished to those who want to make jokes. And  7 so neither will nature desert art nor will intelligence be abandoned by art and observation, for observation is gradually reduced to precepts, but art consists of precepts. If it has not reached the highest point and completion in some things nor has been entirely perfected because these things are numberless or because sometimes negligence is responsible, sometimes the difficulty of the things, sometimes also because it appears sufficient to have reached some understanding and the skill of provoking laughter appears slight, it should completely suffice the orator, as orator, and the urbane man, as citizen, to have achieved from observation just enough to be able to provoke laughter on his own, in accordance with place and time, and to create restoration of mind in the way opened up by witticisms, charming remarks, and a skillful knowledge of joking, which is not particular to the orator but to the witty man. This is what I discuss in this book.

: 2 :

*Artem naturae coniunctam plurimum valere ad facetudinem.*

1 His itaque hunc in modum explicatis, sensim quidem atque exemplis propositis ostendamus artem naturae coniunctam id praestare
ut, quod turpe est suapte natura atque oscenum, id dicatur nec
turpiter nec oscene; quod artis esse quis neget? Perinde enim ut
sterilibus in arboribus insitionis arte utuntur agricolae, quo foe-
cundas illas atque hortenses efficiant e silvaticis, sic faceti homines,
arte adhibita ac translationibus usi, rem naturaliter turpem dictis
honestant et quod ipsum per se oscenum est in lepidum vertunt ac
facetum.

2 Id autem est huiusmodi. Reguli cuiusdam[4] aula inquinabatur
nefandis puerorum amoribus atque huiusce generis libidine. Forte
igitur ex aulicis quispiam aestivo tempore in cubiculo quiescebat
sub meridiem spirantibus zephyris, quorum afflatu, quibus ille
intectus erat linteolis, detegebatur pudendas ad partes corporis.
Forte igitur ea praeteriens Rodoricus Hispalensis, vir et suavis et
qui aulicorum mores notos haberet, cum animadverteret cucurbitulam quasi quandam pendere ad illius ramices, 'Mirum ne,' inquit, 'videatur grandiusculam eam esse, quae in sterquilinio coalue-
rit?' Videtis ne ars ingenio comitata quid praestiterit? Adhibita
enim translatione virilis membri in cucurbitulam, primo verbum
honestavit, deinde rem turpem honestis vocibus et expressit et ac-
cusavit, eadem translatione usus. Cucurbita enim fimo saturata
mirifice grandescit. Quo etiam verborum honestamento turpem
illius usum in re venerea expressit et ridiculum fecit.

3 Haec igitur artis sunt, quae in hac ipsa parte locum quoque
suum optinent, si qui facetiis dant operam artis ipsius oblivisci

: 2 :

*Art joined to nature is very effective for producing wit.*

Having explained these things after this fashion, I will show,   1
gradually and by setting forth examples, how art joined to nature
allows what by its own nature is base and obscene to be said in a
way that is neither base nor obscene. Who would deny that this is
the province of art? For just as farmers use the art of grafting onto
sterile trees to change them from wild to fertile and suited to a
garden, so witty men, applying art and using metaphors, make
naturally base matter appear respectable with their words and turn
what is in itself obscene into something charming and witty.

But here is an example. The court of a young prince was being   2
polluted by the unspeakable love of boys and lust of this sort. So
by chance one of the courtiers was resting in his bedroom in the
heat of summer at noon with the west winds blowing, and by
their breeze the private parts of his body were uncovered by the
bedclothes with which he had been covered. Passing that way by
chance, then, Rodrigo of Seville, a pleasant man who knew the
habits of courtiers, noticed a zucchini, as it were, hanging beside
that man's swollen testes and said, "Is it any wonder that it appears
rather big, since it grew in a dung heap?" Do you see what art accompanied by intelligence can accomplish? For by using the metaphor of a zucchini for the male member, first he made the word
appear respectable, then he expressed and reproached a shameful
thing in decent words by using the same metaphor. For zucchini
saturated in dung grow wonderfully. Also, by making the words
appear respectable he expressed the shameful sexual behavior of
that man and made it ridiculous.

So these things are the province of art, which in this part ob-   3
tain also their own place, unless those who devote their efforts to

noluerint. Nam si facetudo mediocritas quaedam est, sine arte, id
4 est absque prudentia et artificio, perveniri ad illam nequit. Idem
hic Rodoricus, cum vidisset ingredientem Florentinum hominem
in regis atrium, in quo pueri regii se se exercebant ad pilam,
'Macte,' inquit, 'fide ac mercatura vir; arcem hanc ingressus, ad
eius portam, credo, pugiunculum de more reliqueris; et atrium
ingressurus, ne legem quoque atrii ignores, ante eius hostium et
tentigo tibi relinquenda est.' An potuit honestius et turpitudinem
indicare et ludere cum mercatore pudentius?

5 Haec igitur ipsa, ut dixi, artis sunt, quae plurimum apud inge-
niosum hominem ad consequendam retinendamque mediocritatem est praestitura. Artis quoque ipsius est et invenire et conside-
rare locis e quibus dicta ipsa ridiculaque deducantur. In priori
igitur dicto locus praebitus est a translatione, in secundo a rei
similitudine, quemadmodum et hoc quod subiicio.

6 Pepererat infantulum Paschasii Decii nurus, arcis Neapolitanae
praefecti, utque de more est et congratulatum una et visitatum
accesserat idem, de quo dictum est, Rodoricus. Itaque ingressus
ipse cubiculum in quo conquiescebat puerpera comperit hinc Paschasium confectum senio, innisum baculo ac languescentem, illinc
e familiaribus quempiam perinde ac bovem nimia de obesitate
iacentem in scrinio, itemque alterum eo ingenio praeditum parum
qui ab asello iudicaretur differre. Progressus igitur ad cubile ubi
infantulus vagiebat, pedes exosculatus est eius conversusque ad
astantes, 'An,' inquit, 'praesaepe ingressus in quo et asinus et bos
recumberet seniorque una Iosephus, non et ipse ad Christi pedes
exoculandos progrederer?' Potuit ne ars ingenioso suffragata homini commodiore uti atque appositiore similitudine, ut quae ridicula non esset res illam ex arte maxime ridiculam efficeret?

7 Est apud Plautum ex ore et pudicae et permodestae mulieris
dictum eadem e translatione atque officina haustum, quod etiam

wit wish to forget art itself. For if wittiness is a certain kind of mean, without art, that is without prudence and skill, one cannot attain it. When this same Rodrigo saw a Florentine man entering 4 the king's hall where the king's boys were practicing with a ball, he said, "Bravo, man, for your loyalty and enterprise! On entering this castle, you left your dagger at the gate, I believe, as is the custom, and, as you are about to enter the hall, you shouldn't disregard the law of the hall either; leave your lust at its door." Would it have been possible both to reveal his baseness with greater dignity and to joke with the merchant more modestly?

So these things, as I said, are the province of art, which will 5 offer an intelligent man the most help in reaching and keeping to the mean. It is also the province of art to find and consider from which places witticisms and jests are to be drawn. So in the first witticism, the place was suggested by a metaphor, in the second by similarity of situation — like this one too which I now add.

The daughter-in-law of Pasquasio Decio, governor of the castle 6 of Naples, had given birth to a baby, and, as is the custom, this same Rodrigo of whom I have spoken had come to offer congratulations and pay a visit at the same time.[4] And so, having entered the bedroom in which the new mother was resting, he found in one place Pasquasio worn out with age, feeble, and leaning on a staff, and in another place one of the servants, lying from excessive obesity on a book box just like an ox, and likewise another servant, who looked about as intelligent as a donkey. So proceeding to the bed where the infant was crying, he kissed his feet, turned to those present, and said, "Since I've entered the stable in which the ass and ox were reclining together with the aged Joseph, shouldn't I go up and kiss Christ's feet?" Could art, coming to the aid of a clever man, find a more appropriate and apt simile to turn a humorless scene artfully into something funny?

In Plautus there is a witticism from the mouth of a chaste and 7 very modest woman that is drawn from the same workshop of

suppraposui, in re quidem uxoria quae suapte natura perpudenda quidem dictu est: 'Fundum alienum arat, familiarem incultum deserit.' Quod etsi risum non moverit, ostendit tamen ars ipsa quid

8 valeat. Habemus igitur locos duos maxime nobiles et translationis et similitudinis, qui satis quidem aperte vel confirmare possunt vel testificari, praetorio etiam in iudicio, artem quoque vel maximum in his locum sibi vendicare posse, ni hominum defuerit industria laborque ille pertinax, rerum omnium expugnator. Quocirca locos etiam alios percenseamus qui admonere nos et artis possunt et observationis, quae artem ipsam constituere est solita.

: 3 :

## De inveniendis dictorum ac ridiculorum locis.

1 Quoniam autem quos locos appellamus, ii sedes dictorum sunt ac ridiculorum, e quibus ioci, ac si ibidem lateant, extrudendi sunt, ad alias iam regiones proficiscamur, quo palam fiat artem quoque in illis non parum valere.

Sedentibus nobis pro foribus nostris disserentibusque his ipsis de rebus, facti sunt obviam inter se agrestes duo, alter albenti pilleo eoque grandiore intectus caput, alter nudatis pedibus ac plantis. Atque hic quidem e vestigio verbis in illum illatus, 'Quanti,' inquit, 'fungulus iste?,' pilleum videlicet irridens. Ille, sublato statim supercilio, conversis mox ad pedes eius oculis, respondit: 'Quanti calceoli tui ac denariolo pluris?' Statim omnes in risum

2 conversi sumus. Igitur alter a pilleo admonitus est excitusque a natura eaque duce tantum, alter etiam ab arte adiutus, quae illum admonuit pedum excalciatorum. Itaque locus lacessentis videtur a

metaphor (and which I also cited above) concerning marital relations, which by their nature are quite shameful to talk about:
"He plows another's farm; he leaves his family's uncultivated."[5]
Even if this does not provoke laughter, it still shows what art itself
can do. So we have two especially excellent places — metaphor and    8
simile — which clearly enough can confirm or testify, even in a trial
before a judge, that art can also claim for itself the greatest place in
these things, if human effort and perseverance, victor over everything, are present.[6] Therefore, let us also survey other places that
can remind us of art and observation, which usually constitutes art
in itself.

:  3  :

*On finding the places of witticisms and jests.*

But since what we call places are the sources of witticisms and    1
jests, from which jokes, even if they lie hidden there, must be
driven out, let us now proceed to other regions so that it will be
clear that art exerts great power in them too.

While we were sitting in front of our door and discussing these
very things, two peasants met, one with his head covered by a
white, felt hat, and a pretty big one too, the other with his feet and
soles bare.[7] And the latter at once, assailing the former with
words, said, "How much is that little mushroom of yours?," evidently mocking the felt hat. The former immediately raised one
eyebrow, then turning his eyes to the other's feet, responded, "How
much are your little shoes? More than a penny?" At once we all
started laughing. So the one man was prompted by the felt hat    2
and incited by nature alone as his guide, the other was also helped
by art, which put him in mind of the shoeless feet. And so the

vestitu oblatus, respondentis ab arte repraesentatus atque ab oppo-
sito. Alter enim erat intecto capite atque a superiore corporis
3 parte, alter nudatis pedibus, quae pars inferior est corporis. Non
rideas modo, verum etiam dirumpare, cum apud Plautum dicentem illum audies in Trinumo, 'Pol hic quidem fungino est genere:
capite se totum tegit'?

4    Eodem tempore, cum staret forte nobis e regione sutor senex, et
quidem sordidus admodum senex, cui ad nasum pendebat pituita
grandiuscula quidem ac pellucida, praeteriens homullus dicaculus
et ipse 'pannis tamen atque annis obsitus,' ut ille inquit apud Terentium, iocandique opportunitatem nactus, 'Perpulchrum,' inquit,
5 'adamanta et pretiosum.' Tum alter: 'Et anulo tuo dignum.' Tali
igitur tamque inexpectato responso, ars ne an natura, an simul
iunctae, iocari urbanius potuerint nesciam. Ille enim iocatus est,
sumpta occasione senili ab aetate, quae pituitosa est; hic vero ab
6 eo, quod adamantes includi anulis sint soliti. Sumpsit urbanissime
Plautus etiam alibi iocandi opportunitatem a tempore; nam cum
dixisset servus apud lenam de amatore, 'Quam tibi sospitalis fuit,'
tum lena, 'Mortuus est,' inquit, 'qui fuit; qui est vivus est.'

7    Iocabantur aliquando vel rixabantur potius ex iis duo quos maiores nostri appellitabant nebulones: et alteri quidem Asello factum
est nomen, quod ob linguae intemperantiam et pugnis saepe con-
tusus et verberibus ac fustibus honeratus perinde ac asinus esset;
alteri vero Ventritio, quod patrimonium pene omne pitissando
compotandoque in ventrem congessisset. Prior igitur Ventritius
inter conviciandum: 'Quantum, o amice Aselle' — paulo enim ante
et pugnis caesus et quernis etiam fustibus percussus fuerat — 'quantum, inquam, aeris inest tibi in crumena vectura ex hodierna?' Ad

place of the provoker seems to have been offered by clothing, the responder's supplied by art and the opposite. For one had his head covered, the top part of the body; the other was barefoot, the lower part of the body. Wouldn't you not only laugh but also burst when you hear that man in Plautus' *Trinummus* saying, "By Pollux, this man certainly belongs to the mushroom genus: he covers himself entirely with his head"?[8]

At the same time, when by chance an old cobbler — a filthy old man with a bead of snot, large and clear, hanging from his nose — was standing opposite us, a facetious little old man, "covered with rags and years," as the man says in Terence, was passing by and, finding an opportunity to make a joke, said, "What a lovely, precious diamond."[9] The other shot back: "And worthy to go on your ring." I don't know whether art or nature or the two joined together could make a wittier and more surprising response. For the first man joked by taking his opportunity from old age, which is prone to mucus, but the second from the fact that diamonds are customarily set in rings. Elsewhere Plautus with great elegance also took the opportunity for a joke from [the place of] time. For when at a procuress's, a slave said about a lover, "What a lifesaver he was!," the procuress responded, "The one who *was* is dead; the one who *is*, is alive."[10]

Once upon a time two of those men whom our ancestors used to call good-for-nothings were exchanging jokes or rather quarreling. One of them had been given the name of Little Ass because, thanks to his uncontrollable tongue, he had often been beaten with fists and showered with whips and cudgels just like an ass, but the other one was called Potbelly because he had stuffed almost all of his patrimony into his belly by wine-bibbing and drinking parties. So first Potbelly tauntingly says: "How much, Little Ass, my friend" — for a bit earlier he had been pounded with fists and also beaten with oaken cudgels — "how much money, I say, do you have in your purse from today's cartage?" To which

quae confestim Asellus: 'Quantum tibi in ventriculum influxit villi hesterna e vindemia?'

8     Itaque eiusmodi sive dicta sive ridicula et multum habent fellis et maxime apposita sunt ad movendum risum plurimumque in iis pollet natura, tametsi nominum tum interpretatio tum formatio videtur ad artem prorsus referenda. A diverso quoque sensu eorum quae dicuntur ioci et quidem maxime ridiculares depromuntur, ut cum ille inquit in Menechmis, 'Magna cum cura illum curari volo,' tum medicus,

> Quin suspirabo plus sexcentum dies;
> ita ego illum cum cura magna curabo.

Ille diligentiam curationis exigit; hic medici personam sustinens, quod aegre admonitionem ferret quodque cura molestiam quoque animique afflictionem significat, suspiraturum se se obtulit; suspiria enim exagitati ac parum quiescentis animi sunt signa.

9     Forte viator Florentinus, ut ventricosus admodum sic etiam perquam salsus, cum per urbem Senas iter faciens porta exiret quae Romam ducit ac sublato palliolo popam ostentaret et praegrandem et tumidam, atque ibi tum quispiam e portae custodibus per iocum ac risum dixisset, 'Sapit homullus hic, qui neutique pone, sed prae se manticam sibi apposuit,' tum ille ore quam maxime renidenti, 'An tu,' inquit, 'aliter per latronum fines ac sicario-
10   rum securus rebus cum tuis incesseris?' Quid autem mage lepidum aut salsum magis? Iocandi autem locus in dicto priori sumministratus est a corporis sive habitu sive deformitate; in posteriori a morum turpitudine ac rapiendi impotentia et studio. Adminiculata vero est in posteriori plurimum quidem ars, quae illi suggessit ea quae cernantur oculis diligentius custodiri ac cautius. Nam quod tueamur nos nostraque naturali quidem inest a studio; quo nam autem modo quaque fiat via, id artis potius est.

Little Ass immediately replied: "How many sips of wine have flowed into your stomach from yesterday's vintage?"

And so witticisms or jests of this kind both contain much bit- 8 terness and are especially suited to make people laugh, and they are naturally strong, and yet it appears that the explanation and formation of the names must be completely assigned to art. Also, jokes, and in fact the funniest ones, are drawn from a meaning that differs from what is said, as when that man in the *Menaechmi* says, "I want him to be cared for with great care," then the doctor,

> Why, I'll sigh more than six hundred days, and so I will care
> for him with great care.[11]

The first man demands diligence in medical care; the second, play-ing the part of a doctor, offers to sigh because he takes the admo-nition ill and because *care* also means annoyance and affliction of mind. For sighs are signs of an agitated and unquiet mind.

A Florentine traveler, extremely fat as well as sharp-witted, 9 journeying through the city of Siena, happened to be leaving by the gate that leads to Rome, and his raised mantle showed a very large and swollen paunch. And thereupon one of the guards of the gate said, joking and laughing, "This little man is clever because he placed his bag in front, not in back." Then he, beaming for all he was worth, said, "Would you walk safely with your property through this territory of thieves and assassins in any other way?"[12] What could be more charming and witty than that? In the first 10 witticism the place for joking was provided by the condition or deformity of the body; in the latter, from foulness of morals and lack of restraint and eagerness for plundering. But in the latter the greatest support was provided by art, which suggested to him that those things perceived by the eyes are more diligently and cau-tiously guarded. For we protect ourselves and our things by natu-ral inclination, but the manner and way this happens is rather the province of art.

11    Nobis adolescentulis, cum Italiae res maxime florerent vige-
retque rei bellicae honos Italicos apud duces multique ob strenui-
tatem ac rei militaris disciplinam haberentur in pretio, in iisque
Antonellus esset Foroliviensis, qui tamen mercennariam exerceret
militiam singulisque pene aut benniis[5] conductorem mutaret atque ante finitum prius stipendium ad alium transiret conductorem, commendaretureque in senatu Florentino, quod sagax admodum esset, impiger, manu promptus perque laboriosus, tum
Cosmus, 'Et, quod maximum in eo est,' subdidit, 'etiam anteluca-
nus.' Hoc dictum ab arte totum profectum est atque a transfugio-
rum illius observatione; peperit autem risum, quia tanquam obliquo e loco atque ex insidiis repente proruperit.

12    Referre erat mihi solitus inter confabulandum Erricus Pudericus, senex maximi usus summaeque iucunditatis, Neapolitanum
civem, cuius ipse nomen ob familiae respectum ac liberorum ob-
ticebat, nam propudiosus erat morboque laborabat infami, con-
venisse Genuensi cum mercatore ac praefinisse rei frumentariae
summam quandam certam ad diem Neapolitanum in litus com-
portandam. Itaque in praetoris conspectu, cum ab actorum magistro pacta ipsa conventionesque de ritu adnotarentur praetorii,
ex iis, qui tum aderant, testibus inclamasse quempiam, quasi e
loco quodam abdito: Nec licere nec fas esse uxores absque virorum
consensu quippiam omnino transigere quod eae sui iuris non essent. Dictum sane non mordax modo summeque aculeatum, verum illi ipsi in quem inferretur mirifice erubescendum, quippe qui
palam propudii notaretur morbique perpudescendi.

13    Iocandi locum hunc ars ipsa magis quam natura sibi adinvenit
ex lege sumptum constitutisque e civilibus. In eundem quoque
hunc ab matrona perurbana dictum extat generis eiusdem; quae ab
illo vocata in iudicium, cum praetore coram ipsa sisteret, 'Quid mirum,' inquit, 'bone praetor, aut praeter consuetum homo hic facit,

When I was a young man, the affairs of Italy were most flour-  11
ishing, honor in war was thriving among the Italian generals, and
many were valued for their strenuous activity and military disci-
pline. Among these Antonello da Forlì, who was however a condottiere, would change his employer almost every year or two, and
before finishing his service would go over to another employer.[13]
When he was being praised in the Florentine senate as shrewd,
energetic, gallant, and very hardworking, then Cosimo de' Medici
added, "And his greatest quality is that he's also up before dawn."[14]
This witticism entirely proceeded from art and from observation
of his desertions. Moreover, it produced laughter because it suddenly burst forth as if from a hidden place and an ambush.

Enrico Puderico, an old man of the greatest experience and ut-  12
most agreeableness, used to tell me in conversation about a Neapolitan citizen, whose name he kept silent out of respect for his
family and children, since he was disgraceful and suffered from an
infamous disease.[15] He had met with a Genovese merchant and
determined that an amount of grain would be brought on a certain
day to the Neapolitan coast. And so in the presence of the magistrate when the contracts and covenants had been recorded by the
*mastrodatti* according to the usage of the magistrate, one of the
witnesses who was present exclaimed, as if from some hidden
place, that it was not permitted or allowed for wives to conduct
any business at all without the consent of their husbands because
they were not legally competent.[16] A witticism indeed not only
mordant and extremely pointed but also such as to make its target
blush wonderfully, since he was openly censured for a shameful act
and a very shameful disease.

Art itself rather than nature found this place for joking and  13
took it from law and civil ordinances. There is also a witticism of
the same kind against this same man by a very clever matron.
When summoned by him to court, she stood before the judge and
said, "Is this man doing anything astonishing, my good judge, or

si foemellam me eiicere paterno ex agello studet, qui mulieres pene omnes munere iam eiecerit suo bellumque iis indixerit?' Omnino igitur nota haec a morum turpitudine inusta est atque ab infamia usquequaque abominanda ad artemque prorsus referenda, cum abominandum scelus mulier honestis quoad potuit verbis innuerit quibusdamque quasi signis, qua significatione rem tueri suam nitebatur, cum oppressam se ac circumventam intelligeret.

14     Marinus Branchatius, eques Neapolitanus, quique propter dicacitatem et multus esset et invector acerrimus adversum literatos homines, prandente aliquando Ferdinando rege, cuius mensam assiduus inodorabatur, craterculus ei cum esset oblatus vernatii quam suavissimi illumque et ipse labellatim hausisset, interrogatus ab rege qua nam Bacchus is locutus esset lingua, respondit: 'Oppido quam literata,' vinum ex eo commendans. Tum compotor ibidem qui aderat, 'Quid tu,' inquit, 'Marine, tantum literis impartire, adversum literatos ipsos qui tam impotenter atque assiduus

15 inveharis?' Cumque e vestigio illi responsum esset ab non insulso homine inter pares eiusdemque rei studiosos plerumque odium verti atque inimicitias, ibi tum adolescens apprime ingenuus quique vinolentiam eius nosset, 'Nec ad rem,' inquit, 'ista faciunt nec sunt necessaria, cum hos inter literatos nullus profecto sit Marino aut similis aut par.' Primum dictum a genere oblatum est, ab ipsis videlicet literis. Secundum dictum illatum est sive ab eodem genere ductum sive a specie. Tertium autem universa complexum est, cum primas ei concederet inter literatos, hoc est vinosos. Quid his dicas artificiosius?

16     De eodem quoque sic refertur. Occupata Campania ab Carolo octavo, Gallorum rege, cum Alfonsus minor, Neapolitanorum rex, cum Ferdinando filio ac Federico fratre in Siciliam ob metum tam

contrary to his habit, if he is eager to expel me, a poor woman, from my father's little field, since he has already expelled almost all women from his service and declared war on them?" Thus this mark was thoroughly branded [on him] owing to moral turpitude and an infamy always to be abominated, and her words must be totally assigned to art, since the woman intimated an abominable crime with words as honorable as she was able and with certain, as it were, signs. With this hint she was striving to protect her property, since she understood that she had been harassed and cheated.

Marino Brancaccio, a Neapolitan cavalier, thanks to his raillery 14 was a frequent and extremely sharp critic of men of letters.[17] Once when Ferdinando, king of Naples — at whose table he was constantly present[18] — was dining, Marino was offered a little cup of the sweetest Vernaccia. He drained it, smacking his lips, and being asked by the king what tongue this Bacchus spoke, replied, "A most literary one," praising the wine in this way. Then a drinking companion who was there said, "Why, Marino, do you partake of so much literature, you who inveigh so ineffectually and busily against men of letters?" A man of some wit immediately re- 15 sponded to the latter that hatred and enmity usually turn up among peers and men who pursue the same thing, whereupon a very wellborn young man who knew the man's habit of excessive drinking said, "Your remarks are neither apt nor necessary since among literary men like these there is surely no one similar or equal to Marino." The first witticism was brought from the class, namely from letters themselves. The second witticism was introduced, derived either from the same class or from the species. But the third comprehended all together, since it conceded him primacy among men of letters, that is, among excessive drinkers. What more artful jokes than these could you make?

This tale is also told about him. When Campania had been oc- 16 cupied by Charles VIII, king of France, and Alfonso II, king of Naples, with his son Ferdinando and his brother Federico, had

violentis exercitus traiecisset nec Marinus eos comitatus iam esset, demiratus hoc quispiam ac sciscitabundus quaeritabat quaenam huius esset rei causa. Tum adolescens eadem ex aula, argutus ille quidem atque admodum lepidus, 'An non,' inquit, 'is est Marini usus, ea in potando atque in convivendo exercitatio, ea etiam vis ac peritia comessandi, ut Gallicas reformidare debeat lagenas aut gentis eius lancibus terga vertere?' Perbelle dictum, nedum salse.

17  Sedes autem ipsa iocandi et quasi argumentatiuncula posita est in usu atque peritia, quando in artificio quocunque, auctore etiam Aristotele, peritissimo eius cuique adhibenda fides est atque auc-toritas tribuenda.

18  Sunt multa quoque verba duos sensus, ut Quintilianus quoque inquit, significantia, quae et amplum et patentem praebere possunt iocantibus campum, in quo et ars non exiguum ius exercet maxime in respondendo; siquidem, prolato verbo ingenioque lacessito et provocato, statim ars convertit se se ad implorandum auxilium ab altero quidem verbi ipsius sensu, ut cum Mercurius dixisset apud Plautum, 'Malam a me sibi rem arcessit iumento suo,' confestim

19  Sosia subdidit, 'Non enim ullum habeo iumentum.' Itaque duplici-tas sensus, arte iuvante, iocandi locum ei praebuit; cumque alibi dixisset, 'Geminum dum quaeris, gemes,' ipsa literarum ac sylla-

20  barum similitudo et quasi collusio iocandi locum exhibuit. Atque in huiusmodi praecipue vocibus prima quidem occursio tota est naturae, secunda vero ad artem potius referenda: eius enim est et deducere voces et quaerere earum structuram et comparare eas atque inflectere—quam alliterationem alibi vocavimus, cum de poetarum numeris praecepta traderemus.

21  Ea quoque quae insunt a natura ac dicuntur propria, ut 'pastum quaerere,' ut 'prolem appetere,' ut 'hinnire ac mugire' atque eius-modi alia, iocantes mirifice adiuvant, ut cum ludens apud Plautum servus dixisset, 'Boves bini hic sunt in crumena,' alterius servi e vestigio menti occurrit colludere et ipsum posse ab pascendi cupi-ditate quae a natura bubus inest, itaque iocabundus subdidit,

crossed over into Sicily, fearing the French army's violence, and
Marino had not yet joined them, someone wondered at this and
asked inquiringly what the reason for it was.[19] Then a clever and
charming young man from the same court said, "Is it not Marino's
custom, his practice in drinking and banqueting, also his vigor and
skill in reveling, to fear the bottles of the French or flee the dishes
of this people?"[20] A lovely and pointed remark. But this source 17
and, as it were, theme for joking are located in experience and
skill, since in each art, also on the authority of Aristotle, one must
put faith in and attribute authority to the most skilled.[21]

There are also many words having two meanings, as Quintilian 18
also says, that can offer jokers an ample and wide field in which art
exercises no small authority, especially in replying, since after a
word has been thrown out and one's wit stimulated, art at once
turns itself to imploring aid from another sense of this word, as
after Mercury had said in Plautus, "He begs me for trouble with
his own mule," Sosia immediately replied, "I don't have a mule."[22]
And so the doubleness of sense, with the aid of art, provided him 19
the place for joking, and when he said elsewhere, "While you seek
your sib, you sigh," the similarity, almost collusion, of letters and
syllables suggested a place for joking.[23] And especially in words of 20
this kind the first occurrence is completely natural but the second
must rather be attributed to art. For it is the province of art to
adapt words, to examine their structure, to join them together,
and to bend them—which elsewhere I termed "alliteration," when
I was handing down precepts about poetic meters.[24]

Also, statements which are natural and are called proper or lit- 21
eral, like "seek food," "desire offspring," "neigh and low," and others
of this sort, wonderfully help jokers, as when in Plautus a slave
says playfully, "A pair of oxen is here in the purse," it at once comes
into the mind of the other slave that he could play along, and so
he jokingly adds, alluding to the desire to eat natural to oxen,

'Emitte sodes, ne fames enecet, inire pastum.' Quis autem neget artis hoc esse, tametsi, natura repugnante, ars ipsa parum per se omnino in multis potest?

22 Ambigua quoque quaeque aliam atque aliam interpretationem recipiunt maxime exposita sunt iocantibus, ut cum servus apud Plautum et graviter et gratulanter domino dixisset, 'Gaudeo / tibi mea opera liberorum esse amplius,' (filium enim herilem in infantia amissum recuperaverat), illico, nactus herus iocandi opportunitatem, respondit iocabundus, 'Etenim non placet. / Nil moror aliena mihi opera fieri plures liberos.' Quod enim ille dixerat gratulatus — sua quod opera atque industria filium invenisset — in alium ac libidinosum sensum interpretatus herus ioco materiam praebuit.

23 Contraria quoque inter se et ipsa occasionem iocis praebent, ut in Amphitryone cum dixisset Mercurius, 'Dextera vox aures, ut videtur, verberat,' ex adverso contulit Sosia, 'Metuo vocis ne vice hodie hic vapulem.' Et verbero enim et vapulo invicem contraria sunt, perinde ut ago et patior.

24 Datur etiam iocis locus ab interpretatione scripti, cum illud est ambiguum, etiam Cicerone exemplum afferente in altercatione Scauri ac Rutilii de ambitu; cum in eius tabulis ostenderentur hae quatuor literae, 'A.F. P. R.,' et Scaurus interpretaretur, 'Actum fide publica Rutilii,' Rutilius autem, 'Ante factum post relatum,' ibi C. Canium, equitem Romanum qui Rutilio aderat, exclamasse, 'Verum illarum literarum sensum esse hunc scilicet: Aemilius fecit, plectitur Rutilius.' Quod dictum acutum esse vult Cicero et concinnum. Non caruit igitur nec magistro nec arte huiusmodi interpretatio.

25 Consuevere duci etiam ab admonitionibus ac consiliis dicta admodum etiam faceta, quale Granii illud apud Ciceronem. Cum malo patrono, qui vocem in dicendo obtudisset, mulsum frigidum

"Please let them out to eat so that they don't starve to death."[25] Indeed, who could deny that there is art in this, although, if nature is adverse, art itself can do very little in many cases?

Also, ambiguous things and ones that receive different interpre- 22 tations are especially accessible to jokers, as when a slave in Plautus said gravely and joyfully to his master, "I rejoice that you have more children through my work" (for he had recovered his master's son, who had been lost in infancy). Instantly the master took the opportunity for joking and responded with a jest, "Well I don't like it. I'm not fond of having more children through someone else's work."[26] What the other had said joyfully—that he had found the son through his work and industry—the master, interpreting it in another and licentious sense, made into matter for a joke.

Opposites also provide an occasion for jokes, as when Mercury 23 said in *Amphitruo*, "A voice from the right, it seems, is striking my ears," and Sosia replied with the opposite, "I'm afraid I might receive a beating here today instead of a voice."[27] For to strike and to be beaten are opposites, just as to act and to suffer.

A place for jokes is also given from the interpretation of writing 24 when it is ambiguous; even Cicero offers an example in the dispute between Scaurus and Rutilius about corrupt electioneering. When four letters, "A.F. P. R.," were shown in Rutilius' account books, and Scaurus interpreted, "A transaction on the public credit of Rutilius," but Rutilius, "Done earlier, entered later," then Gaius Canius, a Roman equestrian who was assisting Rutilius, exclaimed, "The true sense of those letters is surely this: Aemilius did it; Rutilius is punished."[28] Cicero maintains that that witticism is clever and elegant. Therefore such an interpretation lacked neither a master nor art.

It is common for witticisms, even very witty ones, to be drawn 25 from admonition and advice, like this one of Granius in Cicero. When he advised a bad advocate, who had weakened his voice by

bibendum consuleret illeque, 'Si id fecero, perdam vocem' respondisset, tum Granius,⁶ 'Melius,' inquit, 'quam reos.'

26      Datur etiam iocandi locus a consentaneis moribus, cuius exemplum extat etiam apud Ciceronem. Cum enim Scaurus non nulla
laboraret invidia, quod sine testamento Pompeii cuiusdam locuple-
tis hominis bona possideret funusque quoddam duceretur, tum C.
Memius dixisse fertur et acute et perbelle, 'Quin vides, o Scaure,
mortuus enim rapitur, si potes esse possessor?'

27      Ducuntur etiam ioci et salsi et belli admodum ab responsore in
eo ipso genere quo usus est quis prior, utque Ciceroniano utamur
exemplo: adolescentulus Q. Aquilius male de se audivit; is gran-
dior iam et consularis, factus obviam festivo homini Aegilio, qui
videbatur mollior quamvis nec esset, muliebri usus est nomine,
quo illum vellicaret, 'Quando,' inquit, 'Aegilia, ad me veneris cum
tua colu et lana?,' reddidit statim Aegilius, vel retorsit potius,
'"Non pol," inquit "audeo, nam me ad famosas vetuit mater accedere."' Quid magis artificiosum quam telum idem retorquere et ex
eodem genere dictum eiusdem fellis reiaculari ac repercutere?

28      Est et hoc generis eiusdem. Neapolitanus quidam civis et ipse
male de se quoque audiebat; sub vesperum itaque ad fores eius
accessit iuvenis et ipse propudiosus nec satis bene de se audiens,
cumque clausas illas inveniret et esse illum intus intelligeret,
accommodata vocula maxime mollem in modum atque ad rimulas,
'O mea,' dixit, 'Iacoba, cur non te te mihi cupientissimo ad fores
exhibes?' Tum ille eodem vocis usus lenocinio, 'Quia suas te te ad
fores paratissimus expectat Ambrosius.'

29      Manant et a re non expectata et ab eo quod est ex non sperato
non illepide neque non admodum belle dicta ac diversis quidem
modis, praecipue autem a nominis aut verbi vel derivatione vel

speaking, to drink cold wine with honey, and the other had replied, "If I do, I'll destroy my voice," Granius replied, "Better that than the defendants."[29]

A place for joking is also given by appropriateness to character, 26 an example of which is also in Cicero. For when Scaurus was an object of ill-will because he had taken possession without a will of the goods of one Pompeius, a rich man, and a funeral procession was passing by, Gaius Memmius is supposed to have cleverly and neatly remarked, "Scaurus, a dead man is being rushed along; why don't you see if you can take possession?"[30]

Jokes that are pungent and neat are also to be found by a re- 27 spondent replying in the same vein as the original speaker. To take an example from Cicero: as a young man, Quintus Aquilius had a bad reputation. When he was older and now a former consul, he ran into Aegilius, a jovial man, who appeared effeminate although he was not, and used a woman's name to taunt him. "Aegilia," he said, "when will you come to my house with your distaff and wool?" At once Aegilius replied or rather hurled back, "'I really don't dare,' he said. 'My mother has forbidden me to approach women of ill repute.'"[31] What is more artful than to hurl back the same weapon and to cast back a witticism of the same kind, full of the same bile?

This, too, is of the same kind. A Neapolitan citizen also had a 28 bad reputation. And so toward evening a young man, who was also disgraceful and had no good reputation, approached his door. When he found it shut and realized the other was inside, he made his little voice as effeminate as possible and said to the cracks, "My dear Jacoba, why don't you show yourself at the door to me, who desire you so?" Then the other, using the same alluring tone, "Because Ambrosio is all ready for you at his door."

Rather neat witticisms and ones not lacking in charm flow from 29 something unexpected and unhoped-for in different ways but especially from the derivation or definition of a name or word. For

definitione, ut, cum in senatu ageretur de agris publicis deque lege Thoria et premeretur Lucilius ab iis qui a pecore eius depasci agros publicos et de lege dicerent, 'Non est,' inquit Appius, 'Lucilii pecus illud; erratis; liberum enim esse puto quod qua lubet pascitur.'

30    Est eiusdem generis, nec minore quidem gratia, Charitei dictum non incelebre. Cum enim Neapoli iactaretur numus belli tempore adulterata materia querereturque e notis eius quispiam quod nesciret iam quid haberet, tum ille, vultu quam maxime ad iocum accommodato, 'Est,' inquit, 'diis immortalibus quod gratias agam gratulerque amicitiae nostrae, tandem enim hominem inveni et amicum quidem hominem et vere divitem, quando divitis est hominis nescire quid habeat.'

31    Habet quoque concessio et locum et leporem suum. Id autem est quod Cicero inquit, 'Ut facete concedas adversario id ipsum quod tibi ille detraxit'; quale illud Coelii. Cum enim ei quidam malo genere natus diceret indignum esse suis maioribus, 'At her-
32    cule,' respondit, 'tu tuis dignus.' Simile est familiaris nostri Marini Tomacelli, viri[7] admodum iucundi. Cum enim per iocum obiiceretur ab amico quod nimia ventris eius esset parsimonia, 'Gratulor liberalitati tuae,' respondit, 'quod plura multo des ipse quam accipias.' Laborabat enim ille saepissime ventris profluvio.

33    Ingeniosa sunt haec omnia, non minus tamen artificiosa, singulaque locos habent suos e quibus defluunt. Et peracuta sunt et perquam concinna quae ex collatione personarum deducuntur. Deperibat adolescentulus magno[8] loco natus puellam nobilitate summa excellentique et forma et pudicitia. Cumque inter preces ac blanditias respondisset illa, 'Scito te Lucretiam invenisse,' hic ille, 'Experiere te et Tarquinium comperisse.'

example, when there was a discussion in the senate of public lands and of the *lex Thoria*, and Lucilius was being attacked by those speaking of the law and saying that the public lands were being grazed by his flock, Appius said, "That's not Lucilius' flock; you're wrong. I think it's a free flock because it grazes where it pleases."[32]

A famous witticism of Cariteo is of the same kind and no less 30 pleasing.[33] For when at Naples during wartime money of adulterated metal was being called into question, and one of his acquaintances was complaining because he did not know what he had, Cariteo said, preparing his expression as much as possible for joking, "I must thank the immortal gods and rejoice in our friendship, for I've finally found a man—a man truly a friend and truly rich—since it is the characteristic of a rich man not to know what he has."

Concession also has a place and its own charm. And this is 31 what Cicero says, "Wittily concede to your opponent what he has taken from you," like the following remark of Caelius. For when someone ill-born said to him that he was unworthy of his ancestors, he replied, "But, by Hercules, you're worthy of yours."[34] Similar is the riposte of my friend Marino Tomacelli, a very de- 32 lightful man.[35] For when a friend jokingly upbraided him for the excessive parsimony of his stomach, he replied, "I congratulate you on your liberality, since you give much more than you yourself receive"—the latter suffered from frequent diarrhea.

All these things are ingenious, yet not less artful, and each has 33 its own places from which it is derived. And the ones that are drawn from comparison of persons are very clever and elegant. A young man born to a great position was helplessly in love with a girl of the highest nobility and excellent beauty and modesty. When she responded to his prayers and flattery with the words, "Know that you've found a Lucretia," he replied, "And you'll find that you've met with a Tarquin."

34     Proverbia quoque dictorum in usum adducuntur habentque vim ridiculi. Marinus Tomacellus, de quo paulo ante mentionem feci,[9] functus est compluris annos summa cum laude munere oratorio sub Ferdinando, rege Neapolitanorum; cumque satis longo post tempore quam promissum ei fuisset ab Antonello, epistolarum magistro, satis esset factum, gratulabundus mihi per episto-

35     lam respondit, 'Bene habet: elephanti partum vidimus.' Cumque aliquando compertum habuisset Paschasium Decium, quaestorem regium, secum egisse liberaliter in salario persolvendo — erat enim Paschasius maxime attenuatus — ad me rescripsit, 'Optime actum est: foenicem iam vidimus.'

36     Ab commemoratione etiam versus cuiuspiam celebris poetaeque maxime noti manant facetiae et argutae et gratae. Considerant mecum meis pro foribus idem hic Marinus et Petrus Compater, homo iucundissimus, magna senectute tres, cano capite omnes, nullis dentibus, multis tamen ac prope tercentenis annis. Praeteriens igitur adolescentulus, demiratus cum esset tris annosos vetulos, albentibus capillis, maxime hilari vultu et iocari cum praetereuntibus et arridere salutantibus, hic Marinus in ipsa illa adolescentis admiratione tanto cum lepore Virgilianum effudit illud, 'Tercentum nivei tondent dumeta iuvenci,' ut risum non tenuerint senem qui audierunt eo in consessu tam opportune, adeo praeter expectationem ac perquam concinne modulantem. Isque confestim risus ingeminatus est, nam derisui cum haberetur a nobis qui praeteribat iuvenis obeso corpore, obesiori ingenio, maxime obesis moribus, tum a festivissimo et perquam concinno iuvene Petro Summontio et festive admodum et pervenuste iniectum est Virgilianum aliud, quanquam dimidiatum, e Georgicis, 'Longamque trahens inglorius alvum,' ut protractus risus fuerit in Charitei adventum, qui animadvertens senum trium tam aequalem canitiem,

Proverbs are also introduced for use in witticisms and are ca-    34
pable of producing laughter.[36] Marino Tomacelli, whom I mentioned a little while ago, discharged the office of ambassador for
many years with the highest praise under Ferdinando, king of
Naples. When, after a much longer time than he had been prom-
ised, he was paid by Antonello, the king's secretary, he joyfully replied to me in a letter, "All is well: we've seen the elephant give
birth."[37] Another time when he discovered that Pasquasio Decio,    35
the king's treasurer, had been liberal with him in paying his sal-
ary—for Pasquasio was especially cheap—he wrote back to me,
"It's gone extremely well; now I've seen the phoenix."[38]

Witticisms both clever and pleasing also spring from quoting    36
some famous verse and a particularly well-known poet.[39] This
same Marino and Petrus Compater, a most delightful man, were
sitting with me in front of my door, the three of us very old, all
white-haired, no teeth but many years, almost three hundred of
them.[40] So when a young man passing by wondered at three aged,
little old men with white hair and cheerful faces who were joking
with passersby and smiling on those who greeted them, Marino
poured forth to the young man's surprise that line of Vergil's,
"Three hundred snow-white young bulls are grazing the thorn
bushes," with so much charm that the people in that gathering
who heard the old man reciting so opportunely, so unexpectedly
and elegantly, could not restrain their laughter.[41] And suddenly
this laughter was doubled, for when we were making fun of a
youth—fat, fatter-headed, and in his character fattest of all—who
was passing by, Pietro Summonte, a handsome and elegant youth,
interjected with jovial charm another line of Vergil's, although only
half of it, from the *Georgics*, "Ingloriously dragging his long belly,"
so that the laughter was protracted until Cariteo's arrival.[42] He
took a look at the three men, all equally white-haired, and said,

'Quid,' inquit, 'hic ad fores? An inalgescere cupitis, cum alpes videamus nivibus oppletas undequaque concanescere?'

37 In primis igitur ferax est locorum campus materiaque maxime
opulenta subministrandis iocis, ut recte Quintilianus dixerit, 'Si
species omnis persequi velimus, nec modum reperiemus et frustra
laborabimus.'

38 Neque enim minus numerosi sunt loci ex quibus dicta quam illi
ex quibus eae quas sententias vocamus ducuntur neque alii. Itaque
et sententiae ipsae, quae suapte natura graves sunt et sapientes, si
ridiculum in modum iactatae fuerint, risum etiam ipsae pariturae
sunt, ut, cum Franciscus Puccius, vir in studiis his nostris eminens,
deridere vellet hominem seditiosum ingenioque minime quieto,
qui in corona quadam constiterat, 'Ecce,' inquit, 'concordia parvae
39 res crescunt.' Cum etiam idem hic deridiculum facere vellet, bona
qui patria obliguriisset, iniecit sententiam hanc, 'Parsimonia rei
familiaris, eae demum divitiae magnae sunt,' cumque suis ex auditoribus somniculosum aliquem notare vellet, rorem antelucanum
vocitabat.

40 Itaque hominum industria et ars, de qua hic noster est sermo,
etiam quae gravia fuerint ad ridicula saepe transfert, ut negare qui
voluerit arti suum esse locum comparandis ridiculis dictisque fun-
ditandis nulla ratione id possit, quando gravia etiam ac sententiosa
dicta, ubi arte usus quis fuerit, ac tum temporum tum personarum
delectu adhibito, ad iocum traduci soleant ac risum, et persaepe
quae ipsa per se ridicula non sunt belle tamen agitata rideantur.
Itaque et quod dictorum ridiculorumque ac facetiarum regiones
sint amplissimae quodque in iis ars quoque vel multum etiam
valeat abunde a nobis ostensum videtur et exemplis etiam compro-
batum.

"What are you doing here in the doorway? Do you want to freeze? Don't you see the Alps going white in every direction, loaded down with snow?"

Above all, then, the field for places is fertile and the material 37 very rich for providing jokes, so that Quintilian was right to say, "If we want to pursue every type, we will find no limit and will labor in vain."[43]

Nor are the places from which witticisms are drawn less numer- 38 ous or different from those from which the things we call *sententiae* are drawn.[44] Indeed if *sententiae*, which are naturally serious and wise, are tossed out in a jesting way, they will also produce laughter, as when Francesco Pucci, a man eminent in these studies of ours, wished to mock a seditious man of no peaceful disposition who had stood up in an assembly. Pucci said, "Behold, through concord small things spring up."[45] When this same man also 39 wanted to laugh at someone who had consumed his inheritance, he threw out this *sententia*, "Thrift in household affairs — these in the end are great riches."[46] And when he wanted to reprimand some drowsy person among his auditors, he would call him "the dew of sunrise."

And so the industry and art of men, which this discussion of 40 mine is about, often transfer even things that were serious to jests, so that anyone wishing to deny that art has its place in preparing jests and producing witty sayings can by no means do so, since even serious and sententious statements, where someone has used art and with discrimination of both times and persons, are regularly transformed into jokes and laughter, and very often things not ridiculous in themselves are nevertheless laughed at when handled well. Thus it appears that I have shown abundantly and also confirmed by examples that the topography of witticisms, jests, and funny stories is vast and that in that department art can be of great effect.

## : 4 :

*Neque adversum miseros neque*
*potentes viros utendum esse ridiculis.*

1 Hinc ad alias quoque observationes transeamus quae plurimum convenire videantur ad facetudinem, hoc est, ad eam quam in iocis quaerimus mediocritatem quodque in delectu fere mediocritas ipsa collocata sit; cuiusmodi vero id, et quale sit, ostendendum relin-
2 quitur. Cum praesertim Cicero, de oratore agens oratoriisque muneribus, dicat nec insignem improbitatem nec rursus miseriam rideri statuatque in iocando moderationem retinendam esse et Umber quoque noster dicat facile esse miserum irridere, quocirca et miseris parcendum est, in quibus locus esse misericordiae debeat, ni fortasse superbia maledicentia incontinentia praecipites eant, et a potentibus etiam viris et quibus publica res in manu est continendum. Est enim periculosum perque termerarium lacessere eum qui gladium strictum habeat possitque proscribere. Adhaec et scurrile habeatur ac sit lacessere eum qui ab omnibus ametur et maximis atque infimis aeque carus sit atque acceptus. Quae enim mediocritas esse potest, ubi prudentia munus minime retineat suum? Quid rursum imprudentius quam eorum in se iram provocare in quorum nutu posita sit hominis vita, quando ut a derisu, quod ait Quintilianus, haud procul abest risus, sic ab ira potentis haud longe abest sanguinolentia ac vis?

3 Qua e re efficitur ut quemadmodum oratoria urbanitas parum frequens esse debet minimeque in causis earumque actionibus frequentata, sic et facetiarum usus rarus ac maxime temperatus, nec quotienscunque locus patuerit ad iocandum poteritque, ut
4 Cicero inquit, dictum aliquod dici, dicere id necesse ducamus. Ut

## ∶ 4 ∶

## *Ridicule must not be used against either miserable or powerful men.*

From here let us pass on to other observations that seem most ap- 1
propriate to humor, that is, to that mean we are seeking in jokes,
and to the fact that that mean has been usually placed in discrimination. It remains to show of what type and nature it is. Especially 2
since Cicero, discussing the orator and the orator's duties, says that
neither remarkable wickedness nor, on the other hand, misery is
to be laughed at, and establishes that moderation must be maintained in joking, and also our fellow Umbrian says that it is easy to
laugh at a miserable person, and for this reason one must spare the
miserable, with whom one ought to make room for pity, unless
perhaps they run headlong into pride, slander, and incontinence;
and one must also be restrained with powerful men and those who
have the state in hand.[47] For it is dangerous and very rash to injure
someone who holds a drawn sword and can proscribe.[48] In addition, it might be considered, and in fact it is buffoonish to assail
someone loved by everyone and dear and acceptable to the greatest
and the lowest alike. For what kind of mean can there be when
prudence does not stick to its duty? Besides, what is more imprudent than to provoke against oneself the wrath of those in whose
will the life of man has been placed, since, as laughter is not at all
far from derision, as Quintilian says, so bloodthirstiness and violence are not at all far from the wrath of the powerful?[49]

From this it follows that just as oratorical urbanity must be in- 3
frequent and seldom resorted to in lawsuits and their trials, so also
the use of witticisms must be rare and moderate; nor, whenever an
occasion for joking opens up and a witticism could be uttered, as
Cicero says, should we consider it necessary to do so.[50] For as 4

enim in re omni modus retinendus est, si probari actiones nostras
volumus, sic etiam in iocando. Utque etiam seriis, quae ad usum
spectant, quaedam tamen regula normaque a ratione constituta
est, sic iocosa, quae ad iucunditatem, freno etiam quodam sunt
tanquam praesaepibus alliganda. Si enim iocosa probantur relaxationis gratia, non eo probari debent, quo alteri obsint ac molestiam
afferant, quod nec viri boni nec civis probi officium est, cum facetum hominem et bonum eundem virum et civem item probum
esse dicamus. Nec enim ad maledicentiam descendendum ullo
modo est, aut sponte aut ex provocatione, nisi cum honestas ra-
5 tioque id permiserit. Quocirca dicacitas neutique tam amica est
facetudini tamque coniuncta quam est comitas, cum dicta pleraque salsa sint ac suo nomine sic appellentur ridiculaque ipsa
haudquaquam semper grata, comitas vero a temperamento vix recedat. Itaque facetum hominem aspersum comitate plurima esse
oportet, quod facetudinis ipsius condimentum est.

: 5 :

*Quae servanda sint faceto.*

1 Ipsarum autem facetiarum duo cum sint genera, reque alterum
tractetur ac non nunquam tanquam fabella narretur aliqua, alterum dicto, in utroque modus retinendus est faceto idque diligenter videndum, ne dum alterum cavet, in insulsitatem incidat
pariatque ipse audientibus derisum. Non ab re autem putat Cicero
mendaculis aspergi oportere praesertim fabellas, quod oratori
conducant, cuius finis est iudicem ad benevolentiam suam trahere.

moderation must be retained in everything if we wish our actions to win approval, so it must also be retained in joking. And yet, just as some rule and norm have also been established by reason for serious things that aim for usefulness, so funny things that aim at delight must also be bound by a bridle, as it were in a stable. For if funny things win approval for the sake of relaxation, they must not be approved on the grounds that they hurt or bother someone, which is not the duty either of a good man or a virtuous citizen, since we say that a witty man is both a good man and a virtuous citizen. For one must not descend in any way to abuse, neither spontaneously nor out of provocation, unless honor and reason permit it. For this reason raillery is by no means as friendly and 5 related to good humor as affability, since witticisms are for the most part pungent and are called so with their own name, and ridiculous things are by no means always pleasing, but affability scarcely departs from moderation. And so a witty man must be sprinkled with the greatest affability because it is the seasoning of humor itself.

: 5 :

*What the witty man must observe.*

But since there are two kinds of these witticisms, and one deals 1 with the subject matter and sometimes is told like a story, and the other deals with the words, moderation must be maintained in each by the witty man, and he must diligently see to it that while he avoids one extreme he does not fall into tastelessness and produce derision in his hearers.[51] Cicero, however, correctly thinks that it is to the orator's particular advantage to sprinkle his little stories with fibs, with a view to making the judge well disposed to

2  Facetum quoque nequaquam dedecuerit eiusmodi aspersio, tametsi
   mendacia fugienda sunt, quippe cum ornatus hic quasi quidam
   adhibeatur non fraudis gratia sed delectationis et honestae et natu-
   ralis.

: 6 :

*Dictorum salsorum duplex esse genus.*

1  Sed mihi videtur quod salsum est dupliciter partiendum: et in
   quod molestum sit odiosumque atque in rixam spectet ac contentionem, et quod delectet ac familiariter iocetur, ut hoc sit omnino
   iocosum et liberale, mordax illud ac dentatum. Nam servile quomodo conveniat homini ingenuo?
      Generis utriusque haec erunt exempla: Scipio ille maior, in
   mensa cum accubuisset ac de convivarum more corona capiti eius
   esset imposita eaque et bis et ter rumperetur aegreque fortasse id
   ferret, tum P. Licinius Varus, 'Noli mirari,' inquit, 'parum si conve-
   nit: caput enim magnum est.' Et laudabile et honestum, ut Cicero
   ipse putat: cum enim salsum videri possit, dentem tamen non
2  imprimit. Simile et illud. Invitatus cum esset Erricus[10] Pudericus
   ad prandium appositaque esset ei altilis haud bene assa, conversus
   ad eum qui pullum deartuabat, 'Importune,' inquit, 'accubuimus,
   neque enim ad prandium vocati sed ad coenam fuimus.' Liberale
3  prorsus ac concinnum. Crassus in Parthos proficiscens ad Deio-
   tarum in Bithyniam divertit, novam tunc urbem aedificantem;
   itaque in eum iocatus quod esset senectute iam confectus, 'Duo-
   decima,' inquit, 'diei hora novam urbem aggrederis.' Ad quae Deiotarus, nam et Crassus erat sexagenario maior, 'Nec tu,' respondit,

him.[52] This kind of sprinkling is also by no means unbecoming to 2
the witty man, even though lies must be avoided, since this ornament, as it were, is employed not for the sake of deception but for
honest and natural delight.


: 6 :

*There are two kinds of pungent witticism.*

But it seems to me that what is pungent must be divided in two: 1
into the kind that is annoying and odious and tends to quarreling
and contention, and into the kind that delights and jokes in a
friendly way, so that the latter is entirely a jest worthy of a free
man, the former mordant and biting. For how can anything servile
suit a freeborn man?

Here are examples of each kind. When the famous elder Scipio
was reclining at table, a crown placed on his head, as is the custom
with dinner guests, broke two or three times, and he might be get-
ting annoyed, Publius Licinius Varus said, "Don't be surprised if it
doesn't fit, for the head is great." Both praiseworthy and honorable, as Cicero himself thinks: for while it might look like a sharp
remark, it doesn't bite.[53] The following remark is similar. When 2
Enrico Puderico was invited to lunch and served an underdone
fowl, he turned to the man carving the chicken and said, "We've
taken our seats at table at the wrong moment, for we weren't invited to lunch but to dinner."[54] This is perfectly well-bred and
agreeable. Setting out against the Parthians, Crassus stayed in 3
Bithynia with Deiotarus, who then was building a new city. And
so, making fun of him because he was now stricken in years, he
said, "At the twelfth hour of the day you're beginning a new city."
To which Deiotarus replied, for Crassus too was over sixty, "Nor

'o Crasse, satis matutinus in Parthos proficisceris'—uterque perquam familiariter ac iucunde, neque ut lacesserent verum ut io-
carentur.

4    At haec quae subdam vel uncum praeferunt, quando et scin-
dunt et rapiunt. Barnabas Barolitanus iudicatus est de fide Christiana parum pie sentire. Itaque aliquando dum hiaret deque more
tamen Christiani hominis crucem pollice ad os designaret, tum
Masius Aquosa, qui et iocosus homo esset et peracutus, ut Siculus, atque illi notus, 'Quid hoc,' inquit, 'Barnaba, qui cruce os quasi
carcerem obsignaveris, ne daemon ille malus tuo se e pectore pro-
ripiat?' Quid hoc salso salsius? His enim verbis ut male de Deo
5    sentiens coarguitur. Accubuerat ad mensam Petrus Compater,[11]
cumque pransus iam esset, sacerdos satis importune ad mensam se
se ingessit; vixque accubuerat, cum ad ministrum conversus, statim, 'Sitio,' inquit, 'misce, puer.' Tum Petrus, 'Atqui,' inquit, 'non
putassem praeterita nocte tua te cum commatercula delicias fecisse.' Pupugit enim illum acerrime ex hoc, quod mane sitiant
multum qui se in Venerem noctu resolverint. Haud dissimile multum est in Ciceronem illud: 'Mirum anguste si sedeas, duabus qui
sellis sedere sis solitus.'

: 7 :

*Altera divisio salsorum dictorum.*

1    Est et alia salsorum divisio, ut alterum dicax sit, verumtamen non
urbanum sed rusticanum aut servile potius; alterum autem, quod
urbanam educationem referat. Nanque apud Ciceronem Antonius

are you, Crassus, setting out against the Parthians early enough in the morning."[55] Each was speaking very familiarly and pleasantly, not to provoke but to joke.

But the ones I am about to add show barbs also, since they 4 both split and tear. Barnaba of Barletta was judged to hold impious sentiments about the Christian faith.[56] And so one time while he was yawning, yet in the manner of a Christian man making the sign of the cross over his mouth, an acquaintance of his, Masio Aquosa, who was an amusing man and, being Sicilian, was very sharp, said, "What's this, Barnaba? You make the sign of the cross over your mouth as if it were a prison, so that the evil demon won't rush out of your breast?"[57] What is more pungent than this pungency? For with these words he was exposed as holding wrong beliefs about God. When Petrus Compater had taken his seat at 5 table and had finished eating, a priest rudely rushed to the table.[58] He had barely taken his seat, when he turned to the servant and said at once, "I'm thirsty, boy; pour." Then Petrus said: "But I wouldn't have supposed that last night you had enjoyed yourself with your little concubine." He stung him very sharply indeed from the fact that those who sap themselves at night making love are very thirsty in the morning. This one against Cicero is not very different: "How astonishing that your seat is cramped, since you usually sit on two seats."[59]

## : 7 :

### A second division of pungent witticisms.

There is another division of pungent witticisms: one is caustic yet 1 not urbane but instead rustic or servile, while the other reveals a polite education. For in Cicero Antonius says that Crassus is most

Crassum dicit venustissimum esse atque urbanissimum, pari quoque modo gravissimum atque severissimum.

2     Posterioris generis exempla sunt haec: ostentabat Pomponius et quidem iactanter vulnus ore exceptum in seditione Sulpitiana, quod ipse tamen passum se pro Caesare pugnantem gloriabatur. Ibi Caesar et salse admodum et urbanissimum in modum, 'Nunquam fugiens respexeris,' inquit. Itaque et momordit illum Caesar

3     et ab urbanitate non recessit. Alumnus quidam meus non inurbane educatus, cum obiiceretur ei, quod pater araret, 'At mater,' respondit, 'tua hubera locat.' Itaque in re quamvis conviciosa non minus tamen urbane respondit quam salse.

4     Prioris vero generis haec erunt: contendebant homunculi duo, cumque alter perpupugisset hoc dicto alterum: 'Verba tua neutique mihi bene olent,' tum alter, 'Quod videlicet loqui a tergo

5     consuesti.' Spurce nimis et serviliter, quale Plautinum illud: 'Obturat ne inferiorem gutturem?' Hoc vero perquam rustice; nam dicenti cuipiam inter lacessendum, 'Caprinum bibe quo pulmones refrigeres,' tum alter, 'Tuum si sequar exemplum, hircinum potius demulserim.'

6     Sed haec quae rusticana dicimus ac servilia pleraque oscena sunt et scurrilia. Exemplum est: regii stabuli magister famulos increpabat, equile immundum quod esset; tum unus ex iis: 'Videlicet enitescere stabulum vis quo stabulariorum ipse nuptias celebres.' Eiusmodi haec et spurcantur et civilium conventu hominum omnino indigna sunt et ab ore auribusque facetorum atque ingenuorum hominum procul repellenda.

charming and urbane, also most serious and severe in equal measure.[60]

Here are examples of the latter kind. Pomponius was showing 2
in a boastful manner a face wound he'd received in Sulpitius' re-
volt, which he nevertheless bragged that he had suffered fighting
for Caesar. Then Caesar both very pungently and in the most urbane manner said, "Never look around while you are running
away."[61] And so Caesar both stung him and did not depart from
urbanity. When a certain pupil of mine, a man not without a po- 3
lite education, was taunted with his father's plowing, he replied,
"But your mother rents out her breasts." And so, although he was
trading insults, his reply was as polite as it was pungent.

Here are examples of the former kind. Two little men were 4
quarreling when one stung the other with this witticism, "Your
words don't smell at all good to me." Then the other, "Clearly because you're in the habit of speaking from behind." Too filthy and 5
servile, like this line from Plautus, "Is he stopping up his lower
throat?"[62] This one is exceedingly rustic: For to someone saying,
provokingly, "Suck goat milk to refresh your lungs," another retorts, "If I followed your example, I'd stroke a he-goat instead."

But the things we call rustic and servile are for the most part 6
obscene and buffoonish. An example: the master of the royal stable was chiding the servants because the horse stable was filthy.
One of them shot back: "Obviously you want the stable to shine so
that you yourself can celebrate your nuptials with the stable boys."
Witticisms of this kind defile and are completely unworthy of a
gathering of civil men and must be thrust far from the mouths and
ears of witty and freeborn men.

: 8 :

*Vultum esse dictis ipsis accommodandum et*
*gestum et vocem.*

1  Summo autem studio id videndum, quo dictis ipsis vultus accedat,
et, qua opus est, gestus quoque sit accommodatus ac perquam
concinnus. Secus enim dicteria non modo gratiam suam non retinent, sed is qui dicit apparet etiam absurdior, ut, si non fiat ex eo
ridiculus, efficiatur tamen parum gratus habeaturque haudqua-
2  quam sive politus civis sive satis sodalitii studiosus. Quodque de
vultu praecipimus deque gestu, in voce etiam servandum ducimus,
nam et ipsa inflexiones ac modulos suos habet. Permulta enim
tum inepta apparebunt tum frigida, haec illis si defuerint, quae
suapte quidem natura lepida sunt et bella.

3    Id tamen considerandum aliam rationem esse debere facetorum
atque ingenuorum hominum, aliam mimorum ac theatralium lu-
dionum, in quibus interdum oscenitas ipsa spurcatioque cum scurrilitate ac petulantia non commendetur modo verum etiam, si
abfuerint, desideretur. Quocirca in his ipsis immoderatiores qui
fuerint nimiique imitatores mimorum potius e numero habendi
sunt quam facetorum theatroque ac spectaculis magis digni.

: 8 :

*One must suit one's expression, gesture, and*
*voice to one's witticisms.*

But one must see to it with the greatest attention that one's facial  1
expression suits one's witticisms, and, when necessary, one's gestures also must be appropriate and elegant.[63] For otherwise witty
sayings not only do not retain their charm, but the speaker even
appears absurd, so that, if he is not made ridiculous on this account, he may still be considered lacking in charm and not a polished citizen or a desirable associate. And what I advise about fa-  2
cial expression and gesture I also consider must be observed with
the voice, for it also has its inflections and modulations. For many
witticisms that are naturally elegant and beautiful appear both inept and feeble if they lack these.

Nevertheless one ought to take into account that there should  3
be one way for witty and freeborn men to act and another for
mimes and stage actors, in whom occasionally obscenity itself and
filth with buffoonery and impudence not only are commended but
even, if absent, are missed. For this reason those mimics who are
too unrestrained and excessive in these matters are to be considered rather in the ranks of the mimes than of the wits, and more
worthy of the theater and spectacles.

: 9 :

*Mimica et theatralia parum facetis convenire.*

1   Nec vero imitatio tantum ipsa, dum nimia quidem sit, fugitanda
est verum etiam dicta quaedam quae mimica sint potius aut parasitica quam ingenua consessionibusque ac sermonibus de quibus
dicimus male convenientia, qualia haec ex Plauto quaeque alia eorum similia:

> Qui edistis, multo fecistis sapientius,
> qui non edistis, saturi fite fabulis.

Item:

> Dum ludi fiunt, in popinam, pedissequi,
> irruptionem facite.

2   Delectant haec populum suntque mirum in modum auribus popularium apta et ad invitandum risum et ad detinendum spectatores
in subselliis, seu ne satietate afficiantur seu dum pati nequaquam
possunt spectandi moram. Quid illud quam festivum, quam ridi-
cularium?

> Vin noctuam adferri,
> quae 'tu tu' usque dicat?

Et: ' — Assum apud te, eccum. — At ego elixus sis volo.'

3   Delectant haec mirifice: quid enim histrionica popularius? Ac
fieri quidem potest ut quandoque, quanquam rarenter, in ore tamen ingenui ac faceti viri commendentur haec eadem, quae suapte

4   natura omnino tamen dedeceant. At hoc et populare admodum et
theatricum:

: 9 :

*The mimic and theatrical do not suit the witty.*

But not only is mimicry, when it is excessive, to be shunned but 1
also some witticisms more suitable to mimes or parasites than to
freeborn men; they are inappropriate to the kind of gatherings and
conversations I am talking about. For example, these lines from
Plautus and others similar to them:

> You who have eaten have done much more wisely; you who
> haven't, fill yourselves with stories.

Likewise:

> While the games are taking place, footmen, attack the cook-
> shop.[64]

These things delight the people and are marvelously suited to their 2
ears and to inciting laughter and keeping spectators in their seats,
either to prevent them from being sated or because they can't bear
a delay in the spectacle. What about this one, so jovial, so ridiculous?

> Do you want a night owl to be brought along, which keeps
> saying "You you"?[65]

And: "Look, here I am with you. — But I wish you were boiled."[66]

These things are wonderfully delightful: for what is more popu- 3
lar than the actor's art? But it can happen nevertheless that sometimes, although rarely, things are praised in the mouth of a freeborn and witty man that yet are completely unbecoming by their
nature. But this is both very popular and theatrical: 4

—Digitos in manibus non habent.
—Quid iam?  —Quia incedunt cum anulatis auribus.

Et illud:

—Perpetuon valuisti?  —Varie.
—Caprigenum hominum non placet mihi neque pantherinum
genus.

Haec, inquam, quaeque huiusmodi sunt, vel suavissimum esse
condimentum videri ac iure quidem possunt relaxationum earum,
quas ipsi quaerimus quaeque, ut quaeramus, natura ipsa et hortatur et commonet.

: 10 :

## E silentio interdum risum gigni.

1   Dicere vix quidem ausim, dicam tamen nec parum quidem libenter: etsi facetus vir in dictis responsisque decenter versatur ad iocum quidem honestamque ad relaxationem ac quietem accommodatis, tamen ipse quandoque vidi mirificum excitari risum
suavissimamque gigni recreationem e silentio respondentis, quod
sive motus quispiam oculorum concinnus sequatur ac decens sive
manuum digitorum ve sive dentium subsannatio gesticulatio ve
aliqua sive innutus quispiam extemporaneus sive e loco abitio
praeter expectationem, quae res[12] contemptus ac irrisionis signifi-
cationem habeat.

2   Etenim aliquando loquaculus quidam Hieronymum obtunde-
bat Carbonem, suavissimi ingenii virum, atque, ubi multa ingentem verborum in cumulum congessisset, petebat sibi ab eo ad singula responderi, illum vero memini[13] ad omnia quidem siluisse
conversumque ad astantes dixisse, 'Magnum ranarum proventum

288

—They don't have fingers on their hands. —Why so?
—Because they walk along with rings in their ears.[67]

And this one:

—Have you been continually in good health? —Variably. —I don't like men of the goat or the panther kind.[68]

These things, I say, and ones of this sort, can be seen, and indeed rightly so, as a most pleasant condiment of those relaxations that we are seeking and that nature itself urges and impresses upon us to seek.

: 10 :

*Sometimes laughter arises from silence.*

I would hardly dare to say, yet I will say, and not indeed unwillingly, that although the witty man is properly involved with witticisms and responses suited to joking and honorable relaxation and rest, nevertheless I myself have sometimes seen extraordinary laughter excited and the sweetest relaxation produced from the silence of the responder because some pleasant and becoming movement of the eyes, hands, or fingers followed, or a grimace with the teeth or some gesture or spontaneous nod or unexpected departure from a place, which signifies contempt and derision.

For once some talkative fellow was annoying Girolamo Carbone, a man of the pleasantest disposition.[69] After he had amassed many things into a huge pile of words, he asked Carbone to respond to them individually, but I recall that he remained silent at every one, turned to the bystanders, and said, "This year has

3    hic annus attulit.' Garriebat alius quispiam ⟨ ⟩[14] quem ferre[15] cum
non posset, nullo dato responso, manu sublata monuit nasum ut
emungeret; quo e signo mirificus inter astantes exortus est risus.

4    Et illud quoque Tristani Caracioli perquam iucundum et bellum. Cum enim homo, parum in loquendo temperatus nulliusque
in rem publicam operae aut officii, frequenti in conventu nobilium
virorum dixisset ei, 'Malos rei publicae ministros habemus,' tum
ipse, averso ab illo statim ore ac discessuro similis, 'Nuntium,' inquit, 'habemus, o cives, adventantium peregre gracculorum. Ego
rus eo ne segetibus iam pullulantibus damno sint.'

5    Hortabatur homo minime malus Petrum Compatrem ad uxorem ducendam; has inter adhortationes qui pone eum stabat iuvenis argutius cum sternuisset, nihil ipse respondit; tum ille, 'Quid,
malum, et amico et honesta suadenti non respondes?' Ad ea tum
Compater, 'Nec mihi,' inquit, 'nec uxori male auspicaturus sum.
Cum enim e duobus coniugium, ut scis, constet, Hispani quidem
augures, ubi unum sternutamentum tantum fuerit, et malum illud
et portentosum profitentur: meis igitur nuptiis infelix absit auspi-
cium.' Facetus itaque vir potest e silentio quoque gratiam sibi
comparare ab auditoribus.[16]

: II :

*Quae servanda sint in risu provocando.*

1    Provocandi autem risus hilaritatisque excitandae vel praecipua
causa est, cum is qui dicit sive lacessitus sive lacessens prior ve aut
posterior iocatus ipse quidem minime riserit, ut quaerendum for-

brought forth a great increase of frogs." Another person ⟨. . .⟩ was  3
chattering, whom he could not stand. Giving no response, he advised him with raised hand to wipe his nose, at which sign an extraordinary laugh arose among the bystanders.

And also this one, very delightful and charming, of Tristano  4
Caracciolo.[70] For when a man, intemperate in speech and perform-
ing no service nor holding a position in the state, said to him in a
crowded gathering of noblemen, "We have poor ministers in this
state," he at once turned his face away from him and like a man
about to depart said, "Citizens, we have news of jackdaws arriving
from abroad. I'm going to the country so that they don't harm the
crops sprouting now."

A man, not at all bad, was exhorting Petrus Compater to  5
marry.[71] When in the midst of these exhortations a young man
standing behind him sneezed rather distinctly, he made no reply.
Then the former said, "Why the devil don't you respond to a
friend who's advising you honorably?" Then in reply Compater
said, "I'm not going to make a bad beginning for me or my wife.
Since, as you know, a marriage consists of two people, the Spanish
augurs declare that when there is only one sneeze, that is bad and
portentous. So let an unlucky omen be far from my marriage."
And so the witty man can also make himself agreeable to his listeners by silence.

: 11 :

*What must be observed while provoking laughter.*

A special cause of provoking laughter and exciting hilarity is when  1
the speaker, whether provoked or provoking, before or after he
tells a joke, does not laugh at all himself. So perhaps one ought to

tasse a doctis sit viris, cur tantopere ad commovendum conferat risum dicentis confirmatus vultus verbaque eius cum severitate et pondere.

2    In repercutiendo autem docere exemplum hoc potest quanti sit id ipsum quod nunc dicimus. Vexabat bello Florentinum populum Alfonsus, Neapolitanorum rex, atque in primo quidem adortu expugnarat Rencinum, satis tenue oppidum. Ibi primum ad nuntium civis quidam illatus in Cosmum, qui tum princeps erat administrandae rei publicae, 'Quid hoc,' inquit, 'Cosme? periimus amisso Rencino,' tum Cosmus, vultu maxime sedato et forti, verba illius despicatus, 'Per Christum,' inquit, 'rogatus edoceas: qua nam in parte agri nostri Rencinum situm est? Nam quod te excruciat amissum oppidum, mihi haudquaquam satis cognitum est sit ne illud Florentinae ditionis.' Risit prudens et cautus senex, vultu maxime imperterrito et despicaci, garrulantis illius meticulosum dictum perque degenerantem orationem.

3    Extat exemplum quoque Marini Tomacelli[17] in lacessentem deque dictione met sua prorumpentem in cachinnos; nam cum hiscentem illum Marinus[18] cerneret, 'Hia,' inquit, 'hia mea monedula: en adest mater cum lumbriculo, quae tibi pappam dabit!'

4    Nec vero dicta et ipsa dicentis ipsius risu vultuque non etiam aliquando exhilaranda videantur. Verumtamen quae belle dicuntur ac cum severitate et, pene dixerim, erudite dicuntur, tametsi risum non movent, plerunque laudari nihilominus solent; contra irrideri saepius et sperni quae cum risu emittuntur dicentis, sive is prior 5    dixerit sive posterior. Itaque vultus ille severus reique accommodatus in hoc dicendi statu rideri vix potest, risus autem derideri plerunque et potest et solet; nam suapte natura risus expositus est derisui. Nec vero mirum hoc videri cuiquam debet, quando sedes

ask learned men why a speaker's impassive face and words spoken with severity and gravity contribute so much to moving laughter.[72]

This example, however, can teach the importance for retorts of what I'm now talking about. Alfonso, king of Naples, was plaguing the people of Florence with war and in the first assault had captured Rèncine, a trifling enough town.[73] At the first news of this some citizen flew at Cosimo, who at that time was the first man in the government of the state, and said, "What is this, Cosimo? We're done for now that we've lost Rèncine." Then Cosimo, his face utterly calm and steadfast, showed his contempt for the man's words, saying, "For Christ's sake, remind me, please, just where in our territory is Rèncine situated? I'm not even sure it's under Florentine jurisdiction, this town you're so anxious about." That prudent and cautious old man, his expression imperturbable and contemptuous, mocked the cowardly and base remark of that chatterer.

There's also an example from Marino Tomacelli against an exasperating fellow who broke into a guffaw while he was speaking.[74] Noticing him with his mouth wide open, Marino said, "Open wide, open wide, my jackdaw. Look, your mother's here with a little worm; she'll give you your yum-yums!"

On the other hand sometimes witticisms seem to be enlivened by the laughter and expression of the speaker. Nevertheless, things said with grave charm, even, I might almost say, with learning, even if they do not cause laughter, are generally praised; while on the contrary, statements uttered by the speaker with a laugh are more often derided and scorned, whether he speaks before or after laughing. Hence a severe expression suited to the subject can hardly be laughed at in this kind of speaking, but as a rule laughter both can be derided and commonly is, as laughter by its own nature is exposed to derision.[75] Nor indeed ought this to appear astonishing to anyone, since the very source of laughter has been

ipsa ridendi collocata est, ut apud doctos constat, in deformitate aliqua corporis aut vitio aut in turpitudine morum actionumque earum, quae aut animi solius sunt aut utriusque, corporis scilicet atque animi, aut eorum etiam quae fortuita vocantur suntque in eventu posita.

6    Itaque eorum quae movendo risui apta sunt, alia in natura sunt posita, alia in eventu, quorum omnium animus cum sit observator visque illa rationalis homini naturaliter insita et ab habitu confirmata atque ab observatione, id praestandum est ut ad insitam vim aptitudinemque artem quoque adiungamus, quae naturae ipsius

7    imitatrix est. Quid autem perfectum quod non idem et naturae conveniat et eruditioni? Quocirca facetum hominem volumus et naturae ipsi inniti et arti atque observationi, id est praeceptis consiliisque atque admonitionibus a ratione profectis. Nec vero hac in parte artem ut quaestuosam aliquam intelligimus aut manu comparatam, verum institutionem ingenuo homine dignam, quam qui sequatur, hunc ipsum necesse est, quacunque in actione, sive severa et gravi sive iucunda et lepida, convenientem retinere mensuram seque secundum eam metiri, perinde ut recta dictet ratio.

8    Nec vero ii sumus qui hac in dissertione aut oratoriam respiciamus aut theatralem, verum mediocritatem sequimur libero homine dignam, quam quaerendam a fortissimis etiam viris, natura ipsa duce, decernimus illisque praesertim qui res publicas moderantur. Quibus enim animorum relaxatio quaerenda magis est aut ab quonam hominum genere honestius etiam desideratur quam ab iis qui in assiduis maximis periculosissimisque versantur laboribus rerumque multiplicibus difficultatibus ac curis? Quo fit ut plerique negociosissimorum hominum publicisque in administrationibus obrutorum et sint hodie et fuerint maxime facetiarum appentes ac studiosi.

9    Cicero dat primas Caesari partes in hoc ipso genere virtutis. Quis autem Caesare bellicis in rebus maior? Quis Cicerone in toga, ut non iniuria fortasse dictum sit ab eo, 'Cedant arma togae'?

placed, as the learned agree, in some deformity of body or vice or in baseness of character or of those acts which are either of the mind alone or of both, that is, of both body and mind, or also of those things which are called fortuitous and depend upon chance.[76]

And so some of those things that are apt to move laughter de- 6 pend on nature, others on chance. Since the mind is the observer of all those things and the rational faculty is naturally implanted in man and strengthened by habit and observation, we must see to it that we also add art, which is the imitator of nature itself, to that implanted faculty and aptitude. Moreover, what is perfect that is 7 not suited to nature and learning alike? This is why I maintain that the witty man leans upon nature, art, and observation, that is on precepts, advice, and admonitions originating in reason. But in this part, by "art" I do not mean some profitable trade or manual labor but an education worthy of a freeborn man.[77] He who follows it must, in whatever action, whether severe and grave or pleasant and charming, maintain the appropriate measure, and measure himself by it just as right reason dictates.

But I am not one to consider the oratorical or theatrical mean 8 in this exposition, but rather I pursue the mean worthy of a free man, which I judge must be sought even by the most courageous men with nature as guide, and especially by those who govern states. For by whose minds must relaxation be more sought for, or by what kind of men can relaxation more honorably be desired, than by those who are engaged in the most continual and most dangerous labors and in the midst of numerous difficulties and cares for state affairs? So it happens that most of the men who are busiest and overwhelmed by the administration of public affairs both are today and have been especially desirous of and devoted to humorous stories.

Cicero gives Caesar the principal part in this kind of virtue.[78] 9 Who, however, was greater than Caesar in warfare? Who greater than Cicero in peace? Thus he said perhaps not unjustly, "Arms

10  Sed nec praetereantur imperatores alii maximorumque bellorum exanclatores. Igitur et maximus dux Hannibal facetiis plurimum delectatus est, sive in dicendo sive in respondendo, cuius illud extat dictum in Gisconem maxime quidem salsum. Is enim, cum Romani exercitus ad Cannas miraretur multitudinem, aegre id ferens Hannibal in illum sic iocatus est, ut despicabilem etiam militibus suis faceret, 'Quanto,' inquiens, 'mirabilius est, o Gisco, in tanto hominum numero, qui tuo isto vocetur nomine, esse neminem.'

11  Nec minus etiam iocis huiusmodi libenter Iugurta usus legitur, tametsi cum illo rebus gestis minime comparandus. Neque genere in hoc ab iis superatus est Ponti rex Mithridates. Nam Augusti Caesaris dicta plura fortasse referuntur quam aut Caesaris aut re-

12  gis alicuius. Alfonsus item rex tempestate sua quem non vicit aut dicendo aut, cum dicerentur, applaudendo urbanis atque facetis iocis aut prosequendis facetis viris et muneribus et beneficiis? An non laus haec ipsa olim Atheniensium praecipua fuit eaque in

13  Demosthene, summo et oratore et cive, desiderata? Nostro tempore trium est praecipue in Italia populorum, Perusinorum, Senensium, Florentinorum. Hispaniae regum aula hac a virtute et institutione cum primis commendatur. Gentes vero extremas non tam barbaras ac feras ipsa feritas vocari facit quam sermo ipse rudis agrestisque et oratio ab omni iucunditate ac lepore prorsus aliena.

14  Itaque ut salsum quod non est insulsum id dicimus, quod vero infacetum minime ingenuo viro dignum, sic facetos in verbis quidem iucundis versari ac lepidis quae ioca dicuntur volumus, fontes vero ipsos e quibus facetiae manent e factis fluere, quae qui insectentur, dicaces. Placet autem Marco Fabio dicacitatem sermonem esse cum risu aliquos incessentem sive in rebus sive in verbis.

should yield to the toga."[79] But other generals and those who have    10
endured the greatest wars should not be passed over. So then even
Hannibal, the very great general, delighted very much in witticisms, whether in saying or in responding. That famous bon mot
of his against Gisco, an especially pungent one, is extant. For
when the latter was amazed at the multitude of the Roman army
at Cannae, Hannibal took it ill and mocked the man so as to render him contemptible also to his soldiers, saying, "How much
more amazing is it, Gisco, that in such a number of men there is
no one who has your name."[80]

Nor does one read that Jugurtha was less willing to use jokes of    11
this kind, although he by no means must be compared with
Hannibal in military affairs.[81] Nor did they surpass Mithridates,
king of Pontus, in this kind of humor.[82] Indeed, perhaps more
witticisms of Augustus Caesar are related than of Caesar or any
king.[83] Likewise, whom in his day did not King Alfonso beat in    12
telling urbane and witty jokes or in applauding them when told or
in honoring witty men with gifts and benefits?[84] Was not this once
a principal glory of the Athenians and something missed in Demosthenes, their greatest orator and citizen?[85] In our time it is the    13
glory principally of three peoples in Italy, the Perugians, Sienese,
and Florentines. The court of the kings of Spain is particularly
celebrated for its schooling in this virtue. In truth, it is not so
much their savagery that causes the most remote races to be called
barbarian and savage as their rude and rustic language and their
speech, so completely alien to all delight and charm.

And so just as I call what is not witty insipid[86] but what is not    14
humorous entirely unworthy of a freeborn man, so I maintain that
witty men are concerned with the pleasant and charming words
called jokes, but that the sources from which witticisms flow derive from deeds, and those who censure them are railers. Marcus
Fabius, however, is of the opinion that raillery is speech that attacks someone with laughter either in substance or in words.[87]

297

15 Itaque ridicularia esse dicimus quae risum movere habeant; dicta,
quae salem; qui, si cum asperitate fuerit atque offensione, ad dica-
cem dicta ipsa referenda sunt, etsi risum exciunt; sin cum lepore
sineque offensione, aut si offensiuncula ipsa levior fuerit qua-
damque cum gratia et familiaritate, ad facetum, quem ingenuum
quidem esse volumus. Quocirca eiusmodi dicta commendationem
potius atque approbationem quandam quam risum ingenerant.

16 Fabellas vero facetorum quodammodo proprias esse volumus;
nam et faceti maxime comes sunt eorumque familiarissimas eas
esse superiore libro ostensum est; enarrantur enim eae plerunque
sine offensione et, quod laudabilissimum est, cum gratia etiam
summa; delectant enim et tum risum suavem quidem illum et
gratum inducunt tum approbationem dictorum,[19] ut licet fictae et

17 sint et intelligantur, tamen ad seria videantur inventae. Nugae vero
omnino leves, futiles, inanes, vanae; quocirca ab hoc toto genere
repellendae, ut ne nugaces quidem salsi esse possint ridiculariaque
ipsa derisum potius quam risum afferant, ubi nugis infecta fuerint.

18 Itaque tum dicta, quae salsa videlicet atque aculeata, tum ridicularia, forum, theatra, plebeios homines ipsaque spectacula rixas
conviciaque generaliter pertingunt; nam praeterquam quod habent
spicula ac felle scatent, pleraque oscena sunt scurrilia perque amara
aut rusticana rudia incondita, parum urbe digna, non raro etiam
servilia. Quae vitia ingenuitatem non modo dedecent verum tur-
pissime illam notant ac labefaciunt. Quocirca aliter in dicace consi-
derantur, ridiculo, mimico, histrione, sicophanta, rusticano, servo,
aliter in homine ingenuo quique risum iocumque ex medocritate
quaerat, quae et iucunditatem ratione hac afferat et curarum refrigerationem.

19 Ingenuum autem hominem eundemque facetum non modo levem esse nolumus, verum etiam, qualis Crassus orator refertur, et

And so I say that jests are those things able to move laughter; 15
witticisms, those that have wit. If wit is present with harshness
and aggression, the witticisms must be set down to a railer, even if
they excite laughter, but if wit is combined with charm and does
not offend, or if the little offense is rather slight and is somewhat
agreeable and friendly, they must be set down to a witty man, who
I maintain is freeborn. So witticisms of this kind produce commendation and some approbation rather than laughter.

But I maintain that in some way stories are intrinsically suited 16
to witty men. For witty men are particularly affable, and it has
been shown in the preceding book that telling stories is a habit
with them.[88] For they are narrated for the most part without offense and, what is most praiseworthy, with the highest charm as
well. For they delight and produce both that pleasant and charming laughter as well as approval of what is been said, so that although they are fictional and understood to be so, yet they appear
to have been invented for serious purposes. But trifles are com- 17
pletely lightweight, futile, inane, and empty. So they are to be removed from this whole class: triflers cannot be witty and jests
cause derision rather than laughter when they are infected with
trifles. And so both witticisms, namely the pungent and pointed 18
ones, and jests generally extend to the markets, theaters, plebeian
men, and to spectacles, quarrels and insults. For in addition to being sharp and abounding with bile, they are for the most part obscene, buffoonish, very bitter, or rustic, rude, unseasoned, not
worthy of the city, often even servile. These vices are not only unbecoming to good birth but also mark it with infamy and ruin it.
So they are considered one way in the railer, jester, mime, actor,
sycophant, rustic, and slave, another way in a freeborn man who
seeks laughter and joking according to the mean, which affords
delight in this way and a refreshing of cares.

But I not only do not want the freeborn and witty man to be 19
lightweight, but also I require him to be both severe and serious,

severum et gravem exigimus, vel si natura ab ipsa iucundus fuerit, ne tamen iucunditas ipsa aut insulsa sit aut prorsus ridenda. Rarior, ut est apud Iuvenalem, usus voluptatem commendat, frequentia enim plerunque satietatem gignit. Quam ob rem nimia dictorum frequentatio ususque maior ridiculorum isque immoderatus et, pene dixerim, coacervatus fugiendus est; non solum enim affert satietatem, verum nimiam ob frequentiam dicta ipsa sordescunt

20  fiuntque vilia et vel ad despicientiam pervulgata. Quocirca modus et in iis quoque adhibendus est, ne sordescat ioculatio, quae, ni temperata fuerit, transitura sit in garrulitatem, nugationem, sicophantias, ut, qui eiusmodi sint, magis despiciantur sintque aliis contemptui quam ut ipsi delectent. Erit igitur dictorum quoque ac ridiculorum tum comes tum magistra prudentia, qua remota, quid est quod suo in genere assequi commendationem queat?

21     Et dicta et ridicula et facetiae e verbis constant et vultu et gestu et voce, pro loco videlicet ac tempore dignitateque accommodatis. Coeterum loca ipsa unde ducuntur posita sunt in factis, quae dicentes non verbis modo verum etiam gestibus insectantur. Hoc autem ideo contingit, quod facta ipsa sint turpia. Turpitudo autem et rideri solet et accusari, quando suapte natura irridenda est, ut, cum quis ab obesitate tardiore incessu graditur, ibi quispiam dixerit, 'Nimirum navis ipsa honere gravata est suo.' Et ridiculum dictum est et iocandi locus existit a rei ac facti deformitate, ut cum quispiam vinosus incessitur, quod nimis atrox sit miles adversus exenterandas cupas. Hoc igitur dictum a facto est deque morum turpitudine depravataque e materia dolatum.

22     Nec vero ioca ipsa non quandoque e dictis quoque ac verbis deducuntur, quare sedes eorum ibidem quoque sunt collocatae, cuius rei exemplum est apud Ciceronem. Cum enim orator quidam protulisset, 'Sputatilia,'[20] adversarius, quasi attonitus verbi

as Crassus the orator is said to have been,[89] or if he should be cheerful by nature, yet his cheerfulness should not be insipid or absolutely laughable. Rarer use, as Juvenal says, renders pleasure agreeable, for frequency commonly produces satiety.[90] For this reason, excessive frequency in the use of witticisms and a too great, immoderate, and I might almost say heaping up of jests must be avoided. For it not only brings satiety, but because of their excessive frequency the witticisms themselves become sordid, vile, and common to the point of contempt. So in these things, too, moderation must be used so that joking does not become sordid, for unless tempered it will pass into garrulity, trifling, and sycophancy, so that people of this sort are despised and contemptible to others rather than delightful. Therefore both the companion and master of witticisms and also jests must be prudence; when it is removed, what in its class can achieve commendation? 20

Witticisms, jests, and funny stories consist of words, facial expression, gestures, and voice, suited, of course, to place, time, and rank. Moreover, the places from which they are drawn are located in acts, which speakers inveigh against not only with words but also with gestures. This, however, happens because the acts themselves are base. But baseness is usually laughed at and blamed, since it ought to be mocked on account of its own nature, as, when someone walks with a slower gait from obesity, someone might say, "Surely that ship is laden with its own cargo." The speech is ridiculous, and the place for joking proceeds from the deformity of the thing and the act, as when some drunkard is attacked for being too fierce a soldier against casks that need to be disemboweled. Therefore this speech has been hewn from the act and from baseness of character and out of a depraved substance. 21

But sometimes jokes are drawn from speech and also words because their sources are also located in the same place. An example of this is in Cicero. For when a certain orator produced the word "*Sputatilia*," his opponent, as if astonished by the novelty and 22

novitate ignorantiaque, 'Sputa,'[21] inquit, 'o iudices, quid sit scio,
23  tilia[22] vero nescio,' ex eo autem insidiae verendae. Patet igitur iocu-
lorum sedes in factis dictisque constitutas esse, qualia permulta a
nobis demonstrata sunt, nec enim dictis quam factis minus appa-
rantur. Partes autem respondentis videntur praestabiliores esse,
quando et difficiliores; potuit enim qui lacessit praemeditatus dicta
quasi e domo secum afferre ac tanquam ex improviso aggredi, cum
illi extemporalitas sola subsidio sit. Quo igitur responsa minus
expectata, ex eo vehementius movent praestabilioraque ob id iudi-
cantur.

24    Responsa vero ipsa duplici modo partienda sunt: in ea quae aut
diluant tantum aut quae vel acriter mordeant. Sunt et mista
compositaque, ut duo illa simplicia sint tertium vero hoc congluti-
25  natum. Primi exemplum est: Pallas Stroctius, Florentia pulsus a
factione Medica, fertur dixisse in fuga, 'Incubare nos oportet, o
viri, et ingenio et viribus, quo patriam ab dominatu unius libere-
mus'; quae cum relata essent Cosmo, respondit, 'Pauca haec Pal-
lanti referenda: non posse alitem incubare quae et nidum amisisset
et plumis spoliata sit.' Quo dicto et minas irrisit et verbum verbo
diluit ac belle iocatus est.

26    Exemplum secundi: inter congrediendum homo non inurbanus
irriserat alium eiusdem ordinis hominem, cum, qui suo nomine
Foeniculus esset, eum Ferriculum salutasset. Tum ille, vultu quam
maxime verbis apposito, 'Et tu vale,' inquit, 'Furacule.' Videtis quo
adversarium ictu percussit quamque etiam gravissime?

27    Est et tertium genus exemplo suo confirmandum, quod est
huiusmodi, nam et diluit et mordicus etiam abripit. Erat ad divae

his ignorance of the word, said, "I know, judges, what *sputa* is but not *tilia*," fearing some sort of an ambush.[91] Therefore it is clear 23 that the sources of jokes reside in acts and in speech. I have indicated very many; indeed they are furnished not less by speech than by acts. But the role of the responder is more praiseworthy, since it is also more difficult. For the provoker, having thought of his witticisms in advance, can bring them with him from home, so to speak, and attack almost without warning, while for the other, speaking extemporaneously is his only defense. Therefore, the less expected the responses, the more powerfully they move and the more praiseworthy they are judged on this account.

But responses themselves must be divided in two ways: into 24 those that only weaken the attack or those that bite fiercely back. There are also mixed and composite ones so that two are simple but the third one an amalgam. An example of the first: Palla Stro- 25 zzi, driven from Florence by the Medicean faction, is reported to have said in his exile, "Men, we must brood with our intelligence and our forces so that we can liberate our fatherland from the tyranny of one man." When this was reported to Cosimo, he replied, "Make this brief reply to Palla: a bird that has lost its nest and has been despoiled of its feathers cannot brood."[92] With this witticism he derided the threats, defused the remark with a remark of his own, and made a neat joke.

An example of the second: in an encounter, an urbane man 26 mocked another man of his class whose name was Finocolo by greeting him as Ferricolo. Then the latter, his expression suited to his words as much as possible, said, "And farewell to you, too, Furacolo."[93] Do you see with what a blow he struck his adversary and also how serious the blow was?

There is also a third kind to be confirmed with its example, 27 which is of this sort, for it both weakens and tears off a bite at the same time. It was market day near the basilica of Santa

Mariae templum extra Capuam dies nundinalis; convenerant de more ibidem multi mortales; erant in diversoriis pisces maiusculi et assi et elixi in lancibus expositi; forte mercatores duo; alter, ut montanus rerum maris inscius, percontabatur qui nam tam novae magnitudinis piscis esset qui ad uncum pendebat. Ibi alter, qui esset litoralis, irridenti perquam similis respondit: 'Cacomerdilis.' Ibi tum ille, qui se se irrideri sensisset, 'Hui,' inquit, 'quanta est nominum varietas! Hic idem piscis meos apud Marsos suo nomine est sterquicomedis.' Uterque quidem oscenus, at responsor cum primis mordax.

28    Sunt etiam responsa quaedam minime salsa, valde tamen ridicula, qualia Plautina haec. Cum enim alter dixisset e collocutoribus, 'Terrestris cena est multis holeribus,' confestim alter, 'Curato
29    aegrotos domi.' Et hoc item. Cum enim dari sibi dragmam servus cuperet et alter respondisset, 'Quid nam dragma facere vis?,' illic
30    alter, 'Restem volo / mihi emere quo me faciam pensilem.' Illud vero non tam ridiculum quam probatione dignum et sapiens iudicandum. Nam cum senex dixisset grande se honus ferre alterque respondisset interrogans, quid nam id esset honeris, tum senex retulit,

Annos octoginta quatuor;
    eodem accedit servitus, sudor, sitis.

Responsa igitur multo maiorem prae se ferunt ingenii vim insitamque a natura acrimoniam, cum ea sint extemporalia ferantque secum etiam admirationem, cum appareant repentina minimeque praemeditata.

31    Quae igitur et qualia ioca sint, ridicula, dicteria, fabellae, quae sit oratoris, quae faceti hominis, quae vero mimica, theatralia, parasitica, quae et quot responsorum genera et quibus quaeque a

Maria Maggiore outside Capua. As usual, many people had come together there. In the inns some large fish, both roasted and boiled, had been set out on platters. By chance there were two merchants. One, from the mountains and ignorant of sea matters, was asking what in the world was that fish of such unusual size that was hanging from the hook. Then the other, who was from the seashore, replied mockingly, "A shit-crapper." Then the first man, who sensed he was being mocked, said, "Hah! how great is the variety of names! Among my folk, the Marsi, this same fish goes by the name of dung-eater." Each indeed was obscene, but the respondent was especially biting.

There are also some responses not at all pungent, yet very ri- 28 diculous, like these from Plautus. For when one of the interlocu- tors said, "This is a dinner that comes from the ground—with many vegetables," at once the other, "Take care of your sick at home."[94] And this one, too. For when a slave wanted to be given a 29 drachma and the other had replied, "What in the world do you want with a drachma?," the former replied, "I want to buy me a rope to hang myself."[95] But this next one is not so much to be 30 judged ridiculous as wise and worthy of approbation. For when an old man had said he was carrying a great burden and another had responded by asking what that burden was, the old man replied,

Eighty-four years, to which are added slavery, sweat, and thirst.[96]

Thus responses display much greater force of wit and natural acu- ity when they are extemporaneous and also bring surprise with them, appearing suddenly and without premeditation.

Thus it has been sufficiently explained what and of what sort 31 jokes, jests, witty sayings, and stories are; what kind of humor is proper to an orator, what to a witty man, what to a mime, an ac- tor, a parasite; what and how many kinds of responses there are;

locis ducantur, satis id explicatum est; nec minus aperte etiam declaratum quae a nobis quaeruntur ea ad virtutem tantum spectare quae mediocritas quaedam est ad animorumque pertinere relaxationem ac tum ad laborum recreationem relaxationemque tum praecipue quidem molestiarum. Quocirca ad alia quoque transeamus.

and from which places each are derived. Also, it has been declared no less plainly that those things I have been seeking only concern a virtue that is a kind of mean and pertain to the relaxation of the mind and refreshment and relaxation from labors and especially annoyances. So let us pass on to other things, too.

# LIBER QUINTUS[1]

## [Sine titulo]

1 Primum igitur faceti videtur officium fugitare offensiones, petulantias, subsannationes, sicophantias, oscenitates atque id genus plurima quae honestati quidem adversantur animorumque ipsorum et post labores et inter ipsas quoque insudationes refocillationi. Quod autem plurima inter iocandum accidunt quae aut turpia sint aut parum omnino decora, sive factu dictu ve sive gestu aut voce, id etaim diligentissime praestandum est ab eo, illa ut et dicantur et referantur quin etiam fiant nullo modo turpiter minimeque indecenter, verum his in cunctis rectam sequetur rationem quaeque ab
2 illa dictantur et honesta et decora. Hoc autem ideo praecipimus quod ea fere solum ridentur quae, ut Cicero inquit, vel sola vel maxime notant designantque deformitatem aut turpitudinem aliquam; quae ut dicantur referanturque haudquaquam turpiter aut parum decenter, id vero summo studio praestandum est ingenuo viro. Quod quia difficile est praestare, iccirco virtus haec in iis versari a nobis dicitur. Servare enim honestum in magna morum corruptione ac dicendi licentia, id vero quam difficillimum; iccirco maxime etiam dedecorosum et turpe aliter se gessisse.

# BOOK FIVE

## [Untitled]

It seems, therefore, that the first duty of the witty man is to avoid  1
offense, impudence, derision, sycophancy, obscenity, and many
things of this kind contrary to honor and to the restoration of
mind after labors and exertions alike. Moreover, because many
things happen while joking that are either base or not at all decorous, either in doing or saying, in gesture or in voice, he must also
most diligently see to it that those things are said and related
without becoming in any way base or at all indecent, but that in all
these things he follows right reason and what it dictates as honorable and decorous. Therefore I give this precept: almost the only  2
things that are laughed at, as Cicero says, either solely or for the
most part censure and mark out some deformity or baseness.[1] The
freeborn man must see to it with the greatest zeal that these things
are said and related not at all basely or indecently. It is difficult to
accomplish this, and that is why I say that there is a virtue involved for us in this kind of speech. For to preserve one's honor
amid great corruption of morals and licentiousness of speech is in
truth extremely difficult; for this reason it is also especially indeco-
rous and base to comport oneself otherwise.

### : 2 :

## *Definitio facetudinis.*[2]

1 Domitii Marsi extat apud Quintilianum opinio urbanitatem virtutem esse quandam in breve dictum coactam aptamque ad delectan-
dos movendosque homines in omnem affectum, maxime idoneam
ad resistendum vel lacessendum, prout quaeque res et persona desiderat. Quae definitio nobis parum idonea visa est. Cur autem ita
visum sit, aperiemus. Principio si urbanitatem pro ipsa iocandi
virtute Domitius accipit, a veri cognitione longe aberrat, cum urbanitas, ut superiore libro ostendimus, rusticitati opponatur, nec
genus sit verum species. Deinde urbanitas non in dictis solum
consideratur verum urbanis etiam in moribus ac consuetudinibus.

2 Ad haec cum dicit 'ad resistendum vel lacessendum,' verba haec videntur solum spectare ad ea quae oratoris sunt, minime vero ad
illa quae ad relaxationem spectant, propter quod virtus haec et
laudatur et in maximo habetur honore apud occupatissimos et la-
boriosissimos sive cives sive civitatum rectores. Quod autem dixit
'in omnem affectum,' quanquam id non improbamus, videtur tamen de oratoria tantum innuere, non de hac ipsa virtute quam facetudinem vocavimus quaeque ipsa moralis ac civilis virtus est,

3 nedum oratoria ac forensis seu senatoria. Qua e re efficitur ut et
vera et certa definitio virtutis huius sit: mediocritatem eam esse
quandam iocandi et verbis et gestibus accommodatis, ad laborum
molestiarumque ac curarum doloris quoque honestam et suavem
relaxationem, ingenuo viro dignam.

4 Igitur cum in universum multa a nobis disputata sint, multa
etiam exempla tradita circa iocandi genus omne, dehinc ingenua-
rum facetiarum exempla trademus, carptim tamen, ne multitudine
sordescant ipsa; quibus referendis delectum adhibebimus, quemadmodum adhiberi oportere supra praecepimus iis dicendis.

: 2 :

*Definition of wittiness.*

In Quintilian one finds the opinion of Domitius Marsus that urbanity is a virtue compressed into a brief saying and fit to delight and move men to any emotion, but especially suitable to resistance or provocation, just as the situation or person requires.[2] This definition has not seemed adequate to me. And I will explain why it has seemed so. In the first place, if Domitius takes urbanity for the virtue itself of joking, he is far from understanding the truth, since urbanity, as I showed in a previous book, is opposed to rusticity and is not the class but a species.[3] In the second place, urbanity is not considered only in witticisms but also in manners and habits that are urbane. In addition, when he says "to resistance or provocation," the words appear only to concern things that are the province of an orator but not at all those that concern relaxation, for which this virtue is praised and held in greatest honor by the busiest and most laborious men, whether citizens or rulers of states. Moreover, his phrase "to any emotion," although I do not disapprove of it, yet he seems to indicate only an oratorical virtue, not the one I have called wittiness, which is a moral and civic virtue, not only an oratorical and forensic or senatorial one. From this it follows that the true and sure definition of this virtue is as follows: it is a mean in joking with appropriate words and gestures for the purpose of honorable and pleasant relaxation, worthy of a freeborn man, from labors, annoyances, cares, and also pain.

Therefore, since I have discussed many things generally and also given many examples of every kind of joking, next I will give examples of freeborn witticisms, yet selectively, so that they are not demeaned owing to their great number. In relating them I shall use discrimination, as I taught earlier must be used while

5  Prius tamen de urbanitate Quintilianus quid sentiat, quando ipse
Domitianae huius opinionis relator est, aperiemus. Putat igitur
venustum esse quod cum gratia quadam dicatur ac venere; salsum
autem in consuetudine ait pro ridiculo tantum accipi, non quod
utique id sit, quanquam et ridicula esse oportet salsa, et Cicero,
quod salsum sit, ait esse Atticorum; urbanitatis vero nomine significari sermonem praeferentem in verbis et sono et usu proprium
quendam gestum urbis, ut sumptam e conversatione doctorum
tacitam eruditionem, denique cui contraria sit rusticitas.

6  Ac mihi quidem videntur rhetoricae facultatis scriptores et rusticitatem et urbanitatem circa verba tantum gestusque illa comi-
tantes versari velle, ac si non rusticum sit illotis manibus accum-
bere in mensa nec cedere natu maioribus aut magistratibus in via,
non decedere aut illis non assurgere nec salutare quos, iter faciens,
obvios habueris, contra servare haec omnia neque urbanum hoc
7  sit neque ad urbanitatem referendum. Quocirca urbanitas — quod
distinguendum erat eloquentiae scriptoribus — partim in iocis versatur ac ridiculis urbe dignis coetuque civilium atque ingenuorum
hominum, partim in factis ac moribus quos cives retineant quique
in urbe versati sint conversationibusque civilibus. Quo fit ut Cicero, cum urbis mores admiraretur et sequendos duceret, ad Rufum
familiarem scribens dicat, 'Urbem, mi Rufe, cole et in ista luce
8  vive.' Itaque quod olim esset Atticum — qua e re, id est ab humanitate morumque suavitate, Pomponius ille clarissimus vir agnomi-
natus est Atticus — id ab urbe Roma post dictum est urbanum, ut
asperi mores difficiles, morosi, inconditi, rustici dicti sint, et Caius
Marius, a parum cultis moribus ac vitae duritia quodque nullas
vivendi sequeretur amoenitates, habitus est rusticanus. Contra qui
humanitate praediti essent suavibusque ornati moribus atque

saying them.⁴ But first I will explain what Quintilian thinks about  5
urbanity, since he is the one who relates this opinion of Domitius.
He thinks, then, that what is said with some grace and elegance is
charming, but he says that *salsum* is ordinarily only taken to mean
"ridiculous," not that this is so without fail, although ridiculous
things are necessarily *salsa*, and Cicero says the *salsum* is peculiar to
the Attic orators.⁵ However, by the word *urbanity*, he says, is
meant speech that reveals in words, sound, and usage an attitude
proper to the city, like a silent instruction taken from the conversation of the learned, and, in a word, the opposite of rusticity.

And what is more, writers on rhetorical ability seem to me to  6
want both rusticity and urbanity to be concerned only with words
and the gestures accompanying them, as if it were not rustic to
recline at table with unwashed hands or not to yield in the street
to one's elders or magistrates, not to make way or to rise for them
or not to greet while traveling those whom you meet, and as if, on
the contrary, to observe all of these things were not urbane or to
be ascribed to urbanity. So urbanity—a distinction the writers on  7
eloquence ought to have made—is partially concerned with jokes
and jests worthy of the city and gatherings of civil and freeborn
men, and partially with actions and manners of citizens and those
versed in the city and civil conversation. So it follows that Cicero,
admiring the manners of the city and considering they ought to be
followed, says, writing to his friend Rufus, "Inhabit the city, my
friend Rufus, and live in its light."⁶ And so what once was "At-  8
tic"—from which, that is, from his humanity and the agreeableness of his manners, that very famous man Pomponius was sur-
named "Atticus"—that quality was later called "urbane" from the
city [*urbs*] of Rome, just as harsh, difficult, morose, and uncouth
manners were called "rustic," and Gaius Marius was considered a
rustic from his uncultivated manners and the hardness of his life
and from not pursuing any of the pleasures of life.⁷ On the other
hand, those endowed with humanity and adorned with pleasant

institutis ut urbani et laudati sunt et culti. Quid quod stultos etiam vocavere quos urbano a cultu institutisque usuque ab humano et civili alienos esse intellexere?

9    Igitur vetustas omnis iocum id accepit quod esset serio adversum, cuius opinioni Horatius etiam assentitur inquiens, 'Sed tamen omisso quaeramus seria ludo.' Ludum enim pro ioco posuit. Quo fit ut qui iocantur seria tantisper relinquant, dum refrigerationem concipiant aliquam a seriis ac laboriosis rebus, ut iocatio ipsa ab ingenuis viris omnino suscipiatur recreationis gratia, quae tamen nec ab honestate recedat nec ab ingenuitate. Quid enim urbanum esse potest ac facetum, quod non idem ingenuum? Aut quid iure laudari, praeterquam si honestum? Quocirca in omni actione et vita, delectu adhibito et rerum et personarum itemque et locorum et temporum, iocandi hilaritas haec ac modestia magnopere laudatur nullumque omnino civilis vitae genus dedecet, cum etiam in principibus viris non commendetur solum verum etiam desideretur.

10   In iocando autem ludendisque facetiis duo potissimum cavenda: unum, ne in miseros iocemur, praeterquam si petulantes fuerint, superbi, contumaces; quid enim inhumanius quam irridere eum cuius commoveri et angi miseriis debeas? alterum, ne eos dictis incessamus quorum maior sit auctoritas ac vis, unde eos tibi inimicos facias. Quid enim imprudentius quam potentium iras in se se provocare, dictis eos lacessentem? Eadem quoque animadversione fugiendum ne aut populum universum aut factionem aliquam ordinem ve aut nationem totam lacessamus aut disciplinas artesque laudabiliores aut studia; quo quid esse potest stultius aut quid inconsideratius quam uno dicto integram in se se civitatem irritare?

manners and habits have been praised and honored as urbane. What about the fact that they also called foolish those who they knew were alien to urbane culture and habits and to humane and civil usage?

Therefore all antiquity accepted the jest as the opposite of the serious, to which opinion Horace also assents, saying, "But, nevertheless, let's pursue serious things, having put play aside."[8] He has used *play* for *joke*. So it happens that those who joke leave off serious things for as long as they are taking refreshment from serious and laborious affairs, so that joking itself is undertaken by freeborn men entirely for the sake of recreation of a kind that does not depart from honor or noble-mindedness. What indeed can be urbane and witty that is not also freeborn? Or what can be justly praised unless it is honorable? For this reason, in every action and way of life, when discrimination of things, persons, places and times is used, this cheerfulness and moderation of joking are greatly praised and are not unbecoming at all to any kind of civil life, since even in princes it is not only commended but also desired.

In joking and playing with witticisms, however, two things must especially be avoided.[9] First, we should not joke at the expense of miserable men unless they are impudent, proud, insolent. For what is more inhumane than to mock someone at whose miseries you ought to be moved and distressed? Second, we should not attack with witticisms those who have greater authority and power, such that you make them your enemies. For what is more imprudent than to provoke the wrath of the powerful against yourself by irritating them with your witticisms? Also, with the same care one must avoid provoking the entire populace or some faction or order or the whole nation or the disciplines and praiseworthy arts or studies.[10] For what can be more foolish and inconsiderate than to incite an entire state against oneself with a single witticism?

11    Franciscus Philelphus, et Graece et Latine Mediolani cum pro-
fiteretur, praedicantem Bernardinum, qui post obitum ob merita
inter divos relatus est, dicto aculeatiori ita pupugit ut ex eo omnem eorum ordinem qui Minores Fratres dicuntur non in se modo
verum in omnis literatos armaverit exindeque insectari studia haec
humanitatis ordinis eius praedicatores nunquam publice priva-
12    timque desierint. Dum Demosthenes nec Philippo parcit et Alexandrum nunc ut puerum ridet, nunc ut adolescentulum contem-
nit, quam prudenter rebus suis consuluerit, vitae eius testis est
13    exitus. Cum animadvertisset Augustus equitem Romanum biben-
tem in spectaculis praeter morem dignitatemque eius ordinis mi-
sissetque ad eum qui sub obiurgationis speciem diceret, 'Ego si
prandere velim, domum iverim,' tum illum memoriae proditum est
respondisse et modeste et perquam ingenue nequaquam Augustum timere locum in orchestra si reliquerit, illum ne recuperet.
Quo responso et minax Augusti dictum facete diluit et principis a
se iram per iucunditatem avertit, habita et temporis et loci et personarum ratione.
14    Itaque abstinendum est a principibus. Quin si qua concepta est
ira, suavioribus dictis placanda est, quod Tarentini illi iuvenes
praestitere; nam convicti cum essent quod multa inter coenandum
licentius de rege Pyrrho locuti essent ratioque maledictorum re-
posceretur, tum unum ex iis iocabundum dixisse ferunt, 'Nunquid,
o Pyrrhe rex, hoc mirare et querere? Per Herculem ipsa te in
coena confecissemus, ni lagena nos destituisset.' Quo dicto, ut et
urbano et ingenuo profecto ab homine, omnis e vestigio ira disso-
15    luta est. Accusatus iuvenis quispiam, quod in mensa intemperan-
tius locutus esset adversus sacerdotem vocatusque ob id in iudicium atque interrogatus a iudicibus, 'Si eodem,' respondit, 'pacto
rursus in coena me invitavero, vel duodecim quoque Apostolos

When Francesco Filelfo was teaching Greek and Latin at Mi-  11
lan, he stung the preacher Bernardino, who was canonized after
his death for his merits, with so sharp a witticism that he armed
the entire order who are called the Friars Minor not only against
himself but against all men of letters, and thereafter the preachers
of this order have never stopped attacking the study of the humanities in public and in private.[11] The end of Demosthenes' life  12
bears witness how prudently he considered his own interests when
he did not spare Philip and sometimes mocked Alexander as a
boy, sometimes scorned him as an adolescent.[12] Augustus noticed  13
that a Roman equestrian was drinking at the spectacles in a manner contrary to the custom and dignity of his order and sent someone to say in the form of a reproach, "If I wanted to eat lunch, I'd
go home." That man, it has been recorded, replied both moderately and very like a freeborn man that Augustus wasn't afraid that
he would lose his place in the orchestra if he left it.[13] With this
response he wittily defused Augustus' menacing remark and by
means of his pleasantness averted from himself the wrath of the
emperor, taking account of time, place, and person.

And so one must refrain from attacking princes. But if wrath  14
has been kindled, it must be appeased with more pleasing witticisms, as the young men of Tarentum demonstrated. For when
they had been found guilty of saying during dinner many things
with too little restraint about King Pyrrhus, and the reason for
their abusive remarks was demanded, it is said that one of them
jokingly said, "King Pyrrhus, do you really marvel at and lament
this? By Hercules, we would have finished you off right here at
dinner if the bottle hadn't deserted us."[14] With this witticism, as
coming from an urbane and freeborn man, all wrath was at once
dissipated. A young man, accused of speaking too intemperately at  15
table against a priest, being summoned to trial for it and questioned by the judges, responded, "If I regale myself again in the
same way at dinner, I'll attack even the twelve Apostles with

insectabor fustibus.' Statimque inter iudices, exorto risu cogni-
toque vini vitio, ab illis absolutus est, poena tamen a sacerdote
irrogata uti quatriduum vino abstineret.

16    Genus hoc facetiarum et ingenuo viro dignum est et inter egregios cives relatu atque auditu, quando et obiecta dissolvit et offensione caret, nec delectat solum verum summa quoque cum laude
fert secum audientium approbationem. Id tamen videndum, ne
dicta ipsa aut frigida sint aut absurda quae ve imprudenter exci-
17    dant, ex quo stultitiae accusemur. Gregarius quispiam furti accusatus, dum iram se se praetoris lenire putat, 'Equidem,' inquit, 'o
praetor, artibus his hero me placere intelligebam.' Quid his stultius? Nanque hero dum dicit studere se ut obsequatur, illum ca-
18    lumniatus est. Alius eiusdem ordinis in horto deprehensus, cum
vapulans deprecaretur, 'Non mihi,' inquit, 'poma surripui, verum
asello meo.' Quid hoc frigidius? Habent igitur generis huius dicta
suas ac necessarias cautiones.

19    Utque ad humilis abiectosque ac miserabiles redeamus, quid
indignius quam miserum irridere? Colas quidam Siculus et naturae et fortunae bonis destitutus, cum nobili ab adolescente importune irrideretur, 'Ne tu,' inquit, 'me irrideas, inferior enim sum
quam ut rideri merear, cuius tamen sors deplorari ab summis atque infimis iure debeat; haud multum tamen aberit, cum bonis
ipse exutus omnibus, mecum et fortunam tuam lugebis et mendi-
cabis in patria,' quod non multo post contigit. Habent enim impia
20    et intestabilia tum facta tum dicta Deum ipsum ulctorem. Aliquando etiam miserabilium e numero ac mendicantium existunt
qui dicaces sint ac maxime ipsi quidem ad movendum risum ido-
nei, de quibus dici iure possit Horatianum illud, 'Foenum in cornu
gerit.' Hi igitur ipsi irritati notas maxime cicatricosas relinquunt
immorsionum suarum, ut cum dicaculus quidam lippo insultaret

clubs." And at once the judges burst into laughter, recognizing that the wine was at fault, and they acquitted him, but with a penalty, imposed by the priest, that he abstain from wine for four days.

This kind of witticism is worthy of a freeborn man and of be-  16
ing related and heard among outstanding citizens, since it disarms accusations and does not offend. It not only delights but also carries away with the highest praise the approbation of the listeners. Nevertheless, one must see to it that witticisms are not feeble or absurd or slip out imprudently, owing to which we may be accused of foolishness. A herdsman, accused of theft, while thinking to  17
soften the wrath of the judge, said, "Indeed, judge, I thought I was pleasing my master with these arts." What response could more foolish than this? For while he says that he's endeavoring to gratify his master, he has accused him falsely. Another of the same class  18
was caught in a garden. While being beaten, he pled in excuse, saying, "I didn't steal the apples for myself but for my little donkey." What is more feeble than this? Therefore remarks of this kind necessarily require some caution.

And to return to the humble, abject, and miserable, what is  19
more shameful than to mock a wretch? When a certain Cola, a Sicilian, deprived of the goods of both nature and fortune, was being mocked harshly by a young nobleman, he said, "Don't mock me, for I am too low to deserve being laughed at, and my lot ought justly to be deplored by the highest and lowest. The time is not far off when you yourself, stripped of all goods, will lament your fortune along with me and will go begging in your fatherland," which happened not much later. For impious and detestable acts and words have God himself for their avenger. Sometimes too there  20
are some from among the number of the miserable and the beggars who are railers and especially suited to move laughter, about whom that line of Horace may be justly said, "He carries hay on his horn."[15] Accordingly, these, when provoked, leave deeply scarring marks from their bites, as when a railer insulted a blear-eyed

mendicanti quod ad scrupum pedem offendisset, 'At non offendit pedem tuarum ad limen aedium nocte praeterita adulter, domo cum abesses,' quod quidem et factum erat et ille id minime ignorabat. Quocirca nequaquam committendum, ratione ut aliqua huiusmodi hominum generis sive imprecationibus sive maledicentiae te exponas.

21     Dictorum autem genera facimus duo: unum, quod risum tantum moveat; alterum, quod approbationem. Movent igitur risum non modo acute ac venuste dicta sed non nunquam stulte, iracunde, timide seu dicta seu facta. Efferbuerat Alfonsus minor in famulum stabularium, itaque vocato architriclino iussit illi vinum decimum in diem adimi. Risus illico excitatus est ab astantibus, qui scirent stabularium illum abstemium, quod etsi Alfonso notum erat, ira tamen memoriam praepedierat. Idem Alfonsus, cum

22 fugientem cerneret ab hostium incursu calonem interrogaretque, 'Quo fugis?,' exterritus ille, 'Umbram,' respondit, 'quaerito.' Risit tum Alfonsus ut ignave loquentem atque e consternatione illique tabernam vinariam ostendit, 'Eccam,' inquiens, 'quam quaeritas

23 umbram.' Item pro tribunali ius cum diceret ac stultior ad eum quispiam accessisset clamitans, clementiae uti suae memor esset in iure dicundo, percontatus tum ipse, quod nam officium praestari a se posset facilitatis atque clementiae? Tum ille, 'Clementia,' inquit, 'uxor mea cubito me hac nocte e lecto exposuit et maledictis extra domum prosecuta est. Ego apud te iniuriarum ago.' Difficile dictu est qui risus toto foro exorti fuerint.

24     Haec igitur sive dictorum sive facetiarum genera, etsi in facetum hunc nostrum minime cadunt dicendo, usuveniunt tamen referendo inter confabulandum in circulis atque consessionibus. At quae approbationem adducunt et dictu et relatu digna sunt addecentque utroque modo facetum, ut apud Plautum, cum

beggar because he had hit his foot against a sharp stone, "But the adulterer didn't hit his foot against the doorstep of your house last night while you were away from home," which indeed had happened and was by no means unknown to the railer. So you must not make the mistake of exposing yourself in any way to the imprecations or abuse of men of this kind.

Moreover, I distinguish two classes of witticisms: one, which 21 only produces laughter; the other, approbation. So not only things said sharply and charmingly produce laughter but sometimes also things said or done from foolishness, anger, or fear. Alfonso II had boiled into a rage against a stable boy, and so, having summoned the majordomo, ordered that his wine be taken away for ten days. At once laughter was roused among the bystanders, who knew that the stable boy did not drink. Although Alfonso knew this, anger had impeded his memory. When this same Alfonso per- 22 ceived a soldier's batman fleeing from an attack of the enemy and asked, "Where are you fleeing?," that terrified man replied, "I'm looking for the shade." Then Alfonso laughed at him for speaking in cowardly alarm and pointed out to him a wine tavern, saying, "Over there is the shade you're looking for." Also, when he was 23 administering justice from his tribunal and a rather stupid fellow approached him, crying out for him to remember his clemency in giving judgment, Alfonso inquired what service of courtesy or clemency he could provide. Then that man said, "Clemency, my wife, pushed me out of bed tonight with her elbow and pursued me out of the house with her abuse. In your presence I accuse her of outrage." It is difficult to describe the laughter that arose in the whole court.

Therefore, witticisms and funny stories of this class, although 24 they are not at all appropriate for our man of wit to say himself, nevertheless may be related by him in companies and gatherings.[16] But things that induce approbation are worthy to be both said and related, and they become the witty man in either way, as in

percontaretur alter, 'Quo pacto potis / nupta et vidua esse eadem?,'
respondit alter, 'Quod adulescens nupta sit cum sene.' Dictum
minime ridiculum, quod tamen sententiae loco probationem indu-
25 cat. Quale etiam Ciceronis illud, cum dicentibus sero eum in castra ad Pompeium venisse respondit, 'Minime vero sero, quando
26 nihil hic paratum invenio.' Huiusmodi enim sive dicta sive responsa magis probantur ut concinne, ut graviter, ut prudenter
atque ex tempore et ad rem ipsam accommode dicta quam ut ridicule, cum saepenumero admirationem quoque ingenerent in ani-
27 mis audientium. Cuiusmodi etiam illud Augusti Caesaris: nam
cum auctio bonorum fieret equitis Romani, qui plurimo aere
alieno pressus esset atque undique a creditoribus circumventus,
iussissetque ex illis culcitram sibi tantum cubicularem emi, mirati
cum essent quibus id negocii ab Augusto dabatur, 'An non ea,' inquit, 'habenda a nobis est alliciendum ad somnum culcitra, in qua
ille qui tantum deberet capere somnum potuerit?' Non igitur dicta
omnia risum movent, cum haec ipsa horumque similia approbationem tantummodo secum ferant.

28    Risus vero ipse aut e nobis ipsis petitur aut ex aliis aut e rebus
ipsisque ex eventis. E nobis igitur risus petetur, cum aliqua tanquam subabsurda dicentur, non tamen subabsurde, aut gestus quidam parum erunt compositi atque ob id ridiculi, cum tamen ne-
29 que ipsi per se neque res ipsae nostrae sint ridiculae. Est apud
Plautum in Casina senex qui villico ancillam tradere in uxorem
studeat, cum ipse tamen voluptatem ex ea sibi quaereret. Itaque
quo risum poeta excitaret inter spectatores, errantem inter loquendum illum inducit:

Nam cur [senex inquit] non ego id perpetrem quod coepi,
ut nubat mihi? illud quidem volebam,
nostro servo villico.

Plautus, when one man asks, "In what way can the same woman be both married and a widow?," and the other replies, "Because a young woman married an old man."[17] A witticism not at all ridiculous, which nevertheless wins approval as an aphorism. As also 25 this one of Cicero's: To those saying he had come late to Pompey's camp he replied, "Not at all late, in fact, since I find nothing ready."[18] Indeed, witticisms or repartee of this kind are approved 26 more when spoken elegantly, gravely, prudently, extemporaneously, and appropriately to the situation than when said jestingly, since they also often produce admiration in the minds of the listeners. This witticism of Augustus Caesar's is also of this kind. A Roman 27 equestrian's goods were being auctioned off as the man had been overwhelmed with enormous debts and was beset on all sides by creditors; Augustus bade only a bedroom mattress be purchased on his behalf, which amazed his agents in the transaction. Augustus responded, "Shouldn't I acquire a mattress so sleep inducing that a debtor like that was able to sleep on it?"[19] Thus not all witticisms induce laughter, since these and ones like them only win approval.

But laughter itself is sought from ourselves, others, or things 28 and events.[20] Laughter will be sought from ourselves when (for example) some mildly absurd things are said, yet not in a mildly absurd way, or some physical movements are awkward and on that account ridiculous, although neither we ourselves nor our affairs are ridiculous. In Plautus' *Casina* there is an old man who endeavors 29 to marry a female slave to his steward, although he is seeking pleasure from her for himself. And so to raise laughter in the audience he brings him on stage, making a mistake as he speaks:

For why [says the old man] don't I complete what I've begun: that she marry me? Indeed, I meant this, marry my slave, the steward.[21]

Subabsurdum atque aberrantem illum parumque in verbis consistentem facit, quo risum inde excitet.

30 Gregorius Typhernas, quo praeceptore Graecis in literis usus sum adolescens, ad forum accesserat rerum venalium, dumque rusticano cum homine non potest de mercimonio convenire, sermone enim cum illo nimis composito utebatur, ibi ego, qui rem perpendissem, conversus ad rusticum, 'O bone,' inquam, 'homo, ex hac omni summa quantum ipse vis decorticari?,' quod a me dictum est pro demi. Tum ille, verbo hoc et suo et rusticano cum voluptate audito, renidenti similis aspernatusque Gregorium meque de amoenitate complexus, 'Tu,' inquit, 'sapide adolescens, universo de pretio quantum tibi visum fuerit decorticabis.' Tum ego, 'De cumulo isto tuo vel granulum exgranulabo.' Rursum ille in risum abiens, 'Pro arbitrio,' inquit, 'exgranulabis.' Ad ea ipse, 'Novem igitur tibi granula argenteola crassula atque haec quidem tantum immanuabo.' 'Immanuabis,' inquit, 'quam primulum.' Hac igitur ratione, composito pretio, transacta res est; qui vero aderant omnes in cachinnos resoluti sunt. Feci igitur me ridiculum, hoc est rusticanum, quo agrestis hominis mollirem duritiem.

31 Quaeritur autem ex aliis risus, ut cum Cicero de genero suo, qui exigua esset statura, dixit, 'Quis, obsecro, generum meum ad
32 gladium alligavit?' Item de Quinto fratre, qui et ipse brevi esset statu corporis, cum vidisset imaginem eius maioribus lineamentis ad pectus usque depictam, 'Profecto,' inquit, 'frater meus dimidius
33 maior est quam totus.' Antonius Panhormita,[3] praetereuntem passu maiore ac frequentiore claudum quempiam cum videret, 'Cui nam,' inquit, 'divo sacer hic dies est, o campanator, adeo nam fre-
34 quens tintinnis?' Itaque et a nobis et ab aliis, plurimis etiam modis, iisque maxime diversis, risum excimus. Militabat sub Alfonso eques, cui nomen erat Rostro; hic tegmento capitis quod hodie birretum vocant utebatur rubro atque in cristam porrecto; forte et excubias pro castris agebat. Cum igitur Alfonsus noctu munus

He has him commit a slightly absurd and erroneous verbal inconsistency in order to excite laughter.

Gregorio Tifernate, whom I had as teacher of Greek letters 30 when I was a young man, had gone to the marketplace and was unable to make a deal with a man from the country about some merchandise, since he was using excessively artificial language with him.[22] Then having given the matter some thought, I turned to the rustic and said, "My good fellow, how much are you willing to peel away from this amount?," saying "peel away from" instead of "reduce." The man enjoyed hearing this familiar country word and beamed with pleasure; then disdaining Gregorio and embracing me in his delight, he said, "Smart young fellow, you may peel away from the full price as much as you think right." Then I, "From this heap of yours I'll degrain a small grain." He, once again dissolving in laughter, "Degrain as you please." To which I added, "So I'll slip you nine little solid silver grains — and that's all."[23] "Slip away, as soon as you can," he said. In this way, then, the price having been settled, the business was transacted, but everyone present dissolved into loud laughter. Thus I made myself ridiculous, that is rustic, to mollify the hardness of a man from the country.

Moreover, laughter is sought from others, as when Cicero said 31 of his son-in-law, because he was short in stature, "Who, I pray, girded my son-in-law onto a sword?"[24] Likewise when he saw a 32 half-length portrait of his brother Quintus, who was also of short stature, painted with enlarged features, he said, "Half of my brother is certainly larger than the whole."[25] When Antonio Panormita saw a lame man passing by with longer and faster steps, he 33 said, "To what saint is this day consecrated, bell-ringer, that you ring so fast?"[26] And so we call forth laughter both from ourselves 34 and from others in many and very different ways. A horseman named Beak served as a soldier under Alfonso. He wore the head-covering that today they call a beret, red and stretched to a crest, and happened to be keeping watch in front of the camp. So when

suum obiret, in eum et ob cristam et ob nomen iocatus, 'Quando,'
inquit, 'o galle, matutinum cantabis?' Ad ea ille, 'Male,' inquit, 'ma-
tutinatur qui vespernam non gustavit'; quo quidem ioco delectatus
Alfonsus vestitu illum donavit etiam diversicolore, quo gallum et
crista et appellatione et varietate coloris toto etiam corpore referret. Sed immorari hac in parte, exemplis amplificandae eius gratia
afferendis, omnino videtur importunum.

35     Reliquum est ne partem eam inexemplificatam relinquamus
quae tum a rebus ipsis risum quaerit tum ab eventis. Qua autem
via risus ab iis quae eveniunt comparetur Cicero docuit in Vatinii
consulatum iocatus, cum paucorum admodum dierum fuisset,
'Magnum,' inquit, 'ostentum anno Vatinii factum est, illo enim
consule, nec bruma nec ver nec aestas nec autunnus fuit.' Docuit et
Vatinius ipse, in Ciceronis verba iocatus. Nam cum gloriaretur
Cicero se rei publicae humeris ab exilio reportatum, 'Unde ergo
36 tibi varices?,' Vatinius intulit. Nec minus apud Plautum servus pro
ancilla suppositus in cubili, cum a spectatoribus risum captans
dixit:

> Mihi quidem aedepol insignite facta est iniuria:
> duobus nupsi, neuter fecit quod novae nuptae solet.

37 Extat etiam Catonis dictum admodum facetum; cui renuntiatum
cum esset Albidii, civis Romani qui sua bona per luxum atque
ingluviem consumpsisset, domum, quae una illi esset reliqua, in-
cendio conflagrasse, 'Ut belle,' inquit, 'Albidius proterviam[4] fecit,'
alludens ad sacrificium in quo mos erat quicquid reliquiarum su-
38 peresset ex epulis in ignem id coniici. Extat eodem hoc etiam in
genere Valerii Martialis et bellum et cultum epigramma ad Fausti-
num amicum:

Alfonso was on night duty, he made fun of him both on account
his crest and his name, saying, "When, rooster, will you sing your
morning song?" In reply he said, "Someone who hasn't tasted his
evening meal sings poorly in the morning." Delighted with this
joke, Alfonso also gave him a multicolored garment so that he
would resemble a rooster in his crest, his name, and in variety of
color over the whole body. But to linger on this subject, producing
examples for the sake of amplification, seems entirely unsuitable.

It remains not to leave without examples that part of my sub-  35
ject which seeks laughter both from the material itself and from
events. Cicero showed how events produce laughter when he joked
about Vatinius' consulship, which lasted only few days. His remark was, "A great portent occurred in Vatinius' year, for when he
was consul there was no winter or spring or summer or autumn."
And Vatinius himself also showed how to do this by making fun
of Cicero's words. For when Cicero was boasting that he had been
brought from exile on the shoulders of the republic, Vatinius interjected, "So then where did your varicose veins come from?"[27]
No less did the male slave, being substituted in bed for the slave  36
girl in Plautus, show how to do this, when he said, hoping to raise
a laugh from the audience:

Clearly, by Pollux, an injustice has been done me: I married
two men, but neither did the usual thing to a new bride.[28]

There is also Cato's very witty saying. When it was reported to  37
him that the house of Albidius, a Roman citizen who had consumed his goods in luxury and gluttony, had burned up the only
house he had left in a fire, Cato said, "How beautifully Albidius
did this act of impudence," alluding to the sacrifice in which it was
customary to throw anything left over from feasts into the fire.[29]
There is also in this same class a beautiful and elegant epigram of  38
Valerius Martial to his friend Faustinus:

Lotus nobiscum est, hilaris coenavit, et idem
inventus mane est mortuus Andragoras.
Tam subitae mortis causam, Faustine, requiris?
In somnis medicum viderat Hermocratem.

39     Elicitur etiam rebus ab ipsis risus multipliciter quidem, quando
rerum ipsarum et multiplex et varia et pene infinita supellex est.
Itaque et maximam et perquam idoneam iocantibus praebent materiam, sive ioci sint ipsi liberales atque ingenui, sive serviles aut
rusticani, sive theatro detur opera mimicisque spectaculis. Conabi-
mur itaque quantum memoria nobis ex diutina lectione summinis-
trabit quantumque ipsi ingenio assequi poterimus, pro materia,
qua de agitur, exempla diversi generis variaeque ioculationis afferre, dignitate tamen servata. Philosophamur enim, vel philoso-
phice potius ludimus, non ea tamen licentia ut histrioniis sico-
phantiisque locus detur in scriptis his nostris ullus. Rerum autem
appellatione et negocia et artes et ministeria opificiaque et praedia
et supellectilem censumque et id genus externa omnia intelligi
volumus.

40     Vido Grammaticus, quem ego adolescentulus Perusiae audivi
senem iam, retinentem tamen dignitatem institutore dignam,
fuerat iunior in editiore domus parte cum ancilla deprehensus a
discipulo atque eo quidem in statu, ut, cum discipulus magistro
illudens dixisset repente ad primam deprehensionem, 'Omnis
homo currit,' non discedens a grammatica dialecticaque disciplina,
praeceptore quoque ab ipso, momento eodem, responsum fuerit,
'Praeter me volantem,' statum videlicet considerante in quo deprehensus esset. Res igitur ipsa et discipulum admonuit et doctorem
iisdem sensibus simul ludere eandemque in sententiam iocari.

41     Thomas Pontanus, nobilissimus rhetor, habebat in deliciis ca-
tellam, cui Lusculae erat nomen; ea cum vidisset ancillulam cum

He bathed with us, dined cheerfully, and yet Andragoras was found dead in the morning. You ask, Faustinus, the cause of such a sudden death? In a dream he had seen the doctor Hermocrates.[30]

Laughter is also elicited in many ways from the material itself, 39 since the stock of material is manifold, various, and almost infinite. Thus it provides the greatest and most appropriate subject matter to jokers, whether the jokes are liberal and honorable, servile and rustic, or one applies oneself to the theater or to mimes' spectacles. I will try, then, as much as my memory furnishes from daily reading and as much as I am able to procure from my own wit, to bring forth examples of different kinds and of varied joking in accordance with the matter concerned, while preserving dignity. For I am practicing philosophy, or rather I am playing philosophically, yet not with such license that any place in my writings is given to actors or sycophants. By the appellation *matter* I intend to be understood occupations, arts, employments, works, estates, household goods, property, and all externals of this kind.

When I was a very young man I attended in Perugia the lec- 40 tures of the grammarian Guido, who, though already an old man, nevertheless maintained the dignity worthy of a teacher. When he was younger, he was caught with a maidservant by a pupil in the upper part of the house and in such a position that the pupil, mocking his teacher, said right upon catching him, "Every man runs," keeping to his grammatical and dialectical method. In that same moment his teacher himself replied, "Except for me; I am flying," in view, namely, of the position in which he had been caught.[31] So the situation itself prompted both the pupil and teacher to play with the same senses and at the same time to joke with the same meaning.

Tommaso Pontano, a most famous teacher of rhetoric, was very 41 fond of a little dog whose name was Luscula.[32] When she saw a

hero ludentem deliciosius, in eam mordicus illata est; qua de re, cum illa quereretur ad herum respondissetque ille ioculabundus amorem tenebris gaudere atque inde vulgo caecum dicitari, tum illa, 'Atqui putabam,' retulit, 'de nomine ipso Lusculam caecam

42 esse.' Erant Lucio Manlio pictori deformiores liberi; quod cum animadvertisset, qui apud eum coenitabat, Servilius Geminius dixissetque, 'Quid hoc, Manli, quod nequaquam similem in modum et pingis et fingis?,' ille subdidit illico, 'Quid mirum, qui in

43 tenebris fingam, pingam in luce?' M. Cicero, cum audisset Pompeium in bello illo Macedonico militem Gallum Caesaris e castris qui ad eum transfugisset civitate donasse, 'Perbellum,' inquit, 'hominem, qui Gallis alienam promittat civitatem, cum nostram no-

44 bis non possit reddere.' Iocabundus quispiam, vel tentabundus[5] potius, cum dixisset—nam de somniis coram Alfonso rege erat disceptatio—nocte praeterita somniasse dono se ab rege accipere sacculum aureis gravidum, ibi tum Alfonsus, 'An ignoras adhibendam somniis fidem christiano ab homine nullam esse?'

45 Est Ioviano Pontano, qui de his disserit, Eugenia filia eaque sine liberis; cumque aliquando ea suis e scriniolis protulisset imagunculas quasdam venustissime effigiatas, 'Quanto,' inquit, 'melius, o filia, et patri et viro et tibi ipsi consultum esset, si harum similes

46 aliquas ex utero tuo proferres!' Altera eius filia Aurelia eaque natu maior, amisso Paulo marito, cum a patre ad alterum virum torumque hortaretur secundum, 'Quin tu,' inquit, 'pater, non et nuptias secundas inis?' 'Quia,' respondit, 'nullam matri tuae similem me reperturum confido.' 'Id ipsum,' respondit, 'me me versat, pater, quod mihi placiturum Paulo aeque similem sperem neminem.'

47 Haec ipsa, cum vix duodecim annorum filiam marito despondisset, iubente Federico rege, eaque a viro parum pro aetate atque

maidservant dallying with her master, she attacked and bit her. When the maidservant complained about this to her master, and he had joked that love delights in darkness and therefore is commonly called blind, then she retorted, "But I thought from her name that Luscula was blind."[33] The children of the painter Lucius Manlius were rather ugly. When Servilius Geminius, who was dining at his house, noticed this and said, "What's this, Manlius? You don't paint and produce offspring in the same way at all," he added at once, "Why is that astonishing, since I produce offspring in the dark but paint in the light?"[34] When Marcus Cicero heard that Pompey in that famous Macedonian war had given citizenship to a Gallic soldier who had deserted to him from Caesar's camp, he said, "What a fine fellow; he promises someone else's citizenship to Gauls when he can't restore our own to us!"[35] When someone said jokingly, or rather suggestively — for people were disputing about dreams in the presence of Alfonso — that he had dreamed the previous night how he had received from the king a small bag full of gold coins, Alfonso replied, "Don't you know that a Christian should put no faith in dreams?"[36]

Giovanni Pontano, the narrator of this discussion, has a daughter, Eugenia, who has no children. One time when she was bringing some very elegantly fashioned little images out of boxes, he said, "How much better, daughter, you would have taken care of your father, husband, and yourself, if you had brought some images like these out of your womb!"[37] His other daughter, Aurelia, who is the elder, lost her husband, Paolo.[38] When she was urged by her father to take another husband and a second marriage, she said, "Why don't you, father, marry a second time?" "Because," he replied, "I'm sure that I couldn't find anyone like your mother."[39] "I have the same thought," she replied, "father, since I have no hope that anyone would please me as much as Paolo." At the command of King Federico this same woman had betrothed her daughter, hardly twelve years old, to a husband, and she was not treated

42

43

44

45

46

47

urbanis moribus deliciose tractaretur, interrogataque quam nam
uxorie filiola cum marito ageret, 'Mihi,' inquit, 'mortuus est coniux,

48   filiae vero nullo modo vivus.' Haec vero ipsa responsa, quamvis risum non afferant, afferunt tamen approbationem. Atque ea quidem de causa in medium illa attulimus uti ex hoc quoque genere
quae in utranque partem et risus et approbationis proferri possent
praeteriisse minime videremur.

49     Ioannes Pardus, non minus urbanus consessor quam eruditus
philosophus, consederat in aula principis; constiterat ei ad latus
iurisconsultus vestitu serico, vultu quam maxime severo, oculis in
humum coniectis, qui post multum silentium, corona non inepto-
rum hominum circumstante, voce quam maxime canora atque in
tonum sublata, coepit excantare magis quam dicere. Hic Pardus,
'Ut e concavo,' inquit, 'ac vacuo e loco sonitus hic depromitur.' Vix
ullum unquam tantus risus prosecutus est dictum.

50     Bernardus Vitalis, vir multi usus ac maxime compositis moribus, interrogabatur a Federico rege quid nam esset causae cur in
vescendo alosa pisce oculari uteretur vitro. Respondit, 'Nequaquam ipse miraris, o bone rex, legentem me amicorum epistolas,
quibus legendis nullum immineat periculum, vitro uti, at demira-
ris usum ocularium in edendo maxime spinoso pisce sentibusque
tam spissis atque acutis, quibus singulis insit vel strangulatorius
gladius.' Ibi adolescentulus licentiosior, 'Quid,' inquit, 'o Vitalis,
uteris ne specillis istis tuis, ubi cum uxore lusitas?' 'Quin,' inquit,
'uxoris naso ea admoveo quo mercimonium illi meum crassius
vegetiusque appareat.' Quid aut festivius aut in re licentiore venus-
tius?

51     Prosequebatur quidam mirificis Gallos laudibus, summa celeritate Alpes Apenninumque transgressos paucissimis diebus in
Campaniam contendisse magnis pedestribus atque equestribus copiis; ibi homo, qui aegrius fortasse id ferret, dissimularet tamen,

lovingly by her husband as befitting her age and urbane manners. When asked about her daughter's marital relations with her husband, the mother said, "My husband is dead but my daughter's is not in any sense alive."[40] These replies do not indeed produce 48 laughter, but they do win approval. And for this reason I have made them known so that I may not appear to exclude from this class, too, things that can be brought forth on either side, both laughter and approval.

Giovanni Pardo, no less urbane a companion than he was 49 learned as a philosopher, was sitting in the prince's court.[41] A lawyer, dressed in silk, with a face as grave as possible, his eyes cast down to the ground, was at his side. After a long silence, with a circle of intelligent men standing around, the man began to chant rather than speak with a voice as melodious and high-pitched as possible. At this point Pardo said, "This sound issues forth as from a hollow and the void." Hardly ever has such laughter followed a witticism.

Bernardo Vitale, a man of much experience and placid charac- 50 ter, was asked by King Federico why in the world he used eyeglasses while eating shad. He replied, "You don't at all marvel, my good king, that I use glasses to read my friends' letters, although there's no danger in reading them, but you do marvel at using glasses to eat a very spiny fish with thorns so thick and sharp that there's a sword in every one, if you will, that can choke me." Then a licentious young man said, "What then, Vitale, do you wear those little spectacles when you're sporting with your wife?" "No indeed," he said, "I put them on my wife's nose so that my merchandise will appear thicker and more vigorous to her." What is merrier or more charming in a licentious matter?

Someone was bestowing marvelous praise on the French, who 51 had crossed the Alps and Apennines with the greatest speed in very few days and rushed into Campania with great numbers of infantry and cavalry. Then a man, who perhaps took this rather ill

'At,' inquit, 'multo id admirabilius Federicum tam brevi e rege re-
migem factum esse,' siquidem spoliatus regno pauculas in triremes
se se receperat, quibus post ad Ludovicum regem in Galliam est
52  delatus. Iis in copiis manus quaedam fuit nec exigua nec male
strenua, cuius insigne esset cochlea. Hac e manu cum fama esset
non paucos Romae, tumulto exorto, caesos suoque sanguine Florae
campum cruentasse, hic Chariteus, 'Quid nunc,' inquit, 'dicent
Enniani isti, "Cochleas herbigenas, domiportas, sanguine cassas?"'

53    Erat sermo porticu sub nostra de usu resinae vinaceae quodque
ea summo studio conquireretur a mercatoribus. Erant qui dicerent
Campaniam inopem eius esse, quod vina haberet et tenuiora et
permultum acida. Idem tum Chariteus, quo solet tum suo illo lepore tum summa ingenii dexteritate, 'Si Busta,' inquit, 'Gallica
perscrutari curae sit mercatoribus, nullam eius generis resinae re-
gionem feraciorem hac invenerint.'

54    Ferdinandus rex aegerrime ferebat, ubi quos aut binos aut ter-
nos vidisset deambulantes quique suas invicem res suaque consilia
inter deambulandum conferrent. Quod cum aliquando Pompa pa-
rasitaster deprehendisset, 'Vin,' inquit, 'o rex, aut magnam tibi
molestiam adimere aut non exiguum deambulationibus ex iis
compendium comparare? Portorium iis constitue perinde ut e pis-
cationibus mercimoniorumque invectionibus persolvendum; mihi
55  crede, dives inde vectigal exegeris.' Idem rex commendabat novi
portorii excogitatorem. Erat autem vectigal huiusmodi: stipendia
qui de regio acciperent aerario pro singulis centenis aureis quatuor
annuos in aerarium ut referrent. Ad ea Ferrandus Gevara, qui tum
aderat, eques maxime festivus et comis, 'At ego,' inquit, 'o rex, quo
apud te commendatior multo sim, id tibi consilii dederim, nobis
omnibus, quos et pascis et vestis, ut et victum eripias et vestitum;

but was dissimulating, said, "But it's much more wonderful that Federico in such a short time was made from a ruler into a rower," since, deprived of his kingdom, he retired into a few triremes, in which he afterward was brought to King Louis in France.[42] In those troops there was a band, neither small nor lacking in energy, whose sign was a snail. When rumor had it that a rebellion had arisen and not a few of this band had been killed and had made the field of Flora flow with their blood, Cariteo said, "*Now* what will those verses of Ennius signify, 'Snails born from the grass, carrying their homes, deprived of their blood?'"[43]

There was a conversation under my portico about the use of wine resin and the fact that it was sought by merchants with the greatest eagerness.[44] There were those who said that Campania was poor in it because it had light and very acidic wines. Then that same Cariteo said with his characteristic charm and ready wit, "If the merchants took care to search the Busta Gallica, they'd find that no region is more fertile in this kind of resin."[45]

King Ferdinando used to take it very ill when he would see people in twos and threes strolling about and discussing their mutual affairs and plans while strolling. Once when Pompa, a sorry parasite, detected this, he said, "Do you want, king, to rid yourself of a great annoyance or to make no little profit from these strolls? Impose a tax on them like the ones charged for fishing or transporting merchandise. Believe me, you'll collect rich revenue from it." The same king was praising the inventor of a new tax. The revenue, however, was of this sort: those who received stipends from the king's treasury would return to the treasury each year four gold coins for each hundred. At this Ferrante Guevara, an especially merry and affable cavalier who was then present, said, "But so that I, O king, may recommend myself to you the more, let me give you this counsel. Take away from all of us whom you both feed and clothe our food and clothing. Believe me, no better

52

53

54

55

mihi crede, nullum sive mari sive terra nec maius nec utilius ex-
cogitari a quoquam hoc ipso vectigal poterit.'

56    Est ridiculum et lepidum Valerii Martialis illud:

Potor nobilis, Aule, lumine uno
luscus Phryx erat alteroque lippus.
Huic dicit medicus, 'Bibas caveto:
vinum si biberis, nihil videbis.'
Ridens Phryx oculo, 'Valebis,' inquit.
Misceri sibi protinus deunces,
sed crebros iubet; exitum requiris?
Vinum Phryx, oculus bibit venenum.

57    Est et hoc iocosum ac suave:

Raucae cortis aves et ova matrum
et flavas medio vapore Chias
et foetum querulae rudem capellae
nec iam frigoribus pares olivas
et canum gelidis holus pruinis
de nostro tibi rure missa credis?
O quam, Regule, diligenter erras!
Nil nostri, nisi me, ferunt agelli.
Quidquid villicus Umber aut colonus
aut Thusci tibi Thusculi ve mittunt,
aut rus marmore tertio notatum
id tota mihi nascitur Subura.

58    Marinus Tomacellus Romae agebat quo tempore inter Ferdinandum Aragonensem et Andegaviensem Ioannem de regno
Neapolitano erat certamen, quod totam in se Italiam converterat.
Favebat partibus Andegaviensibus Atrebas Cardinalis. Itaque nun-
tius allatus cum esset Ioannis copias fugatas, Atrebas Marino obviam factus, 'Quid vanitatis,' inquit, 'per ora hominum sparsum
audio? Milites Gallos fugatos esse?' Ad ea Marinus, 'Minime

or more useful revenue on land or sea will ever be invented by anyone than this."[46]

This passage of Valerius Martial is ridiculous and charming:    56

Aulus, Phryx, a well-known drinker, was blind in one eye and blear-eyed in the other. A doctor said to him, "Take care not to drink: if you drink wine, you will see nothing." Laughing, Phryx said to his eye, "Good bye." At once he ordered eleven measures to be mixed for him, one right after the other. You ask about the outcome? Phryx drank wine; his eye, poison.[47]

And this one is also humorous and pleasant:    57

Poultry from the raucous farmyard and eggs from mother birds and Chian figs yellow from the moderate heat and the young offspring of the plaintive she-goat and olives no longer equal to the cold and vegetables gray from the cold frosts — do you think that I've sent you them from my farm? Regulus, how completely wrong you are! My little fields bear nothing except me. Whatever your Umbrian steward or tenant farmer or your Tuscans or Tusculans send you or your farm marked with the third marble milestone — that is grown for me all over Subura.[48]

Marino Tomacelli was living in Rome during the war over the    58 kingdom of Naples between Ferdinando of Aragon and Jean d'Anjou, which had attracted the notice of all Italy.[49] The cardinal of Arras favored the Angevin party.[50] And so when the message was brought that Jean's troops had been put to flight, Arras, having met Marino, said, "What falsehood do I hear spread by the mouths of men? The French soldiers have been put to flight?" To which Marino replied, "Indeed, by no means were they put to

quidem fugatos, nam ne fugere possent ad unum captos omnis esse,' respondit. Tum Atrebas, 'Tu quidem, Marine, versutior es quam pro brevitate corporis'; cui Marinus, 'At tu quidem, o Atrebas, minus es multo et verus et probus quam pro proceritate ista tua.'

59 Faustus, Lucii Syllae filius, compertum cum haberet sororem suam eodem tempore adulteris duobus dare operam, Fulvio uni, fullonis filio, alteri Pompeio, cui cognomen esset Maculae, eaque accusaretur a familiaribus, quod uno tempore duos haberet, Maculam et fullonem, amatores, tum ipse, quasi vix id crederet, 'Miror,' inquit, 'sororem meam habere maculum, cum eadem fullonem

60 habeat.' Lanii cuiusdam Neapolitani, Ditis nomine, uxor erat de se ipsa liberalior quam pudicam deceret; dicaculus quispiam, cum eam per iocum diceret carnem minoris vendere, 'Quid mirum,' subdidit Petrus Compater,[6] 'quae ditem lanium habeat coniugem?'

61 Ex iis igitur quae dicta sunt, ne nimii hac in parte videamur, facile quidem apparet risus unde oriri soleant: sive a nobis petantur sive ab aliis sive a rebus ipsis rerumque eventis. Quo autem secundum philosophorum sententiam apposite magis loquamur, sunt enim tria bonorum genera: aut ridentur in nobis corporis sive deformitates sive vitia aut animi aut quae externis sunt e rebus quaeque ab eventu contingunt.

62 Iocabatur persaepe in semet ipsum Federicus Urbinas, quod oculo altero captus esset, Nicolaus Picininus, quod pede uno minus validus; uterque belli dux, alter maxime strenuus, alter summe cautus; et hic et ille admodum facetus, Urbinas quidem ornatus literis multaque praeditus eruditione, Picininus vero ut qui ad grammaticum profectus nunquam fuerit. Ille igitur nunquam non

flight, for all, to the last man, were captured so they were unable to take flight." Then Arras, "You indeed, Marino, are more cunning than one would expect from your short stature"; to whom Marino, "But you indeed, Arras, are much less truthful and honest than one would expect from that height of yours."

When Faustus, the son of Lucius Sulla, had discovered that his 59 sister was bestowing her attention on two adulterers at the same time, one Fulvius, the son of a launderer, the other Pompeius, whose cognomen was Stain, and she had been accused by her family members of having two lovers at one time, Stain and the launderer, Faustus, as if he could hardly believe it, said, "I marvel that my sister has a stain given that she has a launderer."[51] The wife of 60 a certain Neapolitan butcher, Rich by name, was more generous with herself than befitted a modest woman. When a caustic man said jokingly that she sold meat at a too low a price, Petrus Compater then said, "Why is that astonishing, since she has a rich butcher for a husband?"[52]

Therefore, not to appear excessive in this part, from what has 61 been said it easily appears where laughter usually arises: it is sought from ourselves or from others or from the subject matter itself and related events. To speak, however, in a manner more suited to the opinion of the philosophers, there are three kinds of goods: either deformities of our bodies are laughed at or defects of the mind or what is from external things and what happens by chance.[53]

Federico of Urbino would very often make fun of himself be- 62 cause he had lost an eye; Niccolò Piccinino, because he was not strong in one foot.[54] Each was a general, the one especially vigorous, the other cautious to the highest degree.[55] Each was very witty, Federico in the manner of someone adorned with literary culture and furnished with much learning, but Piccinino like a man who had never gone to a grammarian. The former, therefore,

in iocando elegans atque urbanus, hic qui cuperet esse urbanus,
cum tamen praestare vix id posset.

63     Dicentem audivi saepius Antonium Panhormitam nunquam se
magis in initio deiectum animo, in exitu autem maiore cum hilaritate risisse quam cum obviam Nicolao factus illique ut duci fortis-
simo, ut Mediolanensis rei administratori, et assurrexisset sum-
missius et de more etiam reverentius salutasset. Illum igitur, ut qui
et sublandiri Antonio cuperet et suaviore etiam sermone com-
plecti, 'Dispeream,' dixisse, 'o Antoni, ni oculis me me captum velim quoties te intueor.' Ad ea se quanquam consternatum dixisse,
'Nam quem, o imperator eximie, quem nam, quaeso, tuarum rerum observantiorem me me uno aut inveneris aut facinora qui tua
et vehementius admiretur et maioribus atque huberioribus prosequatur laudibus?' Ibi tum illum in risum conversum statim subdi-
disse blandientem quidem, quamvis blandiri parum posset aut
sciret, 'Quoties,' inquit, 'te te ipsum considero tanta cognitione
praeditum, tot tantisque animi bonis clarum atque illustrem, me
autem contra meamque ignorantiam rursus reputo, odi te ut ad-

64     versarium, veneror ut scientem.' Conatus est vir, qui per omnem
aetatem militiam exercuisset, velle esse urbanus; praestitit quod
potuit, fortasse etiam plus quam cupiit, dum se se ignorantem
professus, illum ut doctum et rerum multarum peritum pariter et
admiratur et colit. In alio igitur homine haec ipsa, ut imprudentius
dicta, iudicari stulta possent, quae, si mentem dicentis respicias,
laudem non ei minorem afferunt quam qua ipse Antonium exor-
nare contendebat. Quocirca dicta quaedam, si imprudenter exci-
dant, ut stulta et ridentur et condemnantur; sin simulanter, venusta habentur ac lepida. Interdum vero, perinde ut in Picinino,
magis voluntas dicentis inspicienda est quam ea ipsa quae dicuntur.

65     Secutus ego aliquando cum essem Alfonsum, Ferdinandi filium,
sub cuius ac patris auspiciis Federicus exercitum ductabat

was always elegant and urbane while joking; the latter wanted to
be urbane but could hardly manage it.

I often heard Antonio Panormita say that he was never more    63
depressed initially or finally laughed with greater hilarity than
when, upon meeting Niccolò, he had stood deferentially and also,
as is customary, greeted him reverentially as a powerful general, an
administrator of the Milanese state. So then the other, since he
wished to flatter Antonio and also welcome him with sweet speech,
said, "May I die, Antonio, if I don't wish myself blind every time I
see you." To this Antonio replied, although alarmed, "Whom indeed, outstanding general, whom indeed, please, will you find
more observant of your affairs than me, or who admires your actions more vehemently and honors them with greater and more
abundant praise?" Then the other, moved to laughter, immediately
added flatteringly, although he did not have the ability or knowledge to flatter, "However often I consider you, furnished as you are
with such knowledge, famous and illustrious for so many and
great mental gifts, and then reflect, on the contrary, upon myself
and my ignorance, I hate you as an enemy, but venerate you as a
man of knowledge." A man who had been a soldier all his life tried    64
to be urbane. He did what he could, perhaps even more than he
desired, while, confessing himself ignorant, he admired and honored the other as learned and equally skilled at many things. These
same remarks, spoken without forethought, might be judged foolish in another man; yet if you examine the intention of the
speaker, they bring him no less praise than he was striving to bestow on Antonio. So some humorous remarks, if they slip out inadvertently, are laughed at and condemned as foolish, but if they
are insincere, they are considered charming and elegant. But sometimes, just as with Piccinino, one must look more to the intention
of the speaker than to the things which are said themselves.

One time when I was attending Alfonso, the son of Ferdi-    65
nando—Federico was leading an army under his and his father's

ingressusque cum essem praetorium, in quo praefecti omnes
consedissent, et assurrexit mihi Federicus et tacere omnes iussit,
'En adest,' inquiens, 'magister. Videtis quantum inter utrumque
intersit'; dubites tamen quae maior aut honoratio fuerit aut com-
mendatio; hic et prudens et sciens praestitit mihi non minus quam
voluit; ille, quanquam ignorans, adnisus tamen praestitit forte in
Antonium plus etiam quam studuit. Dicta igitur pleraque imprudenter ubi exciderint, merito stulta sunt habenda; ubi vero simulata fuerint, et venusta et faceta; sed et temporis tamen et loci
et rerum ipsarum, cum primis vero personae, ratio habenda est.
Denique risus ipsi vel gestu excitantur vel dicto. Accedet autem
gratiae plurimum dictis ipsis, ubi severitas quasi quaedam vultus
dicenti affuerit, quod maxime exigitur in iis quae spiculata sunt
aculeosque infigunt. Nam dicacitatem illam scurrilem atque osce-
nam maxime alienam non a faceto solum verum etiam ab urbanis
et comibus esse volumus; nec tantum autem verbis verum etiam a
rerum significationibus abesse oscenitatem oportere Marcus Cicero ostendit, cum ait putare se facetias quidem in narrando consis-
tere, dicacitatem vero in faciendo.

66

: 3 :

*Lasciva dicta non decere facetum*
*nec contumeliosa.*

1 Quoniam autem tum dicta tum ridicula ipsa aut lasciva sunt aut
iucunda aut contumeliosa aut lenia acerba ve, ita quidem tenen-
dum censeo in convictibus congressionibus quotidianoque in
sermone vix unquam principem virum ac graviorem gerentem

auspices — and had entered the general's headquarters, in which all
of the commanders were seated, Federico rose for me and ordered
everyone to be quiet, saying, "Here is the master. You see how
much a difference there is between the two."[56] Nevertheless, you
might doubt which was the greater honor or commendation. This
man, both prudent and intelligent, gave me no less than he intended; the other, although ignorant yet taking pains, perhaps gave
Antonio more than he wished. Therefore, when most remarks slip    66
out inadvertently, they must deservedly be considered foolish, but
when they are insincere, they must be held both charming and
witty. But, nevertheless, one must take account of the time, the
place, the situation itself, and most of all, the person. Finally,
laughter is excited either by a gesture or a witticism. But the greatest grace is added to witticisms when almost a severity of expression is present in the speaker, which is especially required in things
that are barbed and inflict stings.[57] For I want scurrilous and obscene raillery to be especially alien not only to the witty man but
also to the urbane and affable. Marcus Cicero, however, shows that
obscenity must be absent not only from words but also from the
meanings of things, when he says he thinks witticisms consist in
telling but raillery in doing.[58]

: 3 :

*Lascivious and abusive witticisms are not becoming*
*to the witty man.*

Seeing that both witticisms and jests are lascivious or pleasant or    1
abusive or mild or bitter, I maintain as a firm principle that in
feasts, gatherings, and daily conversation lasciviousness is hardly
ever becoming to a prince or someone playing a more important

personam decere lasciviam, quae tamen in homuntionibus ipsis
humilique in loco constitutis commendari passim solita est, quippe
quibus dignitas minime obstet aliqua nullusque aut respectus aut
2 locus. At ioci hilares, iucundi, grati quique animum honeste re-
creent vel etiam sacerdotibus conveniunt, quod praedicatores usur-
patissime in dicendo servant. Contumeliosa non carent intempe-
rantia atque iniustitia adversanturque recreationi. Eiusdem naturae
videntur esse aspera atque amara, quippe quae inimicitias excitent
et causas afferant civilibus contentionibus.[7] Denique summo id
studio evitandum, salsum ne dictum praeferamus amicitiae ac
tranquillitati, ne ve pluris faciamus dictum quam amicum et notum hominem.


꞉ 4 ꞉

*Cuiusmodi esse debeant fabellarum expositiones.*


1 Fabellarum vero enarrationes universaque earum expositio, res
ipsa, cuius gratia fabellae sunt inventae, hortari nos debet ut cultae
sint elegantes, venustae, concinnae, verbis maxime accommodatis
sententiisque cum primis lepidis ac conditis, tum voce ac vultu
2 perquam convenientibus. Narrare solebat avia mea Leonarda, celebris memoriae matrona, Podagram aliquando sub mulierculae speciem peregrinantem in rusculum divertisse eamque, ubi vidisset
casulas inertissime aedificatas, obsitas araneis, squalidas situ atque
illuvie marcidas, conversam ad pedissequas dixisse, 'Apagete a me
hospitium hoc sentum, informe, foetidum, fumosum, tetrum, apagete diversorium, in quo quid intueare praeter marras, bidentes,
rastros agrestiumque ferramentorum diversa genera aut boum asi-
narumque stercoramenta sive suum excrementa ac capellarum!

role, although it is commonly commended far and wide in little men and those placed in a humble position, since neither rank, reputation, or position stands in their way.[59] But cheerful, delight- 2 ful, and pleasing jokes, such as honorably refresh the mind, are appropriate even for priests, something which preachers practice very often while speaking. Abusive things are not without arrogance and injustice and are opposed to relaxation. Rough and bitter things appear to be of the same nature, seeing that they provoke enmities and bring reasons for civil strife. Finally, one must avoid with the greatest effort preferring a pungent witticism to friendship and tranquility or valuing a piece of wit more than a friend and acquaintance.

: 4 :

*How one ought to tell stories.*

But the very reason for which stories were invented should moti- 1 vate us to make the narrations of stories and their whole presentation polished, elegant, charming, and neatly arranged, with particularly well selected words and especially agreeable and polished maxims and with the appropriate voice and facial expression. My 2 grandmother Leonarda, a matron of famous memory, used to tell a story.[60] One time Gout, traveling under the form of a little woman, lodged in a little farm. When she saw that the cottages were incompetently built, covered with spiderwebs, filthy from neglect, and rotten with mud, she turned to her waiting-women and said, "Away with this rough, misshapen, stinking, smoky, foul lodging, away with this abode where you see nothing but hoes, mattocks, rakes, and various kinds of farm tools or the dung of oxen and asses or the excrement of pigs and goats! And so I say:

Itaque valere iubeo et villas et tegetes tam sordentis; urbs nobis et ocia sunt quaerenda, urbs, quae ocium foveat, ocia, quae urbana sint atque deliciosa'; illatamque ad primum urbis ingressum in fabri ferrarii officinam dixisse, 'Nil mihi cum incude et malleo,' in domum inde aliquanto ab ea remotiorem, cuius ante vestibulum choreae agitarentur atque convivia ibique interrogasse, cuius nam aedes eae essent, responsum illico ocii eas esse inhabitarique ab hominibus desidiosis somnoque et vino marcentibus, e vestigio itaque domum ingressam vultuque quam maxime hilari dixisse, 'Haec domus, haec patria est'; cumque solicitudinem ac laborem ante fores videret satagentes, iussisse procul eas abigi et curas inde exulare, cum primisque sobrietatem atque abstinentiam. Haec avia ipsa nobis pueris referebat et vultu et voce et membrorum assensu, qualis fabulantem deceret puerilem animum ad bonos mores ad negocia laboresque invitandum.

3    Narrare quoque solita est Christiana mater, cum noctu adolescentulus lectitarem ad candelam, extitisse patrem familias, cui gemini essent filii, morientemque illum tum supellectilem multam illis reliquisse tum olei non mediocrem summam, quo nocturna uterentur ad opera tenebrasque evigilandas; alterum itaque ex iis in conviviis ac coenis oleum consumpsisse exque eo brevi in inopiam redactum, alterum vero dedisse operam literis, oleoque nocturnis in lectionibus usus quod esset, pervenisse ex eo ad summas divitias; coeptum igitur cantari per urbem de utroque huiuscemodi carmen:

Hic oleum et se perdit, dum ad candelas coenitat.
Ille arcam et se ditat, dum ad lucernas lectitat.

4    Eiusmodi igitur fabellae, cum sint ad bonos mores institutae atque ad recreandos animos, et delectare debent et prodesse; proderunt

goodbye to such filthy farms and shelters. We must seek the city and leisure, the city, which favors leisure — leisure, which is urbane and delicious." And brought to a blacksmith's shop near the first entrance to the city she said, "I have nothing to do with the anvil and hammer." Then at a house a bit farther from it, before whose entrance-court dances and banquets were being held, she inquired to whom the house belonged, and immediately the response was that it was leisure's and was inhabited by lazy men, languid from sleep and wine. At once she entered the house and said with as cheerful an expression as possible, "This is my house; this my country." And when she saw anxiety and labor bustling about the doors, she ordered them to be driven far away and cares to be exiled thence and especially sobriety and abstinence. My grandmother would relate these things to us children with the facial expression, voice, and gestures becoming to someone telling a story and encouraging the childish mind to good character, to enterprise and labor.

Also, when I would read at night by candle as a boy, my mother 3 Cristiana used to tell of a father who had twin sons. At his death he left them a lot of household goods and no small amount of oil for them to use for working at night and for staying up when it was dark. One of them consumed the oil in banquets and dinners and thus was reduced to poverty in a short time, but the other took pains with letters and because he used the oil to read at night, he arrived at the height of wealth. Therefore a song of this sort began to be sung about the two of them throughout the city:

This one wastes his oil and himself, while he dines by candle. The other enriches his money box and himself, while he reads by the lamp.

Therefore, stories of this sort, when they have been created to 4 teach good morals and to refresh the mind, ought both to delight

autem, si ab auditoribus gratis animis acceptae fuerint; accipientur autem periucunde et grate, si enarratio ipsa ornata et comis fuerit, si oratio suavis et nitida, vultus autem gestusque dicentis rebus ipsis accommodatus.

and to profit.[61] They will be profitable if they are accepted with grateful minds by the listeners. They will be received with delight and gratitude if the narration is elegant and good-humored, if the style is pleasant and clear, and the facial expression and gesture of the speaker appropriate to the subject.

# LIBER SEXTUS[1]

## : I :

*Qualis esse debeat vir facetus.*

1 Erit igitur facetus is, quem nunc instituimus, in iocando suavis et hilaris, vultu placido et ad refocillandum composito, in respondendo gratus ac concinnus, voce nec languida nec subrustica, virili tamen et laeta, in motu urbanus quique nec rus indicet nec nimias urbis delicias, a scurrilitate abhorrebit uti a scopulo, oscenitatem ad parasitos et mimos relegabit; salibus ita utetur ac mordacibus dictis ut, nisi provocatus ac lacessitus, nec remordeat nec revellicet; ita tamen ut nunquam ab honesto recedat ab eaque

2 animi compositione quae ingenui hominis est propria. Fuit Antonius Panhormita admodum urbanus, Thomas vero Pontanus etiam salsus. Hic cum sensisset procaciori e dicto infixum sibi dentem, 'Ego mihi,' inquit, 'vulnus obligabo, dum te interim petulantiae poeniteat tuae.' Ille vero, 'Quod os ipsum impure loquitur, id tutemet, ne aures ipsae audiant, obturato.' Uterque et sapienter et pro dignitate, nec a faceti discessit officio.

3 Erit igitur facetus vir sui compos dictorumque moderator quique ubique consideret sermonem suum ad recreationem spectare; et quamvis ipse et sciat et possit esse salsus ac mordax, tamen genus hoc sive dicacitatis sive aculeationis oratoribus relinquet quique defensitationibus dant operam salsique esse malunt quam faceti. Nam ab histrionicis mimicisque intemperamentis erit prorsus alienus, multo autem maxime parasiticis ab oscenitatibus et verbo-

4 rum et significationum. Erit idem multum etiam comis, cum, ut

# BOOK SIX

## : 1 :

*What kind of man the witty man ought to be.*

Thus the witty man I am now training will be pleasant and cheer-  1
ful when telling jokes, and will have a calm face composed to refresh, pleasing and elegant, when responding, with a voice neither
languid nor coarse but virile and glad, urbane in motion as one
who shows neither any sign of the country nor the overrefinement
of the city. He will shrink from buffoonishness as if from a cliff
and relegate obscenity to parasites and mimes.[1] He will use caustic
and mordant sayings in such a way that, unless provoked and ir-
ritated, he does not bite or taunt back, yet never moves away from
the honorable and that composure of mind characteristic of a
freeborn man. Antonio Panormita was very urbane but Tommaso  2
Pontano was also witty.[2] When the latter felt that a tooth had bit-
ten into him from too bold a piece of wit, he said, "I will bind up
my wound until you repent of your impudence." But the former,
"Block what the mouth speaks impurely so that the ears don't hear
it." Both spoke wisely and in accord with their dignity and without
departing from the duty of the man of wit.

Therefore the witty man will be self-controlled and the gover-  3
nor of his witticisms as one who considers in every case that his
conversation aims at recreation. And although he knows how and
is able to be pungent and mordant, yet he will leave this kind of
raillery or needling to orators and those who attend to defenses
and prefer to be caustic rather than witty. For he will be completely adverse to the excesses of actors and mimes but much more
to the obscenities of parasites, both in words and in meanings. He  4
will also be good-natured, since, as we said at the beginning, good

initio diximus, comitas potissimum in fabellis versetur suavibusque in enarrationibus ac colloquiis; habebit peritiam multam, multam item memoriam tum eorum qui faceti sunt habiti, tum facetiarum ipsarum quarum relationes multum habent gratiae apud
audientes: quibus servandis, delectu quoque adhibito, mediocritatem retinebit eam quae virtutem hanc, de qua sermo est,
5    constituit. Quia vero nec semper dicta ipsa responsa ve risum
movent verum saepenumero approbationem eamque non nunquam cum admiratione, iccirco idem ipse abundare debet sententiis iisque gravioribus ac generosis itemque exemplis atque histo-
riis, versibus itidem gravissimorum poetarum, quos subinde in
medium proferet pro natura rerum quae in sermone versantur.
Quodque dictu quidem ridiculum videri potest, non erit ignarus
etiam anilium fabellarum, quae pro loco quidem ac tempore et
gratae sunt et audientiam sibi comparant, cum etiam animos ipsos
auditorum sive fessos sive exatiatos denuo invitent atque ad audiendum alliciant.

6    Quocirca non in circulis tantum et coronis, sive consessionibus
ac convictibus, verum etiam in concionibus, cumque maioribus de
rebus agitur, facetus vir id etiam praestabit, ut iucundis ac suavi-
bus sive dictis sive sententiis proverbiisque sive etiam fabellis et
astantes ad se audiendum trahat et urbane eos comiterque appella-
tos deliniat et, pene dixerim, lenocinetur suavioribus fabellarum
explicationibus aut exemplorum adductione quae cum primis gra-
7    tae sint exhilarentque auditorium. Postremo autem sic habeto faceti hominis orationem ubique multum gratiae habere oportere, ut
ne gravissimis quidem in rebus sui ipsius obliviscatur, sitque ita
facetus, ut severitatis quoque meminerit, adeo autem severus, ut
sciat laborum comitem esse debere quietem ac ludum aliquem,
honestum tamen ac commendatione dignum.

nature is of particular use in telling stories and pleasant narrations and discourses.[3] He will have much experience and likewise a great memory both for those who have been thought witty and for witticisms whose telling gives great pleasure to listeners. Observing these things, also using discrimination, he will maintain the mean which constitutes this virtue under discussion. But since witticisms or repartee do not always produce laughter but often approval, sometimes with admiration, the witty man must abound in maxims, serious and noble ones, and likewise examples, histories, verses of the most important poets, which he will bring forth from time to time in accordance with the nature of the subjects that come up in conversation. And, although it may appear ridiculous to say, he will not be ignorant even of old wives' tales, which are pleasing, when suited to the time and place, and get attention, since they entertain again even tired or satiated minds of listeners and entice them to listen.

So not only in circles and gatherings, or assemblies and feasts, but also in public meetings when greater affairs are handled, the witty man will also take care to bring the bystanders to listen to him using pleasant and delightful sayings, or maxims and proverbs, or even stories, and to entice by addressing them urbanely and affably and, I might even say, seduce them with pleasant presentations of stories or by adducing examples that are especially pleasing and cheer the audience. But finally, be assured that the speech of a witty man must always be very pleasant, so that he does not forget himself even amid the most serious affairs. Let him be witty in such a way that he also remembers his gravity, but let him be grave in such a way as to recognize that decent and commendable repose and some amount of play must accompany labor.

: 2 :

*Qualia facetorum dicta responsaque esse debeant.*

1    Qualia vero facetorum tum dicta tum responsa esse debeant, ex iis
     paucis quae subiicimus facile apparebit.

     Franciscus Aelius, non in studiis modo his nostris summa cum
     celebritate versatus verum etiam civilibus in actionibus ac negociis,
     cum videret sacerdotem excomptum admodum atque expansiore
     capillo soleisque incedentem editioribus, tunicis quoque laxioribus
     atque in plurimos sinus complicatis pallioque inundante, conversus
     ipse ad eos qui secum constiterant, 'An,' inquit, 'ignoratis quam
2    exculti essent pensiles Semiramidis reginae hortuli?' Idem cum vi-
     disset Gallos milites calciamentis uti pedum, taurinorum in vesti-
     giorum speciem, 'Ubi,' inquit, 'horum sunt taurorum cornua?'
     Cumque Gallicus quispiam ex auditoribus, et ipse quoque facetus,
     subdidisset, 'In manibus hi gerunt cornua,' quod telum scilicet e
     manibus nunquam mitterent, ibi Aelius, 'Horum igitur veruta
3    halabardaeque sunt cyathi.' Extat eius sive dictum sive responsum
     catum admodum: funem qui ducerent, eos prae se quidem oculos,
     pone vero vestigia movere.

4    Franciscus Putius,[2] de quo supra mentionem fecimus, nam
     praeter summam literarum cognitionem summe etiam iucundus
     est et comis, cum animadvertisset matronam et forma et cultu
     praecellentem, oculis tamen lascivioribus et pene amatores voranti-
     bus, 'Quid,' inquit, 'segnes, non et nos ad amplexum eius componi-
5    mus?' Est et illud eiusdem maxime facetum; nam vocatus ad coe-
     nam a sacerdote, cum vinarius promptor nusquam compareret,
6    'Quid moramur,' inquit, 'quin cantemus illi mortualia?' Idem cum
     intelligeret cives non paucos occupatos in laudandis pomeriis
     Neapolitanis, quae a Federico rege promovebantur, in mediis

﹕ 2 ﹕

*What kind of witticisms and replies witty men's ought to be.*

But what kind of sayings and replies witty men's ought to be will 1
easily be illustrated from a few things I shall now add.

When Francesco Elio, famously versed not only in these studies
of ours but also in civil actions and practical business, saw a very
elegant priest with rather long hair walking on shoes too high, his
tunic also too loose and folded up into many folds, and his mantle
flowing, he turned to those standing with him and said, "Can it be
that you don't know how well cultivated the hanging gardens of
queen Semiramis were?"[4] When this same man saw French sol- 2
diers wearing shoes on their feet shaped like bulls' hooves, he said,
"Where are the horns of these bulls?" And when some Frenchman
among the listeners, also a witty man, added, "They carry their
horns in their hands," in other words, because a weapon was never
out of their hands, Elio replied, "So their pikes and halberds are
wine ladles." A very clever saying or response of his is extant: those 3
who play tug-of-war keep their eyes forward but move their feet
backward.[5]

When Francesco Pucci, whom I mentioned earlier — for besides 4
his surpassing knowledge of literature he is also surpassingly pleasant and affable — noticed a matron outstanding for her beauty and
attire yet with excessively lascivious eyes almost devouring her lovers, he said, "Why don't we sluggards get ourselves ready for her
embraces too?"[6] There is also this especially witty saying of the 5
same man: invited to dinner by a priest, when the wine steward
never appeared, he said, "What's the delay? Why not sing dirges
for him?" When this same man perceived that not a few citizens 6
were engaged in singing the praises of the city limits [*pomeriis*] of
Naples, which were being enlarged by King Federico, interrupting

laudationibus interstrepitans, 'Ve,' inquit, 'pomariis.' Quod quidem
secutum est: plerique enim horti vastitatem acceperunt propter
muros fossasque circumductas.

7      Actius Syncerus, rari vir ingenii magnaeque nobilitatis et ipse
quoque admodum facetus, cum in conspectu Federici regis esset
inter physicos quaestio, quid praecipue conferret oculorum perspi-
cuitati, aliique foeniculi afflatum dicerent, alii vitri usum aliique
item aliud, 'At ego,' inquit, 'invidiam aio.' Obstupuerunt hoc dicto
adeo medici ut ab auditoribus derisui haberentur. Tum ipse, 'An
non invidia maiora ac pleniora omnia videri facit? Quid autem
oculis magis praesentaneum quam ut vis ipsa aspiciendi maior
reddatur atque vegetior?'; protulitque statim Ovidianos illos versus:

Fertilior seges est alienis semper in agris
vicinumque pecus grandius huber habet.

8      Idem interrogatus ab amico quid de Marini Minervae negociis haberet certi, respondit quod apud forum cum uxore litigaret. Cumque ille, 'Quid, malum, ex te audio, cum uxore hic ut litiget, qui
eam in Brutiis multos ante annos pene viduam reliquerit?,' tum
Actius rursum, 'Quae nam, malum, ignorantia ista est tua, qui
nescias Marinum, repudiata priore, nuper uxorem duxisse podagram?' Movit repente qui adessent omnium risum, cum pro
lecto ad forum alluserit, ubi perpetua est litium agitatio, pro uxore
ad podagram, quae illi usque in cubili adesset et comes et socia,
nec quiescere eum pateretur.

9      Poetus Fundanus, quem audeo dicere Musarum in hortulis
adolescere, cum audiret familiarem hominem de pedum dolore
heiulatus mittere nec posse illos compescere, accurrit ad clamores,
'Ecquid,' inquiens, 'alii de itinere queruntur assiduo laboribusque
quam plurimis, de perpetua negociorum inquietudine alii, tu, pro

them in the middle of their panegyrics, he said, "Alas for the or-
chards [*pomariis*]!" Which indeed happened, for most of the gardens were devastated by being surrounded with walls and ditches.

Actius Sincerus, a man of rare genius and great nobility as well    7
as very witty, when there was a dispute among physicians in the
presence of King Federico over what most conferred sharpness of
vision, and some said exhalation of fennel, others using eyeglasses,
and others something else, Actius said, "But I say it's envy."[7] The
doctors were so stunned by this statement that they were mocked
by the listeners. Actius then explained, "Doesn't envy make everything appear greater and fuller? And what is more immediately
effective for the eyes than something that makes the power of sight
become greater and more vigorous?" And at once he cited these
verses of Ovid:

> The crops are always more abundant in someone else's fields,
> and the neighbor's flock has larger udders.[8]

This same man, asked by a friend what he knew for sure about the    8
affairs of Marino Minerva, replied that he was disputing with his
wife in court.[9] And when the other said, "Damn, what's this you
say, that he's disputing with his wife? He left her almost a widow
many years ago in Calabria," then Actius replied, "Damn, how can
you be so ignorant? Don't you know that Marino, after repudiat-
ing his first wife, has lately been married to gout?" He made everyone present laugh immediately, since he was playing with the bed
as a court, where there is a constant agitation of lawsuits, and with
his wife as the gout, since it was continually his companion and
partner in bed and would not allow him to rest.

When Peto of Fondi, who, I dare assert, grew up in the gardens    9
of the Muses, when he heard a friend sending up howls over the
pain in his feet and couldn't suppress them, he rushed toward the
shouts, saying, "Is it true that some complain of constant travel
and endless labors, others about the perpetual anxiety of business,

deum atque hominum fidem, de quiete quereris atque ocio? Quod
si tibi molestum est, exurge, age, ac peregre proficiscere.' Quid
quaeris? De lepore dolor in risum conversus est.

10    Audio Romanum Thamyram—Romanum dico et patriam
linguam et disciplinas artisque Romanas referentem—audio, inquam, Thamyram, cum esset ab Antonio Cicuro, noto ac bene-
volente homine, qui blaesus tamen esset, salvere iussus illeque
blaesuriens pro Thamyra, 'Salve,' dixisset, 'o Tumule,' respondisse—
cum tamen et ipse blaesum pariter se se effingeret—'Et tu haue, o
Cucule.' Blaesa illa salutatio fuit admodum ridicula, multo tamen
11   ridiculosior gestus ipse, blaesionem effingens. Etenim meus hic
Thamyras, quanquam pudentissimus, tamen solenni die celeber-
rima in pompa animadversum cum esset Pontificem Maximum
coniecisse in puellam oculos, quae tenerrimae esset aetatis ac for-
mae, mirarenturque qui in id intenti essent tum petulantes Ponti-
ficis Summi oculos tum iocos puellae mutuos, 'Desinite,' inquit,
'obsecro, mirari Papae pupam hanc placere cupere, scit enim piper
ab eo sub peplo ferri, nec ignorat Papa pupae penum piperi con-
servando comparatum.' Nescias quid facetius.

12    Et morum suavitate et studiis his nostris abunde notus est
praestantissimis quibusque viris Suardinus Bergomas; is domi
cum haberet convivas iussissetque de more, exemptis dapibus, bellaria afferri, tum e convivis aliquis, 'Cui bellum,' inquit, ad bellaria
alludens, 'facturi sumus?'; tum ipse, 'Vinariae,' inquit, 'cellae'; 'Bene
habet,' respondit, 'etenim sitimus omnes.' 'Agite, pueri,' tum ipse,
'Setinum approperate.' Rursus ille, 'Bello ex hoc quae spolia nobis
futura?' Ad ea Suardinus, 'Spoletina, pueri, in aciem proferte.'
Tertium ille cum phaleratos commendaret pomorum canistros,

but you, by all that's holy, complain about rest and leisure? If that's bothering you, up now, rise, and set out for foreign lands."[10] What more can I say? From the pleasantry the pain was turned into laughter.

I hear that Tamira the Roman — I say "Roman" because he renews both the language of the fatherland and Roman learning and arts — I hear, I say, that when Tamira was greeted by Antonio Cicuro, a well-known, well-meaning man, although a stammerer, who had said, stammering, "Greetings, Tomb," instead of Tamira, he replied, pretending to be a stammerer too, "And hello to you, too, Cuckoo."[11] The stammering greeting was very ridiculous but the act of pretending to stammer much more ridiculous. When on a holy day in a crowded procession the chief priest had been noticed casting his eyes on a very young and beautiful girl, and those intent on this were marveling at both the wanton eyes of the Supreme Pontiff and the corresponding sportiveness of the girl, my friend Tamira, although very modest, said, "Don't be surprised, please, that this girl wants to please the pope, for she knows that he carries a pepper under his robe, nor is the pope ignorant that the girl's larder is well set up for storing pepper." You couldn't think of anything wittier.[12]

For the pleasantness of his manners and these studies of ours Suardino of Bergamo is very well-known to the outstanding men.[13] When he had dinner guests at his house and had ordered, as is customary, the dessert to be brought out after the meal had been taken away, one of the guests said, playing on *dessert* [*bellaria*], "On whom are we going to make war [*bellum*]?" Suardino replied, "The wine cellar." "Great," the guest said, "we're all thirsty [*sitimus*]." Suardino responded, "Come now, boys, hurry up with that wine from Sezze [*Setinum*]." The other returned, "What spoils [*spolia*] will we bring back from this war?" To which Suardino said, "Boys, wheel the wine from Spoleto [*Spoletina*] into the battle line." A third time, when the other had praised the embossed

'Ne parcite, pocillatores, ne ve falernis abstinete.' Cumque quartum ille subdidisset, 'En munera laetitiamque die,' tum ipse, sublato manu utraque carchesio, canere coepit:

Cecubum prelo domitum Caleno
sit meae lenis requies senectae.

13  Hacque ratione a modestissimis viris comiter traducta est coena.
Docuit igitur Suardinus qui ve ioci, quae ve dicta facetum deceant
in coena praesertim, ut quae et iucunda et comis esse debeat inge-
nuisque convivis digna, non tamen hac ut in parte ferculorum ratio
tradatur sed iocorum tantum ac facetiarum.

14  Celebrantur a Ferdinando rege Hippolytae nurus atque Alfonsi
filii nuptiae apparatu splendidissimo. Erat dies decursionis hasta-
tae flagrabantque sub sole cuncta. Convenerant autem mortales
omnis generis ad spectandum; cumque plurimi ludorum essent
laudatores vel plerique omnes admiratores potius, in media lau-
dantium frequentia et plausu exclamavit Teutonicus, 'O valeant
ludi in quibus nemo bibit!' Nesciam an alias tanta in multitudine
dictum ullum tanto cum risu acceptum fuerit, praesertim ex ore
Germanici hominis.

15  Philopomenes, Acheorum dux, praecipue inter Graecos clarus,
erat diversurus ad hospitium veteris amici. Quo cognito iussit
hospes apparari quae necessaria essent alia ab uxore, dum interim
ipse obsonium appararet. Haec inter Philopomenes solus, ut ipsa
res ferebat, ad hospitium properat; quem venientem hospitandum,[3] ut solum, ut deformem, ut qui nihil ornatus haberet eximii,
arbitratur mulier ex administris esse aliquem qui herum praeveni-
ret; cum esset de adventu Philopomenis mirifice solicita, etiam

[*phaleratos*] fruit baskets, he said, "Hey, cupbearers, don't hold back on the Falernian wine [*falernis*]." And when the other added for a fourth time, "Behold the gifts and the joy of the day,"[14] Suardino raised a drinking cup with both hands and began to sing:

> Let the Caecuban, tamed by the winepress of Cales, be the sweet repose of my old age.[15]

And in this way dinner was affably spent by these very temperate 13 men. So Suardino has taught which jokes and witticisms suit the witty man, especially at dinner, since it ought to be delightful, affable, and worthy of freeborn guests, although in this part an account of the dinner courses is not given but only of the jokes and witticisms.[16]

The wedding of his daughter-in-law Ippolita and his son Al- 14 fonso was being celebrated by King Ferdinando with the most splendid magnificence.[17] It was the day for a parade of spearmen, and everything was burning in the sun. Moreover, people of all kinds had assembled to watch, and while numerous people were praising the games (or rather, while nearly all were admiring them), in the midst of the crowd of praisers and the applause, a German exclaimed, "To hell with games at which no one drinks!" I do not know that at any other time in such a multitude a saying was received with such laughter, especially from the mouth of a German.[18]

Philopoemen, general of the Achaeans, especially famous 15 among the Greeks, was going to lodge as the guest of an old friend. Upon learning this, his host ordered his wife to prepare the other necessaries while in the meantime he prepared the food. Meanwhile, Philopoemen, as the situation required, was hastening alone to his host's house. The woman thought that the man coming to be a guest was one of the servants preceding his master, since he was alone, ugly, and without any uncommon adornment. Since she was extraordinarily anxious about the arrival of

blandienter rogavit eum se uti adiutaret ad dominum comiter acci-
piendum. Tum Philopomenes, ut erat perhumanus, cognito mulieris errore, confestim securi accepta, e cuneo coepit ligna findere
coquendam ad coenam. Hospes interim domum regressus, cum
animadverteret Philopomenem findendis lignis malleo incumbere,
'Pro Iupiter,' inquit, 'quid hoc, Philopomene? Pro pudor deorum
atque hominum, quid agis, dux maxime?' vultumque de dolore simul ac pudore demisit. Ad ea Philopomenes maxima cum iucunditate, 'Pro deformitate,' inquit, 'oris, totius corporis, poenas luo.'
Voluit ipse met praebere de se et risum hospiti et sibi ipsi ridiculus
esse. Res sane festivo ac faceto homine digna quaeque, quo rarior,
eo etiam fuerit facetior.[4]

16    Alfonsus rex, quem liberalissimum aetas nostra experta est,
cum homini de se bene merito de manu praesentem pecuniam
tribuisset, 'Amabo,' inquit, 'hoc age, ne thesaurarius hoc resciscat
meus.' Cumque ille subdidisset, 'Tu ne, o rex, quaestorem vereris?,'
'Vereor,' inquit, 'ne hac e causa de coenis mihi altero tantum demat.' Studebat Alfonsus liberalitatem eam occultam esse; cognito
denique accipientis ingenio, fecit se deridiculum, dum, ne illum
parvifaceret, vult videri.

17    Eundem in Philopomenem cum iocaretur aliquando Titus Flaminius deformitati corporis eius illudens diceretque vultu quam
maxime iocoso et hilari, 'Quid hoc, Philopomene, cum pulchras
manus, crura etiam perquam pulchra habeas, quod ventrem ipse
non habeas?,' ad ea Philopomenes eadem cum hilaritate et vultu,
'Quid, o Romanorum imperator eximie, cum egregios pedites,
strenuos maxime equites habeas, quod pecuniam minime habeas?'
Nam et Flaminius persaepe inopia rei pecuniariae laborabat quemadmodum Philopomenes exiguitate ventris ac medii corporis gra-
cilitate.

Philopoemen, she even coaxingly asked him to help her receive his master affably. Then Philopoemen, since he was very kind, recognizing the woman's mistake, at once took up an ax and began to split wood with a wedge for cooking dinner. Meanwhile when the host returned home and noticed that Philopoemen was working away at chopping the wood, he said, "By Jupiter, Philopoemen, what's this? For shame of gods and men, what are you doing, greatest of generals?," and he cast down his head for sorrow and shame. To this Philopoemen said with the greatest pleasantness, "I'm paying the penalty for my ugly face and my whole ugly body."[19] He wanted to provide his host with a laugh at his own expense and to be ridiculous in his own eyes. This was surely something worthy of a merry and witty man. and all the wittier for its being rarer.

King Alfonso, whom our age learned from experience to be most liberal, was giving ready cash with his own hand to a man who had deserved well of him, saying, "Please take care that my treasurer doesn't find out about this." And when the other added, "You, king, are afraid of a financial magistrate?," he said, "I'm afraid that for this gift he'll deduct the same amount from my dinners." Alfonso endeavored to hide his liberality, but then, recognizing the intelligence of the recipient, he made himself ridiculous as he did not wish to appear to slight him.

Once when Titus Flaminius was making fun of the same Philopoemen, mocking the ugliness of his body, and said with as joking and cheerful an expression as possible, "What's this, Philopoemen? Why, when you have beautiful hands and also very beautiful legs, don't you have a belly?," Philopoemen replied with the same cheerful expression, "Why is it, most excellent general of the Romans, that although you have outstanding infantrymen and extremely vigorous horsemen, you don't have any money?" For Flaminius often suffered from lack of money just as Philopoemen from the smallness of his stomach and the thinness of his torso.[20]

18     Facetissime etiam Themistocles adversus filium matris favore atque auctoritate quaedam exposcentem; nam ad matrem eius conversus, 'Graecis quidem, o uxor,' inquit, 'Athenienses imperitant, ipse ego Atheniensibus, tu autem mihi, tibi vero ipsi filius

19 praescribit.' Non probat Cneus Pompeius in Tusculano aedificatam a Lucullo villam, quod ea aestivae quidem inhabitationi accommodatissima cum esset, hibernae tamen parum omnino prospectum fuisset; ad quae iucundissime magnaque cum festivitate Lucullus, 'Num tibi,' inquit, 'Pompei, quam grues, quam ciconiae minus habere cordis videor, qui nesciam pro temporibus habitatio-

20 nem mutare?' Et illud quoque ab eodem concinniter ac iocose. Cum enim dispensator rei familiaris ab eo accusaretur, quod parciorem parasset coenam, et ille respondisset, 'Quod solus quidem coenaturus esses, non putabam lautiore apparatu opus esse,' ibi ipse vultu quam maxime festivo, 'An ignorabas apud Lucullum ipsum coenaturum esse Lucullum?'

21     Facetum admodum etiam Catonis illud, quanquam dicacitate non caret. Nam maritimum civis quispiam fundum cum vendidisset quod esset ventri ac luxui summum in modum deditus, hoc cognito, quod eius ingenium Catoni perspectum esset, statim inquit, 'Per Herculem, nimis miror hominem hunc quam mare plus etiam pollere,' videlicet quod ille per luxum atque gulam absorpsis-

22 set quod mare fluctibus vix allideret. Est eiusdem Catonis dictum, quanquam sapiens, tamen quod etiam facetum dicas. Filius enim eius, matre mortua, cum mulierculam ad patris cubiculum saepicule itantem torvius aliquando inspexisset idque Catoni esset significatum, confestim alteram despondit uxorem; quod intelligens filius patrem precabatur ignosceret sibi, siquid per incuriam peccasset. Tum ipse, 'Nihil,' respondit, 'eiusmodi est in causa, nisi quod tui similes patriae plures relinquere cives cupiam.'

Themistocles also spoke wittily against his son, who was de-  18
manding something, invoking the favor and authority of his
mother. Turning to the mother he said, "Wife, the Athenians rule
the Greeks, I the Athenians, you me, but your son commands
you."[21] Gnaeus Pompey did not approve of the villa built in Tus-  19
culum by Lucullus because, although it was very well suited to be
inhabited in the summer, yet no care had been taken for inhabiting it in the winter. To which Lucullus said very pleasantly and
with great mirth, "Do I seem to you, Pompey, to have less sense
than cranes and storks, and that I don't know how to change my
habitat with the seasons?"[22] And also there is this elegant and  20
witty remark from the same man. For when he had reprimanded
his steward for preparing too frugal a dinner and his steward had
replied, "Since you were going to dine alone, I didn't think more
sumptuous provision necessary," he replied with an expression as
merry as could be, "Didn't you know that Lucullus was going to
dine with Lucullus'?"[23]

Also, this remark of Cato's is very witty, although it is not with-  21
out raillery. For when some citizen had sold a farm by the sea because he was addicted to his belly and luxury to the highest degree, Cato, because he knew his character, said immediately after
learning this, "By Hercules, I marvel beyond measure that this
man is more powerful than the sea," evidently because the man
had devoured through luxury and gluttony what the sea had hardly
eroded with its waves.[24] There is a saying of the same Cato that,  22
although wise, you might also term witty. For when his son, after
the death of his mother, had regarded with disapproval a common
woman who was going to his father's bed pretty often, and this
had been made known to Cato, he without delay took a second
wife. Learning this, the son begged his father to pardon him if he
had inadvertently done something wrong. Cato replied, "The reason has nothing to do with your disapproval, except that I want to
leave the fatherland more citizens like you."[25]

23    Illud vero Marci Ciceronis et acutum admodum et facetum.
Quidam enim cum ei dixisset, 'Tu ne istud aetatis virgunculam

24  duxisti?,' 'Cras,' respondit, 'mulier erit.' Iulia, Augusti filia, Marci
Agrippae uxor, cum intellexisset suis e consciis mirari quosdam
quod liberi eius tam essent Agrippae similes, 'Desinant,' inquit,
'mirari, quando ipsa nunquam nisi navi plena vectorem tollo.' Hoc,
quanquam facete responsum, significatione tamen oscenitatis minime caret.

25    Emerat Alcibiades canem rarae magnitudinis non exiguo pretio,
nec multis post diebus et caudam illi mutilari et per urbem liberum abire iussit. Hoc viso, cum omnes rem ut ineptam miraren-
tur ac stolidam, alii deridere Alcibiadem, qui id fecisset, alii etiam
ut stultum eum animique parum omnino compositi accusare, esse
e familiaribus atque amicis qui obiurgarent. Quo cognito, Alcibiades in risum versus, 'At mihi,' inquit, 'hoc facto perbelle perque
opportune consultum est; cum enim scirem Atheniensem populum assiduo de me rebusque obloqui de meis ac maledicere, commento hoc, dum ineptam hanc materiam ridiculamque ei maledicendi trado, impudentioribus a maledictis, quibus me quotidie

26  discerpunt, et illum averti et me etiam liberavi.' Atheniensis Anitus, vir et dives et splendidus, paraverat amicis convivium roga-
veratque Alcibiadem eorum uti numero se adiungeret; cumque
recusasset, domum se Alcibiades recepit, vino ibi liberalius indul-
gens; atque, hoc facto, cum servis profectus atque in Aniti coena-
culum irrumpens, iussit abaci ornatum dimidiatum ipsum quidem
a servis rapi, in quo permulta essent ex auro atque argento vascula,
atque ad se impetu eodem ferri. Quod factum a conviviis acriter
cum incesseretur, ibi Anitus, 'Quin,' inquit, 'Alicibiades, toto cum

But this one of Marcus Cicero is both very sharp and witty. For   23
when someone said to him, "At your age you've married a little
girl?," he replied, "She'll be a woman tomorrow."²⁶ When Julia, the   24
daughter of Augustus and wife of Marcus Agrippa, learned that
some people in the know were marveling that her children were so
similar to Agrippa, she said, "Let them stop marveling, since I
never take on a passenger unless the ship is full."²⁷ Although a
witty response, yet it by no means is without obscenity.

Alcibiades had bought a dog of unusual size at no small price,   25
and after not many days he ordered that its tail be cut off and that
it go free throughout the city. When this had been noticed, although everyone wondered at it as something silly and stupid,
some mocked Alcibiades for doing it, while others even accused
him of being foolish and crazy, and some of his acquaintances and
friends rebuked him. When he learned of this, Alcibiades was
moved to laughter and said, "But I did this deliberately, and it's
worked out beautifully and usefully too. For since I knew that the
Athenian people were constantly condemning and slandering me
and my affairs, I provided them with this contrivance as a silly and
ridiculous matter for slander; in so doing I've distracted them and
also freed myself from the more impudent slanders they use to
carp at me every day."²⁸ The Athenian Anitus, a man both rich   26
and magnificent, had prepared a banquet for his friends and had
invited Alcibiades to join their number. And when he had refused,
Alcibiades took himself home and indulged himself there rather
liberally with wine. Having done this, he set out with his slaves,
burst into Anitus' dining room, and ordered the slaves to snatch
up half of the adornments on the sideboard, on which were very
many small vessels of gold and silver, and to carry them to his
house with the same impetuosity. When this act had been sharply
criticized by the guests, Anitus said, "But since Alcibiades was

de hoc abaco pro arbitrio ei facere ius esset, liberalissime mecum egit, quod dimidium mihi eius integrum reliquerit.'

27    Publius Syrus, cuius multae extant praeclaraeque sententiae, interrogatus quid podager quispiam ad solem constitutus ageret, perquam belle respondit ac perargute: 'Aquam calfacit.' Idem quoque interrogatus, quod nam ipse molestum esse ocium duceret,

28    'Pedum podagricorum,' respondit. Delectant autem haec tum dicta tum responsa, nam et lacessunt neminem et oscenitate carent, nec indigna sunt ingenuo homine sive dicendo sive audiendo, nec in referendis fabellis non venustant narrationem ipsam universamque explicationem.

29    Gonnella, sive fabulator facetissimus sive ioculator maxime comis, interrogatus aliquando a Nicolao Marchione Ferrariensi, quarum nam sive artium sive facultatum in urbe Ferraria maior esset numerus, confestim, 'Quis id dubitet medicoruom maiorem esse numerum?' Tum Nicolaus, 'O inanem hominem et urbis huius artium artificumque ignorantissimum, quippe cum vix duo tres ve ad summum Ferraria medicos habeat, sive cives sive externos.' Ad ea Gonnella, 'O principem maioribus rebus deditum, qui ob eas urbem suam suosque cives ignoret penitissime!' Tum Nicolaus, 'Quid, si hoc falsum, quod ipse asseris?' Tum Gonnella: 'Quid, si ego verus?' Ibi sive poena sive mulcta ex compacto ei, qui vanus inventus esset, constituta. Igitur insequenti die sub auroram Gonnella pro templi astans foribus, obvoluto pellibus ore ac gutture, interrogantibus qui in templum ingrediebantur, quo nam morbo laboraret, respondebat singulis, 'Dentium dolore,' singulis etiam remedium aliquod dolori praebentibus, quorum ipse et nomina conscribebat et remedia. Atque hac ratione urbem perrectans perscrutandoque remedia, singulos, qui obviam fierent, percontatus, supra trecentos homines medicinam dolori tradentes notavit in

within his rights to do what he wanted with the whole sideboard, he has acted most liberally with me, since he left me half of it intact."[29]

When Publius Syrus, whose many celebrated maxims are ex- 27 tant, was asked what a gouty man placed in the sun was doing, he replied very prettily and acutely, "He's warming water." Also, when asked what kind of leisure he would consider annoying, he replied, "The leisure of gouty feet."[30] Moreover, these sayings and replies 28 delight, for they harm no one and are without obscenity, are not unworthy to be said or heard by a freeborn man, and, in the telling of stories, make the narration itself and the whole exposition charming.

Once when Gonnella, either the wittiest storyteller or the most 29 affable joker, was asked by Niccolò, marquis of Ferrara, of what arts and professions there was a greater number in the city of Ferrara, he immediately replied, "Who would doubt that the number of doctors is greater?"[31] Niccolò replied, "O what an empty-headed man! You are completely ignorant of the arts and craftsmen of this city, since Ferrara barely has at the most two or three doctors, whether citizens or foreigners." To which Gonnella, "O how devoted to important affairs this prince must be, since on account of them, he is completely ignorant of his city and citizens!" Then Niccolò said, "What if what you assert is false?" Then Gonnella, "What if I'm right?" Then a penalty or fine was set by agreement for the one who was found false. So the next day at dawn Gonnella, standing in front of the doors of the church, his face and throat covered with bandages, replied "Toothache," to each person entering the temple who asked what disease he was suffering from. He also wrote down the names and remedies of the individuals who offered some treatment for his pain. And going through the city in this way, seeking for remedies, and asking one by one everyone he met, he noted down on a tablet more than three hundred men who recommended medicine to him for the pain. This done,

tabella. Quo facto, regiam ingressus, qua hora Nicolaus prandebat, se se obtulit involutis et ore et cervicibus, ingentem dolorem simulans. Nicolaus, astu viri parum cognito, cum intelligeret illum haud bene valere a dentibus, 'Hoc,' statim inquit, 'remedium, Gonnella, adhibe: laudabis Nicolaum, e vestigio enim sanus eris.' His Gonnella acceptis, domum regressus tabulam instruit, remedia illa remediorumque auctores continentem, ac primo loco Marchionem ascribit, inde alios atque alios, delectu adhibito. Tertio die quasi sanus atque a dolore liber, nudata gula ac cervicibus, principem adit, docet quae conquisita et comprobata fuerint, mulctam ab illo expostulat atque in ius illum se se adacturum minatur atque his dictis tabulam Marchioni legendam exponit. Ibi Marchio primum inter medicos locum se se obtinere conspicatus, inde alios atque alios primates viros, a risu continere nequiens seque victum confessus, pecunia illi ut solveretur imperavit.

30     Princeps idem Nicolaus equi Gonnellae huius caudam, quo in loco stabulabatur, clanculum novacula abscindi iussit. Ille, hoc percepto, asellis, qui eodem in stabulo nutribantur, particulam labiorum superiorum abrasit. Delatus apud principem non excusavit factum, rogavit tantummodo damnum uti aestimaretur ipsiusque ad conspectum deligati ducerentur, quo aestimatio ipsa aequius fieri posset. Primo itaque loco reste ducebatur Gonnellae equus, caudae vix frustum motitans; subsequebantur aselli suo ordine illigati. Qui ut ante illius conspectum stetere resque ipsa oculis omnium exposita est atque animadversa, nec princeps ipse nec quisqum ex iis qui aderant fuit quin risu dirumperetur. Tum Gonnella, 'Nec tu, princeps, in solio constitutus nec quisquam e iudicibus, quamvis gravis ac severus, ad hoc ipsum spectaculum tenere risum potuit: tu ne asinos, tu ne bestiolas has a risu

returning to the palace at the hour Niccolò was having lunch, he presented himself with his face and neck wrapped, simulating great pain. When Niccolò, not recognizing the cunning of the man, understood that he was suffering from toothache, he said, "Apply this remedy, Gonnella, and you'll praise Niccolò and get well right away." Having heard these things, Gonnella returned home, drew up an account containing the remedies and their authors, and wrote down the marquis at the head of the list, then another and yet another in order of rank. On the third day, his throat and neck bare as if healthy and free from pain, he approached the prince, showed what had been collected and attested, and demanded the fine from him, threatened to take him to court, and with these words produced the account for the marquis to read. Then the marquis saw that he himself held the first place among the doctors, then another and yet another of the leading men, and unable to keep himself from laughing and confessing himself beaten, he ordered the money to be paid to him.

This same prince Niccolò ordered that the tail of this Gonnel-  30
la's horse be secretly cut off with a razor in the place where it was stabled. When he discovered this, the other shaved off a small part of the upper lips of the donkeys that were fed in the same stable. Accused before the prince, he did not excuse his action but only asked that damages be assessed and that the donkeys be led bound into his master's presence so that the assessment could be fairer. And so, at the head of the line, Gonnella's horse was led out by a rope, barely moving its piece of a tail; the donkeys followed bound in order. When they stood in his presence and the thing was exposed before and noted by everyone's eyes, neither the prince nor anyone who was there could keep from bursting out in laughter. Then Gonnella, "Neither you, prince, though set on your throne, nor any of the judges, no matter how grave and severe, were able to contain your laughter at this spectacle. Could you keep the donkeys, these little beasts, from laughing, when they see a horse

371

continueris, dum equum tam ipsis familiarem decaudatum con-
tuentur?' Quo audito, iteratus est risus Gonnellaque ipse absolutus commendatusque ut facetorum omnium princeps suavissima-
rumque facetiarum artifex suavissimus.

31     Idem tamen ipse aliquando irrisus ac delusus dicitur etiam a
mulierculis, ut cum, iter faciens per Umbriam perque agrum
Treviensem, animadvertisset puellulam prandentem in via resi-
dentemque in lapide ac, despoliato porro, complicantem spolia illa
in epistolae speciem complicataque in os ingerentem dixissetque,
ac si puellam rideret, 'Ad quem nam, o scitula, literas istas compli-
catas mittis?,' tum illa, irrisione viri cognita, exhilarato vultu, 'Ob-
signandas eas anui,' respondit, 'mitto,' dextera etiam anum signifi-
32     cans. Cumque haud multo post puellae alteri obviam factus esset,
quae capellas pastum duceret, dixissetque tentabundus, 'En tibi, o
bellula, argenteolum, petroselinum⁵ mihi si denudaveris,' accepit
illa conditionem atque argenteum statimque, apprehensa capella
annicula caudaque eius sublevata, 'En,' inquit, 'vide atque inspecta,
quod optasti, holusculum.' Huius tamen generis multa, sunt qui
arbitrentur a Gonnella ipso efficta, quo ridiculum se se quacunque
ratione faceret audientibus.

33     Mariotta, Antonii Rebatti mercatoris Florentini uxor, nec insulsa quidem matrona nec parum comis, virum cum intelligeret
noctu per urbem vagari solicitandis scortillis, intranti ei fores do-
mesticas astitit in summis scalis, accensa facula nudatisque puden-
dis; qua ille re inspecta, cum inclamasset, 'Quid, o quid, Mariotta,
hac opus est facula? Quid nudatione?,' tum illa, 'Quo plane inspi-
ceres an hic tantum tibi insit quantum satis esset, ne alibi quaeri-
34     tando labores.' Sed genera haec, sive ludendi sive iocandi, non
carent turpitudine et ingenuo parum digna sunt homine, risum
tamen movent dum in circulis referuntur. Quale illud est rusticani

so familiar to them with its tail cut off?" After this was heard, the laughter was renewed, and Gonnella was absolved and commended as the prince of all witty men and the most pleasant artist of the most pleasant of jokes.

Yet this same man is said once to have been mocked and made 31 fun of by even some little women. For example, when on a journey through Umbria and the district of Trevi he noticed a little girl having lunch by the road, sitting on a stone, and, after stripping a leek and placing it in her mouth, she folded its skins up like a letter. He, as if to laugh at the girl, said, "Pretty one, to whom are you sending this folded letter?" Having recognized the man's mockery, she replied merrily, "I'm sending it to an old woman [anui] to have a seal put on it," indicating, also, her bottom [anum] with her right hand. And when not much later he met another girl 32 who was leading she-goats to pasture, and said temptingly, "Here's a silver coin for you, little beauty, if you uncover your parsley for me," she accepted the condition and the coin, seized a yearling goat, raised her tail, and said, "Here, take a close look at the little vegetable you wanted."[32] Nevertheless, there are some who think that many encounters of this kind were invented by Gonnella, to make himself ridiculous in any way whatsoever to his listeners.

When Mariotta, wife of the Florentine merchant Antonio Re- 33 batto, a clever and affable matron, learned that her husband was wandering through the city at night soliciting prostitutes, she stood on the top of the steps as he was entering the door of their home, having lit a little torch and bared her genitals. When he exclaimed at the sight of this, "What, o what, Mariotta, do you need this little torch for? Why do you need to be naked?," she replied, "So you may see clearly whether there's enough in here to satisfy you so that you don't have to work to seek it out elsewhere." But these kinds of remark, whether mocking or joking, are not 34 without vulgarity and are not worthy of a freeborn man, although they do cause laughter when told in private conversation. Like this

cuiusdam, non insulsi tamen homuntionis; cum enim equo fer-
retur ad nundinas strigoso ac perlongo intrantemque eum in
oppidum vir iocabundus sciscitaretur, quanti venderet panni de-
cempedam, ipseque eo dicto petitum se intelligeret, statim ex equo
descendit sublataque equi cauda podicem illius ostendens, 'Ingre-
dere,' inquit, 'o amice, tabernam, neque enim illiberaliter habeberis
emesque mercatu bono.'

35      Quales igitur faceti esse debeant, qualia etiam facetorum tum
dicta tum responsa, quae allata sunt a nobis exempla docere
abunde possunt. Quoniam autem ipsis e facetiis ac ioculationibus
recreatio quaeritur ac remissio a laboribus molestiisque, ne huic
quoque rei parte ex aliqua desimus, lectio ipsa relatioque[6] tum le-
pidorum versuum tum dialogorum plurimum quoque conferet ad
refocillandos animos, quin historiarum quoque quae avertant auditores, dum attente quidem audiuntur, a curis cogitationibusque
36      gravioribus. Scribendarum fabellarum Luciano, Ioanni item Boc-
catio an aliud fuit consilium quam ut lectores pariter atque auditores delectarent? Idem et Poggio plurimis colligendis quae urbane
dicta essent cumque festivitate et risu itaque de iis libros etiam fe-
37      cit Latine scriptos. Vitae quoque praestantissimorum virorum,
tum Graecis tum Latinis ab auctoribus mandatae literarum monu-
mentis, continent tum salsa tum venusta, quae ad relaxationem
conferant, quae versata in circulis interque conviventes habeant
demulcere curas et tanquam lenocinari molestiis nostris. Nam
praeter ea quae ad hilaritudinem spectent ac iocum, multa iis
continentur lectionibus quae aliis atque aliis rationibus animos
demulceant inducantque eam, quam ipsi quaerimus, relaxationem.
Cuius rei paucis his admonuisse satis fuerit.

38      Illud vero minime omittendum, quod ad relaxationem audien-
tiamque retinendam non parum sibi et ornatus et adiumenti facetus vir comparabit referendis iis sive dictis sive responsis sive

remark of a certain rustic little man, but by no means without wit. When he was being carried on his horse, who was lean and very long, to market day, a joking man had asked him entering the city how much he would sell ten feet of rags for. Understanding that he was being attacked with this remark, at once he descended from his horse, raised his horse's tail, showed its asshole, and said, "Enter the shop, my friend; you'll be treated generously and you'll buy cheaply."

Thus, the examples I have adduced can show abundantly what 35 witty men ought to be as well as what the sayings and responses of witty men should be like. Moreover, since recreation and relaxation from labors and annoyances are sought from witticisms and jokes — not to neglect this subject in any part — the reading and relating of pleasant verses and dialogues also contribute very much to restoring minds, yes, and also the telling of histories that divert listeners, so long as they listen attentively, from cares and serious thoughts. In writing their stories did Lucian and Giovanni Boc- 36 caccio intend anything other than to delight their readers as well as their auditors? And Poggio intended the same thing when he collected very many things that had been said with urbanity, mirth, and laughter and made a book in Latin from them.[33] Also, 37 the lives of the most excellent men, committed by Greek and Latin authors to literary memorials, contain pungent and pleasant things that contribute to relaxation and, when turned over in con- versational circles and among dinner companions, are able to soothe cares and, as it were, entice away our troubles. For in addi- tion to those things that aim at cheerfulness and joking, much is contained in those readings that in one way or another soothes minds and produces the relaxation we are seeking. It suffices to have called this subject to mind in a few words.

But by no means must one omit that the witty man will pro- 38 vide himself with no little distinction and aid for relaxation and for holding his audience through relating witticisms, responses, or

fabellis quas ipse ab aliis acceperit. Ac licet ea ipsa, cum dicerentur, essent sive salsa et aculeata nimis sive oscena et spurca, poterit tamen referre cum modestia, quo efficietur vitiis ut iis careant qualia nunc ipsi referimus.

39    Fuit e senatoribus Petri, Aragoniae regis, Queraldus quidam, tum ore foedo tum reliquo corpore parum composito, tamen qui summa comitate esset praeditus maximisque in negociis exercitatus. Is missus aliquando ad regem Africae, fuit ab illo in coenam adhibitus, quam nostrum in morem rex ipse apparari iussit editioribus in scannis; Afri enim in solo super tapetis discumbunt. Coenitaverunt complures simul. Rex, qui et ipse comis esset et iocandi studiosus, iussit clam ossa colligi omnia eaque ad pedes Queraldi illo nesciente, coniici. Finita igitur coena, cum, aulae magistri iussu, mensae essent sublatae appareretque ossium cumulus, tum quispiam a rege submissus, 'Quid hic,' inquit, 'ossium video? Lupus profecto hic coenitavit, non homo.' Tum Queraldus ad regem conversus, 'Mihi,' inquit, 'o rex, cum lupis fuit in coena negocium, quando luporum est et carnem et ossa simul abrodere, quod comessatores isti tui fecere; ego vero, ut homo, ut conviva comis, carnes absumpsi, ossa in humum abieci, in canum pastum atque oblectamentum.' Haec igitur dictio, ut mordax, tum pupugit, at relatio, ut iucunda, nunc delectat.

40    Idem Queraldus, quo regem delectaret, adhibitus ab illo in cubiculum, in quo constrata essent omnia serico atque exasperatis acu purpuris nullusque relictus esset locus in quo sine nota posset inspui, fieretque illi proximus regiis e famulis quisquim ore foedo atque impuro, e vestigio excreabundus os illius sputo inspurcavit, qui, sublata statim voce, regem appellavit. Hoc cognito, Queraldus, 'Ego,' inquit, 'iucundissime rex, apparatus tui nitorem admiratus, ne aliqua illum parte contaminarem, nullum cum alium,

stories that he has received from others. And although these things, when they were said, were pungent and too pointed or obscene and filthy, yet he will be able to relate them with modesty so that that they will lack the vices that I am mentioning now.

Among the senators of King Pedro of Aragon was a certain 39 Queraldo, whose face was ugly and the rest of his body not well put together, yet he was a very obliging fellow and was experienced in the greatest affairs.[34] Sent one time to a king of Africa, he was invited by him to dinner, which the king ordered, after our fashion, to be served on tables, for Africans recline on the ground upon carpets. Many people dined together. The king, who was affable himself and partial to joking, secretly ordered all the bones to be collected and thrown together by Queraldo's feet without his knowledge. Thus, when dinner was over and the tables removed at the order of the master of the hall, the heap of bones became visible. Then someone dispatched by the king said, "What bones do I see here? Surely a wolf has dined here, not a man." Then Queraldo turned to the king and said, "King, I did have dealings with wolves at dinner, since wolves gnaw off the flesh and bones together, which these revelers of yours have done. But since I'm a human being and an affable guest, I consumed the flesh but threw the bones on the ground as food and amusement for the dogs." This remark was biting and stung at that time, but now it makes an agreeable, delightful story.

The same Queraldo, to amuse the king, was invited by him to 40 his bedroom, in which everything was covered with silk and purple cloth with embroidered needlework, and there was no place one could spit without leaving a stain. Near him was one of the king's servants who had an ugly, filthy face, and suddenly needing to spit Queraldo befouled that man's face with his spittle. The man immediately cried out, calling upon the king. Realizing this, Queraldo said, "Most pleasant king, admiring the brilliance of your magnificent furniture, I wanted to avoid staining it anywhere,

praeter illius os, immundum relictum locum atque spurcosum cernerem, in illum excreatum profudi, quasi a te ob id servatum, quo nitor tibi tuus salvus esset.' Actio quidem ipsa sordida tunc
41 fuit et contumeliosa, at relatio perbella. In eadem legatione quidam e regis aula factus ei obviam, in deformitatem eius illatus, 'Quid,' inquit, 'Petrus rex portenti ad nos misit?' Ad ea ipse confestim, 'Sciebat,' inquit, 'Petrus ad quem me mitteret'; nam et rex ille deformior erat.

42 Haec ipsa et dictio et responsio habent in dicendo spicula at in referendo salem ac ioculationem propter promptitudinem respondendi ac maledicti reiectionem tantopere inexpectatam. Parasito cuidam apposita cum esset in mensa vulva suilla deridiculi gratia, tum ille, sublatis pudibunda e corporis parte vestibus, nudato bacillo, illum in quadram iniecit; cumque esset inclamatum a comessoribus, immurmuravit inquiens talis carnes cultrum talem exigere. Quod quidem actu foedum, oscenum responsu, at relatu, pro loco tamen atque auditoribus, non iniucundum.

43 In hoc autem ipso iocandi genere comis est admodum ac periucundus A. Colotius noster, tum propter insitam ei a natura perraram quandam in dicendo hilaritatem tum propter egregiam literarum peritiam rerumque multarum usum. Quo fit ut in explicandis fabellis, in epigrammatis comicorumque poetarum dictis referendis ac lusibus, mirifice delectet. Quibus in rebus cum primis habenda est pudoris ratio limitesque ipsi verecundiae aut parum aut nihil prorsus transgrediendi. Locus tamen et tempus et auditorum personae non nunquam paulo licentius indulgere solent iis qui verba faciunt.

44 Matrona Mediolanensis, e familia pervetusta et nobili, quaeque aliquando cum amatoribus lusisset, fuerat a sacerdote solicitata, qui e Fratrum Minorum esset ordine. Ea coram solicitanti in hanc sententiam respondisse traditur: se non posse non multum illi

and finding no other place left foul and unclean except for this man's face, I spat on it, as though it had been reserved by you for this purpose, so that your brilliance would be preserved."[35] At that time the action was indeed filthy and abusive, but it makes a lovely story. On that same embassy someone from the king's court encountered him and, in reference to his ugliness, said, "What monstrosity did King Pedro send to us?" To which he said at once, "Pedro knew to whom he was sending me." For the king was even uglier.

This remark and response too have stings in the saying, but in the relating they display humor and wittiness on account of the quickness of response and the surprising way the insult was thrown back. When a pig's womb was placed in front of a sponger at table to ridicule him, he removed his codpiece and bared his rod, laying it upon the morsel. When a shout went up from his fellow diners, the man said in a whisper that flesh like that called for a knife like this. This was certainly a vulgar thing to do, and the man's response was obscene, but nevertheless it is not an unpleasant story to tell in the right place and to the right auditors.

In this kind of joking, however, our Angelo Colocci is most affable and pleasant, both on account of the rare good humor in speaking implanted in him by nature and on account of his extraordinary skill in letters and his experience of many things.[36] Hence he is marvelously delightful in relating stories and epigrams as well as the sayings and jests of the comic poets. In these things one must especially consider propriety, and the limits of modesty must be transgressed either a little or not at all. Nevertheless, the place, time, and character of the auditors sometimes are apt to allow greater license to those who compose the witticisms.

A Milanese matron from a very old and noble family who had dallied sometimes with lovers was propositioned by a priest who was of the order of the Friars Minor. She is said to have replied in the following sense when he openly propositioned her. She could

quidem debere ex eo, quod amaretur; coeterum aegre se illud ferre, quod ab eo eius aetatis esse iudicaretur, cum non esset, in qua quod reliquum esset ut reliquiosum quidem ac male olidum Fraterculorum tunicis sudore ac paedore infectis subiiceretur. Quod responsum per urbem cum percrebuisset ipsaque a gravibus quibusdam viris ac sibi perquam familiaribus interrogata, serenitate quadam oris rem omnem confessa esset, licentior illa festivaque explicatio visa est non solum non ademisse aliquid pudori verum addidisse multum comitati atque inter notos et amicos gratiae.

45    Galeatius Pandonus, Ioannis Andegaviensis partes secutus, cum aliis non paucis in carcere ac squalore complures annos Ferdinando a rege est habitus; coeteri in vinculis assiduo maledicere, lamentari, moerore confici, ipse contra iocari, ridere, paedorem in delicias verbis convertere, nihil illo iucundius esse, denique eam ob rem in pugillatum descendere. Quod Ferdinando renuntiatum cum esset, liberari eum e carceribus statim iussit liberatumque honesto salario est prosecutus. Ille ad mortem usque Ferdinandi sic vixit, ut quae plurima in carcere teterrime passus esset, ea omnia inter enumerandum in risum converteret ac iocum. Cum igitur quae ad fa-

46    cetudinem spectent quaeque ad facetum instituendum a nobis explicata sint, reliquum est uti pauca quaedam de ironicis dicamus, ne pars haec tanquam inculta a nobis relictaque videatur.[7]

only be very obliged to him for loving her, but she took it ill that he judged her of such an age, which she wasn't, that what was left, like an ill-smelling relic, should be placed under tunics of the Little Friars, infected with sweat and filth. When this response had spread through the city and she herself had been questioned by some grave men whom she knew very well, she confessed the whole thing with a certain serenity of expression; and this rather bold and merry story seemed not only not to detract from her modesty but even to add much to her reputation for gentility and the favor she enjoyed among her friends and acquaintances.

Galeazzo Pandone, having taken the side of Jean d'Anjou, was held in a squalid prison with not a few others by King Ferdinando.[37] The others in chains constantly cursed, lamented, and were stricken with sorrow, but he joked, smiled, and turned the filth into sport with his words. No one was pleasanter than him, and at last he got into a fight on this account. When this was announced to Ferdinando, he immediately ordered him to be liberated from prison and bestowed on him, once free, an honorable pension. He lived until Ferdinando's death in such a way that, while recounting them, he turned to laughter and joking all the many foul things he had suffered in prison. Having therefore explained those things that pertain to wittiness and to educating the witty man, it remains to say a few things about self-deprecators so that I will not appear to have left this part, as it were, uncultivated. 45 46

## : 3 :

## De ironicis.[8]

1 Et Aristoteles, virtutum moralium disputator solertissimus, et Graeci scriptores plerique omnes tradunt Socratem fuisse ironicum, quodque dissimulantia eiusmodi a modestia proficisceretur, inde effectum est ut genus quoddam dissimulationis sit ad virtutem referendum, quando eius qui ea utitur nequaquam illud est aut consilium aut finis quo aut fallat ipse quidem nugetur ve aut lucrum inde sibi comparet, verum ut ostentationem defugiat tumoremque vitet, ab insolentia vero sic recedat, ut intra modestiae ac verecundiae fines potius diversetur. 2 De eo enim in quo quis praestat, cum demit sibi particulam vel de se ita quidem loquitur, ut videri nolit aut insolescere ex eo aut non existimare tantum se profecisse quantum aliorum fortasse sit iudicium, utrumque profecto modestiae est, non tergiversationis aut fraudis, qua tamen in re medium quoque retinendum est. Nam velle id quod inest nimium attenuare, id finitimum est inficiationi. 3 Vehementior enim extenuatio non minus fortasse in ostentationem intendit quam arrogatio illa insolens ac vanitatis socia. De cuius principiis, quia multa iam tradita sunt a nobis, reliquum est de hac ipsa ironia, quae virtus est et a multis Socratica est agnominata, quae necessaria visa sunt uti praecipiamus. Agnominabimus itaque libenter Socraticam sive dissimulationem sive ironiam, quo notius appareat alia dissimulationis genera turpia esse quaeque condemnentur digna, sicuti iam docuimus, cum in pluris eam distribuimus partes, hoc vero ipsum genus et honestum esse et ad virtutem referendum.

: 3 :

*On self-deprecators.*

Both Aristotle, who has discussed the moral virtues most skillfully, 1
and almost all Greek writers relate that Socrates was self-
deprecating, and because dissimulation of this kind proceeds from
modesty, it has come about that a certain kind of dissimulation
must be counted a virtue, when it is not at all the intention or goal
of the one who uses it to deceive, trifle, or obtain profit for himself
but to flee from ostentation, to avoid conceit, and to retire from
insolence so that he may instead dwell within the bounds of
modesty and reserve.[38] For when one takes away from himself a 2
small part of what he excels at, or speaks of himself in such a way
that he does not wish to be held insolent on account of it, or to
reckon that his accomplishments are as great as others perhaps
judge them to be, each act is assuredly a matter of modesty, not of
subterfuge or fraud. Nevertheless, in this also the mean must be
maintained. For to wish to diminish too much what is in one is
very close to denial. Indeed, too vehement an extenuation aims 3
perhaps not less at ostentation than that insolent arrogance, companion of vanity. Since I have already related many things about
its principles, it remains to teach what seems necessary about the
kind of self-deprecation that is a virtue and has been called Socratic by many.[39] And so I willingly will call it Socratic dissimulation or self-deprecation so that it will be more obvious that other
kinds of dissimulation are base and worthy to be condemned (as I
have already taught, when I distinguished the several parts of dissimulation),[40] but this kind is honorable and must be counted a
virtue.

## : 4 :

## *Definitio.*[9]

1 Quo igitur Socratica haec, quae et qualis sit, magis appareat, eam sic terminabimus, quaedam ut sit mediocritas pro loco quidem ac tempore proque personae dignitate dissimulandi ea quae nobis insunt et in quibus praestamus sine ostentatione et fraude ac sine lucro. Nam nec Socraticus hic dissimulator pecuniae inhiat ac lucris nec ut demittendo seque et sua altius efferat neque ut inaniter 2 mentiatur aut decipiat. Eritque elevatio ac demissio ipsa sic modesta et prudens, ut neque quod inest prorsus inficietur, perinde ut nihil externum affingit exornat ve se se iis quae sua non sunt, utque ab ingenuitate nullo modo recedat, sed in ea ipsa dissimulantia potius id praestabit quod liberali dignum homine iudicetur. 3 Hos igitur intra fines Socratica haec modestia versabitur iuraque constituet sua; nam si mediocritas est, modum necesse est retineat ac temperationem, aliter enim aut in fraudem declinabit mendacium ve ac veri abnegationem voluntariam aut in ostentationem elatam illam quidem ac superbientem, perinde ut de vestitu Laconico Aristoteles iudicat.

4 Ac primo quidem loco quaerendum videtur an aetatem omnem ac qualemcumque vitae partem deceat dissimulantia, omnem ne etiam personam, sive is filius sit familias sive pater sive cum magistratu sive privata liberaque publicis a muneribus. Cuius quidem rei prudentia ipsa iudex erit et ea ratio quae iure suo recta agnomi- 5 natur. Senex tamen quam iuvenis adolescens ve ad retinendum modestiam quam requirimus ut prorsus magis est idoneus, sic minus facilis ac lubricus ad incurrendum in ostentationem aut in deceptionem ac fraudem propter longiorem vitae usum animumque magis confirmatum adversus inconstantiam ac levitatem, tametsi adolescentulos non nunquam videmus optime constitutos,

## : 4 :

## *Definition.*

To make it clearer, then, what and of what kind this Socratic self-  1
deprecation is, I will define it as a certain mean of dissimulating,
without ostentation, fraud, or profit, in accordance with the place,
the time, and the rank of the person, those things that are in us
and in which we excel. The Socratic dissimulator does not long for
money or profits, nor does he dissimulate to raise himself and his
doings higher by lowering them or to lie vainly or deceive. And  2
this disparagement and lowering will be so modest and prudent
that he will not completely disavow what is in him, just as he will
not feign anything external or adorn himself with qualities that are
not his, or depart in any way from candor, but in this dissimulation he will rather do what is judged worthy of a free man. There-  3
fore, within these boundaries this Socratic modesty will dwell and
establish its own laws. For if it is a mean, it must observe due
measure and fit proportion, for otherwise it will decline into fraud,
lies and willful denial of the truth, or that lofty, proud ostentation,
just as Aristotle judges of the Spartan dress.[41]

But in the first place it seems one must ask if dissimulation  4
suits every age and every stage of life and also every person,
whether a son or father of a family, a magistrate or a private person free from public duties. Prudence and the reason that is properly called "right reason" will be the judge of this. Nevertheless, as  5
an old man is much more suited to preserving the modesty we are
seeking than a youth or a young man, so he is less susceptible and
prone to rushing into ostentation or deception and fraud on account of a longer experience of life and a mind more strengthened
against inconstancy and levity — although we do occasionally see
very young men excellently constituted but old men who are very

senes contra perquam immoderatos. Sed nescio quomodo in sene ironiam hanc, id est elevationem, bene ante actae vitae rerumque gestarum minus admiramur, in iuvene vehementius, fortasse quod aetas haec promptior est ad ostentationem seque resque magnificandas; ab utroque tamen habendus est ante oculos habitus ille Laconicus.

6    Ac, ne nostris a disciplinis discedamus, Iulius Pomponius, exactissimus aetatis nostrae grammaticus Romanaeque vetustatis perpensor quam maxime diligens, nobilitatem generis ita dissimulavit — cum e familia esset Sanseverinia, quae haudquaquam exiguae parti Lucaniae imperitaret ac Brutiae — ut neque ipse genus fateretur, et cum illis quibus notum id esset ita loqueretur, ut videri posset nobilitatem contemnere. Cognitionem vero rerum plurimarum, quae in eo erat non mediocris, ita prae se tulit, ut docens ipse vetustosque auctores interpretans declararet qui et quantus in docendo esset atque in interpretando; coeterum in conventibus familiarique in consuetudine ac sermone mirum est quam verecunde nedum modeste de se aut sentiret aut loqueretur, cumque aliis plurimum tribueret, in se ipsum maxime parcus erat.

7    Contra vero Laurentius Vallensis, multae vir doctrinae ingeniique in primis acuti, popularibus in congressibus ac literatorum circulis ostentandae disciplinae iudicatus est fuisse studiosior, ne dicam parum modestus, ut iis in circulis multo appareret diligentior quam in libris ipsis quos scriptos reliquit; cumque non pauca in dialecticis adinvenisset adversus horum temporum artis eius magistros, eo se se efferebat, palam ut diceret nullam esse logicam praeter Laurentianam.

8    Albertus vero cognomento Magnus, qui multa posteritati physicis in rebus ingenii sui reliquit monumenta, in ultima senectute cum studiosis a viris consuleretur, respondere plerunque est solitus, 'Quaerite Albertum in libris'; adeo non modo non prae se ferebat tot annorum studia lucubrationesque, sed memoriae videri

immoderate. But somehow we admire this self-deprecation, that is disparagement, of a well-lived life and accomplishments less in an old man and more vigorously in a young one, perhaps because youth is more inclined to ostentation and magnifying itself and its affairs. Nevertheless, both must keep in view that Spartan dress.

And not to depart from our own disciplines, Giulio Pomponio, 6 the most precise grammarian of our age and the most diligent examiner of Roman antiquity, so dissimulated the nobility of his birth — since he was of the Sanseverino family, which ruled no small part of Lucania and Bruttium — that he did not himself acknowledge his lineage and spoke in such a way with those who knew it that he could appear to scorn nobility.[42] But he revealed his knowledge of many things, which was by no means middling, in such a way that when teaching and interpreting the old authors he demonstrated who and how great he was in teaching and interpreting. But in assemblies and familiar intercourse and conversation it is wonderful how discreetly, not to mention modestly, he thought and spoke about himself, and although he gave great credit to others, he was very restrained about himself.

On the other hand, Lorenzo Valla, a man of great learning and 7 especially sharp intellect, in public meetings and circles of literary men was regarded as having been too eager to display his learning, not to say immodest, so that in those circles he appeared to take much more pains than in those books that he left in writing.[43] And since he had discovered not a few things in dialectic contrary to the masters of that art in those days, he exalted himself to the point that he would openly say there was no logic besides Lorenzo's.[44]

When Albert, justly named the Great, who left many monu- 8 ments of his intelligence in physical sciences to posterity, was consulted in extreme old age by students, he was accustomed for the most part to reply, "Ask Albert in his books."[45] Thus not only did he not make a parade of the studies and lucubrations of so

volebat timere, cum tamen et memoria optime valeret et obversarentur ei ante oculos physicae inquisitiones etiam iuvenilium annorum.

9 Antonius Panhormita, qui obliteratam nedum languescentem in Italia poeticam restituit in antiquam pene formam, cum a studiosis persaepe hominibus de perveteri dubitataque sive poetae aliqua sive oratoris interrogaretur sententia, quadam etiam cum frontis hilaritudine ac si memoriae diffideret, 'Ite,' respondebat, 'ad Iovianum'; adeo etiam senex et primarius vir in Alfonsi regis aula, quod saepenumero docuisset, scire se dissimulabat. Itaque quem nunc fructum colligit, dissimulatione ex ea colligit.

10 Hae igitur Socraticae sunt dissimulationes et honestae et laudabiles, non ut ostentent, non ut lucrum inde aliquod capiant praeter honestam illam animi conscientiam in se ipsa sibi congratulantem perfruentemque bonis suis, quem tamen fructum eumque maxime huberem admirata posteritas ipsa reddit. Haec est illa despicientia sui ipsius tam liberalis, ut liberalitate ex ea, ne dicam elevatione rerum suarum, tantos colligat redditus, ut centuplum inde summa 11 etiam cum hubertate accipiat. Detrahebat sibi Socrates de cognitione rerum, de scientia, non ut abnegaret quod in luce expositum erat, sed ut alios invitaret ad humanitatem ac modestiam; neque enim videri volebat insolescere ob multarum rerum peritiam.

12 Franciscus Aretinus, genere nobilis, doctrina eximius, aetate provectior, cui Romana non parum debet lingua, inter ipsos quos habebat doctrinae sectatores ita se gerere est solitus, ut post traditam institutionem minores semper inter illos partes quam quae suae essent susciperet. Itaque non solum sibi quod suum non esset

many years, but he wanted to look like he was anxious about his memory, although his memory was extremely strong and the physical investigations of even his youthful years still passed in front of his eyes.

Antonio Panormita restored poetry, which had been obliterated 9 and was not just languishing in Italy, almost to its ancient beauty. Very often when he was asked by studious men about some very old and doubtful passage in either a poet or orator, he would respond, even with a cheerful expression, as if he mistrusted his memory, "Go to Gioviano."[46] To such an extent even an old man, one of the foremost in the court of King Alfonso, would dissimulate his knowledge of what he had often taught. And so the fruit he now gathers, he gathers from this dissimulation.

Therefore, these Socratic dissimulations are both honorable 10 and praiseworthy without showing off, without grasping at any profit besides that honorable consciousness of a mind congratulating itself and enjoying its own good things. Nevertheless, an admiring posterity bestows this reward, and most abundantly. This is a contempt of oneself so freehanded that from this freedom with, not to say disparagement of, its own accomplishments, it gathers such returns that it receives one hundredfold therefrom, and in the greatest abundance. Socrates would detract from his 11 understanding of things and his knowledge, not to deny what had been brought to light, but to urge others to humanity and modesty. For he did not wish to appear to become insolent on account of his experience of many things.

Francesco Aretino, noble by birth, exceptional for his learning, 12 to whom the Roman language owes not a little, when rather advanced in age was accustomed to comport himself with his students in such a way that after imparting his instruction he would always take a lesser role among them than was due to him.[47] And so he not only did not in any way claim for himself what was not

nullo modo arrogabat, verum demebat de proprio et in loquendo et in conversando cum familiaribus.

13    Nec vero quamcumque ad interrogationem sive iocando sive seriis utendo hic ipse ubique erit ironicus ac dissimulans. Nam nec vir fortis quocumque in periculo fortitudine ac robore suo utetur illudque obibit. Nec urbanus et comis in funere iocatur et ad risum invitat dictis suis astantes; delectus sed adhibendus rectaque illa ratio consulenda.

14    Erricus[10] Pudericus, grammaticum cum commonefaceret cuperetque illum minus excandescere erga discipulos temperantiusque illos verberare, vocatum illum ad se huiusmodi agressus est dictis, 'Quid hoc, amabo, quod aliorum quidem grammaticorum discipuli suis de institutoribus queri consuevere ferula quod nimis saeviant, te vero ipsum incusant quod nec irasci scias nec scuticula ferire?' Itaque dissimulanter dum loquitur, grammatico ruborem induxit.

15    Mater mea Christiana, de me admodum puero cum esset solicita sciretque me assiduum agere apud grammaticum primasque ferre inter condiscipulos partes nec laudare coram vellet, alibi his adoriebatur, 'Quid, o fili, de te audio, quod hodie superatus e ludo discesseris in themate latinis verbis explicando?'; alibi, 'At ego mellitum tibi edulium paraveram, quod sperarem te victorem literaria e concertatione rediturum: redis victus? Quod igitur tibi paraveram ad eum sum, qui te vicit, missura.' His igitur atque aliis mater gaudium dissimulabat, dum laudare puerum me coram omnino defugit Socraticamque per dissimulationem hortabatur ad perdiscendas literas.

16    Quin etiam prudens haec dissimulantia plurimum secum fert momenti et in laudando et in vituperando. Actius Syncerus,[11] cum

his own, but he even subtracted from what was his own both in speaking and conversing with those close to him.

But this man will not always be self-deprecating and dissimu- 13 lating in responding to any question whatever, whether jokingly or seriously. Neither will the brave man use his fortitude and strength in any and all dangers, nor will he go to seek them out. Neither does the urbane and affable man joke at a funeral and urge the bystanders to laughter with his sayings. One must use discrimination and consult right reason.

Enrico Puderico, when he was admonishing a grammarian, de- 14 siring that the man would stop bursting into anger at his pupils and control himself when beating them, he summoned him and addressed him in these words, "How is it, pray, that the pupils of other grammarians are accustomed to complain of their teachers because they are too savage with the rod, but yours accuse you because you don't know how to get angry or strike them with the little whip?"[48] And so while he spoke with dissimulation, he made the grammarian blush.

Since my mother Cristiana was very anxious about me as a boy, 15 knew that I was diligent at the grammarian's and took the first place among my fellow pupils, and she did not want to praise me openly, she would accost me at one time with these words, "What is this I hear about you, son, that today you left school beaten in developing the Latin theme?" Or at another time: "But I had prepared a honey cake for you because I expected that you would return victorious from the literary contest. You return defeated? Then I'll send what I'd prepared for you to the one who defeated you." So with these words and others my mother would disguise her joy, while she completely avoided praising me as a boy to my face and would urge me to learn my letters thoroughly by her Socratic dissimulation.

And indeed this prudent dissimulation is of great moment in 16 both praising and blaming. When Actius Sincerus wanted to

irridere vellet philosophantium e classe quempiam, quem honoris causa haud nomino, perinde atque admirabundus, dicebat, 'Hic decimo post anno quicquid profecit, primo quidem studiorum die

17 profecit.' Horatius etiam poeta insectandis vitiis atque irridendis ineptiis magnopere est Socraticus.

Quid quod Hannibal eodem irrisionis genere lusit Antiochum regem? Cum enim rex suas illi ostentaret copias et numero peringentes et armis egregie instructas, percontanti satis ne eae adversus Romanos essent, respondit se satis esse arbitrari, tametsi Romani admodum avari essent. Vide, obsecro, quam Socratice

18 ignaviam illius riserit. Eadem arte summis extulit Scipionem laudibus; nam cum esset, ut traditum est memoriae, sermo inter eos de ducum excellentia dixissetque Hannibal primo sibi videri statuendum loco Alexandrum Macedonem, secundo Pyrrhum Epirotam sibique assereret tertium intulissetque Scipio, 'Quid si te non vicissem?,' tum ille, 'Vel me,' respondit, 'omnibus censerem praeferendum.' Itaque per hos quasi cuniculos iterque dissimulatum pervenit ad exquisitam illam ac maxime celebrem laudem.

19 Iulia Augusti filia, Marci Agrippae uxor, hac etiam via paternam a se avertit reprehensionem; nam cum animadvertisset patrem Augustum permoleste tulisse quadam quod in pompa excultiore ornatu luxuque indulgentiore processisset dieque insequenti matronali solum more culta patri se ostendisset ab illoque mirifice esset laudata quod in eam formam ornata incederet, tum illa, ut erat ad dissimulandum instructa, verbis his hesternum luxum deprecata est luxusque increpationem a se avertit inquiens, 'Heri me viri oculis exornavi, hodie patris.'

mock a certain member of the class of philosophizers, whom I do not name for the sake of his honor, he said, just as if full of admiration, "This man has profited as much after ten years as in fact he did on his first day of studies."[49] The poet Horace is also exceedingly Socratic in attacking vices and mocking absurdities. 17

What about Hannibal's ridiculing of King Antiochus with the same kind of mockery? For when the king was showing him his troops, both immense in number and splendidly equipped with arms, and asked whether they would be enough for the Romans, he replied that he thought they'd be enough, even though the Romans were very greedy.[50] Notice, please, how Socratically he mocked the other's faintheartedness. With the same art he exalted 18 Scipio with the highest praise. For when, as tradition has it, they were conversing about the excellence of generals, and Hannibal had said that it seemed to him that Alexander of Macedon must be put in first place and Pyrrhus of Epirus in second, and was claiming the third for himself, Scipio interjected, "What if I hadn't defeated you?" Hannibal replied, "I suppose I'd think I ought to be placed before everyone."[51] And so by these tunnels, as it were, and a concealed passage he reached the citadel of praise he had been seeking.

Also by this means, Julia, the daughter of Augustus and wife of 19 Marcus Agrippa, deflected her father's censure. For when she noticed that her father Augustus took it very ill that in a procession she appeared in luxurious apparel and self-indulgent splendor, on the next day she showed herself to her father adorned only like a married woman; after she had received exceptional praise from him because she appeared appareled in that form, as one well versed in dissimulation, she deprecated the splendor of the day before in these words and deflected the implied rebuke of her splendor, saying, "Yesterday I adorned myself for my husband's eyes; today, for my father's."[52]

20    Multum itaque has ad res sive in laudem spectent sive in accusationem, sive in respondendo sive in iocando, ipsa valet dissimulatio, ratione duce et comite. Petrus Compater, cuius mors senectuti meae ingens nuper vulnus inflixit, vir utique ad omne genus facetiarum maxime appositus, cum praetereuntem conspicaretur abunde locupletem hominem, maxime tamen attenuatum, 'Hic,'

21    inquit, 'multa dando factus est divitior.' Idem cum videret compluribus cum satellitibus incedentem militarem hominem eundemque purpuratum, 'Nimirum hic,' inquit, 'hoc cum ornatu et clientela ad aram proficiscitur a diis veniam impetraturus quaeque per vim rapinamque abstulit templo arisque oblaturus.'

22    Consederat Laudivius compluribus cum literatis Antonianam ad porticum, utque erat ingenii literarumque ostentator oppido quam gloriosus, cum recitasset versus quosdam a se in laudem editos Bartholmaei Rovarellae, sacerdotis cardinalis, 'Quo,' inquit, 'sciatis versiculi hi nostri quantopere Bartholomaeum delectaverint: iis ipse auditis, confestim de manu quidem aureolos quinquaginta mihi dinumeravit.' Aderat ibi homo qui et levitatem eius nosset et Bartholomaei magis strictas atque attenuatas quam parcas erogationes esse. Is itaque ore quam maxime composito, 'Per Petrum,' inquit, 'et Paulum, adiurarim brevi Laudivium Pontificem Maximum futurum, cum in eum sacerdotes, avarissimum genus hominum, tam sint liberales; Macte ingenio, Laudivi, versus quam plurimos et conde et ede: facile hoc scribendi genere pontificatum

23    tibi comparaveris.' Quae potuit esse insinuatior irrisio et inanissimi simul hominis et inertissimi poetae?

Atque haec quidem ironia agnominari irrisoria recte potest; nam nec Socratica prorsus est, cum aut parum aut omnino nihil demat imminuatque et tamen a modestia non recedat; utuntur au

24    tem ea et oratores et poetae non sine urbanitate. Thomas Pontanus per urbem deambulans, interrogatus a viatore an cancellarius

And so dissimulation, with reason as its guide and companion, 20
is very effective in these matters whether they pertain to praise or
blame, whether in responding or joking. When Petrus Compater,
whose death has recently inflicted a huge wound on my old age,
assuredly a man most suited to every kind of witticism, saw an
abundantly wealthy yet particularly thin man pass by, he said,
"This man has become richer by giving much."[53] When this same 21
man saw a military man clad in purple walking with very many
attendants, he said, "Doubtless this man sets out for the altar with
this apparel and his clients to beg pardon from the gods and to
offer to the temple and altars the things he plundered through
force and robbery."

Laudivio had taken a seat with many literary men in the Anto- 22
nian Portico.[54] As he was an utterly conceited showoff of his talent
and learning, after he had recited some verses he had published in
praise of Bartolomeo Roverella, the cardinal priest, he said, "Just
so you may know the great delight these little verses of mine
brought Bartolomeo: when he had heard them, he at once counted
out with his own hand fifty gold coins."[55] A man was present who
knew both Laudivio's vanity and that Bartolomeo's expenditures
were restricted and reduced rather than stingy. And so this man
said with his expression as composed as possible, "By Peter and
Paul, I'd swear that Laudivio will be pope soon, since priests, the
most avaricious class of men, are so liberal toward him. What a
talent, Laudivio! Compose and publish as many verses as you can:
you'll easily obtain the papacy for yourself with this kind of writing." What could have been a more insinuating mockery of a man 23
who was both extremely vain and an extremely bad poet?

And indeed this irony may be rightly termed mocking, for it
certainly is not Socratic, since it hardly or at all takes away and
lessens anything, and yet it does not depart from moderation.
Moreover, both poets and orators use it not without urbanity.
Strolling through the city and asked by a traveler whether he was 24

esset Perusinus, respondit se viatorem esse impudentique interro-
25 gationi eius hac ratione illusit. Tristanus Caraciolus[12], cum irridere
verbosum hominem honeste vellet, conversus ad astantes, 'Homo
hic,' inquit, 'a muto parum abest.'

26 Quid quod haec ipsa dissimulantia maximam quandoque vim
habet laudationis, ut cum ⟨ ⟩ meus ⟨ ⟩[13] in conventu literatissimo-
rum hominum commendare industriam vellet assiduitatemque
adolescentis cuiuspiam in literis, 'Hic,' inquit, 'adolescens a Musis
aversus est adeo ut etiam noctes in choreis absumat ac palestris'?
Contra cum vituperare hominem maxime sordidum vellet, 'Homo
hic,' inquit, 'domi habet nitelarum omnium magistrum sordiumque
censorem.'

27 Uticensis autem Cato licet ipse in explicanda animi sui sententia apertus admodum ac liber esset, tamen, surdaster cum haberetur, saepenumero ac si non audisset, quorundam dictis nihil omnino respondebat. Itaque dissimulandi genus illud Socraticum ut
ad modestiam referendum est, sic hoc ipsum Catonis ad prudentiam sapientissimumque vivendi usum ac rationem. Nec vero pauci
hoc dissimulationis genere non a maledictis modo se tutantur,
dum, tanquam non audissent, illis non respondent, verum etiam a
malefactis, dum, aliter etiam quam dictum est, se se accepisse fingunt.

28 Adolescens quidam vocatus ad testimonium dicendum in causa
furto subreptae lanae, sumpta occasione a luna, quae biduo ante
deliquium passa esset, dissimulavit se audisse de lana, itaque de
luna respondit. Nanque interrogatus a iudicibus de lanae surrep-
tione, sublatis in coelum oculis, 'Per,' inquit, 'coelum ipsum iuro,
iudices, perque dei potentissimum numen, qui omnia nutu suo
temperat, nunquam me dedisse operam astrologiae neque unquam
me audisse qua ratione lunae surreptio fieret,' addidit et iis fatua
quaedam dicta. Quibus versi in risum iudices arbitratique rudioris

chancellor of Perugia, Tommaso Pontano replied that he was a
traveler and in this way mocked the impudent question.[56] When 25
Tristano Caracciolo wanted to mock a verbose man in a respectable way, he turned to the bystanders and said, "This man hardly
differs from a mute."[57]

What about the fact that this dissimulation sometimes has the 26
greatest power of praise, such as when, in an assembly of most
learned men, my ⟨. . .⟩ wished to commend the industry and assiduity in literature of a young man, he said, "This young man is
so averse to the Muses that he consumes even his nights in danc-
ing and wrestling matches"? On the other hand, when he wished
to censure an especially filthy man, he said, "This man has at
home a master of the mouses and a censor of filth."

Moreover, although Cato of Utica was very open and free in 27
revealing his thoughts, nevertheless since he was thought rather
deaf, he often would not reply at all to the witticisms of some
people, as if he had not heard.[58] Therefore, as the Socratic kind of
dissimulating must be counted as modesty, so Cato's must be
counted as prudence, a very wise practice and plan of living. In
fact, not a few men protect themselves with this kind of dissimulation, not only responding to evil remarks as though they hadn't
heard them, but also pretending to have understood evil deeds in
ways that differ from how they were described.

A young man, called to give testimony in a case of stolen wool, 28
took his pretext from the moon, which two days earlier had suffered eclipse, dissimulated having heard about wool [lana], and so
responded about the moon [luna]. For when he was interrogated
by the judges about the theft of the wool, he raised his eyes to the
heavens and said, "I swear by heaven itself, judges, and the most
powerful will of God, who governs everything by his will, that I
have never paid any attention to astrology and have never heard
how theft of the moon occurs [i.e., an eclipse]," and added some
fatuous remarks. The judges burst into laughter at this, thought

illum ingenii esse ac, prosecuti eum cachinnis, abire e conspectu perinde ac fatuum permiserunt. Ille igitur ratione hac a dicendo testimonio liber evasit. Praetor Neapolitanus per urbem summiserat satellites Focillum quendam qui caperent, furti suspectum. Ii percontati de eo cum essent Erricum Pudericum, equitem Neapolitanum, isque illum sciret proxima delituisse in taberna, 'At,' inquit, 'Facellam scitote domum illam quae est ante oculos paulo ante ingressum'— est enim Neapoli Facellarum familia pervetusta et nobilis—; dumque illi monstratam ingrediuntur domum, interim facultas data est Focillo praetoris satellites evadendi. Itaque, dum se fingit Erricus pro Focillo Facellam audisse, fugae illius consuluit.

29

30    Constans etiam fama est divum Franciscum, dum inter homines ageret, lepusculum canes fugitantem, quo salvum faceret, delatum illum metu ad pedes eius cepisse atque intra tunicae sinistram manicam, quae laxior esset, immissum abscondisse; cumque venatores facti obviam percontarentur qua lepus transisset, dextera levam designans, 'Scitote,' respondit, 'viri, hac illum minime transisse.' Igitur vir sanctissimus dissimulatione ea usus est quo a canum dentibus lepusculum liberaret, quem postea eductum e manica abire liberum permisit. Quod etsi fortasse in exemplum fictum est, tamen et similia quandoque accidisse in rebus hominum palam est. Et hae quidem dissimulationes licet facto magis constent quam dicto, tamen a dicto ut male accepto initium ducunt et causam.

31    Omnino autem rerum publicarum moderatores quique populis praesunt ac nationibus animadvertere vel perpendere potius examinatissime quidem debent qua et via et fronte dissimulatione hac utantur, siquidem eorum dicta sententiaeque et altius

he was rather feebleminded, and, sending him on his way with loud laughter, allowed him to leave their presence like a fool. So by this means he escaped from giving testimony, a free man. A Nea- 29 politan judge had secretly dispatched his assistants to seize a certain Focillo, suspected of theft. When they asked Enrico Puderico, a Neapolitan cavalier, about him and he knew that the man was hiding in the next inn, he said, "Know, then, that just a moment ago Facella entered that house right before your eyes."[59] (The family of the Facella is an ancient and noble one in Naples.) While they were entering the house that had been pointed out, in the meantime Focillo was given the opportunity to escape the judge's assistants. And so, while Enrico was pretending to have heard "Facella" instead of "Focillo," he was looking after that man's flight.

There is also a persistent tradition that Saint Francis, while he 30 was with some men, to save a little hare that was fleeing in haste from the dogs and had been driven by fear to his feet, took it up and hid it in the left sleeve (which was rather spacious) of his tunic. When the hunters came up to him and asked which way the hare had passed, indicating his left hand with his right, he replied, "Know, men, that it has not passed through here." So this most holy man used this dissimulation to free the little hare from the teeth of the dogs. Afterward he took it out of his sleeve and allowed it to go free.[60] Although this may perhaps have been invented as an example, nevertheless it is also evident that similar things have occasionally happened in human affairs. And although these dissimulations consist more of action than words, nevertheless they derive their origin and cause from words wrongly comprehended.

Governors of states, however, and those who rule over peoples 31 and nations absolutely must consider or rather ponder most carefully indeed in what way and with what countenance they use this dissimulation, since their sayings and judgments both penetrate

penetrant in animos audientium et latius tum dicta tum responsa significationes extendunt suas aliique atque alii diversis ea modis interpretantur; ut cum Iacobus Caldora cogitabundus inter deambulandum immurmurasset Capuam Roma quidem minorem at Carthagine maiorem fuisse, tum unus ex iis qui aderant suspicatus agitare animo Iacobum Capuae obsidionem, confestim id Campanis significavit, quod haud multo post Iacobi consiliis incommodi plurimum attulisse constat.

32    Quocirca principibus viris rerumque publicarum administratoribus, et ubi et qua via et apud quos Socratica hac utantur dissimulatione, etiam atque etiam considerandum est. Ferdinandus, Alfonsi filius, patre mortuo, interrogatus a familiaribus amicisque an aerarium relictum esset ei a patre abunde amplum, dum illud dissimulanter extenuat, regulos pene omnes optimatesque civitatum regni ad rebellionem invitavit. Pro tempore tamen ac loco ipsa extenuatio non parum adiicit ad auctoritatem existimationemque.

33    Qua quidem arte Federicus Urbinas saepenumero magna cum prudentia utebatur; nam nec raro quidem nec occulto, aliquando etiam in propatulo, hosti se imparem dicebat partisque suas minores profitebatur, quo, verbis iis hosti significatis, imprudentiorem illum minusque cautum redderet. Quo fit ut haec ipsa omnia ratione metienda sint arteque temperanda, quando ratio ea quae a Peripateticis iure quidem recta dicitur actiones in utranque partem nostras definit.

34    Res autem ipsa et docuit et assiduo docet non in voce solum ac verbis, verum etiam in vultu gestuque ironiam locum ac ius suum retinere, ut cum aliud dicimus, aliud innuimus, aliud vultu, aliud manu significamus. Hinc apud Persium, 'O Iane, a tergo quem nulla ciconia pinsit.'[14] Nam et contemptus ac derisiones quaedam gestu magis ac signis fiunt et maxima sunt ex parte ironicae, cum

more deeply into the minds of their listeners and their sayings and responses stretch their meanings, and different people interpret them in diverse ways. For example, when Giacomo Caldora, meditating during a walk, murmured that Capua was smaller than Rome but larger than Carthage, one of those present suspected that Giacomo was considering besieging Capua and immediately signified this to the Campanians, who, as is well-known, not much later brought the greatest troubles to Giacomo's plans.[61]

So princes and administrators of states must continually con-  32
sider when, in what way and with whom to use this Socratic self-deprecation. After his father's death, Ferdinando, the son of Alfonso, was asked by friends and acquaintances whether his father had left him an ample and abundant treasury. By diminishing it with dissimulation, he invited almost all the barons and nobles of the cities in the kingdom to rebel. Nevertheless, when done with due attention to time and place, this diminishing can add no small amount to one's authority and reputation. Federico of Urbino of-  33
ten used this art with great prudence. For neither rarely nor secretly, sometimes even in public, he would say that he was unequal to the enemy and would confess that his resources were fewer in order to render the enemy more imprudent and less cautious, once his words had been made known to them. So it follows that all these things must be measured by reason and tempered by art, since that reason which is justly called "right reason" by the Peripatetics sets bounds to our actions in both directions.

Reality itself, however, has taught and continually teaches that  34
self-deprecation holds its rightful place not only in the voice and words but also in facial expression and gesture, as when we say one thing but nod another, indicate one thing with facial expression, another with the hand. Hence in Persius, "O Janus, whom no stork pounds from behind."[62] For some acts of contempt and derision occur more in gesture and signs and are for the most part

tamen voce laudem videantur afferre. Nam et praetereuntes sive cives sive peregrinos, postquam eos blande familiariterque salutavimus, aut manuum gestu aut oris irridere consuevimus, ut salutatio
35 ipsa omnino fuerit ironica ac ridicularia. Quid quod verba quaedam maxime sunt ad ironiam idonea? Quale est verbum *vale* et *vive* aliaeque salutandi voces; indeque inductum est, ut saepenumero ab eruditissimis etiam scriptoribus ea verba malam dicantur in partem, ut illud Terentianum, 'Valeant / qui inter nos dissidium volunt,' et Tibullianum illud, 'O valeant silvae deficiantque canes!' Item apud Virgilium, 'Vivite, silvae,' et apud Valerium Catullum, 'Cum suis vivat valeatque moechis.' An non servi interdum ac nequam et scelerati homines verbis dictisque foedis ac contaminatis sibi male dicunt invicemque conviciantur ac detrahunt, cum ipsa tamen detractio laudationis in se vim habeat ac speciem congratulationis quasi cuiuspiam?[15]

36 De ironia igitur Socraticaque dissimulatione hactenus.[16] Absoluta est, ut arbitror, de sermone disputatio communique oratione ac familiari praecipueque pars ea qua requies quaeritur relaxatioque a laboribus ac molestiis. E qua quidem explicatione liquido apparet quae vitia sint inter colloquendum fugienda sermonesque domesticos, quae contra mediocritates complectendae.

37 Tu vero . . .[17] sic habeto ad honestas voluptates relaxationesque a curis ac negociis nihil tam conferre quam sermones illi conferunt collocutionesque quae de deo habentur divinisque de rebus, id quod nuper Petrus Compater moriens declaravit; paulo enim antequam animam ageret, multa cum de deo deque animorum disseruisset aeternitate, sic denique ad astantes nos, quos valere iubebat, conversus et tanquam ultimo in actu constitutus, lingua etiam hebescente, dixit omnes quidem sermones inter notos atque ami-

ironic, although they appear to convey praise by the voice. For after we greet passersby, whether citizens or foreigners, flatteringly and familiarly, we are accustomed to mock them by a gesture of the hands or face, so that the greeting is completely ironic and laughable. What about the fact that some words are especially 35 suited to irony? Such is the word *goodbye* and *farewell* and other words of leave-taking. As a result these words are often used by even very learned writers in a bad sense, as in this line from Terence, "May they fare well who want to separate us," and this one from Tibullus, "O, farewell to forests and may the dogs perish!" Likewise in Vergil, "Farewell, forests," and in Valerius Catullus, "Let her live and be well with her adulterers."[63] Do not sometimes servants and worthless and wicked men revile one another with foul and corrupt words and remarks and taunt and disparage each other by turns, although this disparagement has within it the force of praise and the appearance almost of some sort of congratulation?

So this may suffice for Socratic irony and dissimulation. I think 36 that I have completed the discussion of conversation, common and familiar speech, and especially that part of speech wherein rest and relaxation from labors and annoyances are sought. Indeed, from this exposition it appears clearly which vices are to be avoided while talking together and in domestic conversation, and which virtuous means, on the contrary, are to be embraced. But you . . . 37 be assured that nothing contributes to honorable pleasures and relaxations from cares and business as much as those conversations and discussions about God and religion, as Petrus Compater, dying, recently made evident.[64] For a little before he breathed his last, when he had discoursed much about God and the eternity of the soul, finally turning to us bystanders, whom he bade farewell, and stationed, as it were, in the final act, with his tongue growing dull, he said that indeed all conversations among acquaintances

cos esse suavissimos, illos vero multo suaviores quorum materia deus esset. Quocirca nos ipsos exhortatus prius, post etiam per deum ipsum obtestatus rogabat, uti amicitiae memores quoties conveniremus, nostra omnis oratio a deo inciperet desineretque in deo.

FINIS[18]

and friends were very pleasant, but those were much pleasanter of
which God was the subject. So first he exhorted us, then, calling
God himself also to witness, requested us, that, however often we
came together in memory of his friendship, all our speech would
begin with God and end in God.

THE END

# APPENDIX I

## Summonte's Preface

*P. Summontius Suardino Suardo. S.*

Nequa in re non felix Iovianus Pontanus haberetur: contigit illi Suardine Suarde: ut te quoque amicum haberet. Nam (quae tua est ex antiqua nobilitate generositas) mortui famae ita consuluisti: ut maiora inter vivos officia vix optanda videantur. Omitto: quo vivum semper studio colueris: utque illius Uraniam: paulo ante ipsius obitum: una cum Meteoris: Hesperidum hortis: atque Eclogis quam emendatissime Venetiis edendam curaveris. Idem postea: vix audita eius morte: neque precibus: neque adhortationibus: non etiam pecuniae modum ullum fecisti: donec nos ad excudenda hic deinceps reliqua paratos iam: accinctosque videris. Quo fit: ut tibi non parum omnino debituri sint: quicunque absolutam hanc quam primum editionem videbunt. Nam post haec: quae de Sermone: Aristotelico more scripta sunt: postque Historiam belli Neapolitani: quae duo non dum omnino auctore ab ipso elimata: quodque miserabile magis sit: non dum suis omnibus ornata prooemiis: ita ut erant: suasu tuo praemisimus: insequentur statim qui reliqui sunt in Philosophia: de Fortuna: ac de Immanitate libri. Demum vero: ultimo quasi partu: res Astrologicae (quod unum superest) in lucem prodibunt. Vale.

# APPENDIX I

## Summonte's Preface

*Pietro Summonte to Suardino Suardo, greetings.*[1]

Lest Gioviano Pontano be considered unhappy in any respect, he had the good fortune, Suardino Suardo, to have you also as a friend. For, in keeping with the generosity of your ancient nobility, you had such regard for his fame after his death that greater favors among the living scarcely seem to be desired. I pass over that you honored him always with zeal when he was alive and that you, shortly before his death, took care of the publication at Venice, as faultlessly as possible, of his *Urania*, together with the *Meteora*, *Gardens of the Hesperides*, and *Eclogues*.[2] Likewise afterward, shortly after hearing of his death, you set no limit to prayers or exhortations, nor even to money, until you saw that here we were finally ready and prepared to print his remaining works. Thus it happens that whoever sees this publication completed as soon as possible will not be a little in your debt. For after we have sent forth these works by your advice just as they were— *On Speech*, written after the manner of Aristotle, and the *History of the Neapolitan War*, both of which had not been completely polished by the author, and, more lamentably, had not been furnished with all of his prefaces— at once will follow the remaining books in philosophy, *On Fortune* and *On Cruelty*. And finally, the final act of childbirth, as it were, *Astrological Matters* (the only remaining work) will see the light.[3] Farewell.

# APPENDIX II

## Pontano's Coinages

This appendix reproduces, with a few modifications and additions, the table in Bistagne 2005. A small number of the additions come from Tateo's edition (Pontano 2004). For additional information, see the appropriate entry in Ramminger. Of course, some of these coinages may have been used earlier, and Pontano might have thought he was coining some of the words that are attested earlier.

*aculeatio*, 6.1.3

*aequipensator*, 2.6.3

*afflatim*, 2.13.2

*agrestitas*, 3.8.4

*agrestitudo*, 3.8.4

*alliteratio*, 4.3.20

*anaticulus*, 3.17.13 (*anaticula* appears in Plautus and Cicero)

*argumentatiuncula*, 4.3.17

*blaesio*, 6.2.10

*cacomerdilis*, 4.11.27

*campanator*, 5.2.33

*ciathulus*, 2.17.5

*commatercula*, 4.4.5

*concanesco*, 4.3.36

*contentiositas*, 1.18.2, 1.22.3

*craterculus*, 4.3.14

*cucurbitula*, 4.2.2 ("zuchini"; as "cupping glass" the word appears many times in Celsus, and as "colocynth" it appears once in Scribonius Largus)

*cunnulus*, 6.2.32 (see note *ad loc.*)

*decantito*, 2.5.3

*decaudatus*, 6.2.30

*defensitatio*, 6.1.3

*demorsiuncula*, 3.17.14

*despicax*, 4.11.2

*exanclator*, 4.11.10

*excreabundus*, 6.2.40

*exgranulo*, 5.2.30

*facetitas*, 1.12.9–10, 1.13.3, 3.1.3

*facetudo*, 1.12.9–10, *et passim*

*gratiloquentia*, 1.30.3

*herbigenus*, 5.2.52

*hiberoneus*, 3.17.13

*hilariusculus*, 4.1.1

*hirquiculus*, 3.17.6 (Pontano had used the word in *Antonius* [2012b, 258]; see also Santo 1971)

*illepiditas*, 3.2.4

*immanuo*, 5.2.30

*immarcesco*, 1.18.4

*immorsio*, 5.2.20

*inclamator*, 1.25.2

*inexemplificatus*, 5.2.35

*innutus*, 4.10.1

*inodoror*, 4.3.14

*insudatio*, 3.3.1, 5.1.1

*interstrepito*, 1.21.2, 6.2.6

*labellatim*, 4.3.14

*latebricosus*, 2.17.7

*morsiculate*, 3.16.1

*offensito*, 1.19.2

*perbellus*, 5.2.43, 6.2.40

*peringens*, 6.4.17

*perpudendus*, 4.2.7

*perrecto*, 6.2.29 (Pontano had used the word in *Antonius* [2012b, 232])

*prodigenter*, 3.17.3

*promptor*, 6.2.5

*reiaculor*, 4.3.27

*relaxamentum*, 3.4.2

*reliquiosus*, 6.2.44

*revellico*, 6.1.1

*ridicularius* (as adjective), 6.4.34

*rixatio*, 1.18.2, 1.28.11 (Pontano had used the word in *Antonius* [2012b, 260])

*ruptatilis*, 3.12.3

*rupto*, 3.12.2–3

*sciscitabundus*, 3.17.15, 4.3.16

*scuticula*, 6.4.14

*socratice*, 6.4.17

*sterquicomedis*, 4.11.27

*strangulatorius*, 5.2.50

*subcrassesco*, 3.17.2

*subflavesco*, 2.13.2

*subtitillatio*, 3.18.3

*summorsio*, 3.18.2

*ventricosus*, 4.3.9 (Pontano had used the word in *Charon* [2012b, 98])

*vitrum oculare*, 5.2.50

The following words in Bistagne's table are attested earlier than *De sermone*, as are *aculeate* (3.16.1, 3.17.16), *compoto* (4.3.7; also John of Salisbury, *Policraticus* 1.6), *marcescentia* (1.12.4), and *nugatio* (4.11.20; also Dante, *De vulgari eloquentia* 1.18, and frequently as "nonsense" in scholastic philosophy, e.g., William of Ockham, Francis of Marchia), for which she herself provides earlier examples.

*benedicentia*, 2.2.7, 2.13.4 (Panormita, *De dictis et factis Alphonsi regis Aragonum*; see Rammingar)

*demorsio*, 3.18.1 (Alain de Lille, *De planctu naturae*, chaps. 12, 14, 16, and 18)

*denariolus*, 4.3.1 (Benvenuto da Imola, *Comentum super Dantis Aldigherij Comoediam*; see Rammingar)

*faceties*, 1.12.9–10, 3.1.3, 3.8.1 (see note to 1.12.9)

*litigatorius*, 1.18.5 (Aristotle, *Topica*, trans. after Boethius, 8.11, and John of Salisbury, *Metalogicon* 3.10, refer to a "syllogismus litigatorius")

*matutinor*, 5.2.34 (Benvenuto da Imola, *Comentum super Dantis*

# Note on the Text and Translation

**ชริชริ**

The text of *De sermone* in this edition is based on Vienna, Österreichische Nationalbibliothek, Cod. 3413.[1] This manuscript contains several works by Pontano, including *De bello Neapolitano*, the other work that his friend and pupil Pietro Summonte prepared for the first edition of *De sermone*, published by Sigismund Mayr in Naples in 1509.[2] The manuscript also served as copy-text for this first edition, as Summonte's "La tonsa piu grande se bisogna" on a slip inserted before the preface to the first book and a printer's annotations in the manuscript of page breaks in the first edition indicate.[3] Unlike *De bello Neapolitano*, the original layer of which in the Vienna manuscript was a fair copy of one or more earlier drafts,[4] the original layer of *De sermone* appears to be Pontano's first draft. The manuscript shows no signs that Pontano was copying an earlier draft, nothing like the telltale dittography and cancellation noted by Monti Sabia in *De bello Neapolitano*. Pontano extensively revised and added to the Vienna manuscript, and Summonte modified it for publication.[5]

With a significant exception to be mentioned shortly, Summonte made few substantive changes to his master's work. There is one major addition to the manuscript (3.16.3), and on a few occasions he changed or added a phrase (1.29.1, 2.9.3, 2.17.7, 3.22.4, 4.3.11, 4.3.33, 4.11.22, 5.2.title, 6.2.15, 6.2.35, and 6.4.34).[6] But by far his most numerous interventions modify spelling and capitalization, emphasize letters to make them more legible, or indicate that verse quotations are to be displayed. He also regularized the titles at the beginnings of the books and, from 154v, wrote "De Ser." at the top of each verso (he missed the one on 203v) and "LIB." plus the appropriate Roman numeral at the top of each recto.

If Summonte had done no more than this, one might be willing to accept the assertion in the colophon of the *editio princeps*, "fideliter omnia ex archetypis: Pontani ipsius manu scriptis" (everything faithfully from the autograph written in Pontano's own hand) or to admire Summonte's declaration to Angelo Colocci in a letter from 1519, "omnia tentemus

413

antequam ad emendationem veniamus" (let us try everything before we come to emendation; Percopo 1899, 392). But, as Monti Sabia demonstrated in 1987, Summonte also changed the names of people to whom Pontano attributed witticisms a dozen times—including two that he attributed to himself (2.13.5, 4.6.2, 4.6.5 [Summonte], 4.10.3, 4.11.3, 5.2.33, 5.2.60, 6.2.4 [Summonte], 6.4.14, 6.4.16, 6.4.25, and 6.4.26). Moreover, Summonte changed the dedicatee of the first book from Marcantonio Sabellico, who had died a couple of years before the printing of *De sermone*, to the Dominican friar Giacomo da Mantova (1.pr.1, 4).

Consequently, this edition tries to reproduce Pontano's final intentions—as far as I can ascertain them—in the manuscript and relegates Summonte's substantive changes to the critical notes.[7] I have accepted Monti Sabia's restorations of the names changed by Summonte because of her vast experience with Pontano's manuscripts and knowledge of Pontano, although I can verify the restorations in only three places.[8] I have modernized the punctuation and capitalization. The punctuation in the manuscript—reproduced with remarkable fidelity in the first edition—is very heavy, as can be seen from Summonte's dedicatory letter in Appendix I, in which, *exempli gratia*, I have not modified the punctuation. I add dashes to indicate a change of speaker in Pontano's quotations from drama, but otherwise I do not modify his quotations or indicate when they differ, as they often do, from the readings in modern editions. The numbering of chapters and the division into sections are those of Lupi–Risicato.[9]

Spelling is a well-known headache afflicting Pontano's editors because he expressed some decided views on the subject, but his practice was inconsistent. After considerable back and forth, I have decided to reproduce the spelling of the corrected state of the manuscript, which is almost invariably the spelling of the first edition, as well as that of Lupi–Risicato (and therefore of the other editions of the past sixty years).[10] Often it is easy to see that Pontano made the correction, but often it is not. Furthermore, it is sometimes hard to tell whether Summonte's correction is an effort to restore Pontano's preferred spelling or Summonte's own preference. Finally, I doubt that Pontano would have objected to

Summonte's orthographical changes, since I take Pontano at his word when he urges the dedicatees of *De aspiratione*, his friends Marino Tomacelli and Petrus Compater, to emend in accordance with their judgment.[11]

A couple of examples will give an idea of the difficulties involved in trying to establish Pontano's spelling. First, in *De aspiratione* (1481, 32v), he carefully explains why *Panhormus* and its derivatives should be aspirated in Latin, although they are not in Greek, but in the Vienna manuscript four times (1.18.3, 3.17.4, 3.17.15, 5.2.63) he spells the name of his friend and mentor as *Panormita* and twice (6.1.2, 6.4.9) as *Panhormita*. Summonte added an *h* to the first four instances. Second, Pontano's discussion of *Hispania*, *Hispanus*, and related words does not provide firm guidance about the aspiration (23v). All these words, Pontano says, are unaspirated, but some contend that they should be; he approves and has seen the aspirated forms on some very old monuments. The words appear seventeen times in *De sermone*. Three times Pontano provided an initial *h*, and Summonte capitalized it (1.4.2, 2.17.7 [twice]). The other fourteen times someone added *H*, twelve times with a caret (1.25.4, 2.14.1, 3.17.12, 3.17.13 [twice], 3.17.15, 3.17.15 [first instance in cancellation], 3.17.16 [in cancellation], 3.18.1, 3.18.2, 4.10.5, 4.10.13), twice without a caret (1.pr.2, 3.17.15 [second instance in cancellation]). I would be tempted to say that Summonte was responsible for all fourteen of these additions — the *H*'s look very similar to me, and Pontano often does not capitalize adjectives that come from names of places — if it were not for the fact that three of them (3.17.15 [twice], 3.17.16) occur in two passages that Pontano canceled — although it is not impossible that Summonte canceled the second passage. As far as the text of this edition is concerned, there is no problem; the corrected state in the manuscript always has *H*. But it is not clear who made all of the corrections, and it is not clear what Pontano's preferred spelling was when he composed *De sermone*.

This is not a critical edition. I have not collated the five sixteenth-century editions (1509, 1519, 1520, 1538, and 1566) but simply consulted them whenever in doubt about a reading of the Vienna manuscript.[12] I put in the notes to the text the longer cancellations, the variants relating

to the division of *De sermone* into books, and Summonte's substantive revisions. I believe that Pontano himself was responsible for these longer cancellations, but it is hard to be sure when a passage is only lined out and the ink is the same. I have restored to the text one cancellation that I am positive Summonte made (3.22.4). Two cancellations (2.9.3 and 2.14.3) are particularly difficult to attribute because they contain Summonte's habitual change of Pontano's *Virgilius* to *Vergilius*. Consequently, the critical notes usually just say that a passage has been canceled, not who canceled it. I have not noted cancellations of words or short phrases, interlinear additions of words, or changes to the order of words, nor indicated when Pontano added a passage in the margin, at the foot of the page, or on a separate page. Such revisions are very frequent, and the interested reader should consult Lupi–Risicato or the online manuscript.[13] In accordance with the practice of the I Tatti Renaissance Library, consonantal *u* is printed as *v*, and consonantal *j* is printed as *i*, although Pontano wrote *u*, *ej*, and *ij*. Pontano wrote the enclitics *ve* and *ne* as separate words, and I have followed his practice. Finally, since Pontano rarely divides the chapters into paragraphs, some of the paragraphs are very long; for example, 3.17, which contains 2,305 words, and 4.3, which contains 2,831, are each one paragraph. For the sake of readability, I have created several new paragraphs. The twenty-two paragraphs indicated in the manuscript occur at the beginning of 1.25.4; 2.17.9; 3.18.9; 4.11.16, 21, 24, 31; 5.2.9, 10, 19, 21, 28, 35, 39; 6.2.1 (after the first sentence), 35, 38; and 6.4.4, 13, 31, 34, 36.[14]

One note on the translation:[15] Pontano makes many distinctions among types of wit, and his desire to distinguish conflicts with his fondness for *copia*. I have not tried to establish a one-to-one correspondence between his Latin terminology and English, since he is not always consistent in his usage, but I usually err on the side of consistency (see the note on *salsus*, 1.8.3). One particularly troublesome word is the one that Pontano uses the most — *dictum*. Although "witty saying" or "witticism" is often the appropriate translation, Pontano also uses, though not nearly as frequently, *dicterium*, which also means "witty saying." On some occasions Pontano uses *dictum* to mean "remark" or "saying," so the translation gives no indication of how ubiquitous *dictum* is in *De sermone*.

## NOTES

1. I worked from a scan kindly provided by the library and examined the manuscript in person. The whole manuscript is now available online via the website of the Österreichische Nationalbibliothek. The critical edition of Lupi–Risicato (Pontano 1954) is the only one based on a thorough examination of the manuscript. Although it contains several substantive errors, it is very valuable and has a full critical apparatus. Mantovani (Pontano 2002) reproduces their text photographically, and Tateo (Pontano 2004) reproduces it, occasionally modifying the punctuation. Bistagne states, "Le texte que nous donnons est donc celui du manuscrit autographe de Vienne dégagé des interventions renaissantes ou modernes" (Pontano 2008, 70), but she has relied on the Lupi–Risicato apparatus for the readings of the manuscript. On four occasions, for example, Lupi–Risicato omit a word contained in the manuscript — *populari* (1.15.3), *admodum* (2.7.1), *peto* in "auxilium peto" (3.16.2), and *pene* (6.2.8) — and Bistagne omits all four words, too. Her text is unfortunately full of errors, but her annotation, although to be treated with caution, is the fullest available.

2. In addition to publishing almost all of Pontano's works between 1505 and 1512 (Manzi 1971, 33–34, 40–41, 43–44, 47–49, 60–65), Pietro Summonte (1463–1526) was responsible for the first editions of Sannazaro's *Arcadia* (1504) and the poems of Cariteo (Gareth 1508). (One sees the year of Summonte's birth given as 1453, but his will and the inscription on his tomb clearly indicate that he died at the age of sixty-three, in 1526: see Minieri Riccio 1969, 421–22.) His letter to Marcantonio Michiel is a valuable source for contemporary Neapolitan art (Nicolini 1925). Along with Girolamo Carbone, Summonte succeeded Pontano as director of the Accademia Pontaniana. Pontano joked about Summonte's love for Neaera (*Baiae* 1.24, 2.18–19, *Eridanus* 2.15), recorded his love for her in a poem on her death (*De tumulis* 2.33), and made him a speaker in *Actius* and *Aegidius*. Sannazaro praised him for publishing his friends' works posthumously (*Epigrams* 2.9); see Mancinelli 1923. On Summonte's editing of Pontano, see Monti Sabia in Pontano 1970, iv–x; Monti Sabia 1977; Monti Sabia 1985; Monti Sabia 1986; Monti Sabia 1987; Tateo 1964;

Tateo in Pontano 1969, x–xxxvi; Tateo in Pontano 2012c, 66–72; Tateo in Pontano 2013, 25–31; and Furstenberg-Levi 2016, 136–41.

3. *Littera tonsa* is "the upright roman script as differentiated from the cursive" (Bond 1956, 153), and the compositor did leave space for a drop capital for the first letter of the preface to the first book. Bond's study of another manuscript that Summonte prepared as copy-text for Mayr's first edition of *De prudentia* (1508) discusses the kinds of changes that Summonte made to prepare *De sermone* for the press.

4. Monti Sabia 1995, 55.

5. Monti Sabia 1995, 55, believes that Summonte made his editorial interventions in the manuscript of *De bello Neapolitano* after Pontano's death.

6. The frontispiece of Lupi–Risicato is a facsimile of the page containing the major addition.

7. I have accepted two of Summonte's changes into the text. At 4.10.2 *memini* (or something similar) is needed for the grammatical construction; in 1538 someone hit on the same emendation. At 6.4.34 Pontano's *pinxit* (painted) for the *pinsit* (pounds) of Persius' manuscripts and early prints makes little sense.

8. At 4.3.32 Marinus Tomacellus is surely right, but that is because Pontano refers to him at 4.3.34 as recently mentioned. At 5.2.33 I can see the superscript *h* that Summonte regularly adds to Panormita, and at 5.2.60 I can see the C of Compater. Summonte did an excellent job of obliterating the traces, as one can see from the online version of the manuscript; I was not able to make out much more when I examined it in Vienna.

9. Except at 1.25.6, at which "Quamvis . . . adolescentia" is an addition at the foot of the page and should begin a sentence and not be attached to the preceding sentence, as Lupi–Risicato print it. The 1538 and 1566 editions number chapters, except for the untitled 4.1 and 5.1, but do not divide into sections.

10. I violate this policy with two words that Summonte regretted changing when he edited *De fortuna* (Pontano 1512a, above the colophon): *Vergilius* for Pontano's *Virgilius*, and *vicium* for Pontano's *vitium*. The third

word Summonte mentions—*heremita* instead of *eremita*—appears only once in *De sermone* (2.17.2), and Pontano, contrary to his statement in *De aspiratione* (Pontano 1481, 19v) that *eremus* is not aspirated, writes *heremita*, thus depriving Summonte of the opportunity of inserting the initial *h*. Consequently, I print *Virgilius, vitium/vitiosum* (even when Summonte missed them; the words appear some sixty times), and *heremita*.

11. "Et tamen multa tradendis his omissa esse satis scio: non tam negligentia quam rerum occupatione plurimarum. Quamobrem vosipsos coeterosque omnes: qui haec legerint iterum atque iterum rogo: ea ut addere cura sit: et si qua minus probabuntur: illa aut delere aut mutare: In quo uterque vestrum utetur iudicio et amicorum et suo quo liber emendatior prodeat: Nam quamquam detractores ipse fugio: emendatores non fugio." See *De aspiratione*, Pontano 1481, last page (cf. 30v); Germano 2005, 294 (cf. 293).

12. All of the emendations proposed by Lupi–Risicato that I accept had already been made by a sixteenth-century edition except for two (1.pr.4 and 1.10.4).

13. One kind of addition deserves special mention. All of the chapter titles are marginal additions, more often than not with a paragraph symbol in the middle of the line.

14. Pontano indicated a new paragraph after the first sentence of 1.15.8, but I believe he originally intended to begin a new chapter at that point; see the textual note to the chapter heading of 1.16.

15. I have profited from the translations into Italian by Mantovani (Pontano 2002) and Tateo (Pontano 2004) and French by Bistagne (Pontano 2008), as well as the translation (sometimes very free) into English of a few sections in Speroni 1964, 167–77.

# Notes to the Text

꙳ꙮꙭ꙳

BOOK ONE

1. M. ANTONIUM SABELLICUM *Pigman*: ELOQUENTIS-
SIMUM E PRAEDICATORUM ORDINE FRATREM IA-
COBUM MANTUANUM S. *At the top of 151v, S wrote* Ioannis Ioviani Pontani ad eloquentissimum e Praedicatorum ordine Fratrem
Iacobum Mantuanum de Sermone Liber primus. *He repeated these words
all in capitals on a a slip of paper inserted before the preface. At the bottom of the
slip, S added an instruction for the compositor,* La tonsa piu grande se bisogna.
*Below the title on 151v, Coriolano Martirano (1503–57) wrote* Pontani manu
scripta *(Vecce 1998, 20–21). The preface to the first book is in a slightly larger
hand than the rest of the manuscript — about the same size as the final paragraph
of Book 6 — and the line length is longer than usual.*

2. M. Antoni Sabellice *P*: Iacobe Mantuane *S*

3. M. Antoni *P*: Mantuane *S*

4. geri posse *Lupi–Risicato*: et geri et ~~agitari~~ posse *P*: et geri et posse *prs*

5. homines . . . futiles *are the only words on the page (152v), and Pontano left
the rest of it blank.* 153r *is blank except for something at the very bottom of the
page, which reads* Lucaniae non exiguae parti imperitaret ac Brutiae *(see
6.4.6),* de sermone de, *a mark of separation, followed by* Brutia *in plus four or
five words that I cannot make out. The top of 153v has* Ioan: Iovia: Ponta: de
Sermone liber primus *in a hand that I do not recognize, and the bottom,*
prooemium in primo de Sermone libro, *in Summonte's. At the top of the next
page, Summonte wrote and (I believe) partially erased* IOANNIS IO-
VIANI PONTANI DE SERMONE LIBER PRIMUS.

6. bibulaeque *Ovid's MSS, Lupi–Risicato*: bibulaque *P*

7. *All of the chapter titles are marginal additions, more often than not (as here)
with a paragraph symbol in the middle of the line. I suspect that Pontano, when
revising and adding chapter headings, misplaced* De lascivis. His accedit, *which
begins a new paragraph in the manuscript, introduces a different kind of person*

421

*than the* captator, *and* Qua in re *continues the discussion of the* lascivus. *Pontano rarely divides the chapters into paragraphs (see Note on the Text and Translation, 416), and the paragraph at* His accedit *probably records his original intention to begin a new chapter. Besides making a more sensible division, a new chapter at* His accedit *accords with Pontano's practice. A number of chapters begin with some form of* hic *(1.21, 2.9, 2.12, 3.7, 3.10, 3.11, 3.20, 4.2), and several others end with a sentence beginning* Itaque *(1.8, 1.9, 1.14, 1.17, 2.9, 3.18, 4.3, 4.5). But since Pontano clearly marked the chapter beginning before* Qua in re, *I am reluctant to emend the text.*

8. quaerenda *prs:* queraenda P

9. quae *prs:* que P

10. *After* daturum *P's* idque libro insequenti faciemus *was canceled.*

11. minimeque *prs:* minineque P

12. *Above this title in the margin, S wrote and partially erased* LIB. II.

13. popularitas comitatem P, *prs:* S added communitatem *in the margin with a sign that also appears between* popularitas *and* comitatem.

14. de qua . . . disseremus P. *These words appear in the right margin in P's hand, replacing* cum et clarissimi quidam extiterint viri qui medium quasi quendam inter utrumque secuti sint habitum, ex eoque tum dissimulatores dicti tum Graeco nomine ironici. *In the left margin, S writes* LIB. II. *and immediately below,* lib'. 2. *in the hand of P. On a slip of paper inserted between this page and the next:* finis. IOANNIS IOVIANI PONTANI DE SERMONE LIBER SECUNDUS S. *Immediately below, S wrote and canceled* Ioannis Ioviani Pontani DE SERMONE LIBER SECUNDUS.

## BOOK TWO

1. *Above the title in the margin, P wrote and canceled* Lib III.

2. alazonas 1519: alazontas P. *Pontano's* alazontas *is not classical Greek (he appears to have mistakenly assumed that* ἀλαζών *is a present participle and to have made up a corresponding accusative plural), and all the sixteenth-century editions except 1509 print the correct form in Greek,* ἀλαζόνας. *Since Pontano does not write in Greek in his manuscript, I have transliterated the correct form.*

3. *After* demant *P's* In utroque autem genere multus ac maxime sagax fuit Ferdinandus, Alfonsi filius, Neapolitanorum rex *was canceled. At 2.9.3 Pontano mentions Ferdinando's great ability to compose his expression and his speech.*

4. Ferdinandus *P*: Ferdinandus, Alfonsi filii *S*

5. *After* fallendum *P's* Nec ab inexperto Virgilius dixit: Quippe domum timet ambiguam Tyriosque bilingues *(from* Aeneid *1.661) was canceled.*

6. Umber *added by S over an illegible erasure*

7. Marinus Tomacellus, vir ⟨. . .⟩ *P*: A. Colotius Bassus, vir et doctus pariter et iucundus *S; the last five words are written over an illegible erasure* (*Monti Sabia, 302*).

8. grassatus *prs*: crassatus *P*

9. *After* hominum *P's* transiitque iam in proverbium vel imperatorium potius sive praeceptum, sive consilium Virgilianum illud: Dolus an virtus quis in hoste requirat? *(from* Aeneid *2.390) was canceled.*

10. quo occulto foenore ac *P before correction*: qui ~~occulto foenore ac~~ *P after correction. The change from* quo *to* qui *is not completely clear, but Pontano appears to have changed the left and bottom of the "o" and added a dot above the letter to make an "i." Moreover,* qui *preserves the parallelism with the three other kinds of dissimulators (*alios . . . qui, alios qui, illos qui, hos . . . qui*). All of the sixteenth-century editions, as well as the modern ones, print* quo.

11. ut Iudaeorum gentem exterminaret *P*: ut universam Iudaeorum gentem omnino exterminaret *S*

12. alibi expressius *P after cancellation*: insequenti libro *P before cancellation*

13. *After* exemplis *P's* nullaque omnino virtus tot tantasque tam varias admittat excusationes, quantopere admittit eas prudentia quanvis eadem ipsa quidem et intelligentiae ministra sit atque appetitionum magistra et cupidatum tum moderatrix tum etiam actionum directrixque et *was canceled. After a small space and centered:* FINIS. P. *The second half of 184r and all of 184v–85r are blank. At the top of 185v,* IOANNIS IOVIANI PONTANI DE SERMONE LIBER TERTIUS *S; the rest of the page is blank. At the top of 186r,* Liber ~~secundus: Quartus~~ Tertius *P; immediately below,* LIB. III. *S.*

## BOOK THREE

1. primo P *after cancellation*: superiore P *before cancellation*

2. De fatuis, insulsis et inconditis *added by S in margin*: Insulsi fatui, *and, after a gap* Inconditi P *in margin and canceled*

3. De ineptis *added by S in margin*: Inepti P *in margin and canceled*

4. P *added and canceled in margin*: lib .V.

5. *After* impetum S *added* Paulus Marchesius Neapolitanus clari nominis iurisconsultus, cum audiret notum sibi hominem quique brevi patrimonium omne dissipasset ad divortium ab uxore compelli, quod is, ut erat rei venereae inhabilis, post aliquot annos matrimonium non consumasset: 'Mirum,' inquit 'cur matrimonium non consumarit qui patrimonium tam cito consumpserit.'

6. adiice *prs*: addiice P

7. aeque *prs*: aequae P

8. aequissime *prs*: equissime P

9. *After* captivitatis P *added and canceled* Eiusdem Alfonsi frater, Cantabrorum, hoc est Navarrae, rex, Ioannes priorem duxit uxorem, Blancam nomine, ex ea Galliae gente, quae ad duodecim equites refertur quos hodie, corrupto verbo, Paladinos vocant, qui suo nomine a palatio palatini; ex eaque suscepit Carolum, qui postea fuit Navarrae princeps. Ea mortua, duxit mulierem genere Hispanam, quae tamen originem ex matre duceret a Iudaeis, qui ad Christianos transissent, quod hominum genus Marranum [?] Hispani vocant estque apud eos maxime odibile habeturque infame praecipue ob foenerationem. Solenni igitur convivio multi (uti moris est) nuptialibus cum laetarentur in mensis, gratulantesque plurima facete loquerentur in gratiam, tum mulus filius: 'Quid ni,' inquit, 'o proceres, patri meo vel mirifice sit congratulandum felicibus his e nuptiis? cuius prior uxor, mater ipsa quidem mea, genus duxerit a duodecim antiquissimis illis Galliae patribus posterior vero duodecim a tribubus foetidis [?].' Cui dicto (indignanter enim enuntiatum sacrat) tantum insedit veneni, ut ex eo inter patrem ac filium simultates coe-

perint quae, in dies auctae, manifestum haud multos post annos atroxque in bellum prorupere.

10. *After* Pisanello *P's* homine ignobili, illiterato, impudente, vano, vix sui ipsius compote, cuique nullus omnino rerum usus humanarum esset, praeterquam subreptim coacervandae pecuniae *was canceled.*

11. *After* animi *P's* Quod ita esse haud ita multis post mensibus declaratum est. Propter illius enim praecipue perversissimam pariter ac inconsideratissimam administrationem Federicus regno pulsus ac privatus est, hinc Gallis maximo terrestri ac maritimo exercitu, illinc Hispanis irruentibus *was canceled.*

12. cum illi . . . me vero . . . P *(the second ellipsis is P's):* quam ille a cornicibus fabellam sumpsit S. *Apparently, Summonte originally intended to include Pontano's passage (a bit more than six lines in the manuscript), since he darkened several letters to make them more legible, and then decided to cancel it (the lines are in the same ink as Summonte's final words), substituting the remark that Phocion had taken the fable from the crows.*

## BOOK FOUR

1. L. IIII. P: LIB. IIII. S. *On a slip of paper inserted between this page and the next:* finis. IOANNIS IOVIANI PONTANI DE SERMONE LIBER QUARTUS S

2. relationes *P in margin, prs:* recitationes *P in text*

3. consumata *P, 1509, 1519, 1520:* consummata *1538, 1566, Lupi–Risicato, who say,* 'P vero scr. consumata, sed alibi semper consummare.' *But this is the only passage in* De sermone *in which Pontano wrote the word, and, as one can see from the facsimile, which is the frontispiece in Lupi–Risicato, Summonte wrote the word with one* m *twice in his marginal addition to 3.16.3.*

4. Reguli cuiusdam *P over erasure:* Ferdinandi regis *P under erasure and added and canceled in margin*

5. aut bienniis *P:* annis *S*

6. Granius *is my emendation:* Canius *P. Presumably, Pontano slipped because of* Canius *in the preceding example.*

7. Marini Tomacelli, viri *P (Monti Sabia, 303)*: Colotii Bassi, viri *S*

8. magno *P*: honesto *S*

9. de . . . feci *canceled by S, who added* Familiaris noster *before* Marinus

10. Erricus *P (Monti Sabia, 304)*: Franciscus *S*

11. Compater *P (Monti Sabia, 308)*: Summontius *S*

12. quae res *1538, 1566*: qui *P*: quae *Lupi–Risicato*

13. vero memini *S, 1538, 1566*: vero *P*

14. *Summonte erased the words between* quispiam *and* quem *and wrote* nostra in porticu, *filling the rest of the blank with a horizontal line. Monti Sabia, 305, after an unrecoverable word, with some doubt, suggests that Pontano wrote* eiusdem in aures.

15. ferre *P*: ferre Albericus Pudericus Francisci nostri filii *S*

16. *P added and canceled in margin*: lib. vii. *It appears that the* ii *of* vii *was canceled before the two words were canceled; there seems to be a period after* ii *but I am not positive.*

17. Marini Tomacelli *P (Monti Sabia, 303)*: A. Colotii *S*

18. Marinus *P (Monti Sabia, 303)*: Colotius *S*

19. dictorum *P*: doctorum *Tateo. The emendation is attractive, recalling the praise of Boccaccio's stories by learned and unlearned alike (1.10.4), and perhaps more suited to the serious purpose for which stories are invented. But the reading of the manuscript (and all the sixteenth-century imprints) is better suited to the general contrast that Pontano makes between the laughter and approval that witticisms can produce (4.11.15; 5.2.21, 27, 48; 6.1.5).*

20. Sputatilia *P*: Supputatilica *S*

21. Sputa *P*: Supputa *S*

22. tilia *P*: tilica *S*

## BOOK FIVE

1. .V. liber. *P. On a slip of paper inserted between this page and the next*: finis. IOANNIS IOVIANI PONTANI DE SERMONE LIBER QUINTUS *S*

2. Definitio facetudinis *P in margin just below the line containing* definitio virtutis huius, *which appears on the next page of the manuscript*: Definitio virtutis huius: *S in margin at the beginning of the chapter*

3. Panhormita *P (Monti Sabia, 306)*: Galateus, cui praeter summam rerum doctrinam summus etiam ac rarus quidam inest dicendi lepos *S*

4. proterviam *P*: propteruiam *Bistagne*: propter viam *Tateo. Modern editions of Macrobius read* propter viam, *but some early editions have* proterviam *(e.g., 1485, O2r; 1501, L2r).*

5. tentabundus *prs*: tentatubundus *P*

6. Petrus Compater *P (Monti Sabia, 307)*: Franciscus Puccius *S*

7. *P added and canceled in margin*: VI

### BOOK SIX

1. .VI. liber. *P. On a slip of paper inserted between this page and the next*: finis IOANNIS IOVIANI PONTANI DE SERMONE LIBER SEXTUS ET ULTIMUS. *S*

2. Franciscus Putius *P (Monti Sabia, 309, who has some doubt about restoring the name)*: Petrus Summontius *S*

3. hospitandum *1509, 1519, 1520*: hospita / dum *P*: hospita, dum *1538, 1566. A couple of lines later, Pontano added* mulier *in the margin, which suggests that he did not take* hospita *as "hostess." In any event,* dum *would have no verb, and* hospita . . . mulier *is awkward.*

4. facetior *P*: lepidior *S*

5. ~~cunnulum~~ petroselinum *P*

6. relatioque *P*: communicatioque *S*

7. *In the margin near this sentence, P wrote and S canceled* De ironicis. *The MS page ends with this sentence, and the next page begins with a new paragraph, so it would appear that Pontano did intend this sentence to end chapter 2, not to begin chapter 3.*

8. De ironicis *S; see the previous note.*

9. Definitio *added by S, but P had written it (and S canceled it) at the beginning of the next line, the first line of the next page in the manuscript.*

10. Erricus *P (Monti Sabia, 304)*: Franciscus *S*

11. Actius Syncerus *P (Monti Sabia, 306)*: Antonius Panhormita *S*

12. Tristanus Caraciolus *P (Monti Sabia, 306)*: Actius Syncerus *S*

13. ⟨. . .⟩ meus ⟨. . .⟩ *P (Monti Sabia, 307)*: familiaris noster Suardinus Suardus *S. Bistagne reports that Monti Sabia suggested the name* Iohannes Musephilus *in a personal communication.*

14. pinsit *S*: pinxit *P. See p. 418 n. 7.*

15. *After* cuiuspiam *P wrote and canceled* ut apud Plautum. *In the margin he wrote and canceled* est supplendum; *the bottom half of the page is left blank.*

16. *This final paragraph begins on a new page, is in a slightly larger hand than the rest of the manuscript (about the same size as the preface to Book 1), and the line length is shorter than usual.*

17. *P himself inserted dots to hold a place for an addressee.*

18. M°CCCCCII: *P in margin*

# Notes to the Translation

࿕࿖࿕

## ABBREVIATIONS

| | |
|---|---|
| Bistagne | Giovanni Giovano Pontano, *De Sermone: De la conversation*, ed. Florence Bistagne (Paris: Champion, 2008) |
| DBI | *Dizionario Biografico degli Italiani* (Rome: Istituto della Enciclopedia Italiana, 1960–), online at www.treccani.it/biografie |
| Lupi–Risicato | Giovanni Gioviano Pontano, *De sermone libri sex*, ed. S. Lupi and A. Risicato (Lugano: Thesaurus Mundi, 1954) |
| Monti Sabia | Liliana Monti Sabia, "Manipolazioni onomastiche del Summonte in testi pontaniani," in *Rinascimento meridionale e altri studi in onore di Mario Santoro*, ed. Maria Cristina Cafisse (Naples: Società editrice napoletana, 1987), 293–320. (Also in Monti Sabia and Monti 2010, 257–92.) |
| OLD | *Oxford Latin Dictionary* (Oxford: Oxford University Press, 1968–82) |
| P | Giovanni Pontano's hand in Vienna, Österreichische Nationalbibliothek, Cod. 3413 |
| *prs* | All five of the sixteenth-century print editions (*1509, 1519, 1520, 1538, 1566*) |
| Ramminger | Johann Ramminger, *Neulateinische Wortliste. Ein Wörterbuch des Lateinischen von Petrarca bis 1700*, online at www.neulatein.de |
| S | Pietro Summonte's hand in Vienna, Österreichische Nationalbibliothek, Cod. 3413 |
| Tateo | Edition of *De sermone* in *Lorenzo, Poliziano, Sannazaro nonché Poggio e Pontano*, ed. Francesco Tateo (Rome: Istituto poligrafico e Zecca dello Stato, 2004) |

| | |
|---|---|
| 1509 | *Pontani De bello Neapolitano et De sermone* (Naples: Sigismund Mayr, 1509) |
| 1519 | *Ioannis Ioviani Pontani Opera omnia soluta oratione composita*, vol. 2 (Venice: Heirs of Aldus Manutius, 1519) |
| 1520 | *Ioannis Ioviani Pontani Opera omnia soluta oratione composita in sex partes divisa*, pt. 4 (Florence: Heirs of Filippo Giunta, 1520) |
| 1538 | *Ioannis Ioviani Pontani Librorum omnium, quos soluta oratione composuit omnia*, vol. 2 (Basel: Cratander, 1538) |
| 1566 | *Ioannis Ioviani Pontani viri in philosophia, in civilibus et militaribus virtutibus summi Opera*, vol. 2 (Basel: Henricpetri, 1566) |

## BOOK ONE

1. Since Pontano was born on May 7, 1429 (Monti 1962–63), he would have turned seventy-two in 1501. In that summer the French troops of Louis XII and the Spanish troops of Ferdinando II of Aragon were dividing the kingdom of Naples; the French and Spanish fought over the kingdom until Louis abandoned it in 1503. Marcantonio Sabellico (1436–1506) was a Venetian historian; Pontano addressed *Eridanus* 2.31 to him (Pontano 2014, 316–23). See Francesco Tateo, "Coccio, Marcantonio, detto Marcantonio Sabellico," *DBI* 26 (1982). As Sabellico was dead by the time Summonte was preparing *De sermone*, he dedicated this book to the Dominican friar Giacomo da Mantova.

2. A difficult sentence, but *desidem* must be read ironically; Bistagne's translation, "comment mener une vie tranquile," requires *deses* to be understood in an idiosyncratic sense not attested in standard lexica. For Pontano's praise of Socratic irony, which he understands as understatement, a virtuous species of dissimulation, see Book 6.

3. See Introduction, xi.

4. Cf. Sallust, *Catilinae Coniuratio* 1.1.

5. Cf. Aristotle, *Nicomachean Ethics* 1097b11, *Politics* 1253a2–3, and Seneca, *Epistulae morales* 95.52.

6. "Irony" in the sense of mock modesty or self-deprecation; cf. Aristotle, *Nicomachean Ethics* 1108a22–23.

7. Pontano is alluding to Nonius Marcellus' derivation of *vafrum* (cunning) from *valde Afrum* (very African; Maltby 1991, 629).

8. Horace, *Epistles* 1.18.89. Pontano is alluding to four of his books: *De fortitudine* (1490); *De liberalitate, De splendore, De magnificentia, De conviventia, De beneficentia* (1498); *De magnanimitate* and *De prudentia* (1508); and *De fortuna* (1512).

9. Cf. Horace, *Ars poetica* 71–72.

10. Cf. Cicero, *De officiis* 1.110, and Otto 1890, 225.

11. Cicero, *De officiis* 1.114.

12. Tibullus, *Elegies* 2.6.26.

13. Presumably, to judge from the title and the last sentence of this section, the two virtues are urbanity and truth. Pontano appears to be equating urbanity with the pleasant and, a little later, with charm.

14. John 14:6.

15. Donatus associated *facetus* with "making words," and Isidore of Seville derived it from *facio* (Maltby 1991, 219).

16. Since he rejects the (correct) derivation from *for fāri fātum* (to speak), Pontano explains the transformation of the short *a* of *facio* into the long *a* of *fācundus, fācunditas,* and *fācundia* as the result of the poets' doubling of *c* to make the preceding *a* long by position. Pontano repeats much of 1.8.2 in 3.1.2–3.

17. Although "pungent" sounds awkward when applied to a witty person, Pontano makes such extensive use of *salsus* — almost always applying it to piquant, pungent, or sharp speech, not to people — that I have preferred consistency over the occasional awkwardness. In classical Latin, *salsus,* which literally means "salty" (as in "sapores . . . suaves simul et salsi," 1.9.4), is often best translated as "witty"; see the note to 5.2.5.

18. In "De ortu et genitura Leporum" (*De amore coniugali* 2.7.45), Pontano recounts how the wood-nymph Dulcidia, "released from labor" (*levata labore*) by Mercury, named their twins the Charms (Lepores).

19. Terence, *Heauton Timorumenos* 381–82.

20. Plautus, *Cistellaria* 1–7.

21. Macrobius, *Saturnalia* 2.3.8. Pompey had married Caesar's daughter Julia, and Cicero's daughter Tullia had married P. Cornelius Dolabella.

22. Terence, *Eunuchus* 415.

23. Ibid. 426. Aelius Donatus' commentary on this line suggests various obscene explanations for *lepus*. Cf. Otto 1890, 190–91.

24. Plautus, *Amphitruo* 718–19.

25. Terence, *Eunuchus* 214.

26. For the ancient association of *comis* and *como*, see Maltby 1991, 142–43.

27. Vergil, *Aeneid* 8.364–65.

28. Livy, *Ab urbe condita* 23.16.1.

29. Plautus, *Miles gloriosus* 79–80.

30. Ovid, *Metamorphoses* 14.623–33.

31. Ibid. 14.643–45. Pontano has slipped. Instead of "freno," Ovid's manuscripts read "faeno," and "his temples often bound with fresh hay" is clearly superior.

32. Ibid. 14.655–67. Modern editions usually omit the two lines after 657. Albula is an old name for the Tiber.

33. Plautus, *Poenulus* 417–20.

34. The first phrase does not appear in Plautus, but Pontano may be thinking of *Curculio* 577, in which Therapontigonus swears by a number of tonsorial instruments, including a comb. The second term of endearment comes from *Poenulus* 367, and the third from *Asinaria* 694.

35. Julius Capitolinus, *Pertinax* 12.1–2 (*Historiae Augustae Scriptores*).

36. Cicero distinguishes "banter" (*cavillatio*), which can be spread evenly throughout a speech, from "raillery" (*dicacitas*), something sharp and short

(*De oratore* 2.218). Pontano devotes a brief chapter, a close paraphrase in fact, to Cicero's distinction (3.19). Moreover, Cicero distinguishes two other different kinds of witticism (*De oratore* 2.240); cf. also *Orator* 87.

37. See Introduction, xix.

38. *Deducere*, that is, create an etymology, although the word also wittily refers back to the *acies*, or line of battle, as in the expression "lead away (*deducere*) troops."

39. Pontano is mistaken, since *facetiae* is sometimes used to refer to the quality (wit or facetiousness), not just to witty sayings (*OLD* s.v. 2a).

40. Pontano believed he was coining *facetitas, facetudo*, and *faceties*, although the latter does appear in the Vienna scholia to Horace's *Ars poetica* (Zechmeister 1877, at l. 46), and in the *editio princeps* of Petrarch's *Invective contra medicum* (1496, 2b4r), one finds "quæ faceties Nasonis" (instead of the "que facetie Nasonis" of modern editions). Pontano uses *facetudo* much more frequently than the other two combined. *Facetiae* and *facetus*, of course, are common words for wittiness/witticism and witty and appear frequently in Cicero's discussion of wit (Leeman, Pinkster, and Nelson 1981–89, 3:185).

41. Plautus, *Poenulus* 970. *Sorditudo* (for the normal *sordes*, "filth,") appears nowhere else in classical Latin.

42. The only occurrence in classical Latin of *castitudo* (for the normal *castitas*, "chastity") is in Accius, *Tragedies* 585; *maestitudo* (for the normal *maestitia*, "sorrow") appears only in Accius, *Tragedies* 616, and Plautus, *Aulularia* 732.

43. *Maestities* is not attested in classical Latin.

44. Initially, Aristotle calls the virtue that is the mean between obsequiousness (always praising to give pleasure and never opposing) and sullenness or quarrelsomeness (opposing everything and not caring about giving pain) friendship (*Nicomachean Ethics* 1108a26–28), but when he discusses this mean in more detail, he says that it has no name but most resembles friendship (1126b11–20). A bit later (1.22.4) Pontano alludes to the second passage, and, despite declaring in the next sentence that he will not say anything about this virtue, he does discuss the unnamed virtue at length in 1.26–27.

45. Tortelli 1501 provides both of Pontano's derivations of *adulor*: *aula* (fol. 14r) and *doulos* (fol. 25v).

46. Terence, *Eunuchus* 252.

47. Aristotle, *Nicomachean Ethics* 1107b2, 1108a16–17.

48. Although *captator* refers, in a general sense, to anyone who strives for something, the word is used particularly of legacy hunters, the butt of the Roman satirists to whom Pontano alludes in the next section (especially Horace, *Satires* 2.5, and Juvenal, *Satires* 12).

49. Pontano discusses ambition in *De magnanimitate* (1969, 98–104): *ambitio* is the excess; *ambientia* (Pontano's coinage), the mean; and *abiectio* or *demissio*, the deficiency.

50. Livy, *Ab urbe condita* 3.33.7, uses "aurae popularis captator" to describe the decemvir, Appius Claudius, a patrician who disingenuously sought popular favor for reasons of political expediency. Apparently, Pontano thinks legacy hunting and ambition for popular favor so much more blameworthy that *captatio* may properly exclude legal quibbling (*captiuncula*).

51. Pontano continues to insist on the servility of adulators, since *peculium* often refers to the property that a slave is allowed to amass by his master.

52. Juvenal, *Satires* 3.108, a difficult line, which may not refer to farting but to the gurgling of the last drops leaving the cup (Courtney 1980, 171). The ancient scholia and Mancinelli's and Valla's commentaries (Juvenal 1492, fol. xxxvi r–xxxvii r), offer reasons for taking *crepitus* as "fart," as does Braund in Juvenal 1996, 193. One obvious problem with this interpretation is that the cup is farting, not the man. But a problem with the gurgling interpretation is the anticlimax, since the preceding line refers to the adulator's praise of belching well and pissing straight. Pontano is looking for a climactic example of adulation and probably expected his readers to understand the line in the manner of Mancinelli and Valla.

53. Juvenal, *Satires* 4.126–28. One of Domitian's courtiers is flattering the emperor by taking the gigantic turbot as a triumphal omen. Arviragus, not mentioned elsewhere in classical texts, is said by Geoffrey of Mon-

mouth to have been one of Cymbeline's sons. The Britons fought by running out on their chariot poles.

54. Terence, *Andria* 68. Cicero quotes this line while insisting on the incompatibility of obsequiousness with friendship and freedom (*De amicitia* 89.) Cf. Otto 1890, 368.

55. "In this" refers to the behavior of the people described in the preceding paragraph — those who seek only to give pleasure. Apparently, these people are the *lascivi* described in this chapter; see the textual note to the chapter heading of 1.16.

56. Plautus, *Casina* 91–94. One slave is telling his rival for the hand of Casina that he will stick to him like a fly, to use Pontano's metaphor, to prevent his stealing Casina.

57. Presumably, a member of the same Neapolitan noble family as Pontano's friend Marino Brancaccio; see note on 4.3.14.

58. Antonio Beccadelli (1394–1471), called Panormita after Palermo, the city of his birth, was Pontano's mentor, friend, and the founder of the "Antonian Portico" (6.4.22), the humanist academy that, after Panormita's death, was called the Accademia Pontaniana (Furstenberg-Levi 2016). At the beginning of the dialogue *Antonius*, named for the recently deceased Panormita, he is praised for his "delightful companionship" (Pontano 2012b, 1:123). *De tumulis* 1.20 is written in his memory. Panormita collected witticisms of his patron, Alfonso V of Aragon, in *De dictis et factis Alphonsi regis Aragonum*, for which, Pontano tells us, Alfonso gave him one thousand gold ducats (Pontano 1999, 106). Pontano also refers to Panormita at 3.17.4, 3.17.15, 5.2.63–65, 6.1.2, 6.4.9, and 6.4.16. Panormita and Valla, whom Pontano is about to present as an exemplar of the contentious man, became bitter enemies (Beccadelli 2010, xv, xviii–xix). See Gianvito Resta, "Beccadelli, Antonio," in *DBI* 7 (1970).

59. Pontano is following the distinction made by Isidore, *Differentiae* L 328: "Litigiosus est de quo litigatur, quasi ager; litigator qui litigat" (*Litigiosus* is what the lawsuit is about, like a field; *litigator* is the person engaged in the suit). In classical Latin, *litigiosus* is used both for a litigious person and for the subject of the suit, and *litigatorius* is unattested.

60. Lorenzo Valla (1407–57) notoriously compared Quintilian favorably with Cicero in a lost work that may have recently been found (Pagliaroli 2006). When Pontano, discussing Cicero's and Quintilian's definition of *status*, defends Cicero against "the rabid bites of living grammarians" (Pontano 2012b, 1:173), he may be thinking of Valla. After alluding to contemporaries audacious enough to sharpen their teeth on Vergil, Pontano defends Vergil's description of Mt. Etna against Favorinus' unfavorable comparison with a passage in Pindar (Pontano 2012b, 1:173–93). Poggio Bracciolini, another of Valla's many enemies, accused Valla, when lecturing in Rome in 1453, of daily criticizing Vergil for being "an insufficiently careful and polished poet" (parum consideratum poetam ac politum; Bracciolini 1984–87, 3:220). Valla attacks Aristotle extensively in *Repastinatio dialecticae et philosophiae* (2012). For Pontano's criticism of Valla, see Marsh 1979, 111–15, and for his debt to Valla, see Nauta 2011.

61. The first verses of the *Ilias Latina*, 1,070 hexameters now usually attributed to one Baebius Italicus; see Schubert 2001. I do not know on what occasion Valla preferred "Pindar of Thebes" to Vergil.

62. Valla's *De vero bono* (*On the True Good*) tries to combine Epicurean hedonism with Christian morality; in the first version of this dialogue, *De voluptate* (*On Pleasure*), Panormita was one of the interlocutors.

63. In *Antidotum in Pogium* 4 (Valla 1543, 340–41), Valla defends himself against Poggio's accusation that he responded to Panormita's indignation at his criticism of Jerome's translation of the Bible by claiming to have in reserve some "barbs against Christ."

64. Valla composed many of his important works, including *Elegantiae linguae Latinae* and *Disputationes dialecticae*, at Naples under Alfonso's patronage (1435–47).

65. Cf. Cicero, *Tusculanae disputationes* 4.25, on Timon's misanthropy. He is familiar to English readers from Shakespeare's *Timon of Athens*, which draws heavily on Plutarch's life.

66. Cicero, *De officiis* 3.116, refers to "with horses and men" (i.e., cavalry and infantry) as a proverb. Cf. Otto 1890, 126.

67. Horace, *Ars poetica* 322.

68. Pontano takes the etymology from Isidore, *Etymologiae* 10.114: "a graculis avibus qui inportuna loquacitate semper strepunt" (from jackdaws, birds who always make a noise with their importunate loquacity); Isidore's *strepunt* may have inspired Pontano's coinage, *interstrepito*.

69. See note to 1.13.3.

70. The ubiquitous definition of man as "animal rationale mortale" derives from the third chapter of Porphyry's *Introduction* to Aristotle's logical works, which was translated by Boethius.

71. All phrases from Vergil's *Aeneid*: 1.691, etc.; 1.1 ("horrentia" is from the fourth line that Varius is said to have removed from the beginning of the poem [Donatus, *Vita Vergiliana* 42]); 9.136.

72. Vergil, *Aeneid* 3.522–23; Lucan, *Bellum civile* 4.52; Vergil, *Aeneid* 2.276.

73. Statius, *Thebaid* 6.858. Although some manuscripts of Cicero, *Tusculanae disputationes* 1.69, read "maria patentia," I do not find "patentia" modifying "maria" in the Roman poets.

74. Chapters 11 to 14 of *De liberalitate* (1498) are concerned with discrimination and liberality (Pontano 1999, 68–81). See also Cicero, *De officiis* 1.42–52.

75. Instead of the infinitives *afferre* and *velle*, one expects the subjunctives *afferamus* and *velimus* to parallel *ne . . . declinemus*.

76. Martial, *Epigrammata* 1.pr.20.

77. Vergil, *Aeneid* 6.37. The Sibyl of Cumae is telling Aeneas that it is not time to look at Daedalus' murals but to perform a ritual sacrifice.

78. Cicero, *De officiis* 1.144.

79. See note to 1.13.3.

80. Lampridius, *Alexander Severus* 36.2.

81. Livy, *Ab urbe condita* 22.51.4: the retort of Hannibal's cavalry commander, when Hannibal did not take his advice to follow the victory at Cannae in 216 by immediately marching on Rome.

82. Terence, *Heauton Timorumenos* 77.

83. Sallust, *Bellum Iugurthinum* 10.

84. Livy, *Ab urbe condita* 30.14–15. Modern texts of Livy usually spell the name of Hasdrubal's daughter as "Sophoniba," and she is most widely known as "Sophonisba," but Pontano is not alone in calling her "Sophronisba." "Regem . . . honorem" is a scarcely modified quotation from 30.15.11–12, and several of the gifts indicate that Scipio is honoring Masinissa with the insignia of a triumphing general.

85. Plautus, *Bacchides* 408–10.

86. Plautus, *Poenulus* 297–99.

87. This section is heavily indebted to Aristotle, *Nicomachean Ethics* 1126b11–27a6.

88. Cf. Cicero, *De amicitia* 80.8.

89. Horace, *Satires* 1.3.43–45. Both *Strabo* and *Paetus* were cognomina referring to squinting, but *paetus*, owing to its association with Venus, appears to have been used affectionately (cf. Varro, *Menippeae* 344; Ovid, *Ars amatoria* 2.659). *Poetum*, the reading of the manuscript and the sixteenth-century editions, is a variant of *paetum* and need not be emended.

90. Horace, *Ars poetica* 464–66: "While desiring to be considered an immortal god, Empedocles coolly leaped into burning Etna."

91. Antisthenes, a follower of Socrates and sometimes regarded as the first of the Cynics, is said to have had few pupils and to have reproved them harshly (Diogenes Laertius, *Lives of the Philosophers* 6.4), but it is not clear what act Pontano is referring to.

92. Juvenal, *Satires* 4.81–90. Quintus Vibius Crispus was an adviser who managed to survive Domitian, the "destruction and plague."

93. See 1.10.

94. Livy, *Ab urbe condita* 7.33.1–2.

95. Ibid. 8.36.5.

96. Ibid. 9.42.5.

97. See 1.25.5.

98. Livy, *Ab urbe condita* 10.14.10–12.

99. See 1.10.2.

100. Livy, *Ab urbe condita* 23.15.10–14.

101. Ovid, *Metamorphoses* 8.677–78.

102. Plautus, *Curculio* 23–26, 28–30, 31, 35. Pontano omits all of the replies of Phaedromus, the master, as well as a couple of lines of the slave, Palinurus. *Intestabilis*, here translated in its technical sense, which implies debarring from legal processes, can mean "shameful" or "infamous"; it punningly suggests the loss of the testicles.

103. Pontano is referring to the opposition between *optimates* and *populares*, senatorial factions that espoused the interests of patricians and plebeians. The *quod* clause refers to *studium . . . populi*, not to the devotion to the nobility. Pontano might be referring to Appius Claudius, decemvir in 451 BCE, whom Livy describes as a "seeker of popular favor" (aurae popularis captator; *Ab urbe condita* 3.337), and who supported plebeian claims for written laws, or to Appius Claudius Caecus, censor in 312 BCE, who took various measures to allow plebeians a greater role in politics, including making some freedmen senators. Gaius Marius, an equestrian, admitted the poorest plebeians into the Roman army in 107 BCE but sometimes allied himself with the optimates. His lieutenant, Lucius Cornelius Sulla, came from an old patrician family and, as dictator in 81 BCE, increased the powers of the senate.

104. Antonio De Ferrariis (1448?–1527), called "il Galateo" after his birthplace, Galatone, was a physician, a prolific author, and a member of the Accademia Pontaniana from about 1470. Pontano addressed *Baiae* 2.20 to him (Pontano 2006, 136–37). Later in the manuscript of *De sermone* (5.2.33), Summonte attributed to Galateo a joke that Pontano had attributed to Panormita. For Galateo's admiration for Pontano, see his letter to Girolamo Carbone (De Ferrariis 1959, 117–20; cited by Furstenberg-Levi 2016, 44–45). See Angelo Romano, "De Ferrariis, Antonio," *DBI* 33 (1987).

105. *Bucca*, which in classical Latin usually refers to the lower part of the cheeks or to the jaws, sometimes means mouth and displaced *os* in the Romance languages (e.g., Italian *bocca*, French *bouche*, Spanish and Portu-

guese *boca*). Pontano is referring to the practice of ending a banquet with a sweet, or *bonne bouche*.

106. Giovanni Pardo (d. after 1512), from Aragon, was a secretary in the royal chancellery, a speaker in Pontano's dialogues (*Actius, Aegidius*, and *Asinus*) and *De fortuna*, and the dedicatee of *De rebus coelestibus* 3 and *De conviventia*. Three poems in *Baiae* tell a playful story of Pontano's invitation to Pardo to come to that pleasure-loving resort (2.6), Pardo's refusal (2.10bis), and Pontano's celebration of the baths' coaxing Pardo to visit (2.23). Pontano also addressed *Eridanus* 1.31 to him.

BOOK TWO

1. See 1.13.2. Pontano distinguishes between men who tell the truth from time to time and habitually truthful men, men who display truthfulness as a character trait.

2. Aristotle, *Nicomachean Ethics* 1127a24.

3. See 1.13.2.

4. Cicero, *Epistulae ad familiares* 5.12, especially 1 and 3. Cicero brazenly asks Lucius Lucceius to write a separate monograph about his consulship and exposure of the Catilinarian conspiracy, neglecting the laws of history (including truthfulness) if need be.

5. Rufinus, *Apologia* (*contra Hieronymum*) 2.6, quoting Jerome's famous dream of being scourged for being a Ciceronian, not a Christian (*Epistulae* 22.30.) In his dream Jerome was scourged not for writing like Cicero (as Pontano goes on to imply) but for reading gentile authors, which he vows never to do again.

6. Livy, *Ab urbe condita* 28.43.2–4.

7. Lampridius, *Alexander Severus* 56.2.

8. Caesar, *De bello Gallico* 1.40.7–10, 15.

9. In 1486 in Rome, Pontano, as the ambassador of Ferdinando I (Ferrante I) of Naples, negotiated the peace treaty that ended the second conspiracy of the barons, in which Innocent VIII had supported the barons. Pontano negotiated a second treaty in 1492 after Ferdinando broke the first. See Monti Sabia 1998, 18.

10. The fourth book of Pontano's *De obedientia*, first printed in 1490 but composed in 1472 (Tateo in Pontano 2004, 442), contains a chapter "An sit mentiendum Reipublicae gratia" (Pontano 1518–19, vol. 1, fol. 36r–37r).

11. Ovid, *Metamorphoses* 13.5–6.

12. Cicero, *De officiis* 1.150.

13. Plautus, *Poenulus* 472–73, 477–78, 484–86. For the variants in the manuscript of Plautus in Pontano's hand and in Giorgio Merula's *editio princeps* (1472), see Cappelletto 1988, 83–85. Sextus Pompeius Festus, *De verborum significatione* 238.34 M, says that Plautus was born in Sarsina in Umbria; Pontano, of course, was also from Umbria.

14. Although "fable of Aesop" suggests one of the fables, Pontano may be thinking of the stories of Aesop's life, especially his birth as a slave, a tradition that goes back to Herodotus 2.134.

15. In *Epistula ad adolescentes de legendis gentilium libris* 5, Basil says that "all Homer's poetry is an encomium of virtue" (1934, 395). Leonardo Bruni's translation of Basil's letter was probably the most famous patristic work in the fifteenth century (Hankins 2003–4, 1:531).

16. Horace, *Epistles* 1.2.3–4.

17. For similar allegories of the civilizing power of Orpheus and Amphion, see Horace, *Ars poetica* 391–99, and Macrobius, *Commentarii in Somnium Scipionis* 2.3.8.

18. Aristotle, *Nicomachean Ethics* 1127a14–b22.

19. Plautus, *Miles gloriosus* 86–87.

20. Aristotle, *Nicomachean Ethics* 1127b22–31. Pontano returns to irony, self-deprecation, and dissimulation in 6.3–4.

21. Aristotle, *Nicomachean Ethics* 1127b28. Pontano refers to the Spartan dress on two other occasions (2.17.1 and 6.4.3).

22. Sallust, *Catilinae coniuratio* 5.4; Vergil, *Aeneid* 1.209.

23. Although *commissor* and *commissio* do not appear to be attested as "subversive" and "subversion," the context requires some such sense, which is a natural extension of *committo* a couple of sentences earlier ("to set at variance, set against each other," *OLD* 6).

24. Presumably, by "the former," Pontano is referring to the *commissores* — or at least to those who seek power through subversion — since the other *commissores* are hardly seeking "great and glorious things," not to mention the first and third types of ostentatious men. In any event, "prioribus illis" is not as clear as one could wish.

25. Anonymous [ps. Caesar], *Bellum Alexandrinum* 24.3–5.

26. Ibid. 7.2–3, 24.1; Cicero, *Pro Rabirio Postumo* 35.

27. *Fucus* is a red seaweed that was used as a dye and cosmetic, and *fucatus* can refer to something sham or counterfeit. Cicero joins *fucatus* and *simulatus* (*De amicitia* 95) and uses *fucus* and *fucatus* to disparage artificial language and style (see *Brutus* 36, with Douglas' note in Cicero 1966). Pontano's "fucum illinant" recalls Cicero's "fuco inlitus" (*De oratore* 3.199).

28. Cicero, *De officiis* 1.41.

29. Plautus, *Asinaria* 495.

30. Juvenal, *Satires* 2.1–35.

31. Pontano continues a line of criticism against clerical hypocrites laid out by the Florentine humanists Leonardo Bruni (*Oratio in hypocritas*, 1417) and Poggio Bracciolini (*Contra hypocritas*, 1436).

32. Marino Tomacelli (1429–1515), from a noble Neapolitan family, held important positions under Ferdinando and was the dedicatee of Pontano's *De aspiratione* and *Baiae* and a speaker in his dialopgue, *Aegidius* (Monti Sabia, 317 n. 52). *De tumulis* 1.15 was written in his memory. Summonte substituted Angelo Colocci for Tomacelli here, and at 4.3.32 and 4.11.3; Pontano mentions him at 6.2.58. This Gianni was presumably called Gianni Vitello, or Vitelli. Pontano may intend a veiled attack against Giovanni Vitelleschi, a warrior-cardinal under Eugene IV accused of great cruelty and one of the more repulsive clerical hypocrites of the Quattrocento.

33. Cicero, *De officiis* 1.150.

34. Cf. Anonymous [ps. Caesar], *Bellum Africum* 73.1–2.

35. Diogenes Laertius quotes Democritus, "In reality we know nothing, for truth is in the depths" (*Lives of the Philosophers* 9.72.10; cf. Cicero *Aca-*

*demica* 1.44 and *Lucullus* 32.) The well appears in later authors (Lactantius, *Divinae institutiones* 3.28.12; Isidore, *Etymologiae* 8.6.12).

36. Livy, *Ab urbe condita* 1.56.7–8.

37. Arrian, *Alexandri anabasis* 3.3.1–2; Plutarch, *Alexander* 27.5–28.

38. Livy, *Ab urbe condita* 26.19.5–8.

39. Cf. Bracciolini 1983, §158; see note to 6.2.36. Poggio does not name Bernardino of Siena (1380–1444), whom Pontano also mentions, in 5.2.11.

40. Cicero, *De officiis* 1.44.

41. Condemned as a heretic, Girolamo Savonarola was hanged and burned in Florence in the Piazza della Signoria, May 23, 1498.

42. Catullus 22. Suffenus is there presented as an elegant pretender to the art of poetry.

43. Tommaso (Masio) Aquosa (d. 1507) served at the Aragonese court under Alfonso, Ferdinando, and Federico. Pontano mentions him again at 4.6.4 and addresses *Baiae* 1.31 to him.

44. Cf. Beccadelli 1538, 37–38 (2.9).

45. Aristotle, *Nicomachean Ethics* 1127b28. Pontano refers to the Spartan dress on two other occasions (2.7.2 and 6.4.3).

46. On Pontano's references to Saint Francis, see Monti Sabia 2001, especially 417–18 for *De sermone*.

47. Tacitus, *Annals* 16.32.

48. One of the speakers in *Antonius* says that the greatest waste of time was listening to Franciscus Hispanus (Pontano 2012b, 252).

49. Bayle 1740, 2.99–101 (s.v. Cataldus), champions Pontano's version of this story over the genuine apparition of Saint Cataldus, bishop of Taranto, recounted by D'Alessandro 1522 (3.15). The apparition was said to have appeared to a priest in April 1492, the month after Ferdinando II of Aragon (cousin of Ferdinando I of Naples) and Isabella I of Castille issued the edict ordering the expulsion of the Jews from their territories.

50. Aristotle, *Nicomachean Ethics* 1127b31–2, which Pontano also paraphrases at 2.7.4.

51. See 6.3–4.

52. Plutarch, *Solon* 8.1; see note to 2.15.2 for Brutus.

53. By "administrators of wars," Pontano may be thinking of the civil officials in Renaissance Italy who worked with mercenary captains and were given responsibility for the successful management of wars.

### BOOK THREE

1. For wittiness as a mean, see 1.12. Sections 3.1.2–3 repeat most of 1.8.2.

2. Plautus, *Truculentus* 494.

3. See 1.12.10.

4. See 1.20.

5. Chapter 8 of *De liberalitate* is devoted to the classes of miser (Pontano 1999, 54–61).

6. Pontano is thinking of Aristotle, *Nicomachean Ethics* 1108a23–26, in which wittiness (εὐτραπελία) is the mean between the deficiency of rusticity (ἀγροικία) and the excess of buffoonery (βωμολοχία). Aristotle's manuscripts read ἄγριος (wild, savage) instead of ἄγροικος at 1128b2, and some do at 1128a9.

7. Plautus, *Asinaria* 297–98.

8. Ibid. 31, 35. A jocular reference to ox-hide whips.

9. Ibid. 616–17.

10. Ibid. 624.

11. Plautus, *Casina* 909–14. The steward, Olympio, is telling his master's wife, Cleostrata, about his wedding night with Casina (as he thought, but actually with a male slave who had been substituted for her).

12. Ibid. 921–22. The end of line 921 is missing, and editors now supply something like "mulieres," so "by which you are women."

13. Plautus, *Asinaria* 874, which Pontano also quotes later (4.2.7).

14. Aristotle, *On the Parts of Animals* 673a8, says that man is the only animal that laughs. Man as "the laughing animal" appears in late antiquity (e.g., Martianus Capella, *De nuptiis Philologiae et Mercurii* 4.348) and oc-

curs frequently in the Middle Ages and Renaissance. Boethius, *In Porphyrii Isagogen commenta* 1.8, says that neighing is peculiar to horses as laughing is to man.

15. Pontano coins *agrestitas* and *agrestitudo*, uses them interchangeably, and uses them only in this chapter and the next. I have translated both as "agresticity," since I could not bring myself to make up a second word, such as "agresticness."

16. Horace, *Epistles* 1.18.6; Pontano has substituted *rusticitas* for *asperitas* (roughness, rudeness). For Aristotle see note to 3.3.6.

17. Cf. Cicero, *De oratore* 2.17.

18. Horace, *Ars poetica* 270–73.

19. Festus, Porphyrio, and Isidore all derive *obscenus* from *Oscus*; see Maltby 1991, 421.

20. *Parasitatio* is not a transliteration of a Greek word but rather a hapax from Plautus (*Amphitruo* 521). In Greek a συκοφάντης is an informer or a slanderer, but Plautus often uses *sycophanta* to refer to a cheat or swindler.

21. See note to 1.9.4

22. Plautus, *Poenulus* 513, 532.

23. Plautus, *Pseudolus* 102.

24. Ibid. 748. The wordplay is on *scitus* (clever) and *scitum* (ordinance, decree).

25. Plautus, *Bacchides* 943. An *arx* is properly a citadel, not a castle, and the *arca* referred to is a chest for keeping money. One character is spinning an elaborate parallel between the Trojan horse and his plan to fleece someone else.

26. Plautus, *Pseudolus* 1180–81.

27. Plautus, *Cistellaria* 731–32.

28. Plautus, *Amphitruo* 325–26.

29. Plautus, *Cistellaria* 604. That is, his wife's step-daughter.

30. Plautus, *Asinaria* 306.

31. Ibid. 339–40.

32. Plautus, *Epidicus* 229–34. Pontano is following Merula's *editio princeps* of Plautus, which differs considerably from modern texts and includes four words that do not appear in Lewis and Short's *Latin Dictionary* or the OLD: *croculam, subminiam, cunatile, gerrinum* (*gerinium* in Merula). The meaning of the first, second, and fourth of these can be surmised, but I have no idea what *cunatile* is supposed to mean and have translated *cumatile* from the received text. Many of the words are very rare and some obscure to unknown in meaning. In his manuscript of Plautus, Pontano excerpted glosses for several words from Nonius Marcellus (Cappelletto 1988, 145–46).

33. Plautus, *Epidicus* 400–401, 403.

34. Ibid. 584–85.

35. Following Aristotle, Cicero defines *loci* as "quasi sedes, e quibus argumenta promuntur" (sources, as it were, from which arguments are drawn; *Topica* 7). From this point forward, Pontano often uses *locus* in this rhetorical sense: "a class of considerations where an orator looks for suggestions in treating his theme" (*OLD* s.v. 24b); cf. 3.20.10. Despite the occasional awkwardness, I translate *locus* as "place" and *sedes* as "source." For a succinct discussion of the different rhetorical uses of *locus*, see Mankin in Cicero 2011, 331–32.

36. Cicero discusses the places of verbal wit first in the words themselves (*De oratore* 2.248–63) and then in the substance of the thought (2.264–90), and Quintilian, *Institutio oratoria* 6.3.35–56, 57–65, follows this division.

37. Bracciolini 1983, §211, tells this story of Angelotto Fosco, who was created cardinal in 1431 by Pope Eugene IV.

38. Plautus, *Amphitruo* 1031–32. Pontano's quotations from Plautus in this chapter are freer than usual; he omits and changes words and rearranges the order of the lines.

39. Panormita, *De dictis et factis Alphonsi regis Aragonum* 3.7 (Beccadelli 1538, 71), attributes a more concise version of this saying to Alfonso.

40. Alfonso I appointed Niccolò Porcinari regent of the Gran Corte della Vicaria in 1455, and he held other positions as judge (Dragonetti

1847, 276–77). Pontano mentions him as a type of judicial savagery in *De immanitate* 14.1 (Pontano 1970, 28).

41. Cf. Bracciolini 1983, §66.

42. Charles VIII occupied Naples in February 1495. Louis d'Orléans (the future Louis XII) married his cousin, the daughter of Louis XI, Jeanne of France, in 1476. The marriage was annulled twenty-two years later. Louis, eager to marry the widow of Charles VIII, alleged that it had not been consummated. For rumors about Louis' mother, see De Maulde 1888, 99–106.

43. *Anaticulum* (in the feminine) comes from Plautus, *Asinaria* 693, a passage to which Pontano alludes earlier (1.11.1) and also uses elsewhere (see Cappelleto 1988, 76). Cf. also Cicero, *Tusculanae disputationes* 5.42.

44. Pontano appears to be using the name of this ancient Roman province to refer to the lands of the crown of Aragon, which included part of Hispania Citerior—the kingdom of Valencia and the county of Barcelona—as well as the kingdom of Aragon. Elsewhere Pontano says that Ferdinando I of Naples was born in Valencia "in Hispania citeriore" (Pontano 1509, A2v).

45. In his brief life, Ludovico Pontano (1409–39) had a very distinguished legal career at the Roman curia, the Council of Basel, and elsewhere (Woelki 2011). Pontano refers to his relative similarly ("prince of the jurists of his age") in *De principe* (Pontano 2003, 70.)

46. Vito Pisanello accompanied Federico into exile in France in 1501 (Gino Benzoni, "Federico d'Aragona, re di Napoli," *DBI* 45 [1995]). On the names and duties of secretaries at the Aragonese court in Naples, see Vitale 2008.

47. Prospero Colonna (ca. 1460–1523) was a condottiere in the service of both Ferdinando II and Federico I, whom he accompanied to Ischia in 1501 but not into exile in France. See Franca Petrucci, "Colonna, Prospero," *DBI* 27 (1982).

48. In the passage that he canceled, Pontano held Vito's mismanagement responsible for Federico's loss of the kingdom of Naples.

49. The city referred to in this passage and the next is probably Vibo Valentia in Calabria.

50. Plautus, *Mercator* 138–39.

51. Plautus, *Menaechmi* 923–24.

52. Plautus, *Pseudolus* 841–44. Merula's edition and the manuscripts have "demissis manibus" (with its hands hanging down) in the last line, a reference to the swaying hands of a runner; Pontano originally wrote "manibus" and then changed it to "naribus."

53. Plautus, *Bacchides* 1140–41.

54. Plautus, *Pseudolus* 75, 77.

55. Plautus, *Mercator* 303–4.

56. Plautus, *Amphitruo* 309–10.

57. Ibid. 323–24.

58. Ibid. 664–67. Alcmena is pregnant.

59. Cf. Cicero, *De oratore* 2.248.

60. Plautus, *Casina* 852–53.

61. Plautus, *Rudens* 1304–5. Plautus is playing on *medicus* (doctor) and *mendicus* (beggar).

62. Plautus, *Amphitruo* 367–68.

63. Plautus, *Mercator* 606.

64. Plautus, *Menaechmi* 885–87.

65. Plautus, *Bacchides* 537.

66. Plautus, *Rudens* 886–88.

67. Martial was born and grew up in Bilbilis, a Roman *municipium* in Hispania Tarraconensis, today's autonomous community of Aragón, Spain, and, after more than thirty years in Rome, returned there for the last years of his life.

68. Martial, *Epigrammata* 3.12.

69. Ibid. 2.37.

70. Ibid. 2.11.

71. Ibid. 1.89.

72. Ibid. 4.2.

73. Ibid. 1.83.

74. Ibid. 2.50.

75. Ibid. 3.3.

76. Ibid. 3.80.

77. Ibid. 3.9.

78. Ibid. 4.6. A patron and friend of Martial and Statius, L. Arruntius Stella wrote love elegies (poems in the meter of Tibullus).

79. Ibid. 4.12.

80. Ibid. 4.24.

81. Ibid. 4.76.

82. Ibid. 4.87.

83. Ibid. 4.79.

84. Pontano is borrowing a phrase from Pliny's letter on the death of Martial: "qui plurimum in scribendo et salis haberet et fellis" (*Epistulae* 3.21.1).

85. This chapter is a very close paraphrase of Cicero, *De oratore* 2.218–19; see note to 1.12.5. In this passage, the primary speaker in the excursus on wit, C. Julius Caesar Strabo Vopiscus, a distant relation of the dictator, is explaining why there is not a rational system or art of witticism, the very point with which Pontano takes issue in the following chapters. In fact, it is a major contention of the *De sermone* that wit can be taught. Caesar refers to what Marcus Antonius, the grandfather of Mark Antony, has just said about the utility of witticisms. For a witticism of Caesar's, see 4.7.2.

86. Ovid, *Remedia amoris* 10.

87. *Digesta Iustiniani* 47.10: "De iniuriis et famosis libellis."

88. The first edition prints *logice* in Greek to make the contrast with "nostro . . . nomine" clear. Pontano may be recalling Cicero, *De finibus* 1.22, "in altera philosophiae parte, quae est quaerendi ac disserendi, quae λογική dicitur."

89. Cf. Cicero, *De oratore* 2.236: "Locus autem et regio quasi ridiculi."

90. Ibid. 2.248.

91. Ibid. 2.245.

92. Since jokes are the class, and witticisms, jests, and fables its members, the title of this section is a bit misleading, since it suggests that all four are on an equal footing.

93. Menenius Agrippa's notorious fable of the belly (Livy, *Ab urbe condita* 2.32.8–12) is probably most familiar to English readers from Shakespeare's *Coriolanus* 1.1.85–152. Pontano has conflated two stories about Phocion (Plutarch, *Phocion* 9.1–2). When asked to contribute to a public sacrifice, Phocion said he would be ashamed to contribute before he had paid his debt to a moneylender. He told the fable about the coward and the crows on another occasion.

94. "You won't get a taste of" comes from Plutarch (*Phocion* 9.2); Pontano ended the soldier's words with dots.

## BOOK FOUR

1. Cicero, *De finibus* 2.14, states that *iucundus* is derived from *iuvo*, and Isidore, *Etymologiae* 10.125, states that the delightful person (*iocundus*) is always ready for jokes (*iocis*).

2. Cf. Cicero, *De oratore* 2.236, 239; Quintilian, *Institutio oratoria* 6.3.8.

3. Cf. Cicero, *De oratore* 2.218, 240, 254.

4. Pasquasio Diaz Garlon (d. 1499), count of Alife, went to Naples in the retinue of Alfonso I and served the Aragonese kings of Naples in a number of capacities, including as governor of Castel Nuovo. See Felicita De Negri, "Diaz Garlon, Pasquasio," *DBI* 39 (1991).

5. Plautus, *Asinaria* 874, which Pontano quotes earlier (3.5.2).

6. "Laborque ille pertinax, rerum omnium expugnator" alludes to Vergil's famous words, "labor omnia vicit / improbus" (*Georgics* 1.145–46).

7. In *Antonius*, the speakers, in the Antonian Portico, observe and chat with some passersby (Pontano 2012b, e.g., 130); cf. 4.3.36.

8. Plautus, *Trinummus* 851.

9. Terence, *Eunuchus* 236.

10. Plautus, *Pseudolus* 247–48. A pimp has asked the tricky slave who is delaying him, and the slave replies, "The one who [*qui*] has been your salvation." (Pontano not only changes *qui* to *quam* but turns the pimp, *leno*, into a procuress, *lena*). But his manuscript and Merula's *editio princeps* do read "qui est vivus est" (Cappelletto 1988, 85), not "qui sit usust," the modern vulgate. The joke turns on the perfect of *fuit*, which indicates a completed state: someone who has finished living is dead and thus of no use to the pimp. In fact, it is tempting to take Pontano's "a tempore" to refer to verb tense instead of time of life.

11. Plautus, *Menaechmi* 895–97.

12. Cf. Bracciolini 1983, §197; Poliziano 1983, §423; and Castiglione 1894, 199–200 (2.60). The joke depends on the traditional hatred of Florentines for the Sienese and vice versa.

13. For details of the career of the condottiere Antonello Armuzzi Zampeschi da Forlì—who served under various captains, including Niccolò Piccinino, Francesco Sforza, Carlo Gonzaga, Sigismondo Malatesta, and many others, frequently switching sides—see Damiani, http://condottieridiventura.it. Antonello died in 1482.

14. Cf. Poliziano 1983, §276, and Castiglione 1894, 221–22 (2.74).

15. Enrico Puderico (d. between 1472 and 1475) held various posts under the Aragonese kings and was a close friend of Pontano and a member of his academy. Other sayings of Puderico appear at 4.6.2, 6.4.14, and 6.4.29. He is a speaker in *Antonius* and *Actius* and is praised in *De beneficentia* 7; *De tumulis* 1.28 is written in his memory. See Minieri Riccio 1969, 152–56, and Monti Sabia 1987, 318 n. 61. At 4.6.2 and 6.4.14 Summonte changed "Erricus" to "Franciscus," Enrico's son, and he also inserted Francesco's son Alberico at 4.10.3. Francesco is the subject of Pontano's *Eridanus* 2.30, and Summonte dedicated *Actius* to him.

16. In the kingdom of Naples a *mastrodatti* (magister actorum) was the functionary responsible for redacting and preserving legal documents.

17. Pontano praises Marino Brancaccio (d. 1497), a noble Neapolitan who served the Aragonese kings as a soldier for many years, in *De prudentia* 5. A relative is mentioned in 1.18.4, and *Baiae* 1.18 is for the wedding of Marino's son Giovanni. See Roberto Zapperi, "Brancaccio, Marino," *DBI*

13 (1971). On Brancaccio's witticisms in this chapter, see Tateo 2000, 45–47. Pontano's vocabulary in the first Latin sentence is particularly innovative. He uses *invector* in an unattested sense and apparently coined *inodoror, craterculus,* and *labellatim.*

18. Pontano appears to have coined the deponent *inodoror,* although Columella uses *inodoro* twice to mean "to cause to smell," and it is not clear what he means. I have followed Ramminger's "gegenwärtig sein (eig. 'durch seinen Geruch prägen')" but wonder whether Pontano is intensifying *odoror* and is saying that Marino is "scenting out" Ferdinando's table, that is, he seeks a place at it.

19. Charles VIII entered Naples on February 22, 1495, and departed on May 20. Alfonso II, king of Naples (1448–95), was Pontano's pupil and the dedicatee of *De principe.* See Raffaele Mormone, "Alfonso II, re di Napoli," *DBI* 2 (1960).

20. The clever young man is playing with *lanx* (plate, dish) and *lancea* (lance, spear); *lagena* (bottle) seems to have been a Neapolitan word for a type of gun or cannon.

21. Cf. Aristotle, *Topica* 104a34–37.

22. Quintilian, *Institutio oratoria* 7.9.1; cf. 6.3.48; Plautus, *Amphitruo* 327–28. Erasmus includes "Suo iumento sibi malum accersere" in his collection of adages and says that it means "to be the author of one's own misfortunes," but he only cites this line from Plautus (Erasmus 1703–6, 2.48D; cf. Otto 1890, 154). Sosia is obviously taking Mercury's figurative mule literally, whatever the expression means exactly, so Pontano's point about a double significance for one word is clear.

23. Plautus, *Menaechmi* 257.

24. Pontano, *Actius* (1943, 181).

25. Plautus, *Persa* 317–18.

26. Plautus, *Cistellaria* 776–78. On ambiguity of words and joking, cf. Cicero, *De oratore* 2.250–54.

27. Plautus, *Amphitruo* 333–34. On opposite words and joking, cf. Cicero, *De oratore* 2.263.

28. Cicero, *De oratore* 2.280, which reads "Actum fide P. Rutilii." Only the last four words of the last sentence are quoted; the first part is Pontano's paraphrase. In 115 BCE, P. Rutilius Rufus and M. Aemilius Scaurus unsuccessfully prosecuted each other for *ambitus* after Scaurus' election as consul.

29. Ibid. 2.282.

30. Ibid. 2.283.

31. Ibid. 2.277. See Adams 2016, 148–56, for an excellent translation of and commentary on this joke (I have borrowed a phrase from his translation).

32. Cicero, *De orator* 2.284. For other perceived etymological connections between *liber* and *libet*, see Maltby 1991, 337–38.

33. Benet Gareth (ca. 1450–ca. 1514), called Cariteo ("dear to the Graces") in the Accademia Pontaniana, was Catalan by birth and a close friend and colleague of Pontano's. He is a speaker in *Aegidius* and *Asinus*, the dedicatee of *De splendore* 1, the addressee of *Baiae* 1.30, and the subject of *Eridanus* 1.37. Summonte published the first edition of his works (1508). See Angela Asor Rosa, "Gareth, Benet," *DBI* 52 (1999).

34. Cicero, *De oratore* 2.286, which attributes the remark to C. Laelius.

35. See note to 2.13.6.

36. Cf. Cicero, *De oratore* 2.258.

37. Antonello Petrucci preceded Pontano as secretary to Ferdinando and was executed in 1487 for his part in the second conspiracy of the barons. See Erasmus 1703–6, 2.336D, for the proverb, and the note to 3.17.16 for the designations of secretaries.

38. Pontano also uses *attenuatus* (which usually means "feeble" or "destitute") to mean "cheap" in *De liberalitate* 8 (Pontano 1999, 54 and 56). For Decio see note to 4.2.6, and see Erasmus 1703–6, 2.615C–16B, for the proverb.

39. Cf. Cicero, *De oratore* 2.257.

40. Pietro Golino (1431–1501), called Petrus Compater by the Accademia Pontaniana, was one of Pontano's oldest and closest friends, along with

Marino Tomacelli (see note to 2.13.6). They are, in effect, co-dedicatees of Pontano's first printed work, *De aspiratione* (Pontano 1481, last page). Compater held important positions for the Aragonese kings. Pontano dedicated *De tumulis* and the second book of *Commentationes super centum sententiis Ptolemaei* to him, made him a speaker in *Antonius* and *Actius*, paid tribute to their almost sixty-year friendship in *Aegidius* (Pontano 2013, 38), addressed him in *Baiae* 1.9, and mentioned him in other poems. *De tumulis* 2.19 is written in his memory. See also note to 6.4.20.

41. Vergil, *Georgics* 1.15. See note to 4.3.1 for chatting in the Accademia Pontaniana.

42. Vergil, *Georgics* 4.94. See Note on the Text and Translation, 417 n. 2, for Summonte.

43. Quintilian, *Institutio oratoria* 6.3.35.

44. Cf. Cicero, *De oratore* 2.248.

45. Sallust, *Bellum Iugurthinum* 10, the first half of perhaps the most famous political quotation of the Renaissance; the second half is "but great things collapse as a result of discord." Pontano cites this passage earlier (1.25.4), in which *res* has a political meaning, "state." For this *sententia*, see Otto 1890, 89. Francesco Pucci (1463–1512), a pupil of Poliziano, was a lecturer in the Studio at Naples and a member of the Accademia Pontaniana. He is a speaker in *Aegidius* and is the addressee of *Baiae* 2.9. Pontano relates three more of his witticisms (6.2.4–5). See Santoro 1948.

46. Cf. Cicero, *Paradoxa Stoicorum* 6.49, "non intellegunt homines quam magnum vectigal sit parsimonia" (men don't understand how great an income parsimony is), and Otto 1890, 266.

47. Cicero, *De oratore* 2.237; Plautus, *Curculio* 240. Pontano also claims Plautus as a fellow Umbrian at 2.5.2.

48. Pontano is alluding to C. Asinius Pollio's response to the Fescennine verses written against him by Octavian, "At ego taceo; non est enim facile in eum scribere qui potest proscribere" (But I keep quiet. For it isn't easy to write against a person who can proscribe), as reported by Macrobius, *Saturnalia* 2.4.21.

49. Quintilian, *Institutio oratoria* 6.3.7; Pontano alludes to this passage at 4.11.5. He repeats much of 4.4.2 at 5.2.10.

50. Cicero, *De oratore* 2.244.

51. Cf. ibid. 2.240.

52. Ibid. 2.241.

53. Ibid. 2.250.

54. See note to 4.3.12 for Enrico Puderico.

55. Plutarch, *Crassus* 17. As the day was divided into twelve hours of unequal length, the twelfth hour of the day was the last before the twelve hours of night; so Crassus means "at the last minute" or, to use the expression that alludes to Matthew 20:6, "at the eleventh hour." Crassus' Parthian expedition was one of the greatest Roman military disasters; he died at Carrhae in 53 BCE.

56. Pontano also mentions Barnaba Della Marra, a member of an old and powerful family in Barletta, in *De bello Neapolitano* (Pontano 1509, C8r, F8r).

57. See note to 2.16.6 for Masio Aquosa. Presumably, Christians made the sign of the cross while yawning to keep the devil from entering, not leaving, through their mouths. Polydore Vergil ascribes the origin of the custom of making the sign of the cross while yawning to warding off the plague (Vergil 1528, fol. 110v [6.11]).

58. See note to 4.3.36 for Petrus Compater.

59. Macrobius, *Saturnalia* 2.3.10 and 7.3.8. According to Macrobius, Laberius, the author of mimes, is mocking Cicero for his political inconstancy.

60. Cicero, *De oratore* 2.228.

61. Quintilian, *Institutio oratoria* 6.3.75. C. Julius Caesar Strabo Vopiscus, the main speaker on wit in Cicero's *De oratore*, stood for the consulship in 88 BCE and was opposed by P. Sulpicius Rufus. Cf. Macrobius, *Saturnalia* 2.4.7, where the saying is attributed to Augustus.

62. Plautus, *Aulularia* 304.

63. Cf. Cicero, *De oratore* 2.289.

64. Plautus, *Poenulus* 7–8, 41–42.

65. Plautus, *Menaechmi* 653–54.

66. Plautus, *Poenulus* 279. Plautus is punning on *assum* (a form of *adsum*, as Pontano noted in his manuscript of Plautus [Cappelleto 1988, 156]), "I am present" and "roasted."

67. Plautus, *Poenulus* 980–81.

68. Plautus, *Epidicus* 17–18. Plautus is playing with the variegated color of the animals and of a slave's skin after a beating.

69. Girolamo Carbone (ca. 1565–1528) was a Neapolitan patrician, poet, diplomat, and friend of Pontano and, along with Summonte, succeeded him as leader of the Accademia Pontaniana. He is the dedicatee of *De immanitate*, a speaker in *Aegidius*, and the recipient of a dinner invitation in *Eridanus* 1.40; his grief for a lover is the subject of *De tumulis* 2.32. See Renato Pastore, "Carbone, Girolamo," *DBI* 19 (1976).

70. Tristano Caracciolo (ca. 1437–1522), of an ancient Neapolitan family, wrote several biographies and works of moral and political philosophy. See Monti Sabia 1998 for an edition and translation of his biography of Pontano. Caracciolo is a speaker in *Aegidius* and the dedicatee of *De prudentia*. See Frank Rutger Hausmann, "Caracciolo, Tristano," *DBI* 19 (1976).

71. See note to 4.3.36 for Petrus Compater.

72. Cf. Cicero, *De oratore* 2.289, and Quintilian, *Institutio oratoria* 6.3.25.

73. In 1452 the Aragonese occupied Rèncine, a castle some twenty kilometers northwest of Siena held by the Florentines under Cosimo de' Medici, the de facto ruler of Florence from 1434 to 1464.

74. See note to 2.13.6 for Marino Tomacelli.

75. See note to 4.4.2.

76. See note to 4.1.2.

77. The word *ars* can also be translated "craft" or "guild."

78. Cicero, *De oratore* 2.216, 231. Cicero is referring to the interlocutor C. Julius Caesar Strabo Vopiscus, although the next sentence indicates that Pontano thinks he is speaking of the dictator.

79. Courtney 1993, 172 (frag. 12). Cicero refers to his notorious phrase on other occasions (e.g., *In Pisonem* 72.5–73.1, *De officiis* 1.77).

80. Plutarch, *Fabius Maximus* 15.

81. Cf. Jugurtha's famous saying about Rome, "A city for sale and soon to perish if it finds a buyer" (Sallust, *Bellum Iugurthinum* 35.10).

82. Justin, *Epitome* 38.1.8–10, gives an example.

83. Quintilian, *Institutio oratoria* 6.3.59, 63–65, 77, 79, 95, and Macrobius, *Saturnalia* 2.4.1–18, relate a number of Augustus' jokes. See "Dicta et apophthegmata" in Augustus 1962.

84. Cf. Panormita's "Prooemium" (Beccadelli 1538, A3v–4r).

85. Cf. Plutarch, *Comparatio Demosthenis et Ciceronis* 1.4, 6, and Quintilian, *Institutio oratoria* 6.3.2.

86. Cf. Quintilian, *Institutio oratoria* 6.3.19.

87. Ibid. 6.3.21.

88. See 3.22.4.

89. See note to 4.7.1.

90. Juvenal, *Satires* 11.208.

91. Cicero, *Brutus* 260. *Sputatilia* (or *sputatilica*, the reading in modern editions as well as in the only contemporary edition that I consulted [Cicero 1497, E2r]) means "to be spat upon," coined from *sputum* (spittle).

92. After securing the exile of Cosimo de' Medici in 1433, Palla Strozzi (1372–1462) was exiled the following year by Cosimo and lived the rest of his life in Padua. Cf. Poliziano 1983, §139, Niccolò Machiavelli, *Istorie fiorentine* 7.6, and Castiglione 1894, 209–10 (2.65). Poliziano and Machiavelli attribute their version of the first remark to Rinaldo degli Albizzi (1370–1442), an oligarch ally of Strozzi in the anti-Medicean faction.

93. *Faeniculum* means "fennel"; *ferriculus*, "iron bar"; and in *furaculus*, one hears *fur*, "thief."

94. Plautus, *Captivi* 189–90. The joke turns on the salesman puffing his cheap dinner as locally grown, while the prospective buyer points out that cheap vegetable dishes are usually fed only to sick people.

95. Plautus, *Pseudolus* 88–89.

96. Plautus, *Mercator* 673–74.

### BOOK FIVE

1. Cicero, *De oratore* 2.236; see note to 4.1.2.

2. A word-for-word quotation of Quintilian, *Institutio oratoria* 6.3.104, except that Pontano has transposed direct to indirect discourse.

3. See 3.8.1 and p. xxv n. 22.

4. See 3.8.

5. Quintilian, *Institutio oratoria* 6.3.17–18, citing Cicero, *Orator* 90. By *salsum* Pontano usually means "pungent" (e.g., 1.9, 4.6–7; see note to 1.8.3), but Quintilian is using the word to mean "witty," and "Attic salt/wit" usually refers to simplicity and elegance (as Pontano implies a bit later at 5.2.8), so I have left *salsum* in Latin in this passage.

6. Cicero, *Epistulae ad familiares* 2.12.2.

7. Cf. Plutarch, *Marius* 3.1. Various explanations have been given for the cognomen of Cicero's close friend Titus Pomponius Atticus. Cicero, *De finibus* 5.4, implies that Atticus' settling in Athens (85–65 BCE) was responsible for the cognomen.

8. Horace, *Satires* 1.1.27.

9. In 5.2.10 Pontano repeats some of what he says in 4.4.2.

10. Cf. Quintilian, *Institutio oratoria* 6.3.34.

11. Francesco Filelfo (1398–1481) praises Saint Bernardino of Siena (whom Pontano also mentions in 2.16.2) in his *Satires* 2.3.29–30, but some have taken the attack on Hypocritius in *Satires* 2.5 as an attack on Bernardino. The articles in the *DBI* on Bernardino (9 [1967] by Raoul Manselli) and Filelfo (47 [1997] by Paolo Viti) do not mention a conflict between the two.

12. Plutarch, *Demosthenes* 23.2. A fierce opponent of Macedonian domination of the Greek city-states, Demosthenes committed suicide in 322 BCE to avoid capture by Antipater, who controlled Greece after Alexander's death.

13. Quintilian, *Institutio oratoria* 6.3.63.

14. Ibid. 6.3.10.

15. Horace, *Satires* 1.4.34; cf. Otto 1890, 93. The victims of the satirist are complaining that he will spare no one, not even a friend, provided that he can raise a laugh. Commenting on this passage, Porphyrio explains that hay was put on the horns of a bull to warn people to avoid him.

16. Pontano is distinguishing between saying something on one's own and relating something said by someone else; see 6.2.38.

17. Plautus, *Miles gloriosus* 965–66.

18. Macrobius, *Saturnalia* 2.3.7.

19. Ibid. 2.4.17.

20. Cf. Quintilian, *Institutio oratoria* 6.3.23, although he is writing explicitly about joking at trials. By "others" he means opposing advocates, and his third category is "things in the middle" (ex rebus mediis), that is, things that do not directly affect either advocate. Quintilian proceeds to link the *subabsurdum* with ourselves and to note that the word, which Pontano uses in the next sentence, is Ciceronian (*De oratore* 2.274, 289).

21. Plautus, *Casina* 701–3.

22. Gregorio Tifernate (1414–ca. 1464) taught in Naples from 1447 to 1450 (Monti Sabia 1998, 11). He translated Aristotle's *Eudemian Ethics* and other Greek works. Pontano's *De tumulis* 1.34 is his epitaph. See Stefano Pagliaroli, "Gregorio da Città di Castello," *DBI* 59 (2002).

23. The "grano" was a Neapolitan coin, ideally equal to 1/600 of an ounce of gold, first issued under Ferdinando I of Aragon.

24. Macrobius, *Saturnalia* 2.3.3.

25. Ibid. 2.3.4.

26. Presumably a reference to the custom of handicapped beggars in the streets ringing bells.

27. Macrobius, *Saturnalia* 2.3.5.

28. Plautus, *Casina* 1010–11.

29. Macrobius, *Saturnalia* 2.2.4. See the relevant note to the text (n. 4). Pontano's text substitutes *protervia* (act of impudence) for the *propter viam* (one for the road) of modern critical texts.

30. Martial, *Epigrammata* 6.53.

31. Guido Vannucci di Isola Maggiore sul Trasimeno taught in the Studio in Perugia for many years from 1443; Pontano also recalls him in *De rebus coelestibus* 8.8. See Monti Sabia 1998, 9 n. 7. "Omnis homo currit" was a common example in dialectic (e.g., William of Ockham 1990, 86).

32. Tommaso Pontano, Giovanni's uncle, was professor of rhetoric and chancellor of the University of Perugia from 1440 until his death in 1450 (Grendler 2002, 227). See also Woelki 2011, 75–77. Pontano mentions a puppy, Luscula, in one of his lullabies for his son Lucio (1469–98), so the name of his uncle's dog appears to have remained in the family (*De amore coniugali* 2.9.9). Pontano tells two more stories about his uncle (6.1.2, 6.4.24).

33. *Luscus*, of which *lusculus* is the diminutive, means "blind in one eye."

34. Macrobius, *Saturnalia* 2.2.10.

35. Ibid. 2.3.8.

36. Cf. Castiglione 1894, 233 (2.82). Sirach (Ecclesiasticus) 34:1–7 warns against the vanity of dreams, and from the first council of Ancyra (314) the Catholic Church officially prohibited divination by dreams, but this did not stop many Christians from regarding dreams as foretelling the future. See Pigman.

37. The date of birth of Pontano's second daughter, Eugenia, is unknown; she married Loise di Casalnuovo around 1485/89 (Monti Sabia 1997–98, 450–51). *De amore coniugali* 3.4 is an epithalamium for her.

38. Pontano's first daughter, Aurelia, was born in 1462. She married Paolo di Caivano in 1484, and he died in 1492. *De amore coniugali* 3.3 is an epithalamium for her.

39. For Pontano's love for his wife, Adriana, and grief at her death on March 1, 1490, see Monti Sabia 1986, 166–70.

40. Aurelia's daughter, Adriana, married Giovanni Andrea Caracciolo in 1497.

41. See note to 1.30.3 for Giovanni Pardo.

42. Abandoning all hope of defending Naples in 1501, Federico first went with a small fleet to Ischia and then to France, where he renounced all his rights to the kingdom of Naples to Louis XII.

43. Cicero, *De divinatione* 2.133. Cicero quotes the periphrasis for snail (terrigenam, herbigradam, domiportam, sanguine cassam) as an example of obscurity but does not attribute it to anyone. See note to 4.3.30 for Cariteo.

44. Pontano regularly refers to the Accademia Pontaniana as the Porticus (Furstenberg-Levi 2016, 71–72).

45. The "Gauls' Tombs" took its name from the burial of the Gauls after the Romans retook the city about 390 BCE (Varro, *De lingua latina* 5.157) or from the Gauls' burning their soldiers who died there from pestilence (Livy, *Ab urbe condita* 5.48).

46. Ferdinando (Ferrante) Guevara was made count of Belcastro in 1467 by Ferdinano I. Cariteo praises his wit (Gareth 1892, 2.415), and Don Quixote recalls his victory over a "caballero de la casa del duque de Austria" (1.49). See Croce 1917, 36–37.

47. Martial, *Epigrammata* 6.78.

48. Ibid. 7.31. Subura was a crowded district in Rome known for its markets and shops; Martial makes a similar joke about it as his orchard in 10.94.

49. See note to 2.13.6 for Marino Tomacelli. After the death of Alfonso V of Aragon in 1458, Jean d'Anjou tried to regain the kingdom of Naples for the Angevins from Ferdinando I of Naples. Pontano participated in the war, which lasted until 1464, as both a soldier and a diplomat, and wrote *De bello Neapolitano* about it.

50. Jean Jouffroy, bishop of Arras (1453–62), unsuccessfully urged the Angevin claim to Naples before Pius II, who had appointed him cardinal in 1461; see Pius II 2018, 446 (7.13).

51. Macrobius, *Saturnalia* 2.2.9.

52. See note to 4.3.38 for Petrus Compater.

53. Pontano is applying the division of goods into those of the body, those of the soul, and external (e.g., Plato, *Laws* 697b2–6, and Aristotle, *Nicomachean Ethics* 1098b12–14) to the sources of laughter. See also 4.1.2 and 5.2.28 with notes.

54. Federico da Montefeltro (1422–82), Duke of Urbino, lost his right eye in a joust in 1451, after which he was portrayed in profile (as in the famous painting by Piero della Francesca in the Uffizi). Pontano mentions Federico's bearing the loss of his eye with equanimity and joking about it in *De fortitudine* (1518–19, 1.80). Federico served as condottiere for the Aragonese kings on different occasions. He attended the school of Vittorino da Feltre and became famous for his patronage of the arts and his immense library. Pontano dedicated the first book of *Commentationes super centum sententiis Ptolemaei* to him. See Gino Benzoni, "Federico da Montefeltro," *DBI* 45 (1995). One of Federico's first military commands was under the condottiere Niccolò Piccinino (ca. 1380–1444), the son of a butcher. Wounded in the neck by an arrow in 1431, Piccinino suffered nerve damage and limped for the rest of his life. For almost the last twenty years of his life, he fought for Filippo Maria Visconti, duke of Milan.

55. In *De prudentia*, Pontano says that no one weighed matters more thoroughly or was more circumspect than Federico (Pontano 1508, F7r).

56. Pontano accompanied Alfonso in the war waged by a league of Naples, Florence, and Milan against Bartolomeo Colleoni, captain general of the Venetian troops, in Romagna (1467–68); Federico, at that time count of Urbino, was the captain general of the league (Monti Sabia 1996, 353–56).

57. Cf. Quintilian, *Institutio oratoria* 6.3.26, for the preceding sentence and the beginning of this one.

58. Pontano is combining two passages from Quintilian, *Institutio oratoria* 6.3.29 and 42; the second quotes Cicero, *Orator* 87. The manuscripts of Quintilian read "dicacitatem in faciendo"; "iaciendo" was conjectured by Regius (Quintilian 1493, N6r) and is the reading of *Orator* 87, "in iaciundo mittendoque ridiculo."

59. Cf. Quintilian, *Institutio oratoria* 6.3.28, which Pontano also draws on for the last words of 5.3.

60. Pontano's maternal grandmother, Leonarda, helped her daughter raise him; she lived to 110 (*De tumulis* 2.6). She used to admonish the children with a story about a prodigal who, on his way to the gallows, bit off his mother's nose as a warning to other mothers to raise their children well; see *De liberalitate* 10 (Pontano 1999, 68).

61. Pontano is alluding to the cornerstone of Renaissance literary theory, the Horatian pronouncement that the writer who mixes the pleasant and the profitable will obtain the greatest success (*Ars poetica* 343–44).

### BOOK SIX

1. Pontano may be alluding to Julius Caesar's famous advice to avoid the unusual word as if it were a cliff (Aulus Gellius, *Noctes Atticae* 1.10.pr.1).

2. See note to 1.18.4 for Panormita, and 5.2.41 for Tommaso Pontano.

3. See 1.10.4.

4. Francesco Elio Marchese (d. 1517) edited an early edition of Horace (Rome, 1474–75) and was a member of the Accademia Pontaniana. *Baiae* 1.10 rejoices in his return to Naples from Rome, *Eridanus* 2.17 is addressed to him, and *De tumulis* 2.12 is about his tomb. See Concetta Bianca, "Marchese, Francesco Elio," *DBI* 69 (2007).

5. *Funem ducere*, the game of tug-of-war, a proverbial metaphor for a stiff altercation; see Otto 1890, 150.

6. See 4.3.38 for Francesco Pucci.

7. In 1501 Jacopo Sannazaro (ca. 1456–1530), known as Actius Sincerus within the Accademia Pontaniana, accompanied Federico into exile in France, remaining with him until his death. Sannazaro is especially famous for his *Arcadia*, first published by Summonte (Sannazaro 1504), and *De partu virginis* (Sannazaro 2009). Pontano addresses *Baiae* 1.11 to him, and he is the dedicatee of *De rebus coelestibus* 2, *De liberalitate*, and *Coryle*. The dialogue *Actius* is named after him, and he is one of its interlocutors. In 6.4.16 Pontano relates a mocking witticism of Sannazaro.

8. Ovid, *Ars amatoria* 1.349–50.

9. Marino Minerva was president of the Regia Camera della Sommaria in Naples in 1479 (Accattatis 1895, 593, s.v. Pulicastru).

10. Only a handful of poems by Francesco Peto from Fondi (d. after 1531) survive. He is a speaker in *Aegidius* and one of the dedicatees of *Asinus*. See Lorenzo Miletti, "Peto, Francesco," *DBI* 82 (2015).

11. Piero Tamira is a speaker in *Aegidius*; very little is known about him, although a handful of his poems survives. He was a pupil of Pomponio Leto and may have belonged to a noble Roman family, the Tomarozzi (Gualdo Rosa and Osmond). I know nothing about Antonio Cicuro and have not been able to confirm Bistagne's identification of him (Pontano 2008, 295).

12. Much of the humor of the original comes from the clever alliteration on words beginning with *p*.

13. See Summonte's preface to Suardino Suardo of Bergamo (Appendix I).

14. Vergil, *Aeneid* 1.636.

15. Pontano has modified and combined lines from Horace, *Odes*, 1.20.9 and 2.6.6.

16. Pontano wrote a treatise on the art of banqueting, *De conviventia*, included in Pontano 1999.

17. Ippolita Maria Sforza (1445–84), daughter of Francesco Sforza, Duke of Milan, married Alfonso, Duke of Calabria, in 1465. Pontano was her secretary from 1475 to 1482 (Pontano 2012a, 3–69).

18. According to the long-standing stereotype of late-medieval Italian humor, Germans were particularly given to drunkenness.

19. Cf. Plutarch, *Philopoemen* 2.1–2.

20. Plutarch (ibid. 2.4) says that Titus was alluding to Philopoemen's lack of money when talking about his thinness and contains no reply by Philopoemen.

21. Cf. Plutarch, *Themistocles* 18.7 and *Cato the Elder* 8.5.

22. Cf. Plutarch, *Lucullus* 39.4.

23. Cf. ibid. 41.3.

24. Cf. Plutarch, *Cato the Elder* 8.11.

25. Ibid. 24.1–7 clarifies the first part of Cato's response. The son asks his father if he is giving him a stepmother because he is to blame for something.

26. Cf. Quintilian, *Institutio oratoria* 6.3.75. Cicero was more than sixty when he took a second wife, Publilia, who is thought to have been fourteen or fifteen years old at the time of their marriage.

27. Cf. Macrobius, *Saturnalia* 2.5.9.

28. Cf. Plutarch, *Alcibiades* 9.

29. Cf. ibid. 4.5.

30. Cf. Macrobius, *Saturnalia* 2.7.6. It is now accepted that the name of the author of the *Sententiae* is Publilius.

31. Pietro Gonnella (ca. 1390–1441) was a buffoon at the court of Niccolò III d'Este, marquis of Ferrara (1383–1441). Stories about him — or about an earlier buffoon named Gonnella — appear in Sacchetti and Bandello, as well as in Mainardi, Gonnella, and Barlacchia 1565. The story in this chapter appears on 122–23, and the first part of the next story on 123–24.

32. Initially, the language was much cruder in the manuscript; Pontano substituted "petroselinum" for "cunnulum" (little cunt).

33. Approximately thirty-four editions of the *Facetiae* of Poggio Bracciolini (1380–1459) were printed between 1470 and 1500, and some fifty manuscripts survive (Sozzi 2000, 92). Stories similar to ones told by Pontano appear in Poggio at 2.16.2, 3.17.2, 3.17.7, 4.3.9, and 6.2.39; see Bisanti 1998 and Tateo 2006, 34–48.

34. It is not clear to which Pedro of Aragon Pontano is referring, and Queraldo is unknown to me. The story that follows recalls one that Poggio tells about Dante and Cangrande della Scala (Bracciolini 1983, §58).

35. Cf. Diogenes Laertius, *Lives of the Philosophers* 2.75.

36. Angelo Colocci (1474–1549) met Pontano in Rome in 1486, was a member of the Accademia Pontaniana under the name of Bassus, and

established himself in Rome in 1498, serving, among other things, as apostolic secretary (1511–21). See F. Petrucci, "Colocci, Angelo," *DBI* 27 (1982). Colocci compiled an index of *De sermone* and his own collection of *facetiae* (Vecce 2008, 488). This is Pontano's only reference to Colocci. Summonte substituted his name at 2.13.6, 4.3.32, and 4.11.3, and made similar changes in *De fortuna*, including the dedication of the third book to Colocci (Pontano 2012c, 66–67, 166, 266, 268). He dedicated his edition of Pontano's *De magnanimitate* (1508) and *De immanitate* (1512b) to him.

37. Galeazzo Pandone was the third son of Francesco, first count of Venafro (Ammirato 1651, 66). Pontano mentions that he was besieged at the beginning of the war between Ferdinando and Jean d'Anjou (*De bello Neapolitano* [Pontano 1509, A5v]). See note to 5.2.58 for this war.

38. Cf. Aristotle, *Nicomachean Ethics* 1127b25–26, on Socrates as an εἴρων. Cicero, *De oratore* 2.270, says that Socrates surpasses all men in the refinement and charm of his self-deprecation, and Pontano's counting it a virtue may owe something to Cicero's approval of *ironia:* "Genus est perelegans et cum gravitate salsum cumque oratoriis dictionibus tum urbanis sermonibus accommodatum" (2.271). Aristotle views self-deprecation as a vice related to the unnamed virtue that most resembles friendship, although he does approve of moderate self-deprecation that avoids bombast and regards boasting as the worse extreme (1127b22–32). Compare Pontano's earlier discussion of Aristotle on irony, self-deprecation, and dissimulation at 2.7. On irony see Knox 1989.

39. See 2.17 for the kind of dissimulation that is a form of ostentation. Cf. Plato, *Republic* 337a4, and Cicero, *Brutus* 292 and *Lucullus* 15.16–18, for Socratic irony.

40. See 2.7.

41. Aristotle, *Nicomachean Ethics* 1127b28. Pontano cites the example of Spartan dress on two other occasions (2.7.2 and 2.17.1).

42. Giulio Pomponio Leto (1428–98) was the illegitimate son of Giovanni Sanseverino, prince of Salerno. Founder of a circle later known as the Accademia Romana, Leto wrote various works on Latin grammar

and Roman history and edited and commented on several Latin authors, including Donatus and Festus. Leto studied rhetoric at Rome under Valla, with whom Pontano is about to contrast him. See Maria Accame, "Leto, Giulio Pomponio," *DBI* 84 (2015).

43. In 1.18.6 Pontano presents Valla as an exemplar of the contentious man. See the note ad loc.

44. See Valla 2012.

45. Pontano is referring to Albert the Great (ca. 1200–80), the teacher of Aquinas, not to Albert of Saxony (ca. 1320–90), as Mantovani and Tateo unaccountably say. Ludwig Feuerbach repeats this anecdote (1834, 87).

46. See note to 1.18.4 for Panormita, to whose *Hermaphroditus* (1425–26) Pontano is alluding.

47. Francesco Accolti from Arezzo (ca. 1416–88) taught law at Bologna, Ferrara, Siena, and Pisa; was the secretary of Francesco Sforza, duke of Milan; and published commentaries on the *Decretals*, as well as other legal works. See [anon.], "Accolti, Francesco," *DBI* 1 (1960).

48. See note to 4.3.12 for Enrico Puderico.

49. See note to 6.2.7 for Actius Sincerus (Sannazaro).

50. Cf. Aulus Gellius, *Noctes Atticae* 5.5, repeated almost word for word by Macrobius, *Saturnalia* 2.2.2–3.

51. Cf. Plutarch, *Titus Flamininus* 21.4–5, and Livy, *Ab urbe condita* 35.14.5–11.

52. Cf. Macrobius, *Saturnalia* 2.5.5.

53. This passage and 6.4.37 refer to Compater's recent death, November 17, 1501, while 4.3.36 and 4.10.5 give the impression that he is still living. See Monti 1962–63, 240–41, and note to 4.3.36.

54. This Laudivio was apparently a native of Vessano in Liguria and the author of a tragedy about Jacopo Piccinino, *De captivitate ducis Jacobi,* and other works (Tiraboschi 1791, vol. 6, pt. 3, pp. 892–94). The Antonian Portico was the humanist gathering that, after the death of Antonio Panormita, became more commonly known as the Accademia Pontaniana; see also note to 5.2.53.

55. Bartolomeo Roverella (1406–76) was made a cardinal priest by Pius II in 1461 and supported Ferdinando against Jean d'Anjou (see note to 5.2.58).

56. Tommaso Pontano was in fact chancellor of the University of Perugia; see note to 5.2.41.

57. See note to 4.10.4 for Tristano Caracciolo.

58. Cf. Plutarch, *Cato minor* 63.5.

59. See note to 4.3.12 for Enrico Puderico.

60. Thomas of Celano, *Legenda Prima Beati Francisci miracula* 1.21.60, and other early biographers tell a story of a hare caught in a snare that runs to Saint Francis when released, but he does not speak to anyone, just to the hare. So when Pontano goes on in the next sentence to suggest that this example may have been made up, he may be dissimulating his own invention. See note to 2.17.2.

61. Giacomo Caldora (1369–1439) was a condottiere who served both Alfonso V of Aragon and Joanna II of Naples. After the death of Joanna in 1435, he was one of the few great barons in the kingdom of Naples to support René d'Anjou against the Aragonese. He was one of the generals besieging Capua later that year, and his disagreement with his colleague led to his abandoning the siege. See Marina Raffaeli Cammarota, "Caldora, Giacomo," *DBI* 16 (1973).

62. Persius, *Satires* 1.58. The two-faced Janus need not fear backbiting, since he can see before and behind at the same time. The context in Persius makes it clear that the stork's "pounding" is some sort of mocking gesture, and Jerome's imitation of the passage ("ciconiarum deprehendas post te colla curvari"; see *Epistles* 125.18) suggests that it involves bending the stork's neck, but just what gesture Persius had in mind is obscure.

63. Terence, *Andria* 696–97; Tibullus 3.9.6; Vergil, *Eclogue* 8.58; Catullus 11.17.

64. See note to 1.pr.3 for Pontano's ellipsis and 6.4.20 for Compater's death.

## APPENDIX I

1. Pontano praises Suardo, who was from Bergamo, and relates a few of his remarks (6.2.12–13), and Summonte, writing his name over whatever Pontano himself had written, attributed two remarks to him (6.4.26). Pontano wrote *Baiae* 2.37 for Suardo, made him a speaker in *Aegidius*, and dedicated *Asinus* to him.

2. Suardo was the intermediary between Pontano and Aldus Manutius for the publication of Pontano 1505; see Aldus' letter to Suardo, 2a1rv.

3. Summonte's editions of *De fortuna*, *De immanitate*, and *De rebus coelestibus* were all published (separately) by Sigismondo Mayr in Naples, in 1512.

# Bibliography

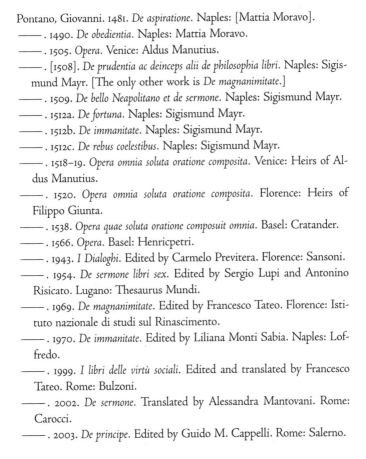

## SELECTED EDITIONS OF PONTANO'S WORKS

Pontano, Giovanni. 1481. *De aspiratione.* Naples: [Mattia Moravo].

——. 1490. *De obedientia.* Naples: Mattia Moravo.

——. 1505. *Opera.* Venice: Aldus Manutius.

——. [1508]. *De prudentia ac deinceps alii de philosophia libri.* Naples: Sigismund Mayr. [The only other work is *De magnanimitate.*]

——. 1509. *De bello Neapolitano et de sermone.* Naples: Sigismund Mayr.

——. 1512a. *De fortuna.* Naples: Sigismund Mayr.

——. 1512b. *De immanitate.* Naples: Sigismund Mayr.

——. 1512c. *De rebus coelestibus.* Naples: Sigismund Mayr.

——. 1518–19. *Opera omnia soluta oratione composita.* Venice: Heirs of Aldus Manutius.

——. 1520. *Opera omnia soluta oratione composita.* Florence: Heirs of Filippo Giunta.

——. 1538. *Opera quae soluta oratione composuit omnia.* Basel: Cratander.

——. 1566. *Opera.* Basel: Henricpetri.

——. 1943. *I Dialoghi.* Edited by Carmelo Previtera. Florence: Sansoni.

——. 1954. *De sermone libri sex.* Edited by Sergio Lupi and Antonino Risicato. Lugano: Thesaurus Mundi.

——. 1969. *De magnanimitate.* Edited by Francesco Tateo. Florence: Istituto nazionale di studi sul Rinascimento.

——. 1970. *De immanitate.* Edited by Liliana Monti Sabia. Naples: Loffredo.

——. 1999. *I libri delle virtù sociali.* Edited and translated by Francesco Tateo. Rome: Bulzoni.

——. 2002. *De sermone.* Translated by Alessandra Mantovani. Rome: Carocci.

——. 2003. *De principe.* Edited by Guido M. Cappelli. Rome: Salerno.

———. 2004. *De Sermone*. In *Lorenzo, Poliziano, Sannazaro nonché Poggio e Pontano*, edited and translated by Francesco Tateo. Rome: Istituto poligrafico e Zecca dello Stato.

———. 2006. *Baiae*. Translated by Rodney G. Dennis. I Tatti Renaissance Library 22. Cambridge, MA: Harvard University Press.

———. 2008. *De Sermone: De la conversation*. Edited and translated by Florence Bistagne. Paris: Champion.

———. 2012a. *Corrispondenza di Giovanni Pontano segretario dei dinasti aragonesi di Napoli: (2 novembre 1474–20 gennaio 1495)*. Edited by Bruno Figliuolo. Battipaglia: Laveglia and Carlone.

———. 2012b. *Dialogues*. Vol. 1. Edited and translated by Julia Haig Gaisser. I Tatti Renaissance Library 53. Cambridge, MA: Harvard University Press.

———. 2012c. *La fortuna*. Edited and translated by Francesco Tateo. Naples: La scuola di Pitagora.

———. 2013. *Aegidius: Dialogo*. Edited by Francesco Tateo. Rome: Roma nel Rinascimento.

———. 2014. *On Married Love. Eridanus*. Translated by Luke Roman. I Tatti Renaissance Library 63. Cambridge, MA: Harvard University Press.

### LITERATURE AND REFERENCE WORKS

Accattatis, Luigi. 1895. *Vocabolario del dialetto Calabrese (Casalino-Apriglianese)*. Castrovillari: Patitucci.

Adams, J. N. 2016. *An Anthology of Informal Latin, 200 BC— AD 900*. Cambridge: Cambridge University Press.

Alfano, Giancarlo. 2000. "La misura e lo scacco: sul *De Sermone* di Gioviano Pontano." *MLN (Modern Language Notes)* 115 (1): 13–33.

Ammirato, Scipione. 1651. *Delle famiglie nobili napoletane. Parte seconda*. Florence: Massi.

Aristotle. 1455–59 and ca. 1473. *Ethica Eudemia, Ethica Nicomachea*, and [ps.-] Aristotle, *Magna moralia*. Translated by Giannozzo Manetti. Vatican City, Biblioteca Apostolica Vaticana, MS Pal. lat. 1021.

———. 1505. *Decem librorum Moralium Aristotelis tres conversiones: Prima*

*Argyropili Byzantii, secunda Leonardi Aretini, tertia vero antiqua.* Paris: Estienne.

——. 1560. *Ethicorum ad Nicomachum libri decem Ioanne Argyropylo interprete . . . et cum Donati Acciaioli Florentini viri doctissimi commentariis.* Paris: de Roigny.

Augustus Caesar. 1962. *Imperatoris Caesaris Augusti Operum fragmenta.* 4th ed. Edited by Enrica Malcovati. Torino: Paravia.

Basil of Caesarea. 1934. *Letters 249–368. On Greek Literature.* Translated by Roy J. Deferrari. Loeb Classical Library 270. Cambridge, MA: Harvard University Press.

Bayle, Pierre. 1740. *Dictionnaire historique et critique.* 5th ed. Amsterdam: Compagnie des Libraires.

Beccadelli, Antonio. 1538. *Antonii Panormitae De dictis et factis Alphonsi regis Aragonum.* Basel: Hervagiana.

——. 2010. *The Hermaphrodite.* Edited and translated by Holt Parker. I Tatti Renaissance Library 42. Cambridge, MA: Harvard University Press.

Bentley, Jerry H. 1987. *Politics and Culture in Renaissance Naples.* Princeton: Princeton University Press.

Bisanti, Armando. 1998. "Le *Facezie* di Poggio nel *De sermone* del Pontano e l'aneddotica dantesca fra Trecento e Quattrocento." *Critica letteraria* 26: 211–40.

Bistagne, Florence. 2000. "Mauvais usages de la parole: flatteurs et querelleurs dans le *De Sermone* de Pontano." *Studi Umanistici Piceni* 20: 196–203.

——. 2005. "Les créations verbales dans le *De Sermone* de Giovanni Pontano." *Studi Umanistici Piceni* 25: 225–29.

——. 2007. "Le *De Sermone* de Giovanni Pontano: est-il un traité de savoir-vivre?" *Silva: Estudios de Humanismo y tradición clásica* 6: 37–59.

Bond, William H. 1956. "A Printer's Manuscript of 1508." *Studies in Bibliography* 8: 147–56.

Botley, Paul. 2004. *Latin Translation in the Renaissance: The Theory and Practice of Leonardo Bruni, Giannozzo Manetti, and Desiderius Erasmus.* Cambridge: Cambridge University Press.

Bracciolini, Poggio. 1983. *Facezie*. Edited and translated by Marcello Ciccuto. Milan: Rizzoli.

———. 1984–87. *Lettere*. Edited by Helene Harth. 3 vols. Florence: Istituto Nazionale di Studi sul Rinascimento.

Cappelletto, Rita. 1988. *La lectura Plauti del Pontano: con edizione delle postille del cod. Vindob. lat. 3168 e osservazioni sull' Itala recensio*. Urbino: QuattroVenti.

Castiglione, Baldassarre. 1894. *Il Cortegiano*. Edited by Vittorio Cian. Florence: Sansoni.

Cicero. 1497. *Tulius [sic] De oratore cum commento et alia opera*. [Nuremberg]: Anton Koberger.

———. 1966. *Brutus*. Edited by A. E. Douglas. Oxford: Clarendon Press.

———. 2011. *De oratore Book III*. Edited by David Mankin. Cambridge: Cambridge University Press.

Croce, Benedetto. 1917. *La Spagna nella vita italiana durante la Rinascenza*. Bari: Laterza.

Courtney, Edward. 1980. *A Commentary on the Satires of Juvenal*. London: Athlone.

———. 1993. *The Fragmentary Latin Poets*. Oxford: Clarendon Press.

D'Alessandro, Alessandro. 1522. *Geniales dies*. Rome: Giacomo Mazzocchi.

Damiani, Roberto. *Note biografiche di capitani di guerra e di condottieri di ventura operanti in Italia nel periodo 1330–1550*. http://condottieridiventura.it.

De Ferrariis, Antonio (Galateo). 1959. *Epistole*. Edited by Antonio Altamura. Lecce: Centro di Studi Salentini.

De Maulde, Robert. 1888. "La mère de Louis XII: Marie de Clèves, duchesse d'Orléans." *Revue historique* 13: 81–112.

Dragonetti, Alfonso. 1847. *Le vite degli illustri Aquilani*. Aquila: Perchiazzi.

Erasmus, Desiderius. 1703–6. *Adagia*. In *Opera Omnia*. Leiden: van der Aa.

Ferroni, Giulio. 1980. "La teoria classicistica della facezia da Pontano a Castiglione." *Sigma* 13: 69–96.

Feuerbach, Ludwig. 1834. *Abälard und Heloise oder der Schriftsteller und der Mensch: Eine Reihe humoristisch-philosophischer Aphorismen.* Ansbach: Brügel.

Floriani, Piero. 1976. *Bembo e Castiglione: Studi sul classicismo del Cinquecento.* Rome: Bulzoni.

Furstenberg-Levi, Shulamit. 2016. *The Accademia Pontaniana: A Model of a Humanist Network.* Leiden: Brill.

Gareth, Benedetto. 1508. *Tutte le opere volgari di Chariteo.* Naples: Sigismund Mayr.

——. 1892. *Le rime di Benedetto Gareth detto il Chariteo.* Edited by Erasmo Percopo. Naples: Accademia delle Scienze.

Germano, Giuseppe. 2005. *Il De aspiratione di Giovanni Pontano e la cultura del suo tempo.* Naples: Loffredo.

Grendler, Paul F. 2002. *The Universities of the Italian Renaissance.* Baltimore: Johns Hopkins.

Gualdo Rosa, Lucia, and Patricia Osmond. "Piero Tamira." *Repertorium Pomponianum.* www.repertoriumpomponianum.it/pomponiani/tamira _piero.htm.

Hankins, James. 2003–4. *Humanism and Platonism in the Italian Renaissance.* 2 vols. Rome: Storia e letteratura.

Juvenal. 1492. *Iuvenalis cum tribus commentariis.* Venice: Giovanni Tacuino.

——. 1996. *Satires: Book I.* Edited by Susanna Morton Braund. Cambridge: Cambridge University Press.

Kidwell, Carol. 1991. *Pontano: Poet and Prime Minister.* London: Duckworth.

Knox, Dilwyn. 1989. *Ironia: Medieval and Renaissance Ideas on Irony.* Leiden: Brill.

Leeman, Anton D., Harm Pinkster, and Hein L. W. Nelson. 1981–89. *M. Tullius Cicero: De oratore libri III: Kommentar.* Heidelberg: Winter.

Luck, Georg. 1958. "Vir Facetus: A Renaissance Ideal." *Studies in Philology* 5 (2): 107–21.

Lupi, Sergio. 1955. "Il *De sermone* di Gioviano Pontano." *Filologia Romanza* 2: 366–417.

Macrobius. 1485. *In Somnium Scipionis expositio et Saturnalia*. Brescia: Bonino Bonini.

———. 1501. *De Somno Scipionis nec non De saturnalibus libri*. Brescia: Angelo Britannico.

Mainardi, Arlotto, Pietro Gonnella, and Domenico Barlacchia. 1565. *Facezie, motti, buffonerie, et burle*. Florence: Giunti.

Maltby, Robert. 1991. *A Lexicon of Ancient Latin Etymologies*. Leeds: Francis Cairns.

Mancinelli, Nicola. 1923. *Pietro Summonte, umanista napoletano*. Rome: Camera dei deputati di C. Colombo.

Manzi, Pietro. 1971. *La tipografia napoletana nel '500: Annali di Sigismondo Mayr — Giovanni A. De Caneto — Antonio De Frizis — Giovanni Pasquet de Sallo (1503–1535)*. Florence: Olschki.

Marsh, David. 1979. "Grammar, Method, and Polemic in Lorenzo Valla's *Elegantiae*." *Rinascimento*, n.s. 19: 91–116.

Minieri Riccio, Camillo. 1969. *Biografie degli Accademici Alfonsini, detti poi Pontaniani, dal 1442 al 1543*. Naples, 1880–81. Reprint, Bologna: Forni.

Monti, Salvatore. 1962–63. "Il problema dell'anno di nascita di Giovanni Gioviano Pontano." *Atti dell'Accademia Pontaniana*, n.s. 12: 225–52. In Monti Sabia and Monti 2010, 1:33–72.

Monti Sabia, Liliana. 1977. "Pietro Summonte e l'*editio princeps* delle opere del Pontano." In *L'Umanesimo Umbro: Atti del IX Convegno di Studi Umbri, Gubbio, 22–23 Settembre 1974*, 451–73. Perugia: Facoltà di lettere e filosofia dell'Università degli studi di Perugia. In Monti Sabia and Monti 2010, 1:215–36.

———. 1980. "L'estremo autografo di Giovanni Pontano: Una lettera a Luigi XII di Francia," *Italia Medievale e Umanistica* 23: 293–314. In Monti Sabia and Monti 2010, 1:139–64.

———. 1985. "Per l'edizione critica del *De prudentia* di Giovanni Pontano." In *Tradizione classica e letteratura umanistica. Per Alessandro Perosa*, edited by Roberto Cardini, Eugenio Garin, Lucia Cesarini Martinelli, and Giovanni Pascucci, 595–615. Rome: Bulzoni. In Monti Sabia and Monti 2010, 2:1073–94.

——. 1986. "Una lettera inedita di Giovanni Pontano ad Eleonora d'Este." *Italia Medievale e Umanistica* 29: 165–82. In Monti Sabia and Monti 2010, 1:173–94.

——. 1987. "Manipolazioni onomastiche del Summonte in testi pontaniani." In *Rinascimento meridionale e altri studi in onore di Mario Santoro*, edited by Maria Cristina Cafisse, 293–320. Naples: Società editrice napoletana. In Monti Sabia and Monti 2010, 1:257–92.

——. 1995. *Pontano e la storia: Dal* De bello Neapolitano *all'*Actius. Rome: Bulzoni.

——. 1996. "Tra realtà e poesia: per una nuova cronologia di alcuni carmi del *De amore coniugali* di Giovanni Pontano (I 5–8)." In *Classicità, Medioevo e Umanesimo: Studi in onore di Salvatore Monti*, edited by Giuseppe Germano, 2:351–70. 2 volumes. Naples: Università degli studi di Napoli, Dipartimento di filologia classica. In Monti Sabia and Monti 2010, 1:477–98.

——. 1997–98. "Vicende belliche e sentimenti del *De amore coniugali* di Giovanni Pontano: Per la cronologia dei libri II e III." *Rendiconti dell'Accademia di archeologia, lettere e belle arti di Napoli* 67: 437–54. In Monti Sabia and Monti 2010, 1:499–518.

——. 1998. *Un profilo moderno e due* Vitae *antiche di Giovanni Pontano.* Naples: Accademia Pontaniana.

——. 2001. "San Francesco nelle opere del Giovanni Pontano." *Pan: Studi dell'Istituto di filologia latina dell'Università di Palermo* 18–19: 409–20. In Monti Sabia and Monti 2010, 2:1215–30.

Monti Sabia, Liliana, Debora D'Alessandro, and Antonietta Iacono. 1998. "Alfonso il Magnanimo nel ricordo di Giovanni Pontano." *Atti dell'Accademia Pontaniana*, n.s. 47: 273–95. In Monti Sabia and Monti 2010, 2:1159–90.

Monti Sabia, Liliana, and Salvatore Monti. 2010. *Studi su Giovanni Pontano.* Edited by Giuseppe Germano. 2 vols. Messina: Centro interdipartimentale di studi umanistici.

Nauta, Lodi. 2011. "Philology as Philosophy: Giovanni Pontano on Language, Meaning, and Grammar." *Journal of the History of Ideas* 72: 481–502.

Nicolini, Fausto. 1925. *L'arte napoletana del Rinascimento e la lettera di Pietro Summonte a Marcantonio Michiel.* Naples: Ricciardi.

Otto, A. 1890. *Die Sprichwörter und sprichwörtlichen Redensarten der Römer.* Leipzig: Teubner.

Pagliaroli, Stefano. 2006. "Una proposta per il giovane Valla: *Quintiliani Tulliique examen.*" *Studi medievali e umanistici* 4: 9–64.

Percopo, Erasmo. 1899. "Una lettera Pontaniana inedita di Pietro Summonte ad Angelo Colocci (1519)." *Studi di letteratura italiana* 1: 388–93.

———. 1907. "Lettere di Giovanni Pontano a principi e amici." *Atti dell'Accademia Pontaniana* 37: 1–86.

Petrarca, Francesco. 1496. *Invective contra medicum.* In *Librorum Francisci Petrarchae Basileae impressorum annotatio.* Basel: Amerbach.

Pighi, Giovanni Battista. 1954. "Sul *De sermone* di Giovanni Pontano." *Convivium* 2: 483–90.

Pigman, G. W., III. Forthcoming. *The Mystical Usurper of the Mind: Conceptions of Dreaming from Homer to Freud and De Sanctis.*

Pius II. 2018. *Commentaries.* Vol. 3. Edited by Margaret Meserve. I Tatti Renaissance Library 83. Cambridge, MA: Harvard University Press.

Plautus. 1472. *Comoediae.* Edited by Giorgio Merula. Venice: Johannes de Colonia.

Poliziano, Angelo. 1983. *Detti piacevoli.* Edited by Tiziano Zanato. Rome: Istituto della Enciclopedia Italiana.

Pugliese, Olga Zorzi, with Lorenzo Bartoli, Filomena Calabrese, Adriana Grimaldi, Ian Martin, Laura Prelipcean, and Antonio Ricci. *The Early Extant Manuscripts of Baldassar Castiglione's* Il libro del cortegiano.https://tspace.library.utoronto.ca/bitstream/1807/32401/1/Transcriptions%20Cortegiano%20MSS%202.pdf.

Quintilian. 1493. *Quintilianus cum commento.* With a commentary by Raphael Regius. Venice: Octavianus Scotus.

Quondam, Amedeo. 2007. *La conversazione: Un modello italiano.* Rome: Donzelli.

Ramminger, Johann. *Neulateinische Wortliste. Ein Wörterbuch des Lateinischen von Petrarca bis 1700.* Online at http://www.neulatein.de.

Sannazaro, Iacopo. 1504. *Arcadia del Sannazaro tutta fornita et tratta emendatissima dal suo originale.* Naples: Sigismund Mayr.

———. 2009. *Latin Poetry*. Translated by Michael C. J. Putnam. I Tatti Renaissance Library 38. Cambridge, MA: Harvard University Press.

Santo, Luigi. 1971. "Hirquitulus, hirquiculus, e pisatilis. Nota pontaniana." *Quaderni dell' Istituto di filologia latina* 3: 79–127.

Santoro, Mario. 1948. *Uno scolaro del Poliziano a Napoli: Francesco Pucci*. Naples: Libreria scientifica.

Schubert, Christoph. 2001. "Wie Pindar zur *Ilias Latina* kam." *Hermes* 129: 386–93.

Sozzi, Lionello. 2000. "Le *Facezie* e la loro fortuna europea." *Journal de la Renaissance* 1: 89–102.

Speroni, Charles. 1964. *Wit and Wisdom of the Italian Renaissance*. Berkeley: University of California Press.

Tateo, Francesco. 1964. "Per l'edizione critica dell'*Actius* di G. Pontano." *Studi mediolatini e volgari* 12: 145–94.

———. 1972. *Umanesimo etico di Giovanni Pontano*. Lecce: Milella.

———. 1975. "Il lessico dei 'comici' nella facezia latina del Quattrocento." In *I classici nel Medioevo e nell'Umanesimo. Miscellanea filologica*, 93–109. Genova: Università di Genova, Istituto di filologia classica e medievale.

———. 2000. "La facezia fra virtù ed arte." In *"Leggiadre donne —": Novella e racconto breve in Italia*, edited by Francesco Bruni, 43–57. Venice: Marsilio.

———. 2006. "Giovanni Pontano e la nuova frontiera della prosa latina: l'alternativa al volgare." In *Sul latino degli umanisti: Studi raccolti*, edited by Francesco Tateo, 11–78. Bari: Cacucci.

Tiraboschi, Girolamo. 1791. *Storia della letteratura italiana*. 2nd ed. Vol. 6, pt. 3. Modena: Società Tipografica.

Tortelli, Giovanni. 1501. *De orthographia*. Venice: Bartolomeo Zani.

Valla, Lorenzo. 1543. *Opera*. Basel: Henricpetri.

———. 2012. *Dialectical Disputations*. 2 vols. Edited and translated by Brian P. Copenhaver and Lodi Nauta. I Tatti Renaissance Library 49–50. Cambridge, MA: Harvard University Press.

Vecce, Carlo. 1998. *Gli zibaldoni di Iacopo Sannazaro*. Messina: Sicania.

———. 2008. "Sannazaro e Colocci." In *Angelo Colocci e gli studi romanzi*, edited by Corradi Bologna and Marco Bernardi, 487–95. Vatican City: Biblioteca Apostolica Vaticana.

Vergil, Polydore. 1528. *De inventoribus rerum*. Paris: Estienne.

Vitale, Giuliana. 2008. "Sul segretario regio al servizio degli Aragonesi di Napoli." *Studi storici* 2: 293–321.

Walser, Ernst. 1908. *Die Theorie des Witzes und der Novelle nach dem De sermone des Jovianus Pontanus: Ein gesellschaftliches Ideal vom Ende des XV. Jahrhunderts*. Strassburg: K. J. Trübner.

William of Ockham. 1990. *Philosophical Writings: A Selection*. Edited and translated by Philotheus Boehner. Indianapolis: Hackett.

Woelki, Thomas. 2011. *Lodovico Pontano (ca. 1409–1439): Eine Juristenkarriere an Universität, Fürstenhof, Kurie und Konzil*. Leiden: Brill.

Zechmeister, Joseph, ed. 1877. *Scholia vindobonensia ad Horatii Artem poeticam*. Vienna: C. Gerold.

# Index

## ᛟᛉᛟᛊ

Bacchus, 261

Baebius Italicus, Publius, *Latin Iliad*, 436n61

Bantius of Nola, 25, 89

Barcelona, 447n44

Barletta, 455n56

Barnaba of Barletta, 281

Basel, council of, 447n45

Basil of Caesarea, Saint, 121; *Address to Young Men on Greek Literature*, 441n15

Bassa, 229

Bassus. *See* Colocci, Angelo

Beak, 325–27

Beccadelli, Antonio. *See* Panormita

Bergamo, 359–61, 469n1

Bernardino of Siena, Saint, 151, 317, 443n39

Bibbiena, Bernardo, xxi–xxii, xxvi n33

Bible, 436n63

biblical books: John, 431n14; Matthew, 455n55; Psalms, 157; Sirach (Ecclesiasticus), 460n36

Bithynia, 279

Boccaccio, Giovanni, 27, 375

Boethius, Anicius Manlius Severinus, 437n70; *Commentary on Porphyry's Isagoge*, 445n14

Bologna, 467n47

Bracciolini, Poggio, xxvii n33, 375, 436n60, 436n63, 443n39, 446n37, 446n41, 465n34; *Against Hypocrites*, 442n31; *Pleasantries*, 465n33

Brancaccio, Giovanni, 451n17

Brancaccio, Marino, viii, 261, 263, 435n57, 451n17, 452n18

Brancaccio, Monte, 53

Britain/British, 47, 145, 434n53

Bruni, Leonardo, xvii, xviii, xxvi n27, xxvi n29, 441n15; *Against Hypocrites*, 442n31

Bruttium, 3, 387

Busta Gallica, 335

Caecilianus, 223

Caecuban (wine), 361

Caelius Rufus, Marcus, 269

Calabria, 357, 447n49

Caldora, Giacomo, 401, 468n61

Cales, 361

Campania/Campanians, 3, 193, 261, 333, 335, 401

Canius, Gaius, 265

Cannae, battle of, 89, 297, 437n81

Capua, 305, 401, 468n61; basilica of Santa Maria Maggiore, 303–5

Caracciolo, Tristano, viii, 291, 397, 456n70

Carbone, Girolamo, viii, 289–91, 439n104, 456n69

Cariteo (Benet Gareth), viii, 269, 271, 335, 453n33, 461n46

Carrasio, Rodorico, 215

Carrhae, 455n55

Carthage/Carthaginians, 11, 401

Casina, 435n56, 444n11

Castel Nuovo, 450n4

Castiglione, Baldassare, xxvi n33; *Book of the Courtier*, xxi–xxii, xxvii n33

· INDEX ·

Pompeius Magnus, Gnaeus (Pompey), 21–23, 133, 197, 199, 323, 331, 365, 432n21
Pomponius, 283
Pomponius Atticus, Titus, 313, 458n7
Pomponius Porphyrio, 445n19, 459n15
Pontano, Giovanni Gioviano (Ioannes Iovianus Pontanus), vii, xxiii n1, 113–15, 331, 389, 407, 440n9, 451n15, 453n33, 453n40, 455n49, 456n69, 469n2; *Actius*, x, 440n106, 451n15, 452n24, 463n7; *Aegidius*, x, 440n106, 442n32, 453n33, 453n40, 454n45, 456nn69–70, 464nn10–11, 469n1; *Antonius*, x, 435n58, 443n48, 450n7, 451n15; *Asinus*, x, 440n106, 453n33, 464n10, 469n1; *Astrologicae*, 407; *Baiae*, x, xxiv n10, 440n106, 442n32, 443n43, 451n17, 453n33, 453n40, 454n45, 463n4, 463n7, 469n1; *Charon*, x; *Commentary on Ptolemy's Centiloquium*, x, 453n40, 462n54; *Coryle*, 463n7; *De amore coniugali*, ix, x, xxiv n10, 432n18, 460n32, 460nn37–38; *De aspiratione*, x, 442n32, 453n40; *De beneficentia*, x, 11, 431n8, 451n15; *De conviventia*, x, 11, 431n8, 440n106, 464n16; *De fortitudine*, 11, 431n8, 462n54; *De immanitate*, x, 446n40, 456n69, 466n36, 469n3; *De laudibus divinis*, ix; *De liberalitate*, x, 11, 431n8, 437n74, 444n5, 453n38, 463n60, 463n7; *De magnanimitate*, x, 11, 431n8, 434n49, 466n36; *De magnificentia*, x, 11, 431n8; *De obedientia*, x, 441n10; *De principe*, x, 447n45, 452n19; *De prudentia*, x, xxiii n4, xxiv n7, 11, 431n8, 451n17, 456n70, 462n55; *De rebus coelestibus*, x, 440n106, 460n31, 463n7, 469n3; *De sermone* (*On Speech*), x–xxiii, 407; *De splendore*, x, 11,431n8, 453n33; *De tumulis*, ix, 435n58, 442n32, 451n15, 453n40, 456n69, 459n22, 463n60, 463n4; *Eclogues*, 407; *Eridanus*, x, xxiv n10, 430n1, 440n106, 451n15, 453n33, 456n69, 463n4; *Garden of the Hesperides*, ix, 407; *History of the Neapolitan War*, viii, x, 407, 455n56, 461n49, 466n37; *Lyra*, ix; *Meteora*, ix, 407; *On Cruelty*, 407; *On Fortune*, x, xi, 11, 407, 431n8, 440n106, 466n36, 469n3; *Parthenopeus*; ix; *Urania*, ix, 407
Pontano, Lucio (son of Pontano), ix, 460n32
Pontano, Ludovico (relative of Pontano), 213, 447n45
Pontano, Tommaso (uncle of Pontano), vii, 329, 351, 397, 460n32, 468n56
Pontano family. *See* Adriana (granddaughter); Aurelia

492

*Publication of this volume has been made possible by*

The Myron and Sheila Gilmore Publication Fund at I Tatti
The Robert Lehman Endowment Fund
The Jean-François Malle Scholarly Programs and Publications Fund
The Andrew W. Mellon Scholarly Publications Fund
The Craig and Barbara Smyth Fund
for Scholarly Programs and Publications
The Lila Wallace–Reader's Digest Endowment Fund
The Malcolm Wiener Fund for Scholarly Programs and Publications